SELECTED POEMS
AND TRANSLATIONS

EZRA POUND

*Edited with an afterword
by Richard Sieburth*

With essays by T. S. Eliot and John Berryman

faber and faber

First published in the US in 2010 by New Directions Books
80 Eighth Avenue, New York, NY 10011
First published in the UK in 2011 by Faber and Faber Ltd
Bloomsbury House, 74–77 Great Russell Street
London WC1B 3DA

Printed in England by T. J. International Ltd, Padstow, Cornwall

10 9 8 7 6 5 4 3 2 1

CONTENTS

CATHAY (1915)

POEMS 1915–1918

TRANSLATIONS 1954–1964

A NOTE ON THIS EDITION

The most recent Faber revision of Eliot's original 1928 selection of Pound's poetry dates back four decades, and the New Directions edition of his *Selected Poems* has barely changed in seventy years. Neither book carries annotation. To read Pound has always involved the invitation to become his student, however, and it is to this end that the notes to this new edition have been prepared. *The Cantos*, no less than Dante's *Commedia* or Milton's *Paradise Lost*, is a didactic poem—although its most characteristic pedagogical gesture is to send the reader on intellectual errands *beyond* its pages to discover the original languages or poetries or world events that lie behind them. Like *The Waste Land*, it is a poem whose notes are part of the text: an editor's job is merely to chart this field of reference for the student or general reader and help them on their journey—"not as land looks on the map/but as sea bord seen by men sailing" (Canto LIX).

The textual skein of the *Cantos* remains something of a philological tangle; the version followed here is that of the latest New Directions reprint of its 1970 revision, considered to be the most reliable available text. For the shorter poems, publication of the *Collected Early Poems* in 1976 added one hundred poems to the canon established in the various editions of *Personæ* (1928, 1949, 1990), but the majority of these pre-*Cantos* texts pose few significant editorial problems, and unless indicated otherwise in the notes, the present selection offers the first book printing of each poem, following the practice established in my edition of Pound's *Poems & Translations* for the Library of America (2003). Unlike the latter volume, however, the early poems are here presented in the chronological order of their original periodical appearance, so as to show how Pound carefully shaped his contributions to such journals as *Poetry* or *The Little Review* into dramatic or musical sequences. Few poets have developed as quickly and as publicly as Pound did between 1912 and 1919, mask after mask donned and discarded on the pages of little magazines.

As its title indicates, this new selection includes both Pound's poems and his translations—although one of his signal contributions to twentieth-century poetics was of course to have erased any easy distinction between "primary" composition and "secondary" translation. Eliot, for his part, omitted *Homage to Sextus Propertius* from his 1928 selection of Pound, precisely on the grounds that it was "not enough a translation" and "too much a translation" to be intelligible to the non-specialist. Pound's *Cathay*, on the other hand, Eliot considered to be an original work, famously commenting (in an insight not lost on Borges) that "Chinese poetry, as we know it today, is something invented by Ezra Pound." So "original" indeed was *Cathay* that when the volume was first published in 1915, it included within its pages a version of the eighth-century Old English poem "The

Seafarer" to serve as a companion piece to Li Po's more-or-less contemporary "Exile's Letter"—both of these renderings constituting, along with "Homage to Sextus Propertius," what Pound called his Major Personæ.

Perhaps the last major poet in the Ovidian tradition, Pound sees the "magic moment" of metamorphosis as defining the mystery at the core of all metaphor and all translation—the elusive persistence of identity within change. The French critic Antoine Berman memorably defined translation as *l'épreuve de l'étranger*—that trial or ordeal or test of the foreign through which a language must pass before returning to itself at once renewed and estranged. Cast as a translation of Book XI of the *Odyssey* (the so-called *nekuia* or "descent" episode), Pound's opening Canto enacts precisely this kind of transformative encounter with the other. As the wandering Odysseus meets with the prophet Tiresias in the kingdom of the dead to receive instructions as to how to accomplish his *nostos* or return home, he is visited by a procession of eloquent shades from the archaic Greek past. The prosody of Canto I is similarly haunted by the revenants of tradition—Homer's pulsing hexameters, Andreas Divus's streamlined Renaissance Latin translation, the alliterative Anglo-Saxon drum-beat of "The Seafarer"—all now returning as spectral echoes within the modernist soundscape of Pound's own epic-to-come.

In our current age of triumphant Anglo-American monolingualism, this willingness to welcome the foreign into his English remains Pound's most attractive legacy. His first-time readers may be annoyed or intimidated by all the "tags" or quotations from the Greek, Latin, Provençal, Italian, French, Spanish, and Portuguese that float like so much mnemonic flotsam and jetsam upon the textual surface of the *Cantos*, but Pound was optimistically convinced that they could easily be navigated. "Skip anything you don't understand and go on till you pick it up again," he wrote a young correspondent in 1934. "All [this] tosh about foreign languages making it difficult. The quotes are all either explained at once by repeat or they are definitely *of* the things indicated. If the reader don't know what an elefant is, then the word is obscure." A few years later he informed another student: "I believe that when finished, *all* foreign words in the *Cantos*, Gk, etc. will be underlining, not necessary, not necessary to the sense, in one way. I mean a complete sense will exist without them; it will be there in the American text, but the Greek, ideograms, etc., will indicate a *duration* from whence or since when. If you find any *briefer* means of getting this repeat or resonance, tell papa and I will try to employ it . . . There is no *intentional* obscurity. There is condensation to maximum attainable. It is impossible to make the deep as quickly comprehensible as the shallow." Like that ideal reader with the ideal case of insomnia whom Joyce envisaged for his *Finnegans Wake*, Pound here sets the interpretative bar for his poem very high indeed; for today's less classically educated student, an annotated edition such as this should at least help fill in some of the blanks within Pound's ellipses while providing translations of key quotations from his Library of Babel.

At times Pound leaves English wholly behind over the course of his "poem including history" to ventriloquize entire passages spoken in foreign tongues. This is the case in Canto XVI, where we move from a montage of various British first-person reports on the horrors of World War I into a long section narrated in the French slang of the *poilus* (as the foot soldiers on the front were known). More notoriously, Pound directly composed two complete Cantos in Ezraic Italian that were published in a small pro-Fascist newspaper in early 1945. Long omitted from the complete editions of his poem, they now figure as Cantos LXXII and LXXIII, tracing the precise moment at which his epic as it were defected into the idiom of the enemy before rediscovering its demotic (African-) American linguistic bearings in prison later that summer in *The Pisan Cantos*. Whether he be translating from Cavalcanti's *dolce stil nuovo* (Canto XXXVI) or from the Chinese classics (Cantos XIII, LII, XCIX), whether he be quoting from Sigismundo Malatesta (Canto IX), Thomas Jefferson (Canto XXXI), John Adams (Canto LXX), or De Mailla's *Histoire génerale de la Chine* (Canto LIII), whether he be constellating the pages of his Cantos with ideograms or hieroglyphs, Pound manages to invent a poetic language that always hovers somewhere *in between* its original historical sources and its contemporary twentieth-century articulation—thereby aiming at that *reine Sprache* (or "pure language") which Walter Benjamin defined as the messianic horizon of all translation.

Nowhere is this liminal interlingual zone—audibly "English" yet no longer "native"—more evident than in Pound's most original acts of translation: his early dramatic monologues, the lyrics of *Cathay*, the elegiacs of *Homage to Sextus Propertius* and, above all, the folk melodies gathered in his *Classic Anthology Defined by Confucius*, composed (and chanted) at St. Elizabeths at the same time that he was attempting to transmogrify Sophoclean tragedy into the ritual "goddance" of Japanese Noh drama through his experimental revoicings of *Elektra* and *The Women of Trachis*. These late dispatches from what he semi-affectionately called "the bughouse" remind us that Pound, proponent of troubadour *motz el son* [words-and-sound], was not just a poet of the printed page. Extracts from his two operas, *Le Testament* (1923) and *Cavalcanti* (1931–33), may be found on the CD issued by Other Minds, *Ego Scriptor Cantilenae: The Music of Ezra Pound*. A sizable body of his recorded readings also exists; it may be accessed and downloaded online at PennSound, together with my *The Sound of Pound: A Listener's Guide*. In the end, after all the dust had settled, Pound hoped that his poetry would simply be judged by the fineness of its *ear*. In a rare, late interview, he broke his silence to observe to Pier Paolo Pasolini: "They say the *Cantos* are a hodge-podge; not so: it's music." ["Dicono che i *Cantos* sono [scritti] a casaccio, ma non è così: è musica."]

. . .

A rich community of commentary has grown up around Pound's poetry. The vast rhizomic root-system of the *Cantos* was first systematically unearthed by Edwards's and Vasse's *Annotated Index to the Cantos* in 1957 and in Achilles Fang's legendary four-volume Harvard doctoral dissertation of the following year, both unthinkable without the publication of Hugh Kenner's *The Poetry of Ezra Pound* in 1951. The sixties through the eighties saw further exegetical work, much of which was published in *Paideuma: A Journal Devoted to Ezra Pound Scholarship*, founded in 1972, the year of Pound's death, and edited by Carroll Terrell. The latter coordinated a team of eminent Pound scholars and synthesized several decades of research in his monumental two-volume *Companion to the* Cantos (1980–1984), now available for consultation online and to which the reader is referred for more detailed annotation. Further guides to the *Cantos* include those of William Cookson, Peter Makin and George Kearns. Pound's earlier poetry in turn received scrupulous commentary and annotation in K. K. Ruthven's 1969 *Guide to Ezra Pound's* Personæ, which laid the ground for Peter Brooker's valuable vademecum to the Faber selection, *A Student Guide to the* Selected Poems of Ezra Pound (1979) and Christine Froula's splendid Baedeker to the New Directions edition, *A Guide to Ezra Pound's* Selected Poems (1982). In my notes, I am continuously grateful to the work of Brooker and Froula, while incorporating glosses included in my own LOA edition of his *Poems & Translations*. In preparing my Editor's Afterword, I have learned a great deal from Hugh Wittemeyer's 1989 article, "The Making of Pound's *Selected Poems*," and from Gregory Barnhisel's informative *James Laughlin, New Directions and the Remaking of Ezra Pound* (2005). For their help in establishing the Table of Contents of this edition, many thanks are owed to David Moody and to my editor at Faber, Paul Keegan. Peggy Fox and Jeffrey Yang of New Directions have serenely shepherded this project along since its inception. Mary de Rachewiltz has been an unswerving tutelary presence.

CHRONOLOGY

1885 Ezra Loomis Pound born in Hailey, Idaho.

1889 His father Homer appointed assistant assayer at the United States Mint in Philadelphia.

1901–1907 Enters the University of Pennsylvania at fifteen, meets William Carlos Williams and H.D., transfers to Hamilton College, New York, then returns to Penn for graduate studies in romance philology and comparative literature. Earns masters degree, travels in Europe on a research fellowship, but never finishes doctorate. Accepts a job as instructor of romance languages at Wabash College, Crawfordsville, Indiana, but is dismissed after a semester.

1908 Sails to Gibraltar, then on to Venice, where he publishes *A Lume Spento* at his own expense. Moves to London in late summer and meets publisher Elkin Mathews, who issues *A Quinzaine for This Yule*.

1909 A series of night-school lectures on the emergence of vernacular literature in the Middle Ages will be published the following year as *The Spirit of Romance*. Meets future wife Dorothy Shakespear, William Butler Yeats, Ford Madox Hueffer [later Ford], T. E. Hulme. Establishes himself as a presence on the London literary scene with the publication of *Personæ* and *Exultations* by Mathews.

1910–11 Returns to the U.S. in early summer, staying in the New York and Philadelphia area. Publication of his first American volume, *Provença* by Small, Maynard & Company of Boston. Sails backs to London the following February to oversee the publication of *Canzoni*, then sets off for a summer in France, Italy, and Germany. Back in London in the fall, becomes a regular contributor to *The New Age*, a Guild Socialist weekly edited by A. R. Orage, to which he will offer literary, music, art, and cultural criticism through 1920.

1912 *Sonnets and Ballate of Guido Cavalcanti* published in Boston, then London. Spring in Paris with H.D. and Richard Aldington; early summer on the roads of southern France, tracking troubadours. *Ripostes* published in the fall; contains first public announcement of the new school of Imagism, which he also promotes to Harriet Monroe, editor of *Poetry* in Chicago.

1913 Advised by its "foreign correspondent" Pound, *Poetry* prints his "A Few Don'ts by an Imagist" and "In a Station of a Metro" as well as work by H.D., Yeats, and Tagore. His early criticism in *Poetry* includes positive reviews of the poetry of Robert Frost and D. H. Lawrence. Travels to Paris in the spring to meet with the newest French poets. Back in London, discovers the young French sculptor Gaudier-Brzeska. Spends the first of three winters as Yeats's secretary at Stone Cottage in Sussex. Meets Mary Fenollosa, widow of the American Orientalist Ernest Fenollosa, and is entrusted by her with her husband's unpublished notebooks on Chinese poetry and Japanese Noh theater.

1914 The inclusion of one of Joyce's poems in his anthology, *Des Imagistes*, initiates Pound's role as unofficial agent and publicist for the subsequent *Dubliners*, *Portrait of the Artist*, and *Ulysses*. Marries Dorothy Shakespear in April. BLAST, co-edited by Pound and Wyndham Lewis, appears in June, proclaiming the birth of the GREAT ENGLISH VORTEX and containing a Vorticist manifesto. Meets T. S. Eliot in London and recommends "Prufrock" to *Poetry*.

1915 *Cathay*, adapted from Fenollosa's notebooks, published in April. Gaudier-Brzeska dies on the front in June. Starts writing "cantos" for "a longish new poem."

1916 *Gaudier-Brzeska: A Memoir. Certain Noble Plays of Japan.* Bowdlerized English version of *Lustra* by Matthews.

1917 Foreign editor of the New-York based *Little Review*. Advisor to Egoist Press, which publishes Joyce's *Portrait*, Eliot's *Prufrock and Other Obervations*, and Wyndham Lewis's novel *Tarr*. Eliot's (anonymous) pamphlet, *Ezra Pound His Metric and Poetry*, promotes the New York edition of *Lustra* by Knopf, which contains Pound's recently published "Three Cantos."

1918 Under Pound's foreign editorship, the *Little Review* publishes chapters from *Ulysses*, special Henry James and contemporary French literature issues, as well as his positive notices of Mina Loy and Marianne Moore. A collection of prose pieces, *Pavannes and Divigations*, with Knopf. Meets the economist Major Douglas, theorist of Social Credit, through A. R. Orage.

1919 Publishes a portion of "Homage to Sextus Propertius" in *Poetry* and *The Fourth Canto* with Ovid Press. The Egoist Press issues a collection of his most recent work to date, *Quia Pauper Amavi*. April through September in France.

1920 Foreign correspondent of the (New York-based) *Dial*. Meets Joyce for the first time on Lake Garda and helps him settle in Paris. New York publication of *Instigations* by Boni Liveright, which includes Fenollosa's "Chinese Written Character as a Medium for Poetry." *Umbra: The Early Poems of Ezra Pound* published by Mathews. Ovid Press brings out his "farewell to London," *Hugh Selwyn Mauberley*. Publicly announces his definitive departure from England in December.

1921 New acquaintances in Paris include Gertrude Stein, E. E. Cummings, Ernest Hemingway, Marcel Duchamp, Francis Picabia, Natalie Barney, Jean Cocteau. Begins working on *Le Testament*, an opera based on the works of François Villon. Edits Brancusi number for the *Little Review*; publishes "Three Cantos" in the Dial. Encourages publication of Marianne Moore's *Poems*. Plays Paris host to his New York publisher, Horace Liveright, who has just issued Pound's *Poems 1918–21: Including Three Portraits and Four Cantos* and who, at his instigation, will bring out *The Waste Land* the following year.

1922 Still in Paris, edits the manuscript of Eliot's *Waste Land* in January; reviews *Ulysses* for the spring *Dial*. Travels through Italy in the summer; discovers Sigismondo Malatesta's Rimini. *The Waste Land* published in the fall *Dial* and *Criterion*. Meets American violinist Olga Rudge.

1923 Travels in Italy with the Hemingways; researches the Malatesta Cantos, published in Eliot's *Criterion* in July. His "autobiography," *Indiscretions*, appears in Paris with Three Mountains Press. Meets Basil Bunting. Edits "Exiles" number of *Little Review*. Fired from *Dial*.

1924 Three Mountains publishes *Antheil and the Treatise on Harmony* and, at Pound's behest, Hemingway's *in our time*. Settles in Rapallo, Italy.

1925 *A Draft of XVI. Cantos for the Beginning of a Poem of Some Length* published by Three Mountains in January. Daughter Mary, with Olga Rudge, born in Italy in July.

1926 Paris premiere of Pound's opera *Le Testament de Villon*. Wife Dorothy gives birth to a son, Omar, in Paris in September. Relations cool with Joyce after receipt of a sample of *Finnegans Wake*. *Personæ*, his collected poems, published by Boni & Liveright in New York.

1927 Launches the short-lived magazine *The Exile*, which will publish Yeats's "Sailing to Byzantium," Zukofsky's "Poem Beginning 'The,'" poems by Carl Rakosi, and portions of Joe Gould's "Oral History."

1928 Publishes his "traduction" of Cavalcanti's "Donna mi prega" in the *Dial* (which awards him its annual prize for 1928). Translates the Confucian *Ta Hsio* ("The Great Learning"). *A Draft of the Cantos 17–27* published by Rodker in London. Eliot edits and introduces Pound's *Selected Poems* for Faber and Gwyer.

1929 Aquila Press in England agrees to publish his Collected Prose, as well as his translations of the Odes of Confucius and Cavalcanti. After Aquila's bankruptcy, George Oppen's To Publishers (Le Beausset, France) takes over the Collected Prose project, the only volume of which will appear in 1932 as *Prolegomena 1–2*.

1930 Organizes local concert series in Rapallo. Travels to Paris to oversee the deluxe edition of *A Draft of XXX Cantos* by Nancy Cunard's Hours Press. Meets German anthropologist Leo Frobenius in Frankfurt.

1931 *How To Read.* BBC broadcast of his opera *Le Testament* encourages him to write another radio opera, *Cavalcanti: A Sung Dramedy in 3 Acts*, which is never produced.

1932 *Guido Cavalcanti Rime* published in Milan, as is his *Profile: An Anthology*. Zukofsky's *An "Objectivist" Anthology* dedicated to Pound. Provides regular contributions over the next eight years to Orage's *New English Weekly*, a forum for Social Credit economics.

1933 Private audience with Mussolini. Faber publishes *ABC of Economics* and *Active Anthology* (featuring the poetry of Williams, Bunting, Zukofsky, Cummings, Moore, Oppen, Eliot, and Aragon's "Red Front").

1934 *ABC of Reading, Make it New, Eleven New Cantos XXXI–XLI.* Note on Frobenius and "A Letter to Ezra Pound" from Langston Hughes in Nancy Cunard's *Negro Anthology*. Prefaces George Oppen's *Discrete Series*.

1935 *Alfred Venison's Poems: Social Credit Themes. Social Credit: An Impact. Jefferson and/or Mussolini.*

1936 "Canto — 'with Usura'" (Canto XLV).

1937 *Polite Essays. The Fifth Decad of Cantos.*

1938 *Guide to Kulchur*, dedicated to Bunting and Zukofksy, "strugglers in the desert."

1939 Travels back to the U.S., unsuccessfully attempting to meet with President Roosevelt to provide advice on American foreign and economic policy. In Cambridge, records a series of *Cantos* for the Harvard Vocarium. In June, receives an honorary degree from his alma mater, Hamilton College.

1940–43 *Cantos LII–LXXI*. Faber publishes *A Selection of Poems* in its Sesame Books series. Begins making short-wave broadcasts on Radio Rome on subjects literary, political, and economic. After the Japanese attack on Pearl Harbor in December 1941, stops broadcasting for a month and half but resumes in early 1942 and continues until the fall of the Mussolini government in July 1943. The scripts of these broadcasts later issued in 1978 as *"Ezra Pound Speaking": Radio Speeches of World War II*. Publishes *Carta da visita* and journalism (in Italian) for the *Meridiano di Roma*.

1943 Officially indicted for treason by the U.S. Department of Justice in July; defends his broadcasts as an exercise of his constitutionally guaranteed right to free speech.

1944 Publication in Italian of six collections of his writings, including two volumes of Confucian translations.

1945 Newspaper publication of Cantos LXXII and LXIII, written in Italian. Early May, arrested by partisans in Rapallo, then voluntarily turns himself over to the American occupiers. After three weeks of interrogation in Genoa, is placed in the U.S. Army's Disciplinary Center in Pisa, where he remains imprisoned until early November. Flown back to Washington, D.C., to face trial for treason, he is diagnosed as "mentally unfit for trial" in December and placed in St. Elizabeths Hospital, a federal mental asylum in Washington, D.C.

1946 Makes final revisions of *The Pisan Cantos*. Receives regular visits from Charles Olson ("Olson saved my life," he writes).

1947 English translation of the Confucian *Unwobbling Pivot* and *The Great Digest*.

1948 New Directions publishes *The Pisan Cantos*. Over next decade receives a steady stream of visitors at St. Elizabeths, ranging from old friends H. L. Mencken, Marianne Moore (whose La Fontaine translation he encourages), William Carlos Williams, Louis Zukofsky, Conrad Aiken, and T. S. Eliot to younger poets Robert Lowell, Allen Tate, Randall Jarrell, John Berryman, Elizabeth Bishop, Robert Duncan, Frederick Seidel, as well as scholars Edith Hamilton, Kenneth Clark, Marshall McLuhan, Hugh Kenner, and Guy Davenport.

1949 Controversy after the Bollingen Prize is awarded to *The Pisan Cantos*. Begins translation of the Confucian Odes. New Directions issues *Selected Poems* in its New Classics series.

1950 *The Letters of Ezra Pound 1907–1941*, edited by D. D. Paige. Charles Olson publishes his manifesto *Projective Verse*, conceived as a "post-modern" advance over the poetics of the *Cantos*. Under Olson's rectorship between 1951–1956, Black Mountain College in North Carolina will transmit the Poundian *paideuma* to a generation of American poets including Robert Duncan, Ed Dorn, Paul Blackburn, John Wieners, Denise Levertov, Jonathan Williams, and Robert Creeley.

1951 Co-translates Sophocles *Elektra* with Rudd Fleming. Young right-wing extremist disciples at St. Elizabeths, John Kasper and David Horton, begin publishing the "Square $" booklet series under Pound's direction: titles include Fenollosa on the Chinese written character, the *Analects* of Confucius, selections from the economists Alexander del Mar and Thomas Benton, and *Gists from Agassiz*, the American naturalist.

1953 Translates Sophocles' *Women of Trachis*. Hugh Kenner edits *The Translations of Ezra Pound*.

1954 *Literary Essays*, edited by T. S. Eliot. *The Classic Anthology Defined by Confucius* published by Harvard.

1955 *Section: Rock-Drill: 86–95 de los cantares* published by Scheiwiller in Milan.

1957 Pound's unsigned contributions to Noel Stock's Australian magazine *Edge* include translations of Rimbaud and Catullus.

1958 Released from St. Elizabeths in April on grounds that he will never be fit for trial. Sails for Italy in June with wife Dorothy and secretary Marcella Spann. The three briefly settle at Schloss Brunnenburg, home of Pound's daughter Mary and her husband, the Egyptologist Boris de Rachewiltz.

1959 *Thrones: 96–109 de los cantares*. Depression. Composition of what will become the *Drafts and Fragments of Cantos CX–CXVII*. Foundation of *Agenda* in England by William Cookson: the magazine and its small press will bring together a new generation of British poets, translators, and publishers under the umbrella of Pound (Peter Russell, Peter Whigham, Michael Alexander, Peter Davidson, Donald Davie, Charles Tomlinson, Thom Gunn).

1960 *Impact: Essays on the Ignorance and Decline of American Civilization.* Publication of Donald Allen's *The New American Poetry 1945–1960*, which influentially maps the impact of the Pound-Williams-Zukofsky tradition on the experimental poetics of the Black Mountain and the San Francisco Renaissance poets (Jack Spicer, Allen Ginsberg, Philip Whalen, Gary Snyder, Michael McClure, etc.)

1962–1972 Moves back into his former Sant'Ambrogio home above Rapallo with Olga Rudge, splitting his time between the Ligurian coast and her small "hidden nest" in Venice. Pound's last major public statement on the *Cantos*, an interview with Donald Hall, appears in the *Paris Review* in 1962.

1964 *Confucius to Cummings*, an anthology of world poetry edited with Marcella Spann.

1965 Attends memorial service for T. S. Eliot in Westminster Abbey; chooses the texts for Faber's *Selected Cantos*. Reads at the Spoleto Festival; travels to Paris for the publication of a French compilation of his work.

1967 Publication of the *Pound/Joyce* correspondence. Pirate edition of *Cantos 110–116* "at a secret location on the lower east side" in New York.

1969 New Directions publishes *Drafts and Fragments*. Pound visits the U.S. in June for an exhibit of Eliot's *Waste Land* manuscript at the New York Public Library.

1972 Dies in Venice, November 1; buried in the San Michele cemetery.

Poems 1908–1912

THE TREE

I stood still and was a tree amid the wood,
Knowing the truth of things unseen before;
Of Daphne and the laurel bough
And that god-feasting couple old
5   That grew elm-oak amid the wold.
'Twas not until the gods had been
Kindly entreated, and been brought within
Unto the hearth of their heart's home
That they might do this wonder thing;
10   Nathless I have been a tree amid the wood
And many a new thing understood
That was rank folly to my head before.

LA FRAISNE
(Scene: The Ash Wood of Melvern)

For I was a gaunt, grave councilor
Being in all things wise, and very old,
But I have put aside this folly and the cold
That old age weareth for a cloak.

5   I was quite strong—at least they said so—
The young men at the sword-play;
But I have put aside this folly, being gay
In another fashion that more suiteth me.

I have curled mid the boles of the ash wood,
10   I have hidden my face where the oak
Spread his leaves over me, and the yoke
Of the old ways of men have I cast aside.

By the still pool of Mar-nan-otha
Have I found me a bride
15   That was a dog-wood tree some syne.
She hath called me from mine old ways
She hath hushed my rancour of council,
Bidding me praise

Naught but the wind that flutters in the leaves.

20 She hath drawn me from mine old ways,
Till men say that I am mad;
But I have seen the sorrow of men, and am glad,
For I know that the wailing and bitterness are a folly.

And I? I have put aside all folly and all grief.
25 I wrapped my tears in an ellum leaf
And left them under a stone
And now men call me mad because I have thrown
All folly from me, putting it aside
To leave the old barren ways of men,
30 Because my bride
Is a pool of the wood and
Tho all men say that I am mad
It is only that I am glad,
Very glad, for my bride hath toward me a great love
35 That is sweeter than the love of women
That plague and burn and drive one away.

Aie-e! 'Tis true that I am gay
  Quite gay, for I have her alone here
  And no man troubleth us.

40 Once when I was among the young men . . . .
And they said I was quite strong, among the young men.
Once there was a woman . . . .
. . . . but I forget . . . . she was . . . .
. . . . I hope she will not come again.

45 . . . . I do not remember . . . .
I think she hurt me once but . . . .
That was very long ago.

I do not like to remember things any more.

I like one little band of winds that blow
50 In the ash trees here:
For we are quite alone
Here mid the ash trees.

CINO

Italian Campagna 1309, the open road

Bah! I have sung women in three cities,
But it is all the same;
And I will sing of the sun.

Lips, words, and you snare them,
5   Dreams, words, and they are as jewels,
Strange spells of old deity,
Ravens, nights, allurement:
And they are not;
Having become the souls of song.

10   Eyes, dreams, lips, and the night goes.
Being upon the road once more,
They are not.
Forgetful in their towers of our tuneing
Once for wind-runeing
15   They dream us-toward and
Sighing, say, "Would Cino,
Passionate Cino, of the wrinkling eyes,
Gay Cino, of quick laughter,
Cino, of the dare, the jibe.
20   Frail Cino, strongest of his tribe
That tramp old ways beneath the sun-light,
Would Cino of the Luth were here!"

Once, twice, a year—
Vaguely thus word they:

25   "Cino?" "Oh, eh, Cino Polnesi
The singer is't you mean?"
"Ah yes, passed once our way,
A saucy fellow, but . . .
(Oh they are all one these vagabonds),
30   Peste! 'tis his own songs?
Or some other's that he sings?
But *you,* My Lord, how with your city?"

But you "My Lord," God's pity!
And all I knew were out, My Lord, you
35 Were Lack-land Cino, e'en as I am,
O Sinistro.

I have sung women in three cities.
But it is all one.
I will sing of the sun.
40 ... eh? ... they mostly had grey eyes,
But it is all one, I will sing of the sun.

    "'Pollo Phoibee, old tin pan, you
    Glory to Zeus' aegis-day,
    Shield o' steel-blue, th' heaven o'er us
45   Hath for boss thy luster gay!

    'Pollo Phoibee, to our way-fare
    Make thy laugh our wander-lied;
    Bid thy 'fulgence bear away care.
    Cloud and rain-tears pass they fleet!

50   Seeking e'er the new-laid rast-way
    To the gardens of the sun . . . ."

    . . . . .

I have sung women in three cities
But it is all one.

I will sing of the white birds
55 In the blue waters of heaven,
The clouds that are spray to its sea.

NA AUDIART
Que be-m vols mal

NOTE: Anyone who has read anything of the troubadours knows well the tale of Bertran of Born and My Lady Maent of Montagnac, and knows also the song he made when she would none of him, the song wherein he, seeking to find or make her equal, begs of each preëminent lady of Langue d'Oc some trait or some fair semblance: thus of Cembelins her "esgart amoros" to wit, her love-lit glance, of Aelis her

speech free-running, of the Vicomtess of Chalais her throat and her two hands, at
Roacoart of Anhes her hair golden as Iseult's; and even in this fashion of Lady Audiart
"although she would that ill come unto him" he sought and praised the lineaments of
the torse. And all this to make "Una dompna soiseubuda" a borrowed lady or as the
Italians translated it "Una donna ideale."

Tho thou well dost wish me ill
                    Audiart, Audiart,
Where thy bodice laces start
As ivy fingers clutching through
5   Its crevices,
          Audiart, Audiart,
Stately, tall and lovely tender
Who shall render
              Audiart, Audiart,
10   Praises meet unto thy fashion?
Here a word kiss!
           Pass I on
Unto Lady "Mels-de-Ben,"
Having praised thy girdle's scope
15   How the stays ply back from it;
I breathe no hope
That thou shouldst . . . .
               Nay no whit
Bespeak thyself for anything.
20   Just a word in thy praise, girl,
Just for the swirl
Thy satins make upon the stair,
'Cause never a flaw was there
Where thy torse and limbs are met:
25   Tho thou hate me, read it set
In rose and gold,[1]
Or when the minstrel, tale half told
Shall burst to lilting at the phrase
                "Audiart, Audiart" . . . .

30   Bertrans, master of his lays,
Bertrans of Aultaforte thy praise
Sets forth, and tho thou hate me well,

[1] *I.e.,* in illumed manuscript.

Yea tho thou wish me ill,
                    Audiart, Audiart.
35   Thy loveliness is here writ till,
                    Audiart,
Oh, till thou come again.[1]
And being bent and wrinkled, in a form
That hath no perfect limning, when the warm
40   Youth dew is cold
Upon thy hands, and thy old soul
Scorning a new, wry'd casement,
Churlish at seemed misplacement,
Finds the earth as bitter
45   As now seems it sweet,
Being so young and fair
As then only in dreams,
Being then young and wry'd,
Broken of ancient pride,
50   Thou shalt then soften,
Knowing, I know not how,
Thou wert once she
                  Audiart, Audiart
For whose fairness one forgave
                      Audiart, Audiart
55   Que be-m vols mal.

HISTRION

No man hath dared to write this thing as yet,
And yet I know, how that the souls of all men great
At times pass through us,
And we are melted into them, and are not
5   Save reflexions of their souls.
Thus am I Dante for a space and am
One François Villon, ballad-lord and thief
Or am such holy ones I may not write,
Lest blasphemy be writ against my name;
10   This for an instant and the flame is gone.

[1] Reincarnate.

'Tis as in midmost us there glows a sphere
Translucent, molten gold, that is the "I"
And into this some form projects itself:
Christus, or John, or eke the Florentine;
15 And as the clear space is not if a form's
Imposed thereon,
So cease we from all being for the time,
And these, the Masters of the Soul, live on.

IN DURANCE

Io am homesick after mine own kind,
Oh I know that there are folk about me, friendly faces,
But I am homesick after mine own kind.

"These sell our pictures"! Oh well,
5 They reach me not, touch me some edge or that,
But reach me not and all my life's become
One flame, that reaches not beyond
My heart's own hearth,
Or hides among the ashes there for thee.
10 "Thee"? Oh, "thee" is who cometh first
Out of mine own soul-kin,
For I am homesick after mine own kind
And ordinary people touch me not.
                              Yea, I am homesick
15 After mine own kind that know, and feel
And have some breath for beauty and the arts.

Aye, I am wistful for my kin of the spirit
And have none about me save in the shadows
When come *they*, surging of power, "DAEMON,"
20 "Quasi KALOUN." S.T. says, Beauty is most that, a
        "calling to the soul."
Well then, so call they, the swirlers out of the mist
        of my soul,
They that come mewards, bearing old magic.

25 But for all that, I am homesick after mine own kind
And would meet kindred e'en as I am,
Flesh-shrouded bearing the secret.
"All they that with strange sadness"
Have the earth in mockery, and are kind to all,
30 My fellows, aye I know the glory
Of th' unbounded ones, but ye, that hide
As I hide most the while
And burst forth to the windows only whiles or whiles
For love, or hope, or beauty or for power,
35 Then smoulder, with the lids half closed
And are untouched by echoes of the world.

Oh ye, my fellows: with the seas between us some be,
Purple and sapphire for the silver shafts
Of sun and spray all shattered at the bows;
40 Of such a "Veltro" of the vasty deep
As bore my tortoise house scant years agone:
And some the hills hold off,
The little hills to east of us, though here we
Have damp and plain to be our shutting in.

45 And yet my soul sings "Up!" and we are one.
Yea thou, and Thou, and THOU, and all my kin
To whom my breast and arms are ever warm,
For that I love ye as the wind the trees
That holds their blossoms and their leaves in cure
50 And calls the utmost singing from the boughs
That 'thout him, save the aspen, were as dumb
Still shade, and bade no whisper speak the birds of how
"Beyond, beyond, beyond, there lies . . ."

SESTINA: ALTAFORTE

LOQUITUR: *En* Bertrans de Born.
Dante Alighieri put this man in hell for that he was a
stirrer up of strife.
Eccovi!
Judge ye!

Have I dug him up again?
The scene is at his castle, Altaforte. "Papiols" is his jongleur.
"The Leopard," The *device* of Richard (Cœur de Lion).

I

Damn it all! All this our South stinks peace.
You whoreson dog, Papiols, come! Let's to music!
I have no life save when the swords clash.
But ah! when I see the standards gold, vair, purple, opposing
5   And the broad fields beneath them turn crimson,
Then howl I my heart nigh mad with rejoicing.

II

In hot summer have I great rejoicing
When the tempests kill the earth's foul peace,
And the lightnings from black heav'n flash crimson,
10   And the fierce thunders roar me their music
And the winds shriek through the clouds mad, opposing,
And through all the riven skies God's swords clash.

III

Hell grant soon we hear again the swords clash!
And the shrill neighs of destriers in battle rejoicing,
15   Spiked breast to spiked breast opposing!
Better one hour's stour than a year's peace
With fat boards, bawds, wine and frail music!
Bah! there's no wine like the blood's crimson!

IV

And I love to see the sun rise blood-crimson.
20   And I watch his spears through the dark clash
And it fills all my heart with rejoicing
And pries wide my mouth with fast music
When I see him so scorn and defy peace,
His lone might 'gainst all darkness opposing.

V

25   The man who fears war and squats opposing
My words for stour, hath no blood of crimson
But is fit only to rot in womanish peace
Far from where worth's won and the swords clash

For the death of such sluts I go rejoicing;
30   Yea, I fill all the air with my music.

VI

Papiols, Papiols, to the music!
There's no sound like to swords swords opposing,
No cry like the battle's rejoicing
When our elbows and swords drip the crimson
35   And our charges 'gainst "The Leopard's" rush clash.
May God damn for ever all who cry "Peace!"

VII

And let the music of the swords make them crimson!
Hell grant soon we hear again the swords clash!
Hell blot black for alway the thought "Peace!"

PIERE VIDAL OLD

It is of Piere Vidal, the fool *par excellence* of all Provence, of whom the tale tells how he ran mad, as a wolf, because of his love for Loba of Penautier, and how men hunted him with dogs through the mountains of Cabaret and brought him for dead to the dwelling of his Loba (she-wolf) of Penautier, and how she and her Lord had him healed and made welcome, and he stayed some time at that court. He speaks:

When I but think upon the great dead days
And turn my mind upon that splendid madness,
Lo! I do curse my strength
And blame the sun his gladness;
5   For that the one is dead
And the red sun mocks my sadness.

Behold me, Vidal, that was fool of fools!
Swift as the king wolf was I and as strong
When tall stags fled me through the alder brakes,
10   And every jongleur knew me in his song.
And the hounds fled and the deer fled
And none fled over-long.

Even the grey pack knew me and knew fear.
God! how the swiftest hind's blood spurted hot
15 Over the sharpened teeth and purpling lips!
Hot was that hind's blood yet it scorched me not
As did first scorn, then lips of the Penautier!
Aye ye are fools, if ye think time can blot

From Piere Vidal's remembrance that blue night.
God! but the purple of the sky was deep!
20 Clear, deep, translucent, so the stars me seemed
Set deep in crystal; and because my sleep
—Rare visitor—came not,—the Saints I guerdon
For that restlessness—Piere set to keep

25 One more fool's vigil with the hollyhocks.
Swift came the Loba, as a branch that's caught,
Torn, green and silent in the swollen Rhone,
Green was her mantle, close, and wrought
Of some thin silk stuff that's scarce stuff at all,
30 But like a mist wherethrough her white form fought,

And conquered! Ah God! conquered!
Silent my mate came as the night was still.
Speech? Words? Faugh! Who talks of words and love?!
Hot is such love and silent,
35 Silent as fate is, and as strong until
It faints in taking and in giving all.

Stark, keen, triumphant, till it plays at death.
God! she was white then, splendid as some tomb
High wrought of marble, and the panting breath
40 Ceased utterly. Well, then I waited, drew,
Half-sheathed, then naked from its saffron sheath
Drew full this dagger that doth tremble here.

Just then she woke and mocked the less keen blade.
Ah God, the Loba! And my only mate!
45 Was there such flesh made ever and unmade!
God curse the years that turn such women grey!
Behold here Vidal, that was hunted, flayed,
Shamed and yet bowed not and that won at last.

And yet I curse the sun for his red gladness,
50   I that have known strath, garth, brake, dale,
And every run-away of the wood through that great madness,
Behold me shrivelled as an old oak's trunk
And made men's mock'ry in my rotten sadness!

No man hath heard the glory of my days:
55   No man hath dared and won his dare as I:
One night, one body and one welding flame!
What do ye own, ye niggards! that can buy
Such glory of the earth? Or who will win
Such battle-guerdon with his "prowesse high"?

60   O Age gone lax! O stunted followers,
That mask at passions and desire desires,
Behold me shrivelled, and your mock of mocks;
And yet I mock you by the mighty fires
That burnt me to this ash.

.   .   .   .

65   Ah! Cabaret! Ah Cabaret, thy hills again!

.   .   .   .

Take your hands off me! . . .   [*Sniffing the air.*
        Ha! this scent is hot!

BALLAD OF THE GOODLY FERE[1]

Simon Zelotes speaketh it somewhile after the Crucifixion

Ha' we lost the goodliest fere o' all
For the priests and the gallows tree?
Aye lover he was of brawny men,
O' ships and the open sea.

5   When they came wi' a host to take Our Man
His smile was good to see,
"First let these go!" quo' our Goodly Fere,
"Or I'll see ye damned," says he.

[1] Fere = Mate, Companion.

Aye he sent us out through the crossed high spears
10 And the scorn of his laugh rang free,
"Why took ye not me when I walked about
Alone in the town?" says he.

Oh we drank his "Hale" in the good red wine
When we last made company,
15 No capon priest was the Goodly Fere
But a man o' men was he.

I ha' seen him drive a hundred men
Wi' a bundle o' cords swung free,
That they took the high and holy house
20 For their pawn and treasury.

They'll no' get him a' in a book I think
Though they write it cunningly;
No mouse of the scrolls was the Goodly Fere
But aye loved the open sea.

25 If they think they ha' snared our Goodly Fere
They are fools to the last degree.
"I'll go to the feast," quo' our Goodly Fere,
"Though I go to the gallows tree."

"Ye ha' seen me heal the lame and blind,
30 And wake the dead," says he,
"Ye shall see one thing to master all:
'Tis how a brave man dies on the tree."

A son of God was the Goodly Fere
That bade us his brothers be.
35 I ha' seen him cow a thousand men.
I have seen him upon the tree.

He cried no cry when they drave the nails
And the blood gushed hot and free,
The hounds of the crimson sky gave tongue
40 But never a cry cried he.

I ha' seen him cow a thousand men
On the hills o' Galilee,
They whined as he walked out calm between,
Wi' his eyes like the grey o' the sea.

45 Like the sea that brooks no voyaging
With the winds unleashed and free,
Like the sea that he cowed at Genseret
Wi' twey words spoke' suddently.

A master of men was the Goodly Fere,
50 A mate of the wind and sea,
If they think they ha' slain our Goodly Fere
They are fools eternally.

I ha' seen him eat o' the honey-comb
Sin' they nailed him to the tree.

PLANH FOR THE YOUNG ENGLISH KING

That is, Prince Henry Plantagenet, elder brother to Richard Cœur de Lion.
From the Provençal of Bertrans de Born "Si tuit li dolh elh plor elh marrimen."

If all the grief and woe and bitterness,
All dolour, ill and every evil chance
That ever came upon this grieving world
Were set together they would seem but light
5 Against the death of the young English King.
Worth lieth riven and Youth dolorous,
The world o'ershadowed, soiled and overcast,
Void of all joy and full of ire and sadness.

Grieving and sad and full of bitterness
10 Are left in teen the liegemen courteous,
The joglars supple and the troubadours.
O'er much hath ta'en Sir Death that deadly warrior
In taking from them the young English King,
Who made the freest hand seem covetous.
15 'Las! Never was nor will be in this world
The balance for this loss in ire and sadness!

O skillful Death and full of bitterness,
Well mayst thou boast that thou the best chevalier
That any folk e'er had, hast from us taken;
20   Sith nothing is that unto worth pertaineth
But had its life in the young English King
And better were it, should God grant his pleasure,
That he should live than many a living dastard
That doth but wound the good to ire and sadness.

25   From this faint world, how full of bitterness
Love takes his way and holds his joy deceitful,
Sith no thing is but turneth unto anguish
And each to-day 'vails less than yestere'en,
Let each man visage this young English King
30   That was most valiant 'mid all worthiest men!
Gone is his body fine and amorous,
Whence have we grief, discord and deepest sadness.

Him, whom it pleased for our great bitterness
To come to earth to draw us from misventure,
35   Who drank of death for our salvacioun,
Him do we pray as to a Lord most righteous
And humble eke, that the young English King
He please to pardon, as true pardon is,
And bid go in with honourèd companions
40   There where there is no grief, nor shall be sadness.

SONNET: CHI È QUESTA?

Who is she coming, that the roses bend
Their shameless heads to do her passing honour?
Who is she coming with a light upon her
Not born of suns that with the day's end end?
5   Say is it Love who hath chosen the nobler part?
Say is it Love, that was divinity,
Who hath left his godhead that his home might be
The shameless rose of her unclouded heart?
If this be Love, where hath he won such grace?
10   If this be Love, how is the evil wrought,

That all men write against his darkened name?
If this be Love, if this . . .
                    O mind give place!
What holy mystery e'er was noosed in thought?
15   Own that thou scan'st her not, nor count it shame!

"BLANDULA, TENELLA, VAGULA"

What hast thou, O my soul, with paradise?
Will we not rather, when our freedom's won,
Get us to some clear place wherein the sun
Lets drift in on us through the olive leaves
5   A liquid glory? If at Sirmio,
My soul, I meet thee, when this life's outrun,
Will we not find some headland consecrated
By aery apostles of terrene delight,
Will not our cult be founded on the waves,
10   Clear sapphire, cobalt, cyanine,
On triune azures, the impalpable
Mirrors unstill of the eternal change?

Soul, if She meet us there, will any rumour
Of havens more high and courts desirable
15   Lure us beyond the cloudy peak of Riva?

ERAT HORA

"Thank you, whatever comes." And then she turned
And, as the ray of sun on hanging flowers
Fades when the wind hath lifted them aside,
Went swiftly from me. Nay, whatever comes
5   One hour was sunlit and the most high gods
May not make boast of any better thing
Than to have watched that hour as it passed.

ROME

From the French of Joachim du Bellay
"Troica Roma resurges."
PROPERTIUS

O thou new comer who seek'st Rome in Rome
And find'st in Rome no thing thou canst call Roman;
Arches worn old and palaces made common,
Rome's name alone within these walls keeps home.

5   Behold how pride and ruin can befall
One who hath set the whole world 'neath her laws,
All-conquering, now conquered, because
She is Time's prey and Time consumeth all.

Rome that art Rome's one sole last monument,
10   Rome that alone hast conquered Rome the town,
Tiber alone, transient and seaward bent,
Remains of Rome. O world, thou unconstant mime!
That which stands firm in thee Time batters down,
And that which fleeteth doth outrun swift time.

TRANSLATIONS AND ADAPTATIONS FROM HEINE
From "Die Heimkehr"

I

Is your hate, then, of such measure?
Do you, truly, so detest me?
Through all the world will I complain
Of *how* you have addressed me.

5   O ye lips that are ungrateful,
Hath it never once distressed you,
That you can say such *awful* things
Of *any* one who ever kissed you?

II

So thou hast forgotten fully
10   That I so long held thy heart wholly,
Thy little heart, so sweet and false and small
That there's no thing more sweet or false at all.

Love and lay thou hast forgotten fully,
And my heart worked at them unduly.
15   I know not if the love or if the lay were better stuff,
But I know now, they both were good enough.

III

Tell me where thy lovely love is,
Whom thou once did sing so sweetly,
When the fairy flames enshrouded
20   Thee, and held thy heart completely.

All the flames are dead and sped now
And my heart is cold and sere;
Behold this book, the urn of ashes,
'Tis my true love's sepulchre.

IV

25   I dreamt that I was God Himself
Whom heavenly joy immerses,
And all the angels sat about
And praised my verses.

V

The mutilated choir boys
30   When I begin to sing
Complain about the awful noise
And call my voice too thick a thing.

When light their voices lift them up,
Bright notes against the ear,
35   Through trills and runs like crystal,
Ring delicate and clear.

They sing of Love that's grown desirous,
Of Love, and joy that is Love's inmost part,
And all the ladies swim through tears
40   Toward such a work of art.

VI

This delightful young man
Should not lack for honourers,
He propitiates me with oysters,
With Rhine wine and liqueurs.

45   How his coat and pants adorn him!
Yet his ties are more adorning,
In these he daily comes to ask me:
"Are you feeling well this morning?"

He speaks of my extended fame,
50   My wit, charm, definitions,
And is diligent to serve me,
Is detailed in his provisions.

In evening company he sets his face
In most spirituel positions,
55   And declaims before the ladies
My *god-like* compositions.

O what comfort is it for me
To find him such, when the days bring
No comfort, at my time of life when
60   All good things go vanishing.

Translator to Translated

O Harry Heine, curses be,
I live too late to sup with thee!
Who can demolish at such polished ease
65   *Philistia's pomp and Art's pomposities!*

21

THE FLAME

'Tis not a game that plays at mates and mating,
Provençe knew;
'Tis not a game of barter, lands and houses,
Provençe knew.
5   We who are wise beyond your dream of wisdom,
Drink our immortal moments; we "pass through."
We have gone forth beyond your bonds and borders,
Provençe knew;
And all the tales they ever writ of Oisin
10   Say but this:
That man doth pass the net of days and hours.
Where time is shrivelled down to time's seed corn
We of the Ever-living, in that light
Meet through our veils and whisper, and of love.

15   O smoke and shadow of a darkling world,
Barters of passion, and that tenderness
That's but a sort of cunning! O my Love,
These, and the rest, and all the rest we knew.

'Tis not a game that plays at mates and mating,
20   'Tis not a game of barter, lands and houses,
'Tis not "of days and nights" and troubling years,
Of cheeks grown sunken and glad hair gone gray;
There *is* the subtler music, the clear light
Where time burns back about th' eternal embers.
25   We are not shut from all the thousand heavens:
Lo, there are many gods whom we have seen,
Folk of unearthly fashion, places splendid,
Bulwarks of beryl and of chrysoprase.

Sapphire Benacus, in thy mists and thee
30   Nature herself's turned metaphysical,
Who can look on that blue and not believe?

Thou hooded opal, thou eternal pearl,
O thou dark secret with a shimmering floor,
Through all thy various mood I know thee mine;

35   If I have merged my soul, or utterly
Am solved and bound in, through aught here on earth,
There canst thou find me, O thou anxious thou,
Who call'st about my gates for some lost me;
I say my soul flowed back, became translucent.
40   Search not my lips, O Love, let go my hands,
This thing that moves as man is no more mortal.
If thou hast seen my shade sans character,
If thou hast seen that mirror of all moments,
That glass to all things that o'ershadow it,
45   Call not that mirror me, for I have slipped
Your grasp, I have eluded.

AU SALON

Her grave, sweet haughtiness
Pleaseth me, and in like wise
Her quiet ironies.
Others are beautiful, none more, some less.

I suppose, when poetry comes down to facts,
When our souls are returned to the gods
            and the spheres they belong in,
Here in the every-day where our acts
5   Rise up and judge us;

I suppose there are a few dozen verities
That no shift of mood can shake from us:

One place where we'd rather have tea
(Thus far hath modernity brought us)
10   "Tea" (Damn you)
            Have tea, damn the Caesars,
Talk of the latest success, give wing to some scandal,
Garble a name we detest, and for prejudice?
Set loose the whole consummate pack
15   to bay like Sir Roger de Coverley's.

This our reward for our works,
                    sic crescit gloria mundi:
Some circle of not more than three
                    that we prefer to play up to,

20   Some few whom we'd rather please
                    than hear the whole aegrum vulgus
Splitting its beery jowl
                    a-meaowling our praises.

Some certain peculiar things,
25   cari laresque, penates,
Some certain accustomed forms,
            the absolute unimportant.

THE SEAFARER
(From the early Anglo-Saxon text)

May I, for my own self, song's truth reckon,
Journey's jargon, how I in harsh days
Hardship endured oft.
Bitter breast-cares have I abided,
5   Known on my keel many a care's hold,
And dire sea-surge, and there I oft spent
Narrow nightwatch nigh the ship's head
While she tossed close to cliffs. Coldly afflicted.
My feet were by frost benumbed.
10   Chill its chains are; chafing sighs
Hew my heart round and hunger begot
Mere-weary mood. Lest man know not
That he on dry land loveliest liveth,
List how I, care-wretched, on ice-cold sea,
15   Weathered the winter, wretched outcast
Deprived of my kinsmen;
Hung with hard ice-flakes, where hail-scur flew,
There I heard naught save the harsh sea
And ice-cold wave, at whiles the swan cries,
20   Did for my games the gannet's clamour,
Sea-fowls' loudness was for me laughter,

The mews' singing all my mead-drink.
Storms, on the stone-cliffs beaten, fell on the stern
In icy feathers; full oft the eagle screamed
25　With spray on his pinion.
　　　　　　　　　　　　Not any protector
May make merry man faring needy.
This he little believes, who aye in winsome life
Abides 'mid burghers some heavy business,
30　Wealthy and wine-flushed, how I weary oft
Must bide above brine.
Neareth nightshade, snoweth from north,
Frost froze the land, hail fell on earth then,
Corn of the coldest. Nathless there knocketh now
35　The heart's thought that I on high streams
The salt-wavy tumult traverse alone.
Moaneth away my mind's lust
That I fare forth, that I afar hence
Seek out a foreign fastness.
40　For this there's no mood-lofty man over earth's midst,
Not though he be given his good, but will have in his youth greed;
Nor his deed to the daring, nor his king to the faithful
But shall have his sorrow for sea-fare
Whatever his lord will.
45　He hath not heart for harping, nor in ring-having
Nor winsomeness to wife, nor world's delight
Nor any whit else save the wave's slash,
Yet longing comes upon him to fare forth on the water.
Bosque taketh blossom, cometh beauty of berries,
50　Fields to fairness, land fares brisker,
All this admonisheth man eager of mood,
The heart turns to travel so that he then thinks
On flood-ways to be far departing.
Cuckoo calleth with gloomy crying,
55　He singeth summerward, bodeth sorrow,
The bitter heart's blood. Burgher knows not —
He the prosperous man — what some perform
Where wandering them widest draweth.
So that but now my heart burst from my breastlock,
60　My mood 'mid the mere-flood,
Over the whale's acre, would wander wide.
On earth's shelter cometh oft to me,

Eager and ready, the crying lone-flyer,
Whets for the whale-path the heart irresistibly,
65   O'er tracks of ocean; seeing that anyhow
My lord deems to me this dead life
On loan and on land, I believe not
That any earth-weal eternal standeth
Save there be somewhat calamitous
70   That, ere a man's tide go, turn it to twain.
Disease or oldness or sword-hate
Beats out the breath from doom-gripped body.
And for this, every earl whatever, for those speaking after —
Laud of the living, boasteth some last word,
75   That he will work ere he pass onward,
Frame on the fair earth 'gainst foes his malice,
Daring ado, . . .
So that all men shall honour him after
And his laud beyond them remain 'mid the English,
80   Aye, for ever, a lasting life's-blast,
Delight 'mid the doughty.
                              Days little durable,
And all arrogance of earthen riches,
There come now no kings nor Cæsars
85   Nor gold-giving lords like those gone.
Howe'er in mirth most magnified,
Whoe'er lived in life most lordliest,
Drear all this excellence, delights undurable!
Waneth the watch, but the world holdeth.
90   Tomb hideth trouble. The blade is layed low.
Earthly glory ageth and seareth.
No man at all going the earth's gait,
But age fares against him, his face paleth,
Grey-haired he groaneth, knows gone companions,
95   Lordly men, are to earth o'ergiven,
Nor may he then the flesh-cover, whose life ceaseth,
Nor eat the sweet nor feel the sorry,
Nor stir hand nor think in mid heart,
And though he strew the grave with gold,
100   His born brothers, their buried bodies
Be an unlikely treasure hoard.

THE PLUNGE

I would bathe myself in strangeness:
These comforts heaped upon me, smother me!
I burn, I scald so for the new,
New friends, new faces,
5   Places!
Oh to be out of this,
This that is all I wanted
        — save the new.

And you,
10   Love, you the much, the more desired!
Do I not loathe all walls, streets, stones,
All mire, mist, all fog,
All ways of traffic?
You, I would have flow over me like water,
15   Oh, but far out of this!
Grass, and low fields, and hills,
And sun,
Oh, sun enough!
Out, and alone, among some
20   Alien people!

N.Y.

My City, my beloved, my white! Ah, slender,
Listen! Listen to me, and I will breathe into thee a soul.
Delicately upon the reed, attend me!

Now do I know that I am mad,
5   *For here are a million people surly with traffic;*
This is no maid.
Neither could I play upon any reed if I had one.

My City, my beloved,
Thou art a maid with no breasts,
10   Thou art slender as a silver reed.
Listen to me, attend me!

And I will breathe into thee a soul,
And thou shalt live for ever.

A GIRL

The tree has entered my hands,
The sap has ascended my arms,
The tree has grown in my breast—
Downward,
5   The branches grow out of me, like arms.

Tree you are,
Moss you are,
You are violets with wind above them.
A child—*so* high—you are,
10   And all this is folly to the world.

THE PICTURE[1]

The eyes of this dead lady speak to me,
For here was love, was not to be drowned out.
And here desire, not to be kissed away.

The eyes of this dead lady speak to me.

PORTRAIT D'UNE FEMME

Your mind and you are our Sargasso Sea,
London has swept about you this score years
And bright ships left you this or that in fee:
Ideas, old gossip, oddments of all things,
5   Strange spars of knowledge and dimmed wares of price.
Great minds have sought you—lacking someone else.
You have been second always. Tragical?

[1] *Venus Reclining,* by Jacopo del Sellaio (1442–1493).

No. You preferred it to the usual thing:
One dull man, dulling and uxorious,
10   One average mind—with one thought less, each year.
Oh, you are patient, I have seen you sit
Hours, where something might have floated up.
And now you pay one. Yes, you richly pay.
You are a person of some interest, one comes to you
15   And takes strange gain away:
Trophies fished up; some curious suggestion;
Fact that leads nowhere; and a tale or two,
Pregnant with mandrakes, or with something else
That might prove useful and yet never proves,
20   That never fits a corner or shows use,
Or finds its hour upon the loom of days:
The tarnished, gaudy, wonderful old work;
Idols and ambergris and rare inlays,
These are your riches, your great store; and yet
25   For all this sea-hoard of deciduous things,
Strange woods half sodden, and new brighter stuff:
In the slow float of different light and deep,
No! there is nothing! In the whole and all,
Nothing that's quite your own.
30   Yet this is you.

SUB MARE

It is, and is not, I am sane enough,
Since you have come this place has hovered round me,
This fabrication built of autumn roses,
Then there's a goldish colour, different.

5   And one gropes in these things as delicate
Algæ reach up and out, beneath
Pale slow green surgings of the underwave,
'Mid these things older than the names they have,
These things that are familiars of the god.

Δώρια

Be in me as the eternal moods
        of the bleak wind, and not
As transient things are —
        gaiety of flowers.
5   Have me in the strong loneliness
        of sunless cliffs
And of grey waters.
        Let the gods speak softly of us
In days hereafter,
10   The shadowy flowers of Orcus
Remember Thee.

APPARUIT

Golden rose the house, in the portal I saw
thee, a marvel, carven in subtle stuff, a
portent. Life died down in the lamp and flickered,
        caught at the wonder.

5   Crimson, frosty with dew, the roses bend where
thou afar, moving in the glamorous sun,
drinkst in life of earth, of the air, the tissue
        golden about thee.

Green the ways, the breath of the fields is thine there,
10   open lies the land, yet the steely going
darkly hast thou dared and the dreaded æther
        parted before thee.

Swift at courage thou in the shell of gold, cast-
ing a-loose the cloak of the body, camest
15   straight, then shone thine oriel and the stunned light
        faded about thee.

Half the carven shoulder, the throat aflash with
strands of light inwoven about it, loveli-
est of all things, frail alabaster, ah me!
20   swift in departing.

30

Clothed in goldish weft, delicately perfect,
gone as wind! The cloth of the magical hands!
Thou a slight thing, thou in access of cunning
      dar'dst to assume this?

THE RETURN

See, they return; ah, see the tentative
    Movements, and the slow feet,
      The trouble in the pace and the uncertain
    Wavering!

5   See, they return, one, and by one,
    With fear, as half-awakened;
    As if the snow should hesitate
    And murmur in the wind,
             and half turn back;
10   These were the "Wing'd-with-Awe,"
      Inviolable.

Gods of the wingèd shoe!
With them the silver hounds,
          sniffing the trace of air!

15   Haie! Haie!
    These were the swift to harry;
    These the keen-scented;
    These were the souls of blood.

    Slow on the leash,
20   pallid the leash-men!

TO WHISTLER, AMERICAN

On the loan exhibit of his paintings at the Tate Gallery.

You also, our first great,
Had tried all ways;
Tested and pried and worked in many fashions,
And this much gives me heart to play the game.

5   Here is a part that's slight, and part gone wrong,
And much of little moment, and some few
Perfect as Dürer!

"In the Studio" and these two portraits,[1] if I had my choice!
And then these sketches in the mood of Greece?

10   You had your searches, your uncertainties,
And this is good to know—for us, I mean,
Who bear the brunt of our America
And try to wrench her impulse into art.

You were not always sure, not always set
15   To hiding night or tuning "symphonies";
Had not one style from birth, but tried and pried
And stretched and tampered with the media.

You and Abe Lincoln from that mass of dolts
Show us there's chance at least of winning through.

[1] "Brown and Gold—de Race."
"Grenat et Or—Le Petit Cardinal."

Poems 1913–1915

TENZONE

Will people accept them?
        (i.e. these songs).
As a timorous wench from a centaur
        (or a centurion),
5   Already they flee, howling in terror.

Will they be touched with the verisimilitudes?
        Their virgin stupidity is untemptable.
I beg you, my friendly critics,
Do not set about to procure me an audience.

10   I mate with my free kind upon the crags;
        the hidden recesses
Have heard the echo of my heels,
        in the cool light,
        in the darkness.

THE GARRET

Come, let us pity those who are better off than we are.
Come, my friend, and remember
        that the rich have butlers and no friends,
And we have friends and no butlers.
5   Come, let us pity the married and the unmarried.

Dawn enters with little feet
        like a gilded Pavlova,
And I am near my desire.
Nor has life in it aught better
10   Than this hour of clear coolness,
        the hour of waking together.

THE GARDEN

En robe de parade.

Samain

Like a skein of loose silk blown against a wall
She walks by the railing of a path in Kensington Gardens,
And she is dying piece-meal
            of a sort of emotional anæmia.

5   And round about there is a rabble
Of the filthy, sturdy, unkillable infants of the very poor.
They shall inherit the earth.

In her is the end of breeding.
Her boredom is exquisite and excessive.
10   She would like some one to speak to her,
And is almost afraid that I
            will commit that indiscretion.

ORTUS

How have I laboured?
How have I not laboured
To bring her soul to birth,
To give these elements a name and a centre!

5   She is beautiful as the sunlight, and as fluid.
She has no name, and no place.
How have I laboured to bring her soul into separation;
To give her a name and her being!

Surely you are bound and entwined,
10   You are mingled with the elements unborn;
I have loved a stream and a shadow.

I beseech you enter your life.
I beseech you learn to say "I"
When I question you:
15   For you are no part, but a whole;
No portion, but a being.

SALUTATION THE SECOND

You were praised, my books,
      because I had just come from the country;
I was twenty years behind the times
      so you found an audience ready.
5   I do not disown you,
      do not you disown your progeny.

Here they stand without quaint devices,
Here they are with nothing archaic about them.
Observe the irritation in general:

10   "Is this," they say, "the nonsense
      that we expect of poets?"
"Where is the Picturesque?"
      "Where is the vertigo of emotion?"
"No! his first work was the best."
15   "Poor Dear! he has lost his illusions."

Go, little naked and impudent songs,
Go with a light foot!
(Or with two light feet, if it please you!)
Go and dance shamelessly!
20   Go with an impertinent frolic!

Greet the grave and the stodgy,
Salute them with your thumbs at your noses.

Here are your bells and confetti.
Go! rejuvenate things!
25   Rejuvenate even "The Spectator."
      Go! and make cat calls!
Dance and make people blush,
Dance the dance of the phallus
      and tell anecdotes of Cybele!
30   Speak of the indecorous conduct of the Gods!
      (Tell it to Mr. Stachey)

Ruffle the skirts of prudes,
      speak of their knees and ankles.

But, above all, go to practical people —
go! jangle their door-bells!
35   Say that you do no work
and that you will live forever.

COMMISSION

Go, my songs, to the lonely and the unsatisfied,
Go also to the nerve-wracked, go to the enslaved-by-convention,
Bear to them my contempt for their oppressors.
Go as a great wave of cool water,
5   Bear my contempt of oppressors.

Speak against unconscious oppression,
Speak against the tyranny of the unimaginative,
Speak against bonds.
Go to the bourgeoise who is dying of her ennuis,
10   Go to the women in suburbs.
Go to the hideously wedded,
Go to them whose failure is concealed,
Go to the unluckily mated,
Go to the bought wife,
15   Go to the woman entailed.

Go to those who have delicate lust,
Go to those whose delicate desires are thwarted,
Go like a blight upon the dulness of the world;
Go with your edge against this,
20   Strengthen the subtle cords,
Bring confidence upon the algæ and the tentacles of the soul.

Go in a friendly manner,
Go with an open speech.
Be eager to find new evils and new good,
25   Be against all forms of oppression.
Go to those who are thickened with middle age,
To those who have lost their interest.

Go to the adolescent who are smothered in family —
Oh how hideous it is

30 To see three generations of one house gathered together!
    It is like an old tree with shoots,
    And with some branches rotted and falling.

    Go out and defy opinion,
    Go against this vegetable bondage of the blood.
35 Be against all sorts of mortmain.

A PACT

    I make a pact with you, Walt Whitman —
    I have detested you long enough.
    I come to you as a grown child
    Who has had a pig-headed father;
5   I am old enough not to make friends.
    It was you that broke the new wood,
    Now is a time for carving.
    We have one sap and one root —
    Let there be commerce between us.

IN A STATION OF THE METRO

    The apparition   of these faces   in the crowd   :
    Petals   on a wet, black   bough   .

APRIL

Nympharum membra disjecta

    Three spirits came to me
    And drew me apart
    To where the olive boughs
    Lay stripped upon the ground:

    Pale carnage beneath bright mist.

GENTILDONNA

She passed and left no quiver in the veins, who now
Moving among the trees, and clinging

                  in the air she severed,
Fanning the grass she walked on then, endures:

Grey olive leaves beneath a rain-cold sky.

THE REST

O helpless few in my country,
O remnant enslaved!

Artists broken against her,
A-stray, lost in the villages,
5   Mistrusted, spoken-against,

Lovers of beauty, starved,
Thwarted with systems,
Helpless against the control;

You who can not wear yourselves out
10   By persisting to successes,
You who can only speak,
Who can not steel yourselves into reiteration;

You of the finer sense,
Broken against false knowledge,
15   You who can know at first hand,
Hated, shut in, mistrusted:

Take thought:
I have weathered the storm,
I have beaten out my exile.

LES MILLWIN

The little Millwins attend the Russian Ballet.
The mauve and greenish souls of the little Millwins
Were seen lying along the upper seats
Like so many unused boas.

5   The turbulent and undisciplined host of art students —
The rigorous deputation from "Slade" —
Was before them.
With arms exalted, with fore-arms
Crossed in great futuristic X's, the art students
10   Exulted, they beheld the splendours of *Cleopatra*.

And the little Millwins beheld these things;
With their large and anæmic eyes they looked out upon this configuration.

Let us therefore mention the fact,
For it seems to us worthy of record.

ALBA

As cool as the pale wet leaves
                        of lily-of-the-valley
She lay beside me in the dawn.

THE BATH TUB

As a bathtub lined with white porcelain,
When the hot water gives out or goes tepid,
So is the slow cooling of our chivalrous passion,
O my much praised but-not-altogether-satisfactory lady.

ARIDES

The bashful Arides
Has married an ugly wife,
He was bored with his manner of life,
Indifferent and discouraged he thought he might as
5   Well do this as anything else.

Saying within his heart, "I am no use to myself,
"Let her, if she wants me, take me."
He went to his doom.

THE ENCOUNTER

All the while they were talking the new morality
Her eyes explored me.
And when I arose to go
Her fingers were like the tissue
Of a Japanese paper napkin.

SIMULACRA

Why does the horse-faced lady of just the unmentionable age
Walk down Longacre reciting Swinburne to herself, inaudibly?
Why does the small child in the soiled-white imitation fur coat
Crawl in the very black gutter beneath the grape stand?
5   Why does the really handsome young woman approach me in
        Sackville Street
Undeterred by the manifest age of my trappings?

COITUS

The gilded phaloi of the crocuses
          are thrusting at the spring air.
Here is there naught of dead gods
But a procession of festival,
5   A procession, O Giulio Romano,
Fit for your spirit to dwell in.
Dione, your nights are upon us.

The dew is upon the leaf.
The night about us is restless.

LIU CH'E

The rustling of the silk is discontinued,
Dust drifts over the court-yard,
There is no sound of foot-fall, and the leaves
Scurry into heaps and lie still,
5   And she the rejoicer of the heart is beneath them:

A wet leaf that clings to the threshold.

FAN-PIECE, FOR HER IMPERIAL LORD

O fan of white silk,
        clear as frost on the grass-blade,
You also are laid aside.

TS'AI CHI'H

The petals fall in the fountain,
        the orange-coloured rose-leaves,
Their ochre clings to the stone.

EPITAPHS

FU I

Fu I loved the high cloud and the hill,
Alas, he died of alcohol.

LI PO

And Li Po also died drunk.
He tried to embrace a moon
In the Yellow River.

"IONE, DEAD THE LONG YEAR"

Empty are the ways,
Empty are the ways of this land
And the flowers
        Bend over with heavy heads.
5   They bend in vain.
Empty are the ways of this land
            Where Ione
Walked once, and now does not walk
But seems like a person just gone.

PAPYRUS

Spring . . .
Too long . . .
Gongula . . .

Ἰμέρρω

Thy soul
Grown delicate with satieties,
Atthis.
        O Atthis,
5   I long for thy lips.
I long for thy narrow breasts,
Thou restless, ungathered.

PROVINCIA DESERTA

At Rochechouart
Where the hills part
                in three ways,
And three valleys, full of winding roads,
5   Fork out to south and north,
There is a place of trees ... gray with lichen.
I have walked there
                thinking of old days.
At Chalais
10   is a pleached arbour;
Old pensioners and old protected women
Have the right there —
                it is charity.
I have crept over old rafters,
15   peering down
Over the Dronne,
                over a stream full of lilies.
Eastward the road lies,
                Aubeterre is eastward,
20 With a garrulous old man at the inn.
I know the roads in that place:
Mareuil to the north-east,
                La Tour,
There are three keeps near Mareuil,
25 And an old woman,
                glad to hear Arnaut,
Glad to lend one dry clothing.

I have walked
                    into Perigord,
30 I have seen the torch-flames, high-leaping,
Painting the front of that church;
Heard, under the dark, whirling laughter.
I have looked back over the stream
                    and seen the high building,
35 Seen the long minarets, the white shafts.
I have gone in Ribeyrac
                    and in Sarlat,
I have climbed rickety stairs, heard talk of Croy,
Walked over En Bertran's old layout,
40 Have seen Narbonne, and Cahors and Chalus,
Have seen Excideuil, carefully fashioned.

I have said:
                    "Here such a one walked.
"Here Cœur-de-Lion was slain.
                    "Here was good singing.
45 "Here one man hastened his step.
                    "Here one lay panting."
I have looked south from Hautefort,
                    thinking of Montaignac, southward.
50 I have lain in Rocafixada,
                    level with sunset,
Have seen the copper come down
                    tingeing the mountains,
I have seen the fields, pale, clear as an emerald,
55 Sharp peaks, high spurs, distant castles.
I have said: "The old roads have lain here.
"Men have gone by such and such valleys
"Where the great halls were closer together."
I have seen Foix on its rock, seen Toulouse, and
60   Arles greatly altered,
I have seen the ruined "Dorata."
                    I have said:
"Riquier! Guido."
                    I have thought of the second Troy,
65 Some little prized place in Auvergnat:
Two men tossing a coin, one keeping a castle,
One set on the highway to sing.

He sang a woman.
Auvergne rose to the song;
70   The Dauphin backed him.
"The castle to Austors!"
        "Pieire kept the singing—
A fair man and a pleasant."
        He won the lady,
75 Stole her away for himself, kept her against armed force:
So ends that story.
That age is gone;
Pieire de Maensac is gone.
I have walked over these roads;
80 I have thought of them living.

IMAGE FROM D'ORLÉANS

Young men riding in the street
In the bright new season
Spur without reason,
Causing their steeds to leap.

5 And at the pace they keep
Their horses' armoured feet
Strike sparks from the cobbled street
In the bright new season.

THE SPRING

Ἦρι μὲν αἵ τε κυδώνιαι—Ibycus

Cydonian Spring with her attendant train,
Mælids and water-girls,
Stepping beneath a boisterous wind from Thrace,
Throughout this sylvan place
5 Spreads the bright tips,
And every vine-stock is
Clad in new brilliancies.
        And wild desire

Falls like black lightning.
10   O bewildered heart,
Though every branch have back what last year lost,
She, who moved here amid the cyclamen,
Moves only now a clinging tenuous ghost.

THE COMING OF WAR: ACTAEON

An image of Lethe,
        and the fields
Full of faint light
        but golden,
5   Gray cliffs,
        and beneath them
A sea
Harsher than granite,
        unstill, never ceasing;
10   High forms
        with the movement of gods,
Perilous aspect;
        And one said:
"This is Actæon."
15   Actæon of golden greaves!
        Over fair meadows,
        Over the cool face of that field,
        Unstill, ever moving
        Hosts of an ancient people,
20   The silent cortège.

THE GYPSY

"Est-ce que vous avez vu des autres — des camarades —
avec des singes ou des ours?"
                    A Stray Gipsy — A.D. 1912

That was the top of the walk, when he said:
"Have you seen any others, any of our lot,

With apes or bears?"
                        —A brown upstanding fellow
5   Not like the half-castes,
                        up on the wet road near Clermont.
The wind came, and the rain,
And mist clotted about the trees in the valley,
And I'd the long ways behind me,
10   gray Arles and Beaucaire,
And he said, "Have you seen any of our lot?"
I'd seen a lot of his lot . . .
                        ever since Rhodez,
Coming down from the fair
15   of St. John,
With caravans, but never an ape or a bear.

THE GAME OF CHESS

Dogmatic Statement Concerning the Game of Chess:
Theme for a Series of Pictures

Red knights, brown bishops, bright queens,
Striking the board, falling in strong "L"s of colour,
Reaching and striking in angles,
                        holding lines in one colour.
5   This board is alive with light;
                        these pieces are living in form,
Their moves break and reform the pattern:
                        luminous green from the rooks,
Clashing with "X"s of queens,
10   looped with the knight-leaps.

"Y" pawns, cleaving, embanking!
Whirl! Centripetal! Mate! King down in the vortex,
Clash, leaping of bands, straight strips of hard colour,
Blocked lights working in. Escapes. Renewal of contest.

ANCIENT MUSIC

Winter is icummen in,
Lhude sing Goddamm,
Raineth drop and staineth slop,
And how the wind doth ramm!
5   Sing: Goddamm.
Skiddeth bus and sloppeth us,
An ague hath my ham,
Freezeth river, turneth liver,
                        Damn you, sing: Goddamm.
10   Goddamm, Goddamm, 'tis why I am, Goddamm,
                        So 'gainst the winter's balm.
Sing goddamm, damm, sing Goddamm.
Sing goddamm, sing goddamm, DAMM.

NOTE: This is not folk music, but Dr. Ker writes that the tune is to be found under
the Latin words of a very ancient canon.

ET FAIM SALLIR LES LOUPS DES BOYS

I cling to the spar,
Washed with the cold salt ice
I cling to the spar —
Insidious modern waves, civilization, civilized hidden snares.
5   Cowardly editors threaten: "If I dare"
Say this or that, or speak my open mind,
Say that I hate my hates,
            Say that I love my friends,
Say I believe in Lewis, spit out the later Rodin,
10   Say that Epstein can carve in stone,
That Brzeska can use the chisel,
Or Wadsworth paint;
                        Then they will have my guts;
They will cut down my wage, force me to sing their cant,
15   Uphold the press, and be before all a model of literary decorum.
                        Merde!
Cowardly editors threaten,
Friends fall off at the pinch, the loveliest die.
That is the path of life, this is my forest.

THE TEA SHOP

The girl in the tea shop
               Is not so beautiful as she was,
The August has worn against her.
She does not get up the stairs so eagerly;
Yes, she also will turn middle-aged,
And the glow of youth that she spread about us
               As she brought us our muffins
Will be spread about us no longer.
               She also will turn middle-aged.

PHYLLIDULA

Phyllidula is scrawny but amorous,
Thus have the gods awarded her
That in pleasure she receives more than she can give;
If she does not count this blessed
Let her change her religion.

SHOP GIRL

For a moment she rested against me
Like a swallow half blown to the wall,
And they talk of Swinburne's women,
And the shepherdess meeting with Guido.
And the harlots of Baudelaire.

ANOTHER MAN'S WIFE

She was as pale as one
Who has just produced an abortion.

Her face was beautiful as a delicate stone
With the sculptor's dust still on it.

5   And yet I was glad that it was you and not I
Who had removed her from her first husband.

POEM

Abbreviated from the Conversation of Mr. T. E. H.

Over the flat slope of St Eloi
A wide wall of sandbags.
Night,
In the silence desultory men
5   Pottering over small fires, cleaning their mess-tins:
To and fro, from the lines,
Men walk as on Piccadilly,
Making paths in the dark,
Through scattered dead horses,
10   Over a dead Belgian's belly.

The Germans have rockets. The English have no rockets.
Behind the lines, cannon, hidden, lying back miles.
Before the line, chaos:

My mind is a corridor. The minds about me are corridors.
15   Nothing suggests itself. There is nothing to do but keep on.

Cathay
(1915)

SONG OF THE BOWMEN OF SHU

Here we are, picking the first fern-shoots
And saying: When shall we get back to our country?
Here we are because we have the Ken-nin for our foemen,
We have no comfort because of these Mongols.
5   We grub the soft fern-shoots,
When anyone says "Return," the others are full of sorrow.
Sorrowful minds, sorrow is strong, we are hungry and thirsty.
Our defence is not yet made sure, no one can let his friend return.
We grub the old fern-stalks.
10   We say: Will we be let to go back in October?
There is no ease in royal affairs, we have no comfort.
Our sorrow is bitter, but we would not return to our country.
What flower has come into blossom?
Whose chariot? The General's.
15   Horses, his horses even, are tired. They were strong.
We have no rest, three battles a month.
By heaven, his horses are tired.
The generals are on them, the soldiers are by them.
The horses are well trained, the generals have ivory arrows and quivers
20   ornamented with fish-skin.
The enemy is swift, we must be careful.
When we set out, the willows were drooping with spring,
We come back in the snow,
We go slowly, we are hungry and thirsty,
25   Our mind is full of sorrow, who will know of our grief?

By Kutsugen
4th Century B.C.

THE BEAUTIFUL TOILET

Blue, blue is the grass about the river
And the willows have overfilled the close garden.
And within, the mistress, in the midmost of her youth,
White, white of face, hesitates, passing the door.
5   Slender, she puts forth a slender hand;

And she was a courtesan in the old days,
And she has married a sot,
Who now goes drunkenly out
And leaves her too much alone.

By Mei Sheng
B.C. 140

THE RIVER SONG

This boat is of shato-wood, and its gunwales are cut magnolia,
Musicians with jewelled flutes and with pipes of gold
Fill full the sides in rows, and our wine
Is rich for a thousand cups.
5   We carry singing girls, drift with the drifting water,
Yet Sennin needs
A yellow stork for a charger, and all our seamen
Would follow the white gulls or ride them.
Kutsu's prose song
10   Hangs with the sun and moon.

King So's terraced palace
                  is now but barren hill,
But I draw pen on this barge
Causing the five peaks to tremble,
15   And I have joy in these words
                    like the joy of blue islands.
(If glory could last forever
Then the waters of Han would flow northward.)

And I have moped in the Emperor's garden, awaiting an order-to-write!
20   I looked at the dragon-pond, with its willow-coloured water
Just reflecting the sky's tinge;
And heard the five-score nightingales aimlessly singing.

The eastern wind brings the green colour into the island grasses at
        Yei-shu,
25   The purple house and the crimson are full of Spring softness.
South of the pond the willow-tips are half-blue and bluer,
Their cords tangle in mist, against the brocade-like palace.

Vine-strings a hundred feet long hang down from carved railings,
And high over the willows, the fine birds sing to each other, and listen,
30 Crying—"Kwan, Kuan," for the early wind, and the feel of it.
The wind bundles itself into a bluish cloud and wanders off.
Over a thousand gates, over a thousand doors are the sounds of spring
        singing,
And the Emperor is at Ko.
35 Five clouds hang aloft, bright on the purple sky,
The imperial guards come forth from the golden house with their
        armour a-gleaming.
The Emperor in his jewelled car goes out to inspect his flowers,
He goes out to Hori, to look at the wing-flapping storks,
40 He returns by way of Sei rock, to hear the new nightingales,
For the gardens at Jo-run are full of new nightingales,
Their sound is mixed in this flute,
Their voice is in the twelve pipes here.

By Rihaku
8th century A.D.

THE RIVER-MERCHANT'S WIFE: A LETTER

While my hair was still cut straight across my forehead
I played about the front gate, pulling flowers.
You came by on bamboo stilts, playing horse,
You walked about my seat, playing with blue plums.
5 And we went on living in the village of Chokan:
Two small people, without dislike or suspicion.

At fourteen I married My Lord you.
I never laughed, being bashful.
Lowering my head, I looked at the wall.
10 Called to, a thousand times, I never looked back.

At fifteen I stopped scowling,
I desired my dust to be mingled with yours
Forever and forever and forever.
Why should I climb the look out?

15 At sixteen you departed,
    You went into far Ku-to-yen, by the river of swirling eddies,
    And you have been gone five months.
    The monkeys make sorrowful noise overhead.
    You dragged your feet when you went out.
20 By the gate now, the moss is grown, the different mosses,
    Too deep to clear them away!
    The leaves fall early this autumn, in wind.
    The paired butterflies are already yellow with August
    Over the grass in the West garden;
25 They hurt me. I grow older.
    If you are coming down through the narrows of the river Kiang,
    Please let me know beforehand,
    And I will come out to meet you
                    As far as Cho-fu-Sa.

                                    By Rihaku

POEM BY THE BRIDGE AT TEN-SHIN

    March has come to the bridge head,
    Peach boughs and apricot boughs hang over a thousand gates,
    At morning there are flowers to cut the heart,
    And evening drives them on the eastward-flowing waters.
5   Petals are on the gone waters and on the going,
    And on the back-swirling eddies,
    But to-day's men are not the men of the old days,
    Though they hang in the same way over the bridge-rail.

    The sea's colour moves at the dawn
10 And the princes still stand in rows, about the throne,
    And the moon falls over the portals of Sei-go-yo,
    And clings to the walls and the gate-top.
    With head gear glittering against the cloud and sun,
    The lords go forth from the court, and into far borders.
15 They ride upon dragon-like horses.
    Upon horses with head-trappings of yellow metal,
    And the streets make way for their passage.
                    Haughty their passing,
    Haughty their steps as they go in to great banquets,

20   To high halls and curious food,
To the perfumed air and girls dancing,
To clear flutes and clear singing;
To the dance of the seventy couples;
To the mad chase through the gardens.
25   Night and day are given over to pleasure
And they think it will last a thousand autumns,
           Unwearying autumns.
For them the yellow dogs howl portents in vain,
And what are they compared to the lady Riokushu,
30   That was cause of hate!
Who among them is a man like Han-rei
        Who departed alone with his mistress,
With her hair unbound, and he his own skiffsman!

                         By Rihaku

THE JEWEL STAIRS' GRIEVANCE

The jewelled steps are already quite white with dew,
It is so late that the dew soaks my gauze stockings,
And I let down the crystal curtain
And watch the moon through the clear autumn.

                         By Rihaku

NOTE.—Jewel stairs, therefore a palace. Grievance, therefore there is something to complain of. Gauze stockings, therefore a court lady, not a servant who complains. Clear autumn, therefore he has no excuse on account of weather. Also she has come early, for the dew has not merely whitened the stairs, but has soaked her stockings. The poem is especially prized because she utters no direct reproach.

LAMENT OF THE FRONTIER GUARD

By the North Gate, the wind blows full of sand,
Lonely from the beginning of time until now!
Trees fall, the grass goes yellow with autumn.
I climb the towers and towers
5   to watch out the barbarous land:

Desolate castle, the sky, the wide desert.
There is no wall left to this village.
Bones white with a thousand frosts,
High heaps, covered with trees and grass;
10 Who brought this to pass?
Who has brought the flaming imperial anger?
Who has brought the army with drums and with kettle-drums?
Barbarous kings.
A gracious spring, turned to blood-ravenous autumn,
15 A turmoil of wars-men, spread over the middle kingdom.
Three hundred and sixty thousand,
And sorrow, sorrow like rain.
Sorrow to go, and sorrow, sorrow returning.
Desolate, desolate fields,
20 And no children of warfare upon them,
    No longer the men for offence and defence.
Ah, how shall you know the dreary sorrow at the North Gate,
With Riboku's name forgotten,
And we guardsmen fed to the tigers.

            By Rihaku

EXILE'S LETTER

To So-Kin of Rakuyo, ancient friend, Chancellor of Gen.
Now I remember that you built me a special tavern
By the south side of the bridge at Ten-Shin.
With yellow gold and white jewels, we paid for songs and laughter
5 And we were drunk for month on month, forgetting the kings and princes.
Intelligent men came drifting in from the sea and from the west border,
And with them, and with you especially
There was nothing at cross purpose,
And they made nothing of sea-crossing or of mountain-crossing,
10 If only they could be of that fellowship,
And we all spoke out our hearts and minds, and without regret.
And then I was sent off to South Wei,
    smothered in laurel groves,
And you to the north of Raku-hoku,
15 Till we had nothing but thoughts and memories in common.
And then, when separation had come to its worst,

We met, and travelled into Sen-Go,
Through all the thirty-six folds of the turning and twisting waters,
Into a valley of the thousand bright flowers,
20   That was the first valley;
And into ten thousand valleys full of voices and pine-winds.
And with silver harness and reins of gold,
Out came the East of Kan foreman and his company.
And there came also the "True man" of Shi-yo to meet me,
25   Playing on a jewelled mouth-organ.
In the storied houses of San-Ko they gave us more Sennin music,
Many instruments, like the sound of young phœnix broods.
The foreman of Kan Chu, drunk, danced
                    because his long sleeves wouldn't keep still
30   With that music playing,
And I, wrapped in brocade, went to sleep with my head on his lap,
And my spirit so high it was all over the heavens,
And before the end of the day we were scattered like stars, or rain.
I had to be off to So, far away over the waters,
35   You back to your river-bridge.

And your father, who was brave as a leopard,
Was governor in Hei Shu, and put down the barbarian rabble.
And one May he had you send for me,
                    despite the long distance.
40   And what with broken wheels and so on, I won't say it wasn't hard going.
Over roads twisted like sheep's guts.
And I was still going, late in the year,
                    in the cutting wind from the North,
And thinking how little you cared for the cost,
45   and you caring enough to pay it.
And what a reception:
Red jade cups, food well set on a blue jewelled table,
And I was drunk, and had no thought of returning.
And you would walk out with me to the western corner of the castle,
50   To the dynastic temple, with water about it clear as blue jade,
With boats floating, and the sound of mouth-organs and drums,
With ripples like dragon-scales, going grass green on the water,
Pleasure lasting, with courtezans, going and coming without hindrance.
With the willow flakes falling like snow,
55   And the vermilioned girls getting drunk about sunset,
And the water, a hundred feet deep, reflecting green eyebrows

—Eyebrows painted green are a fine sight in young moonlight,
Gracefully painted—
And the girls singing back at each other,
60   Dancing in transparent brocade,
And the wind lifting the song, and interrupting it,
Tossing it up under the clouds.
          And all this comes to an end.
          And is not again to be met with.
65   I went up to the court for examination,
Tried Layu's luck, offered the Choyo song,
And got no promotion,
          and went back to the East Mountains White-headed.
And once again, later, we met at the South bridge-head.
70   And then the crowd broke up, you went north to San palace,
And if you ask how I regret that parting:
    It is like the flowers falling at Spring's end
        Confused, whirled in a tangle.
What is the use of talking, and there is no end of talking,
75   There is no end of things in the heart.

I call in the boy,
Have him sit on his knees here
        To seal this,
And send it a thousand miles, thinking.

                            By Rihaku

FOUR POEMS OF DEPARTURE

Light rain is on the light dust
The willows of the inn-yard
Will be going greener and greener,
But you, Sir, had better take wine ere
    your departure,
For you will have no friends about
    you
When you come to the gates of Go.

              (Rihaku or Omakitsu)

Separation On the River Kiang

Ko-jin goes west from Ko-kaku-ro,
The smoke-flowers are blurred over the river.
His lone sail blots the far sky.
And now I see only the river,
     The long Kiang, reaching heaven.

Rihaku

Taking Leave of A Friend

Blue mountains to the north of the walls,
White river winding about them;
Here we must make separation
And go out through a thousand miles of dead grass.

Mind like a floating wide cloud,
5 Sunset like the parting of old acquaintances
Who bow over their clasped hands at a distance.
Our horses neigh to each other
     as we are departing.

Rihaku

Leave-Taking Near Shoku
"Sanso, King of Shoku, built roads"

They say the roads of Sanso are steep,
Sheer as the mountains.
The walls rise in a man's face,
Clouds grow out of the hill
5   at his horse's bridle.
Sweet trees are on the paved way of the Shin,
Their trunks burst through the paving,
And freshets are bursting their ice
     in the midst of Shoku, a proud city.

10 Men's fates are already set,
There is no need of asking diviners.

Rihaku

The City of Choan

The phœnix are at play on their terrace.
The phœnix are gone, the river flows on alone.
Flowers and grass
Cover over the dark path
5   where lay the dynastic house of the Go.
The bright cloths and bright caps of Shin
Are now the base of old hills.

The Three Mountains fall through the far heaven,
The isle of White Heron
10   splits the two streams apart.
Now the high clouds cover the sun
And I can not see Choan afar
And I am sad.

Rihaku

SOUTH-FOLK IN COLD COUNTRY

The Dai horse neighs against the bleak wind of Etsu,
The birds of Etsu have no love for En, in the north,
Emotion is born out of habit.
Yesterday we went out of the Wild-Goose gate,
5 To-day from the Dragon-Pen.[1]
Surprised. Desert turmoil. Sea sun.
Flying snow bewilders the barbarian heaven.
Lice swarm like ants over our accoutrements.
Mind and spirit drive on the feathery banners.
10 Hard fight gets no reward.
Loyalty is hard to explain.

[1] *I.e.*, we have been warring from one end of the empire to the other, now east, now west, on each border.

Who will be sorry for General Rishogu,
       the swift moving,
Whose white head is lost for this province?

SENNIN POEM BY KAKUHAKU

The red and green kingfishers
       flash between the orchids and clover,
One bird casts its gleam on another.

Green vines hang through the high forest,
5   They weave a whole roof to the mountain,
The lone man sits with shut speech,
He purrs and pats the clear strings.
He throws his heart up through the sky,
He bites through the flower pistil
10   and brings up a fine fountain.
The red-pine-tree god looks at him and wonders.
He rides through the purple smoke to visit the sennin,
He takes "Floating Hill"[1] by the sleeve,
He claps his hand on the back of the great water sennin.

15   But you, you dam'd crowd of gnats,
Can you even tell the age of a turtle?

A BALLAD OF THE MULBERRY ROAD

The sun rises in south east corner of things
To look on the tall house of the Shin
For they have a daughter named Rafu,
       (pretty girl)
5   She made the name for herself: "Gauze Veil,"
For she feeds mulberries to silkworms.
She gets them by the south wall of the town.
With green strings she makes the warp of her basket,

[1] Name of a sennin.

She makes the shoulder-straps of her basket
10   from the boughs of Katsura.
And she piles her hair up on the left side of her head-piece.

Her earrings are made of pearl,
Her underskirt is of green pattern-silk,
Her overskirt is the same silk dyed in purple,
15   And when men going by look on Rafu
          They set down their burdens,
They stand and twirl their moustaches.

(Fenollosa Mss., very early)

OLD IDEA OF CHOAN BY ROSORIU

I

The narrow streets cut into the wide highway at Choan,
Dark oxen, white horses,
          drag on the seven coaches with outriders.
The coaches are perfumed wood,
5   The jewelled chair is held up at the crossway,
Before the royal lodge
          a glitter of golden saddles, awaiting the princess,
They eddy before the gate of the barons.
The canopy embroidered with dragons
10   drinks in and casts back the sun.

Evening comes.
          The trappings are bordered with mist.
The hundred cords of mist are spread through
          and double the trees,
15   Night birds, and night women,
          spread out their sounds through the gardens.

II

Birds with flowery wing, hovering butterflies
          crowd over the thousand gates,
Trees that glitter like jade,
20   terraces tinged with silver,
The seed of a myriad hues,

A net-work of arbours and passages and covered ways,
Double towers, winged roofs,
       border the net-work of ways:
25   A place of felicitous meeting.
Riu's house stands out on the sky,
       with glitter of colour
As Butei of Kan had made the high golden lotus
       to gather his dews,
30   Before it another house which I do not know:
How shall we know all the friends
       whom we meet on strange roadways?

TO-EM-MEI'S "THE UNMOVING CLOUD"

"Wet springtime," says To-Em-Mei,
"Wet spring in the garden."

I

The clouds have gathered, and gathered,
       and the rain falls and falls,
The eight ply of the heavens
       are all folded into one darkness,
5   And the wide, flat road stretches out.
I stop in my room toward the East, quiet, quiet,
I pat my new cask of wine.
My friends are estranged, or far distant,
I bow my head and stand still.

II

10   Rain, rain, and the clouds have gathered,
The eight ply of the heavens are darkness,
The flat land is turned into river.
       "Wine, wine, here is wine!"
I drink by my eastern window.
15   I think of talking and man,
And no boat, no carriage, approaches.

III

The trees in my east-looking garden
    are bursting out with new twigs,
They try to stir new affection,
And men say the sun and moon keep on moving
    because they can't find a soft seat.

The birds flutter to rest in my tree,
    and I think I have heard them saying,
"It is not that there are no other men
But we like this fellow the best,
But however we long to speak
He can not know of our sorrow."

T'ao Yuan Ming,
A.D. 365–427

Poems 1915–1918

NEAR PERIGORD

A Perigord, pres del muralh
Tan que i puosch' om gitar ab malh

You'd have men's hearts up from the dust
And tell their secrets, Messire Cino,
Right enough? Then read between the lines of Uc St. Circ,
Solve me the riddle, for you know the tale.

5   Bertrans, En Bertrans, left a fine canzone:
"Meant, I love you, you have turned me out.
The voice at Montfort, Lady Agnes' hair,
Bel Miral's stature, the viscountess' throat,
Set all together, are not worthy of you . . . ."
10   And all the while you sing out that canzone,
Think you that Maent lived at Montagnac,
One at Chalais, another at Malemort
Hard over Brive — for every lady a castle,
Each place strong.

15   Oh, *is* it easy enough?
Tairiran held hall in Montagnac,
His brother-in-law was all there was of power
In Perigord, and this good union
Gobbled all the land, and held it later for some hundred years.
20   And our En Bertrans was in Altafort,
Hub of the wheel, the stirrer-up of strife,
As caught by Dante in the last wallow of hell —
The headless trunk "that made its head a lamp,"
For separation wrought out separation,
25   And he who set the strife between brother and brother
And had his way with the old English king,
Viced in such torture for the "counterpass."

How would you live, with neighbours set about you —
Poictiers and Brive, untaken Rochechouart,
30   Spread like the finger-tips of one frail hand;
And you on that great mountain of a palm —
Not a neat ledge, not Foix between its streams,
But one huge back half-covered up with pine,

Worked for and snatched from the string-purse of Born—
35   The four round towers, four brothers—mostly fools:
What could he do but play the desperate chess,
And stir old grudges?
        "Pawn your castles, lords!
Let the Jews pay."
40   And the great scene—
(That, maybe, never happened!)
        Beaten at last,
Before the hard old king:
        "Your son, ah, since he died
45   My wit and worth are cobwebs brushed aside
In the full flare of grief. Do what you will."

Take the whole man, and ravel out the story.
He loved this lady in castle Montagnac?
The castle flanked him—he had need of it.
50   You read to-day, how long the overlords of Perigord,
The Talleyrands, have held the place; it was no transient fiction.
And Maent failed him? Or saw through the scheme?

And all his net-like thought of new alliance?
Chalais is high, a-level with the poplars.
55   Its lowest stones just meet the valley tips
Where the low Dronne is filled with water-lilies.
And Rochechouart can match it, stronger yet,
The very spur's end, built on sheerest cliff,
And Malemort keeps its close hold on Brive,
60   While Born, his own close purse, his rabbit warren,
His subterranean chamber with a dozen doors,
A-bristle with antennæ to feel roads,
To sniff the traffic into Perigord.
And that hard phalanx, that unbroken line,
65   The ten good miles from there to Maent's castle,
All of his flank—how could he do without her?
And all the road to Cahors, to Toulouse?
What would he do without her?

    "Papiol,
70   Go forthright singing—Anhes, Cembelins.
There is a throat; ah, there are two white hands;

There is a trellis full of early roses,
And all my heart is bound about with love.
Where am I come with compound flatteries —
75　What doors are open to fine compliment?"
And every one half jealous of Maent?
He wrote the catch to pit their jealousies
Against her; give her pride in them?

Take his own speech, make what you will of it —
80　And still the knot, the first knot, of Maent?

Is it a love poem? Did he sing of war?
Is it an intrigue to run subtly out,
Born of a jongleur's tongue, freely to pass
Up and about and in and out the land,
85　Mark him a craftsman and a strategist?
(St. Leider had done as much at Polhonac,
Singing a different stave, as closely hidden.)
Oh, there is precedent, legal tradition,
To sing one thing when your song means another,
90　*"Et albirar ab lor bordon—"*
Foix' count knew that. What is Sir Bertrans' singing?

Maent, Maent, and yet again Maent,
Or war and broken heaumes and politics?

II
End fact. Try fiction. Let us say we see
95　En Bertrans, a tower-room at Hautefort,
Sunset, the ribbon-like road lies, in red cross-light,
Southward toward Montagnac, and he bends at a table
Scribbling, swearing between his teeth; by his left hand
Lie little straps of parchment covered over,
100　Scratched and erased with *al* and *ochaisos.*
Testing his list of rhymes, a lean man? Bilious?
With a red straggling beard?
And the green cat's-eye lifts toward Montagnac.

Or take his "magnet" singer setting out,
105　Dodging his way past Aubeterre, singing at Chalais
　　　　In the vaulted hall,

Or, by a lichened tree at Rochechouart
Aimlessly watching a hawk above the valleys,
Waiting his turn in the mid-summer evening,
110   Thinking of Aelis, whom he loved heart and soul . . .
To find her half alone, Montfort away,
And a brown, placid, hated woman visiting her,
Spoiling his visit, with a year before the next one.
Little enough?
115   Or carry him forward. "Go through all the courts,
My Magnet," Bertrans had said.

       We came to Ventadour
In the mid love court, he sings out the canzon,
No one hears save Arrimon Luc D'Esparo—
120   No one hears aught save the gracious sound of compliments.
Sir Arrimon counts on his fingers, Montfort,
Rochechouart, Chalais, the rest, the tactic,
Malemort, guesses beneath, sends word to Cœur-de-Lion:
The compact, de Born smoked out, trees felled
125   About his castle, cattle driven out!
Or no one sees it, and En Bertrans prospered?

And ten years after, or twenty, as you will,
Arnaut and Richard lodge beneath Chalus:
The dull round towers encroaching on the field,
130   The tents tight drawn, horses at tether
Further and out of reach, the purple night,
The crackling of small fires, the bannerets,
The lazy leopards on the largest banner,
Stray gleams on hanging mail, an armourer's torch-flare
135   Melting on steel.

       And in the quietest space
They probe old scandals, say de Born is dead;
And we've the gossip (skipped six hundred years).
Richard shall die to-morrow—leave him there
140   Talking of *trobar clus* with Daniel.
And the "best craftsman" sings out his friend's song,
Envies its vigour . . . and deplores the technique,
Dispraises his own skill?—That's as you will.
And they discuss the dead man,

145   Plantagenet puts the riddle: "Did he love her?"
      And Arnaut parries: "Did he love your sister?
      True, he has praised her, but in some opinion
      He wrote that praise only to show he had
      The favour of your party; had been well received."

150   "You knew the man."
                "*You* knew the man.
      I am an artist, you have tried both métiers."
      "You were born near him."
                "Do we know our friends?"
155   "Say that he saw the castles, say that he loved Maent!"
      "Say that he loved her, does it solve the riddle?"
                End the discussion, Richard goes out next day
      And gets a quarrel-bolt shot through his vizard,
      Pardons the bowman, dies,

160   Ends our discussion. Arnaut ends
      "In sacred odour" — (that's apocryphal!)
      And we can leave the talk till Dante writes:
      Surely I saw, and still before my eyes
      Goes on that headless trunk, that bears for light
165   *Its own head swinging, gripped by the dead hair,*
      And like a swinging lamp that says, "Ah me!
      I severed men, my head and heart
      Ye see here severed, my life's counterpart."

      Or take En Bertrans?

                        III
170   *Ed eran due in uno, ed uno in due;*
                     Inferno, XXVIII, 125

      "Bewildering spring, and by the Auvezere
      Poppies and day's eyes in the green émail
      Rose over us; and we knew all that stream,
175   And our two horses had traced out the valleys;
      Knew the low flooded lands squared out with poplars,
      In the young days when the deep sky befriended.
            And great wings beat above us in the twilight,
      And the great wheels in heaven

180   Bore us together . . . surging . . . and apart . . .
      Believing we should meet with lips and hands,

      High, high and sure . . . and then the counter-thrust:
      'Why do you love me? Will you always love me?
      But I am like the grass, I can not love you,'
185   Or, 'Love, and I love and love you,
      And hate your mind, not *you,* your soul, your hands.'

      So to this last estrangement, Tairiran!

      There shut up in his castle, Tairiran's,
      She who had nor ears nor tongue save in her hands,
190   Gone — ah, gone — untouched, unreachable!
      She who could never live save through one person,
      She who could never speak save to one person,
      And all the rest of her a shifting change,
      A broken bundle of mirrors . . . !"

VILLANELLE: THE PSYCHOLOGICAL HOUR

      I had over-prepared the event,
            that much was ominous.
      With middle-ageing care
            I had laid out just the right books.
5   I had almost turned down the pages.

            Beauty is so rare a thing.
            So few drink of my fountain.

      So much barren regret,
      So many hours wasted!
10   And now I watch, from the window,
            the rain, the wandering busses.

      "Their little cosmos is shaken" —
            the air is alive with that fact.
      In their parts of the city
15   they are played on by diverse forces.

How do I know?
        Oh, I know well enough.
For them there is something afoot.
        As for me;
20   I had over-prepared the event —

    Beauty is so rare a thing,
    So few drink of my fountain.

Two friends: a breath of the forest . . .
Friends? Are people less friends
25   because one has just, at last, found them?
Twice they promised to come.
    "Between the night and morning?"

Beauty would drink of my mind.
Youth would awhile forget
30   my youth is gone from me.

                    II
("Speak up! You have danced so stiffly?
    Someone admired your works,
    And said so frankly.

    "Did you talk like a fool,
35   The first night?
    The second evening?"

"*But* they promised again:
    'To-morrow at tea-time.'")

                    III
Now the third day is here —
40   no word from either;
No word from her nor him,
Only another man's note:
    "Dear Pound, I am leaving England."

FISH AND THE SHADOW

The salmon-trout drifts in the stream,
The soul of the salmon-trout floats over the stream
        Like a little wafer of light.

The salmon moves in the sun-shot, bright shallow sea. . . .

5   As light as the shadow of the fish
              that falls through the water,
She came into the large room by the stair,
Yawning a little she came with the sleep still upon her.

"I am just from bed. The sleep is still in my eyes.
10   Come. I have had a long dream."
And I: "That wood?
And two springs have passed us."
"Not so far, no, not so far now,
There is a place — but no one else knows it —
15   A field in a valley . . .
                Qu'ieu sui avinen,
Ieu lo sai."

She must speak of the time
Of Arnaut de Mareuil, I thought, *"qu'ieu sui avinen."*

20   Light as the shadow of the fish
That falls through the pale green water.

PAGANI'S, NOVEMBER 8

Suddenly discovering in the eyes of the very beautiful
        Normande cocotte
The eyes of the very learned British Museum assistant.

THE LAKE ISLE

O God, O Venus, O Mercury, patron of thieves,
Give me in due time, I beseech you, a little tobacco-shop,
With the little bright boxes
      piled up neatly upon the shelves
5   And the loose fragrant cavendish
      and the shag,
And the bright Virginia
      loose under the bright glass cases,
And a pair of scales not too greasy,
10   And the whores dropping in for a word or two in passing,
For a flip word, and to tidy their hair a bit.

O God, O Venus, O Mercury, patron of thieves,
Lend me a little tobacco-shop,
      or install me in any profession
15   Save this damn'd profession of writing,
        where one needs one's brains all the time.

IMPRESSIONS OF FRANÇOIS-MARIE AROUET
(DE VOLTAIRE)

I

Phyllidula and the Spoils of Gouvernet

Where, Lady, are the days
When you could go out in a hired hansom
Without footmen and equipments?
And dine in a soggy, cheap restaurant?
5   Phyllidula now, with your powdered Swiss footman
Clanking the door shut,
          and lying;
And carpets from Savonnier, and from Persia,
And your new service at dinner,
10 And plates from Germain,
And cabinets and chests from Martin (almost lacquer),
And your white vases from Japan,
And the lustre of diamonds,
Etcetera, etcetera, and etcetera?

II
To Madame du Châtelet

If you'd have me go on loving you
Give me back the time of the thing.

Will you give me dawn light at evening?
Time has driven me out from the fine plaisaunces,
5   The parks with the swards all over dew,
And grass going glassy with the light on it,
The green stretches where love is and the grapes
Hang in yellow-white and dark clusters ready for pressing.

And if now we can't fit with our time of life
10   There is not much but its evil left us.

Life gives us two minutes, two seasons —
            One to be dull in;
Two deaths — and to stop loving and being lovable,
That is the real death,
15   The other is little beside it.

Crying after the follies gone by me,
Quiet talking is all that is left us —
Gentle talking, not like the first talking, less lively;
And to follow after friendship, as they call it,
20   Weeping that we can follow naught else.

III
To Madame Lullin

You'll wonder that an old man of eighty
Can go on writing you verses. . . .

Grass showing under the snow,
Birds singing late in the year!

5   And Tibullus could say of his death, in his Latin:
"Delia, I would look on you, dying."

And Delia herself fading out,
Forgetting even her beauty.

CANTICO DEL SOLE

The thought of what America would be like
If the Classics had a wide circulation
       Troubles my sleep,
The thought of what America,
5   The thought of what America,
The thought of what America would be like
If the Classics had a wide circulation
       Troubles my sleep.
Nunc dimittis, now lettest thou thy servant,
10 Now lettest thou thy servant
       Depart in peace.
The thought of what America,
The thought of what America,
The thought of what America would be like
15 If the Classics had a wide circulation . . .
       Oh well!
       It troubles my sleep.

L'AURA AMARA

from Arnaut Daniel

I

The bitter air
Strips panoply
From trees
Where softer winds set leaves,
5   And glad
Beaks
Now in brakes are coy,
Scarce peep the wee
Mates
10 And un-mates.
    What gaud's the work?
    What good the glees?
What curse
I strive to shake!
15 Me hath she cast from high,

In fell disease
I lie, and deathly fearing.

II

So clear the flare
That first lit me
20   To seize
Her whom my soul believes;
If cad
Sneaks,
Blabs, slanders, my joy
25   Counts little fee
Baits
And their hates.
        I scorn their perk
        And preen, at ease.
30   Disburse
Can she, and wake
Such firm delights, that I
Am hers, froth, lees
Bigod! from toe to earring.

III

35   Amor, look yare!
Know certainly
The keys:
How she thy suit receives;
Nor add
40   Piques,
'Twere folly to annoy
I'm true, so dree
Fates;
No debates
45   Shake me, nor jerk,
        My verities
Turn terse,
And yet I ache;
Her lips, not snows that fly
50   Have potencies
To shake, to cool my searing.

IV

Behold my prayer,
(Or company
Of these)
55   Seeks whom such height achieves;
Well clad
Seeks
Her, and would not cloy.
Heart apertly
60   States
Thought. Hope waits
    'Gainst death to irk:
    False brevities
And worse!
65   To her I raik,
Sole her; all others' dry
Felicities
I count not worth the leering.

V

Ah, fair face, where
70   Each quality
But frees
One pride-shaft more, that cleaves
Me; mad frieks
(O' thy beck) destroy,
75   And mockery
Baits
Me, and rates.
    Yet I not shirk
    Thy velleities,
80   Averse
Me not, nor slake
Desire. God draws not nigh
To Dome, with pleas
Wherein's so little veering.

VI

85   Now chant prepare,
And melody
To please

The king, who'll judge thy sheaves.
Worth, sad,
90   Sneaks
Here; double employ
Hath there. Get thee
Plates
Full, and cates,
95   Gifts, go! Nor lurk
         Here till decrees
Reverse,
And ring thou take
Straight t'Arago I'd ply:
100   Cross the wide seas
But 'Rome' disturbs my hearing.

Coda

At midnight mirk
In secrecies
105   I nurse
My served make
In heart; nor try
My melodies
At other's door not mearing.

ALBA

When the nightingale to his mate
    Sings day-long and night late
    My love and I keep state
    In bower,
5   In flower,
    'Till the watchman on the tower
Cry:
        "Up! Thou rascal, Rise,
      I see the white
10   Light
          And the night
             Flies."

AVRIL

When the springtime is sweet
And the birds repeat
Their new song in the leaves.
'Tis meet
5   A man go where he will.

But from where my heart is set
No message I get;
My heart all wakes and grieves;
Defeat
10   Or luck, I must have my fill.

Our love comes out
Like the branch that turns about
On the top of the hawthorne,
With frost and hail at night
15   Suffers despite
'Till the sun come, and the green leaf on the bough.

I remember the young day
When we set strife away,
And she gave me such gesning,
20   Her love and her ring:
God grant I die not by any man's stroke
'Till I have my hand 'neath her cloak.

I care not for their clamour
Who have come between me and my charmer,
25   For I know how words run loose,
Big talk and little use.
Spoilers of pleasure,
We take their measure.

Guilhem de Peitieu

from MŒURS CONTEMPORAINES

"Nodier raconte . . ."

I

At a friend of my wife's there is a photograph,
A faded, pale, brownish photograph,
Of the times when the sleeves were large,
Silk, stiff and large above the *lacertus*,
That is, the upper arm,
And décolleté. . . .

It is a lady,
She sits at a harp,
Playing.

And by her left foot, in a basket,
Is an infant, aged about 14 months,
The infant beams at the parent,
The parent re-beams at its offspring.
The basket is lined with satin,
There is a satin-like bow on the harp.

2

And in the home of the novelist
There is a satin-like bow on a harp.

You enter and pass hall after hall,
Conservatory follows conservatory,
Lilies lift their white symbolical cups,
Whence their symbolical pollen is excerpted,
Near them I notice an harp
And the blue satin ribbon,
And the copy of "Hatha Yoga"
And the neat piles of unopened, unopening books,

And she spoke to me of the monarch,
And of the purity of her soul.

Stele

After years of continence
    he hurled himself into a sea of six women.
Now, quenched as the brand of Meleagar,
    He lies by the poluphloisboious sea-coast.

5   Παρὰ Θῖνα Πολυφλοίσβοιο Θαλάσσης.

SISTE VIATOR.

I Vecchii

They will come no more,
The old men with beautiful manners.

Il était comme un tout petit garçon
With his blouse full of apples
5   And sticking out all the way round;
Blagueur! "Con gli occhi onesti e tardi,"

And he said:
    "Oh! Abelard!" as if the topic
Were much too abstruse for his comprehension,
10   And he talked about "the Great Mary,"
And said: "Mr. Pound is shocked at my levity,"
When it turned out he meant Mrs. Ward.

And the other was rather like my bust by Gaudier,
Or like a real Texas colonel,
15   He said: "Why flay dead horses?
There was once a man called Voltaire."

And he said they used to cheer Verdi,
In Rome, after the opera,
And the guards couldn't stop them,

20   And that was an anagram for Vittorio
Emanuele Re D' Italia,
And the guards couldn't stop them.

Old men with beautiful manners,
Sitting in the Row of a morning,
25 Walking on the Chelsea Embankment.

Ritratto

And she said:
   "You remember Mr. Lowell,
He was your ambassador here?"
And I said: "That was before I arrived."
5 And she said:
   "He stomped into my bedroom. . . .
(By that time she had got on to Browning.)
. . . stomped into my bedroom. . . .
And said: 'Do I,
10 I ask you, Do I
Care too much for society dinners?'
And I wouldn't say that he didn't.
Shelley used to live in this house."

She was a very old lady,
15 I never saw her again.

Homage to Sextus Propertius
(1918 / 19)

ORFEO
"Quia Pauper Amavi"

I

Shades of Callimachus, Coan ghosts of Philetas
It is in your grove I would walk,
I who come first from the clear font
Bringing the Grecian orgies into Italy,
                        and the dance into Italy.
Who hath taught you so subtle a measure,
              in what hall have you heard it;
What foot beat out your time-bar,
           what water has mellowed your whistles?

Out-weariers of Apollo will, as we know, continue their Martian generalities.
      We have kept our erasers in order,
A new-fangled chariot follows the flower-hung horses;
A young Muse with young loves clustered about her
            ascends with me into the aether, . . .
And there is no high-road to the Muses.

Annalists will continue to record Roman reputations,
Celebrities from the Trans-Caucasus will belaud Roman celebrities
And expound the distentions of Empire,
But for something to read in normal circumstances?
For a few pages brought down from the forked hill unsullied?
I ask a wreath which will not crush my head.
           And there is no hurry about it;
I shall have, doubtless, a boom after my funeral,
Seeing that long standing increases all things
              regardless of quality.
And who would have known the towers
          pulled down by a deal-wood horse;
Or of Achilles withstaying waters by Simois
Or of Hector spattering wheel-rims,
Or of Polydmantus, by Scamander, or Helenus and Deiphoibos?
Their door-yards would scarcely know them, or Paris.
Small talk O Ilion, and O Troad
           twice taken by Oetian gods,
If Homer had not stated your case!

And I also among the later nephews of this city
          shall have my dog's day,
With no stone upon my contemptible sepulchre;

My vote coming from the temple of Phoebus in Lycia, at Patara,
And in the mean time my songs will travel,

40   And the devirginated young ladies will enjoy them
               when they have got over the strangeness,
For Orpheus tamed the wild beasts—
                 and held up the Threician river;
And Cithaeron shook up the rocks by Thebes

45   and danced them into a bulwark at his pleasure,
And you, O Polyphemus? Did harsh Galatea almost
Turn to your dripping horses, because of a tune, under Aetna?
We must look into the matter.
Bacchus and Apollo in favour of it,

50   There will be a crowd of young women doing homage to my palaver.
Though my house is not propped up by Taenarian columns from Laconia
         (associated with Neptune and Cerberus),
Though it is not stretched upon gilded beams:
My orchards do not lie level and wide

55   as the forests of Phaecia,
                   the luxurious and Ionian,
Nor are my caverns stuffed stiff with a Marcian vintage,
My cellar does not date from Numa Pompilius,
Nor bristle with wine jars,

60   Nor is it equipped with a frigidaire patent;
Yet the companions of the Muses
           will keep their collective nose in my books,
And weary with historical data, they will turn to my dance tune.

Happy who are mentioned in my pamphlets,

65   the songs shall be a fine tomb-stone over their beauty.
          But against this?
Neither expensive pyramids scraping the stars in their route,
Nor houses modelled upon that of Jove in East Elis,
Nor the monumental effigies of Mausolus,

70   are a complete elucidation of death.

Flame burns, rain sinks into the cracks
And they all go to rack ruin beneath the thud of the years.
Stands genius a deathless adornment,
         a name not to be worn out with the years.

II

I had been seen in the shade, recumbent on cushioned Helicon,
The water dripping from Bellerophon's horse,
Alba, your kings, and the realm your folk
            have constructed with such industry
Shall be yawned out on my lyre — with such industry.
My little mouth shall gobble in such great fountains,
"Wherefrom father Ennius, sitting before I came, hath drunk."

I had rehearsed the Curian brothers, and made remarks on the Horatian
    javelin
(Near Q. H. Flaccus' book-stall).
"Of" royal Aemilia, drawn on the memorial raft,
"Of" the victorious delay of Fabius, and the left-handed
                battle at Cannae,
Of lares fleeing the "Roman seat" . . .
                I had sung of all these
And of Hannibal,
           and of Jove protected by geese.
And Phoebus looking upon me from the Castalian tree,
Said then "You idiot! What are you doing with that water:
Who has ordered a book about heroes?
           You need, Propertius, not think
About acquiring that sort of a reputation.
      Soft fields must be worn by small wheels,
Your pamphlets will be thrown, thrown often into a chair
Where a girl waits alone for her lover;
       Why wrench your page out of its course?
No keel will sink with your genius
      Let another oar churn the water,
Another wheel, the arena; mid-crowd is as bad as mid-sea."
He had spoken, and pointed me a place with his plectrum:

    Orgies of vintages, an earthen image of Silenus
Strengthened with rushes, Tegaean Pan,
The small birds of the Cytharean mother
      their Punic faces dyed in the Gorgon's lake;
Nine girls, from as many countrysides
      bearing her offerings in their unhardened hands,

Such my cohort and setting. And she bound ivy to his thyrsos;
Fitted song to the strings;

Roses twined in her hands.
40   And one among them looked at me with face offended.
Calliope:
      "Content ever to move with white swans!
Nor will the noise of high horses lead you ever to battle;
Nor will the public criers ever have your name
45   in their classic horns,
Nor Mars shout you in the wood at Aeonia,
      Nor where Rome ruins German riches,
Nor where the Rhine flows with barbarous blood,
        and flood carries wounded Suevi.
50   Obviously crowned lovers at unknown doors,
Night dogs, the marks of a drunken scurry,
These are your images, and from you the sorcerizing of shut-in
     young ladies,
The wounding of austere men by chicane."
55   Thus Mistress Calliope,
      Dabbling her hands in the fount, thus she
Stiffened our face with the backwash of Philetas the Coan.

III

Midnight, and a letter comes to me from our mistress:
    Telling me to come to Tibur:
               At once!!
"Bright tips reach up from twin towers,
5   Anienan spring water falls into flat-spread pools."

What *is* to be done about it?
    Shall I entrust myself to entangled shadows,
Where bold hands may do violence to my person?

Yet if I postpone my obedience
10   because of this respectable terror,
I shall be prey to lamentations worse than a nocturnal assailant.
And I shall be in the wrong,
       and it will last a twelve month,
For her hands have no kindness me-ward,

15   Nor is there anyone to whom lovers are not sacred at midnight
    And in the Via Sciro.
If any man would be a lover

   he may walk on the Scythian coast,
No barbarism would go to the extent of doing him harm,
20 The moon will carry his candle,
     the stars will point out the stumbles,
Cupid will carry lighted torches before him
      and keep mad dogs off his ankles.
Thus all roads are perfectly safe
25   and at any hour;
Who so indecorous as to shed the pure gore of a suitor?!
  Cypris is his cicerone.

What if undertakers follow my track,
     such a death is worth dying.
30 She would bring frankincense and wreathes to my tomb,
  She would sit like an ornament on my pyre.

Gods' aid, let not my bones lie in a public location
With crowds too assiduous in their crossing of it;
For thus are tombs of lovers most desecrated.

35 May a woody and sequestered place cover me with its foliage
Or may I inter beneath the hummock
    of some as yet uncatalogued sand;
At any rate I shall not have my epitaph in a high road.

IV
Difference of Opinion with Lygdamus

Tell me the truths which you hear of our constant young lady,
   Lygdamus,
And may the bought yoke of a mistress lie with
   equitable weight on your shoulders;
5 For I am swelled up with inane pleasurabilities
    and deceived by your reference
To things which you think I would like to believe.

No messenger should come wholly empty,
   and a slave should fear plausibilities;
10 Much conversation is as good as having a home.
Out with it, tell it to me, all of it, from the beginning,
I guzzle with outstretched ears.

Thus? She wept into uncombed hair,
>And you saw it.

15 Vast waters flowed from her eyes?
>You, you Lygdamus

Saw her stretched on her bed, —
>it was no glimpse in a mirror;

No gawds on her snowy hands, no orfevrerie,
20 Sad garment draped on her slender arms.
Her escritoires lay shut by the bed-feet.
Sadness hung over the house, and the desolated female attendants
Were desolated because she had told them her dreams.

She was veiled in the midst of that place,
25 Damp woolly hankerchiefs were stuffed into her undryable eyes,
And a querulous noise responded to our solicitous reprobations.
For which things you will get a reward from me,
>Lygdamus?

To say many things is equal to having a home.
30 And the other woman "has not enticed me
>by her pretty manners,

She has caught me with herbaceous poison,
>she twiddles the spiked wheel of a rhombus,

She stews puffed frogs, snake's bones, the moulded feathers of screech owls,

35 She binds me with ravvles of shrouds.
>Black spiders spin in her bed!

Let her lovers snore at her in the morning!
>May the gout cramp up her feet!

Does he like me to sleep here alone,
40 >Lygdamus?

Will he say nasty things at my funeral?"

And you expect me to believe this
>after twelve months of discomfort?

V

I
Now if ever it is time to cleanse Helicon;
>to lead Emathian horses afield,

And to name over the census of my chiefs in the Roman camp.

If I have not the faculty, "The bare attempt would be praiseworthy."
5   "In things of similar magnitude
          the mere will to act is sufficient."

The primitive ages sang Venus,
          the last sings of a tumult,
And I also will sing war when this matter of a girl is exhausted.
10   I with my beak hauled ashore would proceed in a more stately manner,
My Muse is eager to instruct me in a new gamut, or gambetto,
Up, up my soul, from your lowly cantilation,
          put on a timely vigour,

Oh august Pierides! Now for a large-mouthed product.
15   Thus:
"The Euphrates denies its protection to the Parthian and
     apologizes for Crassus,"
And "It is, I think, India which now gives necks to your triumph,"
And so forth, Augustus. "Virgin Arabia shakes in her inmost dwelling."
20   If any land shrink into a distant seacoast,
     it is a mere postponement of your domination.
And I shall follow the camp, I shall be duly celebrated
      for singing the affairs of your cavalry.
May the fates watch over my day.

2
25   Yet you ask on what account I write so many love-lyrics
And whence this soft book comes into my mouth.
Neither Calliope nor Apollo sung these things into my ear,
    My genius is no more than a girl.

If she with ivory fingers drive a tune through the lyre,
30   We look at the process
How easy the moving fingers; if hair is mussed on her forehead,
If she goes in a gleam of Cos, in a slither of dyed stuff,
There is a volume in the matter; if her eyelids sink into sleep,
There are new jobs for the author;
35   And if she plays with me with her shirt off,
    We shall construct many Illiads.
And whatever she does or says
    We shall spin long yarns out of nothing.

Thus much the fates have allotted me, and if, Mæcenas,
40 I were able to lead heroes into armour, I would not,
Neither would I warble of Titans, nor of Ossa
        spiked onto Olympus,
Nor of causeways over Pelion,
Nor of Thebes in its ancient respectability,
45   nor of Homer's reputation in Pergamus,
Nor of Xerxes' two barreled kingdom, nor of Remus and his royal family,
Nor of dignified Carthaginian characters,
Nor of Welsh mines and the profit Marus had out of them.
I should remember Caesar's affairs . . .
50   for a background,
Although Callimachus did without them,
       and without Theseus,
Without an inferno, without Achilles attended of gods,
Without Ixion, and without the sons of Menœtius and the Argo and
55   without Jove's grave and the Titans.

And my ventricles do not palpitate to Cæsarial *ore rotundos*,
Nor to the tune of the Phrygian fathers.
Sailor, of winds; a plowman, concerning his oxen;
Solider, the enumeration of wounds; the sheep-feeder, of ewes;
60 We, in our narrow bed, turning aside from battles:
Each man where he can, wearing out the day in his manner.

3
It is noble to die of love, and honourable to remain
      uncuckolded for a season.
And she speaks ill of light women,
65   and will not praise Homer
Because Helen's conduct is "unsuitable."

        VI
When, when, and whenever death closes our eyelids,
Moving naked over Acheron
Upon the one raft, victor and conquered together,
70 Marius and Jugurtha together,
      one tangle of shadows.

Cæsar plots against India
Tigris and Euphrates shall from now on, flow at his bidding,

Tibet shall be full of Roman policemen,
75 The Parthians shall get used to our statuary
       and acquire a Roman religion;
One raft on the veiled flood of Acheron,
   Marius and Jugurtha together.

Nor at my funeral either will there be any long trail,
80   bearing ancestral lares and images;
No trumpets filled with my emptiness,
Nor shall it be on an Attalic bed;
   The perfumed cloths shall be absent.
A small plebeian procession.
85   Enough, enough and in plenty
There will be three books at my obsequies
Which I take, my not unworthy gift, to Persephone.

You will follow the bare scarified breast
Nor will you be weary of calling my name, nor too weary
90   To place the last kiss on my lips
When the Syrian onyx is broken.

   "He who is now vacant dust
   "Was once the slave of one passion:"
Give that much inscription
95   "Death why tardily come?"

You, sometimes, will lament a lost friend
   For it is a custom:
This care for past men,

Since Adonis was gored in Idalia, and the Cytherean
100 Ran crying with out-spread hair,
   In vain, you call back the shade,
In vain, Cynthia. Vain call to unanswering shadow,
   Small talk comes from small bones.

VII

Me happy, night, night full of brightness;
Oh couch made happy by my long delectations;
How many words talked out with abundant candles;
Struggles when the lights were taken away;

5   Now with bared breasts she wrestled against me,
                  Tunic spread in delay;
And she then opening my eyelids fallen in sleep,
Her lips upon them; and it was her mouth saying: Sluggard!

In how many varied embraces, our changing arms,
10   Her kisses, how many, lingering on my lips.
"Turn not Venus into a blinded motion,
             Eyes are the guides of love,
Paris took Helen naked coming from the bed of Menelaus,
Endymion's naked body, bright bait for Diana."
15   —such at least is the story.

While our fates twine together, sate we our eyes with love;
For long night comes upon you
               and a day when no day returns.
Let the gods lay chains upon us
20   so that no day shall unbind them.

Fool who would set a term to love's madness,
For the sun shall drive with black horses,
            earth shall bring wheat from barley,
The flood shall move toward the fountain
25   Ere love know moderations,
          The fish shall swim in dry streams.
No, now while it may be, let not the fruit of life cease.

          Dry wreathes drop their petals,
             their stalks are woven in baskets,
30   To-day we take the great breath of lovers,
                  to-morrow fate shuts us in.
Though you give all your kisses
               you give but a few.

Nor can I shift my pains to other,
35   Hers will I be dead,
If she confer such nights upon me,
             long is my life, long in years,
If she give me many,
        God am I for the time.

VIII

Jove, be merciful to that unfortunate woman
    Or an ornamental death will be held to your debit,
The time is come, the air heaves in torridity,
The dry earth pants against the canicular heat,
But this heat is not the root of the matter:
    She did not respect all the gods;
Such derelictions have destroyed other young ladies aforetime.
    And what they swore in the cupboard
        wind and wave scattered away.

Was Venus exacerbated by the existence of a comparable equal?
    Is the ornamental goddess full of envy?
Have you contempted Juno's Pelasgian temples,
    Have you denied Pallas good eyes?
Or is it my tongue that wrongs you
    with perpetual ascription of graces?
There comes, it seems, and at any rate
    through perils, (so many) and of a vexed life,
The gentler hour of an ultimate day.

Io mooed the first years with averted head,
    And now drinks Nile water like a god,
Ino in her young days fled pellmell out of Thebes,
    Andromeda was offered to a sea-serpent
        and respectably married to Perseus,
Callisto, diguised as a bear,
    wandered through the Arcadian prairies
    While a black veil was over her stars,
What if your fates are accelerated,
    your quiet hour put forward,
You may find interment pleasing,

You will say that you succumbed to a danger identical,
    charmingly identical, with Semele's,
And believe it, and she also will believe it,
    being expert from experience,
And amid all the gloried and storied beauties of Mæonia
There shall be none in a better seat, not
    one denying your prestige,

Now you may bear fate's stroke unperturbed,
Or Jove, harsh as he is, may turn aside your ultimate day.
Old lecher, let not Juno get wind of the matter,
40   Or perhaps Juno herself will go under,
                If the young lady is taken?

There will be, in any case, a stir on Olympus.

IX

1

The twisted rhombs ceased their clamour of accompaniment;
The scorched laurel lay in the fire-dust;
And the moon still declined wholly to descend out of heaven,

But the black ominous owl hoot was audible.

5   And one raft bears our fates
              on the veiled lake toward Avernus
Sails spread on cerulean waters, I would shed tears for two;
I shall live, if she continue in life,
        If she dies, I shall go with her.
10   Great Zeus, save the woman,
          or she will sit before your feet in a veil,
          and tell out the long list of her troubles.

2

Persephone and Dis, Dis, have mercy upon her,
There are enough women in hell,
15   quite enough beautiful women,
Iope, and Tyro, and Pasiphae, and the formal girls of Achaia,
And out of Troad, and from the Campania,
Death has its tooth in the lot,
          Avernus lusts for the lot of them,
20   Beauty is not eternal, no man has perennial fortune,
Slow foot, or swift foot, death delays but for a season.

3

My light, light of my eyes,
          you are escaped from great peril,
Go back to great Dian's dances bearing suitable gifts,
25   Pay up your vow of night watches

                    to Dian goddess of virgins,
And unto me also pay debt:
The ten nights of your company you have promised me.

                              X
Light, light of my eyes, at an exceeding late hour I was wandering,
And intoxicated,
                    and no servant was leading me,
And a minute crowd of small boys came from opposite,
5   I do not know what boys,
And I am afraid of numerical estimate,
And some of them shook little torches,
                    and others held onto arrows,
And the rest laid their chains upon me,
10   and they were naked, the lot of them,
And one of the lot was given to lust.

"That incensed female has consigned him to our pleasure."
So spoke. And the noose was over my neck.
And another said "Get him plumb in the middle!
15   "Shove along there, shove along!"
And another broke in upon this:
                    "He thinks that we are not gods."
"And she has been waiting for the scoundrel,
                    and in a new Sidonian night cap,
20   And with more than Arabian odours,
                        God knows where he has been,
She could scarcely keep her eyes open
                    enter that much for his bail.
                        Get along now!"

25   We are coming near to the house,
                and they gave another yank to my cloak,
And it was morning, and I wanted to see if she was alone, and resting,
And Cynthia was alone in her bed.
                        I was stupified.
30   I had never seen her looking so beautiful
                No, not when she was tunick'd in purple.

Such aspect was presented to me, me recently emerged from my visions,
You will observe that pure form has its value.

"You are a very early inspector of mistresses.

35   Do you think I have adopted your habits?"
                There were upon the bed no signs of a voluptuous encounter,
                No signs of a second incumbent.

She continued:
                "No incubus has crushed his body against me,
40   Though spirits are celebrated for adultery.
                And I am going to the temple of Vesta . . ."
                                        and so on.

Since that day I have had no pleasant nights.

                        XI

1
The harsh acts of your levity!
                        Many and many,
I am hung here, a scare-crow for lovers.

2
Escape! There is, O Idiot, no escape,
5   Flee if you like into Tanais,
                        desire will follow you thither,
Though you heave into the air upon the gilded Pegasean back,
                Though you had the feathery sandals of Perseus
To lift you up through split air,
10   The high tracks of Hermes would not afford you shelter.

Amor stands upon you, Love drives upon lovers,
                        a heavy mass on free necks.

It is our eyes you flee, not the city,
You do nothing, you plot inane schemes against me,
15   Languidly you stretch out the snare
                        with which I am already familiar,

And yet again, and newly rumour strikes on my ears.

Rumors of you throughout the city,
                        and no good rumour among them.

20   "You should not believe hostile tongues,
              "Beauty is slander's cock-shy,
    All lovely women have known this,"
                Your glory is not outblotted by venom,
    Phoebus our witness, your hands are unspotted."
25   A foreign lover brought down Helen's kingdom
               and she was lead back, living, home;
    The Cytherean brought low by Mars' lechery
             reigns in respectable heavens, ...
    Oh, oh, and enough of this,
30   by dew-spread caverns,
    The Muses clinging to the mossy ridges;
               to the ledge of the rocks:
    Zeus' clever rapes, in the old days,
            combusted Semele's, of Io strayed.
35   Of how the bird flew from Trojan rafters,
    Ida has lain with a shepherd, she has slept between sheep.

          Even there, no escape
    Not the Hyrcanian seaboard, not in seeking the shore of Eos.

    All things are forgiven for one night of your games. . . .
40   Though you walk in the Via Sacra, with a peacock's tail for a fan.

XII

    Who, who will be the next man to entrust his girl to a friend?
    Love interferes with fidelities;
    The gods have brought shame on their relatives;
    Each man wants the pomegranate for himself;
5   Amiable and harmonious people are pushed incontinent into duels,
    A Trojan and adulterous person came to Menelaus under the rites
        of hospitium,
    And there was a case in Colchis, Jason and that woman in Colchis;
    And besides, Lynceus,
10   you were drunk.
    Could you endure such promiscuity?
            She was not renowned for fidelity;
    But to jab a knife in my vitals, to have passed on a swig of poison,
    Preferable, my dear boy, my dear Lynceus,
15   Comrade, comrade of my life, of my purse, of my person;
    But in one bed, in one bed alone, my dear Lynceus.

I deprecate your attendance;
I would ask a like boon of Jove.

And you write of Achelöus, who contended with Hercules,
20 You write of Adrastus' horses and the funeral rites of Achenor,
And you will not leave off imitating Aeschylus
        Though you make a hash of Antimachus,
You think you are going to do Homer.
        And still a girl scorns the gods,
25 Of all these young women
            not one has enquired the cause of the world,
Nor the modus of lunar eclipses
        Nor whether there be any patch left of us
After we cross the infernal ripples,
30   nor if the thunder fall from predestination;
Nor anything else of importance.

Upon the Actian marshes Virgil is Phoebus' chief of police,
        He can tabulate Cæsar's great ships.
He thrills to Ilian arms,
35   He shakes the Trojan weapons of Aeneas,
And casts stores on Lavinian beaches.
Make way, ye Roman authors,
                clear the street, O ye Greeks,
For a much larger Iliad is in the course of construction
40 (and to Imperial order)
Clear the streets O ye Greeks!

And you also follow him "neath Phrygian pine shade:"
        Thyrsis and Daphnis upon whittled reeds,
And how ten sins can corrupt young maidens;
45   Kids for a bribe and pressed udders,
Happy selling poor loves for cheap apples.

Tityrus might have sung the same vixen;
        Corydon tempted Alexis,
Head farmers do likewise, and lying weary amid their oats
50 They get praise from tolerant Hamadryads.
Go on, to Ascraeus' prescription, the ancient,
                respected, Wordsworthian:
"A flat field for rushes, grapes grow on the slope."

And behold me, small fortune left in my house.
55   Me, who had no general for a grandfather!
I shall triumph among young ladies of indeterminate character.
My talent acclaimed in their banquets.
       I shall be honoured with yesterday's wreaths.
And the god strikes to the marrow.

60   Like a trained and performing tortoise,
I would make verse in your fashion, if she should command it,
With her husband asking a remission of sentence,
       And even this infamy would not attract numerous readers
Were there an erudite or violent passion,
65   For the nobleness of the populace brooks nothing below its own altitude.
One must have resonance, resonance and sonority . . . like a goose.

Varro sang Jason's expedition,
       Varro, of his great passion Leucadia,
There is song in the parchment; Catullus the highly indecorous,
70   Of Lesbia, known above Helen;
And in the dyed pages of Calvus,
       Calvus mourning Quintilia,
And but now Gallus had sung of Lycoris.
       Fair, fairest Lycoris—
75   The waters of Styx poured over the wound:
And now Propertius of Cynthia, taking his stand among these.

Hugh Selwyn Mauberley
Contacts and Life
(1920)

"Vocat æstus in umbram"
–Nemesianus Ec. IV.

E. P. ODE POUR L'ÉLECTION DE SON SÉPULCHRE

For three years, out of key with his time,
He strove to resuscitate the dead art
Of poetry; to maintain "the sublime"
In the old sense. Wrong from the start—

5   No, hardly, but, seeing he had been born
In a half savage country, out of date;
Bent resolutely on wringing lilies from the acorn;
Capaneus; trout for factitious bait;

Ἴδμεν γάρ τοι πάνθ᾽, ὅσ᾽ ἐνὶ Τροίῃ
10   Caught in the unstopped ear;
Giving the rocks small lee-way
The chopped seas held him, therefore, that year.

His true Penelope was Flaubert,
He fished by obstinate isles;
15   Observed the elegance of Circe's hair
Rather than the mottoes on sun-dials.

Unaffected by "the march of events,"
He passed from men's memory in *l'an trentuniesme*
De son eage; the case presents
20   No adjunct to the Muses' diadem.

II

The age demanded an image
Of its accelerated grimace,
Something for the modern stage,
Not, at any rate, an Attic grace;

5   Not, not certainly, the obscure reveries
Of the inward gaze;
Better mendacities
Than the classics in paraphrase!

The "age demanded" chiefly a mould in plaster,
10   Made with no loss of time,
A prose kinema, not, not assuredly, alabaster
Or the "sculpture" of rhyme.

III

The tea-rose tea-gown, etc.
Supplants the mousseline of Cos,
The pianola "replaces"
Sappho's barbitos.

5   Christ follows Dionysus,
Phallic and ambrosial
Made way for macerations;
Caliban casts out Ariel.

All things are a flowing,
10   Sage Heracleitus says;
But a tawdry cheapness
Shall outlast our days.

Even the Christian beauty
Defects—after Samothrace;
15   We see τὸ καλόν
Decreed in the market place.

Faun's flesh is not to us,
Nor the saint's vision.
We have the press for wafer;
20   Franchise for circumcision.

All men, in law, are equals.
Free of Pisistratus,
We choose a knave or an eunuch
To rule over us.

25   O bright Apollo,
τίν' ἄνδρα, τίν' ἥρωα, τίνα θεόν,
What god, man, or hero
Shall I place a tin wreath upon!

IV

These fought, in any case,
and some believing,
          pro domo, in any case . . .

Some quick to arm,
5 some for adventure,
some from fear of weakness,
some from fear of censure,
some for love of slaughter, in imagination,
learning later . . .
10 some in fear, learning love of slaughter;
Died some, pro patria,
     non "dulce" non "et decor" . . .
walked eye-deep in hell
believing in old men's lies, then unbelieving
15 came home, home to a lie,
home to many deceits,
home to old lies and new infamy;
usury age-old and age-thick
and liars in public places.

20 Daring as never before, wastage as never before.
Young blood and high blood,
Fair cheeks, and fine bodies;

fortitude as never before

frankness as never before,
25 disillusions as never told in the old days,
hysterias, trench confessions,
laughter out of dead bellies.

V

There died a myriad,
And of the best, among them,
For an old bitch gone in the teeth,
For a botched civilization,

5 Charm, smiling at the good mouth,
Quick eyes gone under earth's lid,

For two gross of broken statues,
For a few thousand battered books.

YEUX GLAUQUES

Gladstone was still respected,
When John Ruskin produced
"Kings' Treasuries"; Swinburne
And Rossetti still abused.

5   Fœtid Buchanan lifted up his voice
When that faun's head of hers
Became a pastime for
Painters and adulterers.

The Burne-Jones cartons
10   Have persevered her eyes;
Still, at the Tate, they teach
Cophetua to rhapsodize;

Thin like brook-water,
With a vacant gaze.
15   The English Rubaiyat was still-born
In those days.

The thin, clear gaze, the same
Still darts out faun-like from the half-ruin'd face
Questing and passive. . . .
20   "Ah, poor Jenny's case" . . .

Bewildered that a world
Shows no surprise
At her last maquero's
Adulteries.

"SIENA MI FE'; DISFECEMI MAREMMA"

Among the pickled fœtuses and bottled bones,
Engaged in perfecting the catalogue,
I found the last scion of the
Senatorial families of Strasbourg, Monsieur Verog.

5   For two hours he talked of Gallifet;
      Of Dowson; of the Rhymers' Club;
      Told me how Johnson (Lionel) died
      By falling from a high stool in a pub . . .

10   But showed no trace of alcohol
      At the autopsy, privately performed—
      Tissue preserved—the pure mind
      Arose toward Newman as the whiskey warmed.

      Dowson found harlots cheaper than hotels;
15   Headlam for uplift; Image impartially imbued
      With raptures for Bacchus, Terpsichore and the Church.
      So spoke the author of "The Dorian Mood,"

      M. Verog, out of step with the decade,
      Detached from his contemporaries,
20   Neglected by the young,
      Because of these reveries.

BRENNBAUM

      The sky-like limpid eyes,
      The circular infant's face,
      The stiffness from spats to collar
      Never relaxing into grace;

5   The heavy memories of Horeb, Sinai and the forty years,
      Showed only when the daylight fell
      Level across the face
      Of Brennbaum "The Impeccable."

MR. NIXON

      In the cream gilded cabin of his steam yacht
      Mr. Nixon advised me kindly, to advance with fewer
      Dangers of delay. "Consider
           Carefully the reviewer.

5   I was as poor as you are;
When I began I got, of course,
Advance on royalties, fifty at first," said Mr. Nixon,
"Follow me, and take a column,
Even if you have to work free.

10   Butter reviewers. From fifty to three hundred
I rose in eighteen months;
The hardest nut I had to crack
Was Dr. Dundas.

I never mentioned a man but with the view
15   Of selling my own works.
The tip's a good one, as for literature
It gives no man a sinecure.

And no one knows, at sight, a masterpiece.
And give up verse, my boy,
20   There's nothing in it."

                      ★   ★   ★

Likewise a friend of Blougram's once advised me:
Don't kick against the pricks,
Accept opinion. The "Nineties" tried your game
And died, there's nothing in it.

X

Beneath the sagging roof
The stylist has taken shelter,
Unpaid, uncelebrated,
At last from the world's welter

5   Nature receives him;
With a placid and uneducated mistress
He exercises his talents
And the soil meets his distress.

The haven from sophistications and contentions
10   Leaks through its thatch;
He offers succulent cooking;
The door has a creaking latch.

XI

"Conservatrix of Milésien"
Habits of mind and feeling,
Possibly. But in Ealing
With the most bank-clerkly of Englishmen?

5   No, "Milesian" is an exaggeration.
No instinct has survived in her
Older than those her grandmother
Told her would fit her station.

XII

"Daphne with her thighs in bark
Stretches toward me her leafy hands," —
Subjectively. In the stuffed-satin drawing-room
I await The Lady Valentine's commands,

5   Knowing my coat has never been
Of precisely the fashion
To stimulate, in her,
A durable passion;

Doubtful, somewhat, of the value
10   Of well-gowned approbation
Of literary effort,
But never of the Lady Valentine's vocation:

Poetry, her border of ideas,
The edge, uncertain, but a means of blending
15   With other strata
Where the lower and higher have ending;

A hook to catch the Lady Jane's attention,
A modulation toward the theatre,
Also, in the case of revolution,
20   A possible friend and comforter.

                  ★   ★   ★

Conduct, on the other hand, the soul
"Which the highest cultures have nourished"
To Fleet St. where
Dr. Johnson flourished;

25   Beside this thoroughfare
The sale of half-hose has
Long since superseded the cultivation
Of Pierian roses.

ENVOI (1919)

Go, dumb-born book,
Tell her that sang me once that song of Lawes:
Hadst thou but song
As thou hast subjects known,
5   *Then were there cause in thee that should condone*
Even my faults that heavy upon me lie,
And build her glories their longevity.

Tell her that sheds
Such treasure in the air,
10   *Recking naught else but that her graces give*
Life to the moment,
I would bid them live
As roses might, in magic amber laid,
Red overwrought with orange and all made
15   *One substance and one colour*
Braving time.

Tell her that goes
With song upon her lips
But sings not out the song, nor knows
20   *The maker of it, some other mouth,*
May be as fair as hers,
Might, in new ages, gain her worshippers,
When our two dusts with Waller's shall be laid,
Siftings on siftings in oblivion,
25   *Till change hath broken down*
All things save Beauty alone.

MAUBERLEY (1920)
"Vacuos exercet in aera morsus."

I

Turned from the "eau-forte
Par Jaquemart"
To the strait head
Of Messalina:

5   "His true Penelope
Was Flaubert,"
And his tool
The engraver's.

Firmness,
10   Not the full smile,
His art, but an art
In profile;

Colourless
Pier Francesca,
15   Pisanello lacking the skill
To forge Achaia.

II

"Qu'est ce qu'ils savent de l'amour, et qu'est ce qu'ils peuvent comprendre?
*   S'ils ne comprennent pas la poésie, s'ils ne sentent pas la musique, qu'est ce*
qu'ils peuvent comprendre de cette passion en comparaison avec laquelle la rose
est grossière et le parfum des violettes un tonnerre?"   —CAID ALI

For three years, diabolus in the scale,
He drank ambrosia,
All passes, ANANGKE prevails,
Came end, at last, to that Arcadia.

5   He had moved amid her phantasmagoria,
Amid her galaxies,
NUKTOS AGALMA

                ★   ★   ★

Drifted . . . drifted precipitate,
Asking time to be rid of . . .

10 Of his bewilderment; to designate
 His new found orchid. . . .

 To be certain . . . certain . . .
 (Amid ærial flowers) . . . time for arrangements—
 Drifted on
15 To the final estrangement;

 Unable in the supervening blankness
 To sift TO AGATHON from the chaff
 Until he found his sieve . . .
 Ultimately, his seismograph:

20 —Given, that is, his "fundamental passion,"
 This urge to convey the relation
 Of eye-lid and cheek-bone
 By verbal manifestation;

 To present the series
25 Of curious heads in medallion—

 He had passed, inconscient, full gaze,
 The wide-banded irides
 And botticellian sprays implied
 In their diastasis;

30 Which anæsthesis, noted a year late,
 And weighed, revealed his great affect,
 (Orchid), mandate
 Of Eros, a retrospect.

     ★ ★ ★

 Mouths biting empty air,
35 The still stone dogs,
 Caught in metamorphosis were
 Left him as epilogues.

"THE AGE DEMANDED"

Vide Poem II, page III

 For this agility chance found
 Him of all men, unfit

As the red-beaked steeds of
The Cytheræan for a chain-bit.

5   The glow of porcelain
Brought no reforming sense
To his perception
Of the social inconsequence.

Thus, if her colour
10   Came against his gaze,
Tempered as if
It were through a perfect glaze

He made no immediate application
Of this to relation of the state
15   To the individual, the month was more temperate
Because this beauty had been.

            The coral isle, the lion-coloured sand
            Burst in upon the porcelain revery:
            Impetuous troubling
20   Of his imagery.

Mildness, amid the neo-Nietzschean clatter,
His sense of graduations,
Quite out of place amid
Resistance to current exacerbations,

25   Invitation, mere invitation to perceptivity
Gradually led him to the isolation
Which these presents place
Under a more tolerant, perhaps, examination.

By constant elimination
30   The manifest universe
Yielded an armour
Against utter consternation,

A Minoan undulation,
Seen, we admit, amid ambrosial circumstances
35   Strengthened him against
The discouraging doctrine of chances,

And his desire for survival,
Faint in the most strenuous moods,
Became an Olympian *apathein*
40   In the presence of selected perceptions.

A pale gold, in the aforesaid pattern,
The unexpected palms
Destroying, certainly, the artist's urge,
Left him delighted with the imaginary
45   Audition of the phantasmal sea-surge,

Incapable of the least utterance or composition,
Emendation, conservation of the "better tradition,"
Refinement of medium, elimination of superfluities,
August attraction or concentration.

50   Nothing, in brief, but maudlin confession,
Irresponse to human aggression,
Amid the precipitation, down-float
Of insubstantial manna
Lifting the faint susurrus
55   Of his subjective hosannah.

Ultimate affronts to
Human redundancies;

Non-esteem of self-styled "his betters"
Leading, as he well knew,
60   To his final
Exclusion from the world of letters.

IV

Scattered Moluccas
Not knowing, day to day,
The first day's end, in the next noon;
The placid water
5   Unbroken by the Simoon;

Thick foliage
Placid beneath warm suns,
Tawn fore-shores
Washed in the cobalt of oblivions;

10   Or through dawn-mist
      The grey and rose
      Of the juridical
      Flamingoes;

      A consciousness disjunct,
15   Being but this overblotted
      Series
      Of intermittences;

      Coracle of Pacific voyages,
      The unforecasted beach;
20   Then on an oar
      Read this:

      "I was
      And I no more exist;
      Here drifted
25   An hedonist."

MEDALLION

      Luini in porcelain!
      The grand piano
      Utters a profane
      Protest with her clear soprano.

5   The sleek head emerges
      From the gold-yellow frock
      As Anadyomene in the opening
      Pages of Reinach.

      Honey-red, closing the face-oval
10   A basket-work of braids which seem as if they were
      Spun in King Minos' hall
      From metal, or intractable amber;

      The face-oval beneath the glaze,
      Bright in its suave bounding-line, as,
15   Beneath half-watt rays,
      The eyes turn topaz.

The Cantos
(1925–1969)

CANTO I

AND then went down to the ship,
  Set keel to breakers, forth on the godly sea, and
  We set up mast and sail on that swart ship,
  Bore sheep aboard her, and our bodies also
5   Heavy with weeping, and winds from sternward
Bore us out onward with bellying canvas,
Circe's this craft, the trim-coifed goddess.
Then sat we amidships, wind jamming the tiller,
Thus with stretched sail, we went over sea till day's end.
10 Sun to his slumber, shadows o'er all the ocean,
Came we then to the bounds of deepest water,
To the Kimmerian lands, and peopled cities
Covered with close-webbed mist, unpierced ever
With glitter of sun-rays
15 Nor with stars stretched, nor looking back from heaven
Swartest night stretched over wretched men there.
The ocean flowing backward, came we then to the place
Aforesaid by Circe.
Here did they rites, Perimedes and Eurylochus,
20 And drawing sword from my hip
I dug the ell-square pitkin;
Poured we libations unto each the dead,
First mead and then sweet wine, water mixed with white flour.
Then prayed I many a prayer to the sickly death's-heads;
25 As set in Ithaca, sterile bulls of the best
For sacrifice, heaping the pyre with goods,
A sheep to Tiresias only, black and a bell-sheep.
Dark blood flowed in the fosse,
Souls out of Erebus, cadaverous dead, of brides
30 Of youths and of the old who had borne much;
Souls stained with recent tears, girls tender,
Men many, mauled with bronze lance heads,
Battle spoil, bearing yet dreory arms,
These many crowded about me; with shouting,
35 Pallor upon me, cried to my men for more beasts;
Slaughtered the herds, sheep slain of bronze;
Poured ointment, cried to the gods,
To Pluto the strong, and praised Proserpine;
Unsheathed the narrow sword,

40 I sat to keep off the impetuous impotent dead,
    Till I should hear Tiresias.
    But first Elpenor came, our friend Elpenor,
    Unburied, cast on the wide earth,
    Limbs that we left in the house of Circe,
45 Unwept, unwrapped in sepulchre, since toils urged other.
    Pitiful spirit. And I cried in hurried speech:
    "Elpenor, how art thou come to this dark coast?
    "Cam'st thou afoot, outstripping seamen?"
          And he in heavy speech:
50 "Ill fate and abundant wine. I slept in Circe's ingle.
    "Going down the long ladder unguarded,
    "I fell against the buttress,
    "Shattered the nape-nerve, the soul sought Avernus.
    "But thou, O King, I bid remember me, unwept, unburied,
55 "Heap up mine arms, be tomb by sea-bord, and inscribed:
    "A man of no fortune, and with a name to come.
    "And set my oar up, that I swung mid fellows."

    And Anticlea came, whom I beat off, and then Tiresias Theban,
    Holding his golden wand, knew me, and spoke first:
60 "A second time? why? man of ill star,
    "Facing the sunless dead and this joyless region?
    "Stand from the fosse, leave me my bloody bever
    "For soothsay."
          And I stepped back,
65 And he strong with the blood, said then: "Odysseus
    "Shalt return through spiteful Neptune, over dark seas,
    "Lose all companions." And then Anticlea came.
    Lie quiet Divus. I mean, that is Andreas Divus,
    In officina Wecheli, 1538, out of Homer.
70 And he sailed, by Sirens and thence outward and away
    And unto Circe.
          Venerandam,
    In the Cretan's phrase, with the golden crown, Aphrodite,
    Cypri munimenta sortita est, mirthful, orichalchi, with golden
75 Girdles and breast bands, thou with dark eyelids
    Bearing the golden bough of Argicida. So that:

CANTO II

H ANG it all, Robert Browning,
    there can be but the one "Sordello."
    But Sordello, and my Sordello?
    Lo Sordels si fo di Mantovana.
5 So-shu churned in the sea.
Seal sports in the spray-whited circles of cliff-wash,
Sleek head, daughter of Lir,
        eyes of Picasso
Under black fur-hood, lithe daughter of Ocean;
10 And the wave runs in the beach-groove:
"Eleanor, ἑλέναυς and ἑλέπτολις!"
      And poor old Homer blind, blind, as a bat,
Ear, ear for the sea-surge, murmur of old men's voices:
"Let her go back to the ships,
15 Back among Grecian faces, lest evil come on our own,
Evil and further evil, and a curse cursed on our children,
Moves, yes she moves like a goddess
And has the face of a god
      and the voice of Schoeney's daughters,
20 And doom goes with her in walking,
Let her go back to the ships,
    back among Grecian voices."
And by the beach-run, Tyro,
      Twisted arms of the sea-god,
25 Lithe sinews of water, gripping her, cross-hold,
And the blue-gray glass of the wave tents them,
Glare azure of water, cold-welter, close cover.
Quiet sun-tawny sand-stretch,
The gulls broad out their wings,
30   nipping between the splay feathers;
Snipe come for their bath,
      bend out their wing-joints,
Spread wet wings to the sun-film,
And by Scios,
35   to left of the Naxos passage,
Naviform rock overgrown,
      algæ cling to its edge,
There is a wine-red glow in the shallows,
      a tin flash in the sun-dazzle.

40 The ship landed in Scios,
      men wanting spring-water,
And by the rock-pool a young boy loggy with vine-must,
    "To Naxos? Yes, we'll take you to Naxos,
Cum' along lad." "Not that way!"
45 "Aye, that way is Naxos."
      And I said: "It's a straight ship."
And an ex-convict out of Italy
    knocked me into the fore-stays,
(He was wanted for manslaughter in Tuscany)
50   And the whole twenty against me,
Mad for a little slave money.
     And they took her out of Scios
And off her course . . .
     And the boy came to, again, with the racket,
55 And looked out over the bows,
     and to eastward, and to the Naxos passage.
God-sleight then, god-sleight:
    Ship stock fast in sea-swirl,
Ivy upon the oars, King Pentheus,
60   grapes with no seed but sea-foam,
Ivy in scupper-hole.
Aye, I, Accœtes, stood there,
    and the god stood by me,
Water cutting under the keel,
65 Sea-break from stern forrards,
     wake running off from the bow,
And where was gunwale, there now was vine-trunk,
And tenthril where cordage had been,
     grape-leaves on the rowlocks,
70 Heavy vine on the oarshafts,
And, out of nothing, a breathing,
    hot breath on my ankles,
Beasts like shadows in glass,
    a furred tail upon nothingness.
75 Lynx-purr, and heathery smell of beasts,
    where tar smell had been,
Sniff and pad-foot of beasts,
    eye-glitter out of black air.
The sky overshot , dry, with no tempest,
80 Sniff and pad-foot of beasts,

fur brushing my knee-skin,
Rustle of airy sheaths,
      dry forms in the *æther*.
And the ship like a keel in ship-yard,
85   slung like an ox in smith's sling,
Ribs stuck fast in the ways,
      grape-cluster over pin-rack,
      void air taking pelt.
Lifeless air become sinewed,
90   feline leisure of panthers,
Leopards sniffing the grape shoots by scupper-hole,
Crouched panthers by fore-hatch,
And the sea blue-deep about us,
      green-ruddy in shadows,
95 And Lyæus: " From now, Acœtes, my altars,
Fearing no bondage,
      fearing no cat of the wood,
Safe with my lynxes,
      feeding grapes to my leopards,
100 Olibanum is my incense,
      the vines grow in my homage."

The back-swell now smooth in the rudder-chains,
Black snout of a porpoise
      where Lycabs had been,
105 Fish-scales on the oarsmen.
      And I worship.
I have seen what I have seen.
      When they brought the boy I said:
"He has a god in him,
110   though I do not know which god."
And they kicked me into the fore-stays.
I have seen what I have seen:
      Medon's face like the face of a dory,
Arms shrunk into fins. And you, Pentheus,
115 Had as well listen to Tiresias, and to Cadmus,
      or your luck will go out of you.
Fish-scales over groin muscles,
      lynx-purr amid sea . . .
And of a later year,
120   pale in the wine-red algæ,

If you will lean over the rock,
        the coral face under wave-tinge,
Rose-paleness under water-shift,
        Ileuthyeria, fair Dafne of sea-bords,
125   The swimmer's arms turned to branches,
Who will say in what year,
        fleeing what band of tritons,
The smooth brows, seen, and half seen,
        now ivory stillness.

130   And So-shu churned in the sea, So-shu also,
        using the long moon for a churn-stick . . .
Lithe turning of water,
        sinews of Poseidon,
Black azure and hyaline,
135   glass wave over Tyro,
Close cover, unstillness,
        bright welter of wave-cords,
Then quiet water,
        quiet in the buff sands,
140   Sea-fowl stretching wing-joints,
        splashing in rock-hollows and sand-hollows
In the wave-runs by the half-dune;
Glass-glint of wave in the tide-rips against sunlight,
        pallor of Hesperus,
145   Grey peak of the wave,
        wave, colour of grape's pulp,

Olive grey in the near,
        far, smoke grey of the rock-slide,
Salmon-pink wings of the fish-hawk
150   cast grey shadows in water,
The tower like a one-eyed great goose
        cranes up out of the olive-grove,

And we have heard the fauns chiding Proteus
        in the smell of hay under the olive-trees,
155   And the frogs singing against the fauns
        in the half-light.
And . . .

CANTO III

ISAT on the Dogana's steps
For the gondolas cost too much, that year,
And there were not "those girls," there was one face,
And the Buccentoro twenty yards off, howling "Stretti,"
5   And the lit cross-beams, that year, in the Morosini,
And peacocks in Koré's house, or there may have been.
     Gods float in the azure air,
Bright gods and Tuscan, back before dew was shed.
Light: and the first light, before ever dew was fallen.
10   Panisks, and from the oak, dryas,
And from the apple, mælid,
Through all the wood, and the leaves are full of voices,
A-whisper and the clouds bowe over the lake,
And there are gods upon them,
15   And in the water, the almond-white swimmers,
The silvery water glazes the upturned nipple,
     As Poggio has remarked.
Green veins in the turquoise,
Or, the gray steps lead up under the cedars.

20   My Cid rode up to Burgos,
Up to the studded gate between two towers,
Beat with his lance butt, and the child came out,
Una niña de nueve años,
To the little gallery over the gate, between the towers,
25   Reading the writ, voce tinnula:
That no man speak to, feed, help Ruy Diaz,
On pain to have his heart out, set on a pike spike
And both his eyes torn out, and all his goods sequestered,
"And here, Myo Cid, are the seals,
30   The big seal and the writing."
And he came down from Bivar, Myo Cid,
With no hawks left there on their perches,
And no clothes there in the presses,
And left his trunk with Raquel and Vidas,
35   That big box of sand, with the pawn-brokers,
To get pay for his menie;
Breaking his way to Valencia.
Ignez da Castro murdered, and a wall

Here stripped, here made to stand.
40   Drear waste, the pigment flakes from the stone,
Or plaster flakes, Mantegna painted the wall.
Silk tatters, "Nec Spe Nec Metu."

CANTO IV

PALACE in smoky light,
  Troy but a heap of smouldering boundary stones,
  ANAXIFORMINGES! Aurunculeia!
  Hear me. Cadmus of Golden Prows!
5 The silver mirrors catch the bright stones and flare,
Dawn, to our waking, drifts in the green cool light;
Dew-haze blurs, in the grass, pale ankles moving.
Beat, beat, whirr, thud, in the soft turf
   under the apple trees,
10 Choros nympharum, goat-foot, with the pale foot alternate;
Crescent of blue-shot waters, green-gold in the shallows,
A black cock crows in the sea-foam;

And by the curved, carved foot of the couch,
   claw-foot and lion head, an old man seated
15 Speaking in the low drone . . . :
     Ityn!
Et ter flebiliter, Ityn, Ityn!
And she went toward the window and cast her down,
   "All the while, the while, swallows crying:
20 Ityn!
    "It is Cabestan's heart in the dish."
    "It is Cabestan's heart in the dish?
    "No other taste shall change this."
And she went toward the window,
25   the slim white stone bar
Making a double arch;
Firm even fingers held to the firm pale stone;
Swung for a moment,
    and the wind out of Rhodez
30 Caught in the full of her sleeve.
    . . . the swallows crying:
'Tis, 'Tis, Ytis!
   Actæon . . .
    and a valley,
35 The valley is thick with leaves, with leaves, the trees,
The sunlight glitters, glitters a-top,
Like a fish-scale roof,
   Like the church roof in Poictiers

If it were gold.
40   Beneath it, beneath it
Not a ray, not a slivver, not a spare disc of sunlight
Flaking the black, soft water;
Bathing the body of nymphs, of nymphs, and Diana,
Nymphs, white-gathered about her, and the air, air,
45 Shaking, air alight with the goddess,
    fanning their hair in the dark,
Lifting, lifting and waffing:
Ivory dipping in silver,
   Shadow'd, o'ershadow'd
50 Ivory dipping in silver,
Not a splotch, not a lost shatter of sunlight.
Then Actæon: Vidal,
Vidal. It is old Vidal speaking,
   stumbling along in the wood,
55 Not a patch, not a lost shimmer of sunlight,
   the pale hair of the goddess.

The dogs leap on Actæon,
"Hither, hither, Actæon,"
Spotted stag of the wood;
60 Gold, gold, a sheaf of hair,
   Thick like a wheat swath,
Blaze, blaze in the sun,
   The dogs leap on Actæon.
Stumbling, stumbling along in the wood,
65 Muttering, muttering Ovid:
   "Pergusa . . . pool . . . pool . . . Gargaphia,
"Pool . . . pool of Salmacis."
   The empty armour shakes as the cygnet moves.

Thus the light rains, thus pours, *e lo soleills plovil*
70 The liquid and rushing crystal
   beneath the knees of the gods.
Ply over ply, thin glitter of water;
Brook film bearing white petals.
The pine at Takasago
75   grows with the pine of Isé!
The water whirls up the bright pale sand in the spring's mouth
"Behold the Tree of the Visages!"

Forked branch-tips, flaming as if with lotus.
　　　　Ply over ply
80　The shallow eddying fluid,
　　　　　beneath knees of the gods.

Torches melt in the glare
　　　　set flame of the corner cook-stall,
Blue agate casing the sky (as at Gourdon that time)
85　　　　　the sputter of resin,
Saffron sandal so petals the narrow foot: Hymenæus Io!
　　　　Hymen, Io Hymenæe! Aurunculeia!
One scarlet flower is cast on the blanch-white stone.

　　　　And Sō-Gyoku, saying:
90　"This wind, sire, is the king's wind,
　　　　This wind is wind of the palace,
Shaking imperial water-jets."
　　　　And Hsiang, opening his collar:
"This wind roars in the earth's bag,
95　　　　it lays the water with rushes."
No wind is the king's wind.
　　　　Let every cow keep her calf.
"This wind is held in gauze curtains . . ."
　　　　No wind is the king's . . .

100　The camel drivers sit in the turn of the stairs,
　　　　Look down on Ecbatan of plotted streets,
"Danaë! Danaë!
　　　　What wind is the king's?"
Smoke hangs on the stream,
105　The peach-trees shed bright leaves in the water,
Sound drifts in the evening haze,
　　　　The bark scrapes at the ford,
Gilt rafters above black water,
　　　　Three steps in an open field,
110　Gray stone-posts leading . . .

Père Henri Jacques would speak with the Sennin, on Rokku,
Mount Rokku between the rock and the cedars,
Polhonac,
As Gyges on Thracian platter set the feast,

115   Cabestan, Tereus,
          It is Cabestan's heart in the dish,
    Vidal, or Ecbatan, upon the gilded tower in Ecbatan
    Lay the god's bride, lay ever, waiting the golden rain.
    By Garonne. "Saave!"
120   The Garonne is thick like paint,
    Procession, — "Et sa'ave, sa'ave, sa'ave Regina!" —
    Moves like a worm, in the crowd.
    Adige, thin film of images,
    Across the Adige, by Stefano, Madonna in hortulo,
125   As Cavalcanti had seen her.
          The Centaur's heel plants in the earth loam.
    And we sit here . . .
          there in the arena . . .

CANTO VII

ELEANOR (she spoiled in a British climate)
          Ελανδρος and Ελεπτολις, and
          poor old Homer blind,
          blind as a bat,
5   Ear, ear for the sea-surge;
               rattle of old men's voices.
     And then the phantom Rome,
               marble narrow for seats
     "Si pulvis nullus" said Ovid,
10   "Erit, nullum tamen excute."
     Then file and candles, e li mestiers ecoutes;
     Scene for the battle only, but still scene,
     Pennons and standards y cavals armatz
     Not mere succession of strokes, sightless narration,
15   And Dante's "ciocco," brand struck in the game.

     Un peu moisi, plancher plus bas que le jardin.

     "Contre le lambris, fauteuil de paille,
     "Un vieux piano, et sous le baromètre . . ."

     The old men's voices, beneath the columns of false marble,
20   The modish and darkish walls,
     Discreeter gilding, and the panelled wood
     Suggested, for the leasehold is
     Touched with an imprecision . . . about three squares;
     The house too thick, the paintings
25   a shade too oiled.
     And the great domed head, *con gli occhi onesti e tardi*
     Moves before me, phantom with weighted motion,
     Grave incessu, drinking the tone of things,
     And the old voice lifts itself
30   weaving an endless sentence.
     We also made ghostly visits, and the stair
     That knew us, found us again on the turn of it,
     Knocking at empty rooms, seeking for buried beauty;
     And the sun-tanned, gracious and well-formed fingers
35   Lift no latch of bent bronze, no Empire handle
     Twists for the knocker's fall; no voice to answer.

A strange concierge, in place of the gouty-footed.
Sceptic against all this one seeks the living,
Stubborn against the fact. The wilted flowers
40   Brushed out a seven year since, of no effect.
Damn the partition! Paper, dark brown and stretched,
Flimsy and damned partition.
            Ione, dead the long year
My lintel, and Liu Ch'e's lintel.
45   Time blacked out with the rubber.
            The Elysée carries a name on
And the bus behind me gives me a date for peg;
Low ceiling and the Erard and the silver,
These are in "time." Four chairs, the bow-front dresser,
50   The panier of the desk, cloth top sunk in.
            "Beer-bottle on the statue's pediment!
"That, Fritz, is the era, to-day against the past,
"Contemporary." And the passion endures.
Against their action, aromas. Rooms, against chronicles.
55   Smaragdos, chrysolithos; De Gama wore striped pants in Africa
And "Mountains of the sea gave birth to troops";

Le vieux commode en acajou:
            beer-bottles of various strata,
But *is* she dead as Tyro? In seven years?
60   Ελέναυς, έλανδρος, ελέπτολις
The sea runs in the beach-groove, shaking the floated pebbles,
Eleanor!
            The scarlet curtain throws a less scarlet shadow;
Lamplight at Buovilla, e quel remir,
65   And all that day
Nicea moved before me
And the cold grey air troubled her not
For all her naked beauty, bit not the tropic skin,
And the long slender feet lit on the curb's marge
70   And her moving height went before me,
            We alone having being.
And all that day, another day:
            Thin husks I had known as men,
Dry casques of departed locusts
75   speaking a shell of speech . . .
Propped between chairs and table . . .

Words like the locust-shells, moved by no inner being;
      A dryness calling for death;

Another day, between walls of a sham Mycenian,
80   "Toc" sphinxes, sham-Memphis columns,
And beneath the jazz a cortex, a stiffness or stillness,
      Shell of the older house.
Brown-yellow wood, and the no colour plaster,
Dry professorial talk . . .
85   now stilling the ill beat music,
House expulsed by this house.

      Square even shoulders and the satin skin,
Gone cheeks of the dancing woman,
      Still the old dead dry talk, gassed out —
90   It is ten years gone, makes stiff about her a glass,
A petrefaction of air.
      The old room of the tawdry class asserts itself;
The young men, never!
      Only the husk of talk.
95   O voi che siete in piccioletta barca,
Dido choked up with sobs, for her Sicheus
Lies heavy in my arms, dead weight
      Drowning, with tears, new Eros,

And the life goes on, mooning upon bare hills;
100   Flame leaps from the hand, the rain is listless,
Yet drinks the thirst from our lips,
      solid as echo,
Passion to breed a form in shimmer of rain-blur;
But Eros drowned, drowned, heavy-half dead with tears
105   For dead Sicheus.

Life to make mock of motion:
For the husks, before me, move,
      The words rattle: shells given out by shells.
The live man, out of lands and prisons,
110   shakes the dry pods,
Probes for old wills and friendships, and the big locust-casques
Bend to the tawdry table,
Lift up their spoons to mouths, put forks in cutlets,

And make sound like the sound of voices.
115   Lorenzaccio
Being more live than they, more full of flames and voices.
Ma se morisse!
   Credesse caduto da sè, ma se morisse.
And the tall indifference moves,
120   a more living shell,
Drift in the air of fate, dry phantom, but intact.
O Alessandro, chief and thrice warned, watcher,
   Eternal watcher of things,
Of things, of men, of passions.
125   Eyes floating in dry, dark air,
E biondo, with glass-grey iris, with an even side-fall of hair
The stiff, still features.

CANTO IX

ONE year floods rose,
One year they fought in the snows,
One year hail fell, breaking the trees and walls.
Down here in the marsh they trapped him
5   in one year,
And he stood in the water up to his neck
    to keep the hounds off him,
And he floundered about in the marsh
    and came in after three days,
10   That was Astorre Manfredi of Faenza
    who worked the ambush
    and set the dogs off to find him,
In the marsh, down here under Mantua,
And he fought in Fano, in a street fight,
15   and that was nearly the end of him;
And the Emperor came down and knighted us,
And they had a wooden castle set up for fiesta,
And one year Basinio went out into the courtyard
    Where the lists were, and the palisades
20   had been set for the tourneys,
And he talked down the anti-Hellene,
    And there was an heir male to the seignor,
    And Madame Ginevra died.
And he, Sigismundo, was Capitan for the Venetians.
25   And he had sold off small castles
    and built the great Rocca to his plan,
And he fought like ten devils at Monteluro
    and got nothing but the victory
And old Sforza bitched us at Pesaro;
30   (*sic*) March the 16th:
"that Messir Alessandro Sforza
    is become lord of Pesaro
through the wangle of the Illus. Sgr. Mr. Fedricho d'Orbino
Who worked the wangle with Galeaz
35   through the wiggling of Messer Francesco,
Who waggled it so that Galeaz should sell Pesaro
    to Alex and Fossembrone to Feddy;
and he hadn't the right to sell.
And this he did *bestialmente;* that is Sforza did *bestialmente*

40   as he had promised him, Sigismundo, *per capitoli*
                to see that he, Malatesta, should have Pesaro"
        And this cut us off from our south half
                and finished our game, thus, in the beginning,
        And he, Sigismundo, spoke his mind to Francesco
45   and we drove them out of the Marches.

        And the King o' Ragona, Alphonse le roy d'Aragon,
                was the next nail in our coffin,
        And all you can say is, anyway,
        that he Sigismundo called a town council
50   And Valturio said "as well for a sheep as a lamb"
                and this change-over (*hæc traditio*)
        As old bladder said *"rem eorum, saluavit"*
        Saved the Florentine state; and that, maybe, was something.
        And "Florence our natural ally" as they said in the meeting
55   for whatever that was worth afterward.
        And he began building the TEMPIO,
                and Polixena, his second wife, died.
        And the Venetians sent down an ambassador
        And said "speak humanely,
60   But tell him it's no time for raising his pay."
        And the Venetians sent down an ambassador
                with three pages of secret instructions
        To the effect: Did he think the campaign was a joy-ride?
        And old Wattle-wattle slipped into Milan
65   But he couldn't stand Sidg being so high with the Venetians
        And he talked it over with Feddy; and Feddy said "Pesaro"
        And old Foscari wrote *"Caro mio*
        "If we split with Francesco you can have it
        "And we'll help you in every way possible."
70   But Feddy offered it sooner.
        And Sigismundo got up a few arches,
        And stole that marble in Classe, "stole" that is,
        Casus est talis:
                Foscari doge, to the prefect of Ravenna
75   "Why, what, which, thunder, damnation????"

        Casus est talis:
                Filippo, commendatary of the abbazia
        Of Sant Apollinaire, Classe, Cardinal of Bologna

That he did one night (*quadam nocte*) sell to the
80   Illmo D°, D° Sigismund Malatesta
Lord of Arimininum, marble, porphyry, serpentine,
Whose men, Sigismundo's, came with more than an hundred
two wheeled ox carts and deported, for the beautifying
of the *tempio* where was Santa Maria in Trivio
85   Where the same are now on the walls. Four hundred
ducats to be paid back to the *abbazia* by the said swindling
Cardinal or his heirs.
        grnnh! rrnnh, pthg.
wheels, plaustra, oxen under night-shield,
90   And on the 13th of August: Aloysius Purtheo,
The next abbot, to Sigismundo, receipt for 200 ducats
Corn-salve for the damage done in that scurry.

And there was the row about that German-Burgundian female
And it was his messianic year, Poliorcetes,
95   but he was being a bit too POLUMETIS
And the Venetians wouldn't give him six months vacation.

And he went down to the old brick heap of Pesaro
        and waited for Feddy
And Feddy finally said "I am coming! . . .
100   . . . to help Alessandro."
And he said: "This time Mister Feddy has done it."
He said: "Broglio, I'm the goat. This time
        Mr. Feddy has done it (*m'l'ha calata*)."
And he'd lost his job with the Venetians,
105   And the stone didn't come in from Istria:
And we sent men to the silk war;
And Wattle never paid up on the nail
        Though we signed on with Milan and Florence;
And he set up the bombards in muck down by Vada
110   where nobody else could have set 'em
        and he took the wood out of the bombs
        and made 'em of two scoops of metal
And the jobs getting smaller and smaller,
        Until he signed on with Siena;
115   And that time they grabbed his post-bag.
And what was it, anyhow?
        Pitigliano, a man with a ten acre lot,

Two lumps of tufa,
>and they'd taken his pasture land from him,

120 And Sidg had got back their horses,
>and he had two big lumps of tufa
>with six hundred pigs in the basements.

And the poor devils were dying of cold.

And this is what they found in the post-bag:

125 *Ex Arimino die xxii Decembris*
>"*Magnifice ac potens domine, mi singularissime*

"I advise yr. Lordship how

"I have been with master Alwidge who

"has shown me the design of the nave that goes in the middle,

130 "of the church and the design for the roof and . . ."

"JHesus,

"*Magnifico exso.* Signor Mio

"Sence to-day I am recommanded that I have to tel you my

"father's opinium that he has shode to Mr. Genare about the

135 "valts of the cherch . . . etc . . .

"Giovane of Master alwise P. S. I think it advisabl that

"I shud go to rome to talk to mister Albert so as I can no

"what he thinks about it rite.

"Sagramoro . . ."

140 "*Illustre signor mio*, Messire Battista . . ."

"First: Ten slabs best red, seven by 15, by one third,

"Eight ditto, good red, 15 by three by one,

"Six of same, 15 by one by one.

"Eight columns 15 by three and one third

145 >etc . . . with carriage, danars 151

"Monseigneur:

"Madame Isotta has had me write today about Sr. Galeazzo's

"daughter. The man who said young pullets make thin

"soup, knew what he was talking about. We went to see the

150 "girl the other day, for all the good that did, and she denied

"the whole matter and kept her end up without losing her

"temper. I think Madame Ixotta very nearly exhausted the

"matter. *Mi pare che avea decto hogni chossia.* All the

"children are well. Where you are everyone is pleased and

155 "happy becasue of your taking the chateau here we are the

"reverse as you might say drifting without a rudder. Madame
"Lucrezia has probably, or should have, written to you, I
"suppose you have the letter by now. Everyone wants to be
"remembered to you.   21 Dec. D. de M."

160   ". . . *sagramoro* to put up the derricks. There is a supply of
"beams at . . ."

"MAGNIFICENT LORD WITH DUE REVERENCE:
"Messire Malatesta is well and asks for you every day. He
"is so much pleased with his pony, It wd. take me a month
165   "to write you all the fun he gets out of that pony. I want to
"again remind you to write to Georgio Rambottom or to his
"boss to fix up that wall to the little garden that madame Isotta
"uses, for it is all flat on the ground now as I have already told
"him a lot of times, for all the good that does, so I am writing
170   "to your lordship in the matter I have done all that I can, for
"all the good that does as noboddy hear can do anything
"without you.
              "your faithful
                              LUNARDA DA PALLA.
175   20 Dec. 1454."

" . . . gone over it with all the foremen and engineers. And
"about the silver for the small medal . . ."

"*Magnifice ac potens* . . .
              "because the walls of . . ."

180   "*Malatesta de Malatestis ad Magnificum Dominum Patremque*
"*suum.*

"Ex^so D^no et D^no sin D^no Sigismundum Pandolfi Filium
              "Malatestis Capitan General

"Magnificent and exalted Lord and Father in especial my
185   "lord with due recommendation: your letter has been pre-
"sented to me by Gentilino da Gradara and with it the bay
"pony (ronzino baiectino) the which you have sent me, and
"which appears in my eyes a fine caparison'd charger, upon
"which I intend to learn all there is to know about riding,

190   in "consideration of yr. paternal affection for which I thank
"your excellency thus briefly and pray you continue to hold
"me in this esteem notifying you by the bearer of this that
"we are all in good health, as I hope and desire your Ex^ct "Lord-
ship is also: with continued remembrance I remain

195   "Your son and servant
                MALATESTA DE MALATESTIS.
            Given in Rimini, this the 22nd day of December
                    anno domini 1454"
                (in the sixth year of his age)

200   "ILLUSTRIOUS PRINCE:
"Unfitting as it is that I should offer counsels to Hannibal . . ."

     "   *Magnifice ac potens domine, domine mi singularissime,*
"*humili recomendatione premissa* etc. This to advise your
"Mgt Ldshp how the second load of Veronese marble has
205   "finally got here, after being held up at Ferrara with no end
"of fuss and botheration, the whole of it having been there
"unloaded.
"I learned how it happened, and it has cost a few florins to
"get back the said load which had been seized for the skipper's
210   "debt and defalcation; he having fled when the lighter was
"seized. But that Yr Mgt Ldshp may not lose the moneys
"paid out on his account I have had the lighter brought here
"and am holding it, against his arrival. If not we still have
"the lighter.
215   "As soon as the Xmas fêtes are over I will have the stone
"floor laid in the sacresty, for which the stone is already cut.
"The wall of the building is finished and I shall now get the
"roof on.
"We have not begun putting new stone into the martyr
220   "chapel; first because the heavy frosts wd. certainly spoil
"the job; secondly because the aliofants aren't yet here and
"one can't get the measurements for the cornice to the columns
"that are to rest on the aliofants.
"They are doing the stairs to your room in the castle . . . I
225   "have had Messire Antonio degli Atti's court paved and the
"stone benches put in it.
"Ottavian is illuminating the bull. I mean the bull for
"the chapel. All the stone-cutters are waiting for spring

"weather to start work again.

230 "The tomb is all done except part of the lid, and as soon as
"Messire Agostino gets back from Cesena I will see that he
"finishes it, ever recommending me to y^r M^{gt} Ld^{shp}

"believe me yr faithful
PETRUS GENARIIS."

235 That's what they found in the post-bag
And some more of it to the effect that
    he "lived and ruled"

"*et amava perdutamente Ixotta degli Atti*"
e "*ne fu degna*"
240   "*constans in proposito*
"*Placuit oculis principis*
"*pulchra aspectu*"
"*populo grata (Italiaeque decus)*
"and built a temple so full of pagan works"
245   i. e. Sigismund
and in the style "Past ruin'd Latium"
The filigree hiding the gothic,
    with a touch of rhetoric in the whole
And the old sarcophagi,
250   such as lie, smothered in grass, by San Vitale.

CANTO XIII

KUNG walked
   by the dynastic temple
  and into the cedar grove,
   and then out by the lower river,
5   And with him Khieu, Tchi
  and Tian the low speaking
And "we are unknown," said Kung,
"You will take up charioteering?
   Then you will become known,
10 "Or perhaps I should take up charioteering, or archery?
"Or the practice of public speaking?"
And Tseu-lou said, "I would put the defences in order,"
And Khieu said, "If I were lord of a province
I would put it in better order than this is."
15 And Tchi said, "I would prefer a small mountain temple,
"With order in the observances,
   with a suitable performance of the ritual,"
And Tian said, with his hand on the strings of his lute
The low sounds continuing
20   after his hand left the strings,
And the sound went up like smoke, under the leaves,
And he looked after the sound:
   "The old swimming hole,
  "And the boys flopping off the planks,
25 "Or sitting in the underbrush playing mandolins."
   And Kung smiled upon all of them equally.
And Thseng-sie desired to know:
   "Which had answered correctly?"
And Kung said, "They have all answered correctly,
30 "That is to say, each in his nature."
And Kung raised his cane against Yuan Jang,
   Yuan Jang being his elder,
For Yuan Jang sat by the roadside pretending to
   be receiving wisdom.
35 And Kung said
   "You old fool, come out of it,
Get up and do something useful."
   And Kung said
"Respect a child's faculties

40   "From the moment it inhales the clear air,
     "But a man of fifty who knows nothing
           Is worthy of no respect."
     And "When the prince has gathered about him
     "All the savants and artists, his riches will be fully employed."
45   And Kung said, and wrote on the bo leaves:
           If a man have not order within him
     He can not spread order about him;
     And if a man have not order within him
     His family will not act with due order;
50   And if the prince have not order within him
     He can not put order in his dominions.
     And Kung gave the words "order"
     and "brotherly deference"
     And said nothing of the "life after death."
55   And he said
           "Anyone can run to excesses,
     It is easy to shoot past the mark,
     It is hard to stand firm in the middle."

     And they said: If a man commit murder
60   Should his father protect him, and hide him?
     And Kung said:
           He should hide him.

     And Kung gave his daughter to Kong-Tch'ang
           Although Kong-Tch'ang was in prison.
65   And he gave his niece to Nan-Young
           although Nan-Young was out of office.
     And Kung said "Wang ruled with moderation,
           In his day the State was well kept,
     And even I can remember
70   A day when the historians left blanks in their writings,
     I mean for things they didn't know,
     But that time seems to be passing."
     And Kung said, "Without character you will
           be unable to play on that instrument
75   Or to execute the music fit for the Odes.
     The blossoms of the apricot
           blow from the east to the west,
     And I have tried to keep them from falling."

CANTO XIV

Io venni in luogo d'ogni luce muto;
The stench of wet coal, politicians
. . . . e and . . . . . n, their wrists bound to
        their ankles,
5   Standing bare bum,
Faces smeared on their rumps,
            wide eye on flat buttock,
Bush hanging for beard,
            Addressing crowds through their arse-holes,
10 Addressing the multitudes in the ooze,
        newts, water-slugs, water-maggots,
And with them. . . . . . . r,
            a scrupulously clean table-napkin
Tucked under his penis,
15   and . . . . m
Who disliked colloquial language,
Stiff-starched, but soiled, collars
            circumscribing his legs,
The pimply and hairy skin
20   pushing over the collar's edge,
Profiteers drinking blood sweetened with sh-t,
And behind them . . . . . . f and the financiers
            lashing them with steel wires.

And the betrayers of language
25   . . . . . . n and the press gang
And those who had lied for hire;
the perverts, the perverters of language,
            the perverts, who have set money-lust
Before the pleasures of the senses;

30 howling, as of a hen-yard in a printing-house,
            the clatter of presses,
the blowing of dry dust and stray paper,
fœtor, sweat, the stench of stale oranges,
dung, last cess-pool of the universe,
35 mysterium, acid of sulphur,
the pusillanimous, raging;
plunging jewels in mud,

and howling to find them unstained;
sadic mothers driving their daughters to bed with decrepitude,
40 sows eating their litters,
and here the placard EIKΩN ΓΗΣ,
and here: THE PERSONNEL CHANGES,

melting like dirty wax,
decayed candles, the bums sinking lower,
45 faces submerged under hams,
And in the ooze under them,
reversed, foot-palm to foot-palm,
hand-palm to hand-palm, the agents provocateurs
The murderers of Pearse and MacDonagh,
50 Captain H. the chief torturer;
The petrified turd that was Verres,
bigots, Calvin and St. Clement of Alexandria!
black-beetles, burrowing into the sh-t,
The soil a decrepitude, the ooze full of morsels,
55 lost contours, erosions.

Above the hell-rot
the great arse-hole,
broken with piles,
hanging stalactites,
60 greasy as sky over Westminister,
the invisible, many English,
the place lacking in interest,
last squalor, utter decrepitude,
the vice-crusaders, fahrting through silk,
65 waving the Christian symbols,
. . . . frigging a tin penny whistle,
Flies carrying news, harpies dripping sh-t through the air,

The slough of unamiable liars,
bog of stupidities,
70 malevolent stupidities, and stupidities,
the soil living pus, full of vermin,
dead maggots begetting live maggots,
slum owners,
usurers squeezing crab-lice, pandars to authority,
75 pets-de-loup, sitting on piles of stone books,

obscuring the texts with philology,
>hiding them under their persons,
the air without refuge of silence,
>the drift of lice, teething,
80 and above it the mouthing of orators,
>the arse-belching of preachers.
>And Invidia,
the corruptio, fœtor, fungus
liquid animals, melted ossifications,
85 slow rot, fœtid combustion,
>chewed cigar-butts, without dignity, without tragedy,
. . . . .m Episcopus, waving a condom full of black-beetles,
monopolists, obstructors of knowledge,
>obstructors of distribution.

CANTO XVI

AND before hell mouth; dry plain
                and two mountains;
            On the one mountain, a running form,
                and another
5   In   the turn of the hill; in hard steel
The road like a slow screw's thread,
The angle almost imperceptible,
            so that the circuit seemed hardly to rise;
And the running form, naked, Blake,
10   Shouting, whirling his arms, the swift limbs,
Howling against the evil,
            his eyes rolling,
Whirling like flaming cart-wheels,
            and his head held backward to gaze on the evil
15   As he ran from it,
            to be hid by the steel mountain,
And when he showed again from the north side;
            his eyes blazing toward hell mouth,
His neck forward,
20   and like him Peire Cardinal.
And in the west mountain, Il Fiorentino,
Seeing hell in his mirror,
            and lo Sordels
Looking on it in his shield;
25   And Augustine, gazing toward the invisible.

And past them, the criminal
            lying in blue lakes of acid,
The road between the two hills, upward
            slowly,
30   The flames patterned in lacquer, crimen est actio,
The limbo of chopped ice and saw-dust
And I bathed myself with the acid to free myself
            of the hell ticks,
Scales, fallen louse eggs.
35   Palux Laerna,
the lake of bodies, aqua morta,
of limbs fluid, and mingled, like fish heaped in a bin,
and here an arm upward, clutching a fragment of marble,

And the embryos, in flux,
40   new inflow, submerging,
Here an arm upward, trout, submerged by the eels;
          and from the bank, the stiff herbage
the dry nobbled path, saw many known, and unknown,
for an instant;
45   submerging,
The face gone, generation.

            Then light air, under saplings,
the blue banded lake under æther,
          an oasis, the stones, the calm field,
50   the grass quiet,
           and passing the tree of the bough
The grey stone posts,
          and the stair of gray stone,
the passage clean-squared in granite:
55   descending,
and I through this, and into the earth,
          patet terra,
entered the quiet air
          the new sky,
60   the light as after a sun-set,
          and by their fountains, the heroes,
Sigismundo, and Malatesta Novello,
          and founders, gazing at the mounts of their cities.

The plain, distance, and in fount-pools
65   the nymphs of that water
rising, spreading their garlands,
          weaving their water reeds with the boughs,
In the quiet,
          and now one man rose from his fountain
70   and went off into the plain.

Prone in that grass, in sleep;
          et j'entendis des voix: . . .
                    wall . . . Strasbourg
Galliffet led that triple charge . . . Prussians
75   and he said   [Plarr's narration]
          it was for the honour of the army.

And they called him a swashbuckler.
                    I didn't know what it was
But I thought: This is pretty bloody damn fine.
80 And my old nurse, he was a man nurse, and
He killed a Prussian and he lay in the street
there in front of our house for three days
And he stank. . . . . . .
                    Brother Percy,
85 And our Brother Percy . . .
                    old Admiral
He was a middy in those days,
And they came into Ragusa
. . . . . . place those men went for the Silk War. . . . .
90 And they saw a procession coming down through
A cut in the hills, carrying something
The six chaps in front carrying a long thing
                    on their shoulders,
And they thought it was a funeral,
95   but the thing was wrapped up in scarlet,
And he put off in the cutter,
                    he was a middy in those days,
To see what the natives were doing,
And they got up to the six fellows in livery,
100 And they looked at it, and I can still hear the old admiral,
"Was it? it was
                    Lord Byron
Dead drunk, with the face of an A y n. . . . .
He pulled it out long, like that:
105   the face of an a y n . . . . gel."

And because that son of a bitch,
                    Franz Josef of Austria. . . . . .
And because that son of a bitch Napoléon Barbiche . . .
They put Aldington on Hill 70, in a trench
110   dug through corpses
With a lot of kids of sixteen,
Howling and crying for their mamas,
And he sent a chit back to his major:
                    I can hold out for ten minutes
115 With my sergeant and a machine-gun.
                    And they rebuked him for levity.

And Henri Gaudier went to it,
     and they killed him,
And killed a good deal of sculpture,
120   And ole T. E. H. he went to it,
With a lot of books from the library,
London Library, and a shell buried 'em in a dug-out,
And the Library expressed its annoyance.
     And a bullet hit him on the elbow
125   . . . gone through the fellow in front of him,
And he read Kant in the Hospital, in Wimbledon,
in the original,
And the hospital staff didn't like it.

And Wyndham Lewis went to it,
130   With a heavy bit of artillery,
     and the airmen came by with a mitrailleuse,
And cleaned out most of his company,
     and a shell lit on his tin hut,
While he was out in the privvy,
135   and he was all there was left of that outfit.

Windeler went to it,
     and he was out in the Ægæan,
And down in the hold of his ship
     pumping gas into a sausage,
140   And the boatswain looked over the rail,
     down into amidships, and he said:
     Gees! look a' the Kept'n,
The Kept'n's a-gettin' 'er up.

And Ole Captain Baker went to it,
145   with his legs full of rheumatics,
So much so he couldn't run,
     so he was six months in hospital,
Observing the mentality of the patients.

And Fletcher was 19 when he went to it,
150   And his major went mad in the control pit,
     about midnight, and started throwing the 'phone about
And he had to keep him quiet
     till about six in the morning,

And direct that bunch of artillery.

155 And Ernie Hemingway went to it,
    too much in a hurry,
And they buried him for four days.

Et ma foi, vous savez,
    tous les nerveux. Non,
160 Y a une limite; les bêtes, les bêtes ne sont
Pas faites pour ça, c'est peu de chose un cheval.
Les hommes de 34 ans à quatre pattes
    qui criaient "maman." Mais les costauds,
La fin, là à Verdun, n'y avait que ces gros bonshommes
165   Et y voyaient extrêmement clair.
Qu'est-ce que ça vaut, les généraux, le lieutenant,
on les pèse à un centigramme,
    n'y a rien que du bois,
Notr' capitaine, tout, tout ce qu'il y a de plus renfermé
170   de vieux polytechnicien, mais solide,
La tête solide. Là, vous savez,
Tout, tout fonctionne, et les voleurs, tous les vices,
Mais les rapaces,
    y avait trois dans notre compagnie, tous tués.
175 Y sortaient fouiller un cadavre, pour rien,
    y n'seraient sortis pour rien que ça.
Et les boches, tout ce que vous voulez,
    militarisme, et cætera, et cætera.
Tout ça, mais, MAIS,
180   l'français, i s'bat quand y a mangé.
Mais ces pauvres types
A la fin y s'attaquaient pour manger,
    Sans ordres, les bêtes sauvages, on y fait
Prisonniers; ceux qui parlaient français disaient:
185   "Poo quah? Ma foi on attaquait pour manger."

C'est le corr-ggras, le corps gras,
    Leurs trains marchaient trois kilomètres à l'heure,
Et ça criait, ça grincait, on l'entendait à cinq kilomètres.
(Ça qui finit la guerre.)

190   Liste officielle des morts 5,000,000.

I vous dit, bè, voui, tout sentait le pétrole.
Mais, Non! je l'ai engueulé.
Je lui ai dit: T'es un con! T'a raté la guerre.

O voui! tous les hommes de goût, y conviens,
195   Tout ça en arrière.
               Mais un mec comme toi!
Ct' homme, un type comme ça!
            Ce qu'il aurait pu encaisser!
Il était dans une fabrique.
200   What, burying squad, terrassiers, avec leur tête
            en arrière, qui regardaient comme ça,
On risquait la vie pour un coup de pelle,
Faut que ça soit bien carré, exact . . .

Dey vus a bolcheviki dere, und dey dease him:
205   Looka vat youah Trotzsk is done, e iss
           madeh deh zhamefull beace!!
"He iss madeh deh zhamefull beace, iss he?
        "He is madeh de zhamevul beace?
"A Brest-Litovsk, yess? Ain't yuh herd?
210   "He vinneh de vore.
"De droobs iss released vrom de eastern vront, yess?
"Un venn dey getts to deh vestern vront, iss it
          "How many getts dere?
"And dose doat getts dere iss so full off revolutions
215   "Venn deh vrench is come dhru, yess,
"Dey say, "Vot?" Un de posch say:
         "Aint yeh heard? Say, ve got a rheffolution."

That's the trick with a crowd,
         Get 'em into the street and get 'em moving.
220   And all the time, there were people going
Down there, over the river.

        There was a man there talking,
To a thousand, just a short speech, and
Then move 'em on. And he said:
225   Yes, these people, they are all right, they
Can do everything, everything except act;
And go an' hear 'em, but when they are through,

Come to the bolsheviki . . .
And when it broke, there was the crowd there,
230 And the cossacks, just as always before,
But one thing, the cossacks said:
            "Pojalouista."
And that got round in the crowd,
And then a lieutenant of infantry
235 Ordered 'em to fire into the crowd,
            in the square at the end of the Nevsky,
In front of the Moscow station,
And they wouldn't,
And he pulled his sword on a student for laughing,
240 And killed him,
And a cossack rode out of his squad
On the other side of the square
And cut down the lieutenant of infantry
And that was the revolution . . .
245   as soon as they named it.

And you can't make 'em,
Nobody knew it was coming. They were all ready, the old gang,
Guns on the top of the post-office and the palace,
But none of the leaders knew it was coming.

250 And there were some killed at the barracks,
But that was between the troops.

So we used to hear it at the opera,
That they wouldn't be under Haig;
            and that the advance was beginning;
255 That it was going to begin in a week.

CANTO XVII

So that the vines burst from my fingers
And the bees weighted with pollen
Move heavily in the vine-shoots:
    chirr—chirr—chir-rikk—a purring sound,
5 And the birds sleepily in the branches.
        ZAGREUS! IO ZAGREUS!
With the first pale-clear of the heaven
And the cities set in their hills,
And the goddess of the fair knees
10 Moving there, with the oak-woods behind her,
The green slope, with white hounds
        leaping about her;
And thence down to the creek's mouth, until evening,
Flat water before me,
15   and the trees growing in water,
Marble trunks out of stillness,
On past the palazzi,
          in the stillness,
The light now, not of the sun.
20   Chrysophrase,
And the water green clear, and blue clear;
On, to the great cliffs of amber.
             Between them,
Cave of Nerea,
25   she like a great shell curved,
And the boat drawn without sound,
Without odour of ship-work,
Nor bird-cry, nor any noise of wave moving,
Nor splash of porpoise, nor any noise of wave moving,
30 Within her cave, Nerea,
          she like a great shell curved
In the suavity of the rock,
        cliff green-gray in the far,
In the near, the gate-cliffs of amber,
35 And the wave
        green clear, and blue clear,
And the cave salt-white, and glare-purple,
      cool, porphyry smooth,
      the rock sea-worn.

40   No gull-cry, no sound of porpoise,
        Sand as of malachite, and no cold there,
                the light not of the sun.

        Zagreus, feeding his panthers,
                the turf clear as on hills under light.
45   And under the almond-trees, gods,
                with them, *choros nympharum*. Gods,
        Hermes and Athene,
                                As shaft of compass,
        Between them, trembled—
50   To the left is the place of fauns,
                        sylva nympharum;
        The low wood, moor-scrub,
                the doe, the young spotted deer,
                leap up through the broom-plants,
55   as dry leaf amid yellow.
        And by one cut of the hills,
                the great alley of Memnons.
        Beyond, sea, crests seen over dune
        Night sea churning shingle,
60   To the left, the alley of cypress.
                                A boat came,
        One man holding her sail,
        Guiding her with oar caught over gunwale, saying:
        "   There, in the forest of marble,
65   "   the stone trees—out of water—
        "   the arbours of stone—
        "   marble leaf, over leaf,
        "   silver, steel over steel,
        "   silver beaks rising and crossing,
70   "   prow set against prow,
        "   stone, ply over ply,
        "   the gilt beams flare of an evening"
        Borso, Carmagnola, the men of craft, *i vitrei,*
        Thither, at one time, time after time,
75   And the waters richer than glass,
        Bronze gold, the blaze over the silver,
        Dye-pots in the torch-light,
        The flash of wave under prows,
        And the silver beaks rising and crossing.

80   Stone trees, white and rose-white in the darkness,
Cypress there by the towers,
       Drift under hulls in the night.

        "In the gloom the gold
Gathers the light about it." . . .

85   Now supine in burrow, half over-arched bramble,
One eye for the sea, through that peek-hole,
Gray light, with Athene.
Zothar and her elephants, the gold loin-cloth,
The sistrum, shaken, shaken,
90   the cohorts of her dancers.
And Aletha, by bend of the shore,
      with her eyes seaward,
    and in her hands sea-wrack
Salt-bright with the foam.
95   Koré through the bright meadow,
      with green-gray dust in the grass:
"For this hour, brother of Circe."
Arm laid over my shoulder,
Saw the sun for three days, the sun fulvid,
100 As a lion lift over sand-plain;
                and that day,
And for three days, and none after,
Splendour, as the splendour of Hermes,
And shipped thence
105   to the stone place,
Pale white, over water,
        known water,
And the white forest of marble, bent bough over bough,
The pleached arbour of stone,
110 Thither Borso, when they shot the barbed arrow at him,
And Carmagnola, between the two columns,
Sigismundo, after that wreck in Dalmatia.
    Sunset like the grasshopper flying.

CANTO XX

S OUND slender, quasi tinnula,
　　Ligur' aoide: Si no'us vei, Domna don plus mi cal,
　　Negus vezer mon bel pensar no val."
　　Between the two almond trees flowering,
5　The viel held close to his side;
And another: s'adora".
"Possum ego naturae
non meminisse tuae!" Qui son Properzio ed Ovidio.

The boughs are not more fresh
10　where the almond shoots
take their March green.
And that year I went up to Freiburg,
And Rennert had said: Nobody, no, nobody
Knows anything about Provençal, or if there is anybody,
15　It's old Lévy."
And so I went up to Freiburg,
And the vacation was just beginning,
The students getting off for the summer,
Freiburg im Breisgau,
20　And everything clean, seeming clean, after Italy.

And I went to old Lévy, and it was by then 6.30
in the evening, and he trailed half way across Freiburg
before dinner, to see the two strips of copy,
Arnaut's, settant'uno R. superiore (Ambrosiana)
25　Not that I could sing him the music.
And he said: "Now is there anything I can tell you?"
And I said: I dunno, sir, or
"Yes, Doctor, what do they mean by *noigandres*?"
And he said: Noigandres! NOIgandres!
30　"You know for seex mon's of my life
"Effery night when I go to bett, I say to myself:
"Noigandres, eh, *noigandres*,
"Now what the DEFFIL can that mean!"
Wind over the olive trees, ranunculae ordered,
35　By the clear edge of the rocks
The water runs, and the wind scented with pine
And with hay-fields under sun-swath.

Agostino, Jacopo and Boccata.
You would be happy for the smell of that place
40 And never tired of being there, either alone
Or accompanied.
Sound: as of the nightingale too far off to be heard.
Sandro, and Boccata, and Jacopo Sellaio;
The ranunculæ, and almond,
45 Boughs set in espalier,
Duccio, Agostino; *e l'olors*—
The smell of that place—*d'enoi ganres*.
Air moving under the boughs,
The cedars there in the sun,
50 Hay new cut on hill slope,
And the water there in the cut
Between the two lower meadows; sound,
The sound, as I have said, a nightingale
Too far off to be heard.
55 And the light falls, *remir*,
from her breast to thighs.

He was playing there at the palla.
Parisina—two doves for an altar—at the window,
"E'l Marchese
60 *Stava per divenir pazzo*
after it all." And that was when Troy was down
And they came here and cut holes in rock,
Down Rome way, and put up the timbers;
And came here, condit Atesten . . .
65   "Peace! keep the peace, Borso."
And he said: Some bitch has sold us
        (that was Ganelon)
"They wont get another such ivory."
And he lay there on the round hill under the cedar
70 A little to the left of the cut (Este speaking)
By the side of the summit, and he said:
        "I have broken the horn, bigod, I have
"Broke the best ivory, l'olofans." And he said:
"Tan mare fustes!"
75   pulling himself over the gravel,
"Bigod! that buggar is done for,
"They wont get another such ivory."

And they were there before the wall, Toro, las almenas,
(Este, Nic Este speaking)

80   Under the battlement
(Epi purgo) peur de la hasle,
And the King said:
              "God what a woman!
My God what a woman" said the King telo rigido.

85 "Sister!" says Ancures, "'s your sister!"
Alf left that town to Elvira, and Sancho wanted
It from her, Toro and Zamora.
              "Bloody spaniard!
Neestho, le'er go back . . .

90   in the autumn."
"Este, go' damn you." between the walls, arras,
Painted to look like arras.
                Jungle:
Glaze green and red feathers, jungle,

95 Basis of renewal, renewals;
Rising over the soul, green virid, of the jungle,
Lozenge of the pavement, clear shapes,
Broken, disrupted, body eternal,
Wilderness of renewals, confusion

100 Basis of renewals, subsistence,
Glazed green of the jungle;
Zoe, Marozia, Zothar,
                 loud over the banners,
Glazed grape, and the crimson,

105 HO BIOS,
             cosi Elena vedi,
In the sunlight, gate cut by the shadow;
And then the faceted air:
Floating. Below, sea churning shingle.

110 Floating, each on invisible raft,
On the high current, invisible fluid,
Borne over the plain, recumbent,
The right arm cast back,
            the right wrist for a pillow,

115 The left hand like a calyx,
Thumb held against finger, the third,
The first fingers petal'd up, the hand as a lamp,
A calyx.

From toe to head
120 The purple, blue-pale smoke, as of incense;
Wrapped each in burnous, smoke as the olibanum's,
Swift, as if joyous.
Wrapped, floating; and the blue-pale smoke of the incense
Swift to rise, then lazily in the wind
125   as Aeolus over bean-field,
As hay in the sun, the olibanum, saffron,
As myrrh without styrax;
Each man in his cloth, as on raft, on
  The high invisible current;
130 On toward the fall of water;
And then over that cataract,
In air, strong, the bright flames, V shaped;
  Nel fuoco
D'amore mi mise, nel fuoco d'amore mi mise . . .
135 Yellow, bright saffron, croceo;
And as the olibanum bursts into flame,
The bodies so flamed in the air, took flame,
  ". . . Mi mise, il mio sposo novello."
Shot from stream into spiral,

140 Or followed the water. Or looked back to the flowing;
Others approaching that cataract,
As to dawn out of shadow, the swathed cloths
Now purple and orange,
And the blue water dusky beneath them,
145   pouring there into the cataract,
With noise of sea over shingle,
   striking with:
   hah hah ahah thmm, thunb, ah
   woh woh araha thumm, bhaaa.
150 And from the floating bodies, the incense
  blue-pale, purple above them.
Shelf of the lotophagoi,
Aerial, cut in the aether.
    Reclining,
155 With the silver spilla,
The ball as of melted amber, coiled, caught up, and turned.
Lotophagoi of the suave nails, quiet, scornful,
Voce-profondo:

"Feared neither death nor pain for this beauty;
160   If harm, harm to ourselves."
And beneath: the clear bones, far down,
Thousand on thousand.
          "What gain with Odysseus,
"They that died in the whirlpool
165   "And after many vain labours,
"Living by stolen meat, chained to the rowingbench,
"That he should have a great fame
       "And lie by night with the goddess?
"Their names are not written in bronze
170   "Nor their rowing sticks set with Elpenor's;
"Nor have they mound by sea-bord.
       "That saw never the olives under Spartha
"With the leaves green and then not green,
       "The click of light in their branches;
175   "That saw not the bronze hall nor the ingle
"Nor lay there with the queen's waiting maids,
"Nor had they Circe to couch-mate, Circe Titania,
"Nor had they meats of Kalüpso
"Or her silk skirts brushing their thighs.
180   "Give! What were they given?
                     Ear-wax.
"Poison and ear-wax,
             and a salt grave by the bull-field,
"*neson amumona*, their heads like sea crows in the foam,
185   "Black splotches, sea-weed under lightning;
"Canned beef of Apollo, ten cans for a boat load."
Ligur' aoide.

And from the plain whence the water-shoot,
Across, back, to the right, the roads, a way in the grass,
190   The Khan's hunting leopard, and young Salustio
And Ixotta; the suave turf
Ac ferae familiares, and the cars slowly,
And the panthers, soft-footed.
Plain, as the plain of Somnus,
195   the heavy cars, as a triumph,
Gilded, heavy on wheel,
       and the panthers chained to the cars,
Over suave turf, the form wrapped,

Rose, crimson, deep crimson,
200 And, in the blue dusk, a colour as of rust in the sunlight,
Out of white cloud, moving over the plain,
Head in arm's curve, reclining;
The road, back and away, till cut along the face of the rock,
And the cliff folds in like a curtain,
205 The road cut in under the rock
Square groove in the cliff's face, as chiostri,
The columns crystal, with peacocks cut in the capitals,
The soft pad of beasts dragging the cars;
Cars, slow, without creak,
210 And at windows in inner roadside:
le donne e i cavalieri
smooth face under hennin,
The sleeves embroidered with flowers,
Great thistle of gold, or an amaranth,
215 Acorns of gold, or of scarlet,
Cramoisi and diaspre
slashed white into velvet;
Crystal columns, acanthus, sirens in the pillar heads;
And at last, between gilded barocco,
220 Two columns coiled and fluted,
Vanoka, leaning half naked,
waste hall there behind her.
"Peace!
Borso . . . , Borso!"

from CANTO XXX

COMPLEYNT, compleynt I hearde upon a day,
Artemis singing, Artemis, Artemis
Agaynst Pity lifted her wail:
Pity causeth the forests to fail,
5   Pity slayeth my nymphs,
Pity spareth so many an evil thing.
Pity befouleth April,
Pity is the root and the spring.
Now if no fayre creature followeth me
10   It is on account of Pity,
It is on account that Pity forbideth them slaye.
All things are made foul in this season,
This is the reason, none may seek purity
Having for foulnesse pity
15   And things growne awry;
No more do my shaftes fly
To slay. Nothing is now clean slayne
But rotteth away.

In Paphos, on a day
20   I also heard:
. . . goeth not with young Mars to playe
But she hath pity on a doddering fool,
She tendeth his fyre,
She keepeth his embers warm.

25   Time is the evil. Evil.
                A day, and a day
Walked the young Pedro baffled,
            a day and a day
After Ignez was murdered.
30   Came the Lords in Lisboa
            a day, and a day
In homage. Seated there
            dead eyes,
Dead hair under the crown,
35   The King still young there beside her.

.   .   .

CANTO XXXI

TEMPUS loquendi,
    Tempus tacendi.
    Said Mr Jefferson: It wd. have given us
      time.
5   "modern dress for your statue. . . . .
     "I remember having written you while Congress sat at Annapolis,
     "on water communication between ours and the western country,
     "particularly the information . . . . of the plain between
     "Big Beaver and Cayohoga, which made me hope that a canal
10   . . . . . navigation of Lake Erie and the Ohio. You must have had
     "occasion of getting better information on this subject
     "and if you have you wd. oblige me
     "by a communication of it. I consider this canal,
     "if practicable, as a very important work.
15   T. J. to General Washington, 1787

     . . . . . no slaves north of Maryland district . . . .
     . . . . . flower found in Connecticut that vegetates when suspended
           in air . . .
     . . . screw more effectual if placed below surface of water.
20   Suspect that a countryman of ours, Mr Bushnell of Connecticut
     is entitled to the merit of prior discovery.
     Excellency Mr Adams. Excellency Dr. Franklin.
     And thus Mr Jefferson (president) to Tom Paine:
     "You expressed a wish to get a passage to this country
25   in a public vessel. Mr. Dawson is charged with orders
     to the captain of the 'Maryland' to receive and accommodate you
     with passage back, if you can depart on so short a warning . . . .
     in hopes you will find us returned to sentiments
     worthy of former time . . . . . in these you have laboured as
30   much as any man living. That you may long live to
     continue your labours and to reap their fitting reward . . . .
     Assurances of my high esteem and attachment."

     "English papers . . . their lies . . . . .

     in a few years . . . no slaves northward of Maryland . . .

35   "Their tobacco, 9 millions, delivered in port of France;

6 millions to manufacture
on which the king takes thirty million
that cost 25 odd to collect
so that in all it costs 72 millions livres to the
40   consumer . . . . . .
persuaded (I am) in this branch of the revenue
the collection absorbs too much.
(from Paris, 1785).
. . . . . . for our model, the Maison Quarrée of Nismes . . . . .

45   With respect to his respect to his motives (Madison writing) I acknowledged
I had been much puzzled to divine any natural ones
without looking deeper into human nature
than I was willing to do.
(in re / Mr Robert Smith)
50   So critical the state of that country
moneyed men I imagine are glad to place their money abroad
Mr Adams could borrow there for us.
This country is really supposed to be on the eve of a XTZBK49HT
(parts of this letter in cypher)
55   Jefferson, from Paris, to Madison, Aug. 2, 1787
I hear that Mr Beaumarchais means to make himself heard . . .
. . . turn through the Potomac, . . commerce of Lake Erie . . . .
I can further say with safety there is not a crowned head
in Europe whose talents or merits would entitle him
60   to be elected a vestryman by an American parish.
T. J. to General Washington, May 2. '88.
"When Lafayette harangued you and me and John Quincy Adams
"through a whole evening in your hotel in the Cul de Sac . . . .
". . . . silent as you were. I was, in plain truth as astonished
65   "at the grossness of his ignorance of government and history,
"as I had been for years before at that of Turgot,
"La Rochefoucauld, of Condorcet and of Franklin."
To Mr Jefferson, Mr John Adams.

. . . care of the letters now enclosed. Most of them are
70   of a complexion not proper for the eye of the police.
From Monticello, April 16th. 1811
To Mr Barlow departing for Paris.

. . . indebted to nobody for more cordial aid than to Gallatin . . .

"Adair too had his kink. He believed all the Indians of

75 "America to be descended from the jews."
        Mr Jefferson to Mr Adams.

"But observe that the public were at the same time praying
on it an interest of exactly the same amount
(four million dollars). Where then is the gain to either

80 party which makes it a public blessing?"
        to Mr Eppes, 1813

"Man, a rational creature!" said Franklin.
"Come, let us suppose a rational man.
"Strip him of all his appetites, especially his hunger and thirst.

85 "He is in his chamber, engaged in making experiments,
"Or in pursuing some problem.
"At this moment a servant knocks, 'Sir,
" 'dinner is on the table.'
" 'Ham and chickens?' 'Ham!'

90 " 'And must I break the chain of my thoughts to
" 'go down and gnaw a morsel of damned hog's arse?
" 'Put aside your ham; I will dine tomorrow;'"
Take away appetite, and the present generation would not
Live a month, and no future generation would exist;

95 and thus the exalted dignity of human nature etc. . . . . .
        Mr Adams to Mr Jefferson, 15 Nov. 1813.

". . wish that I cd. subjoin Gosindi's Syntagma
"of the doctrines of Epicurus.
        (Mr Adams.)

100 ". . this was the state of things in 1785 . . ."
        (Mr Jefferson.)

. . met by agreement, about the close of the session—
Patrick Henry, Frank Lee and your father,
Henry Lee and myself . . . to consult . . measures

105 circumstances of times seemed to call for . . .
produce some channel of correspondence . . . this was in '73.
        Jefferson to D. Carr

. . church of St. Peter . . . . . human reason, human conscience,
though I believe that there are such things . . . .

110   Mr Adams.

A tiel leis . . . . en ancien scripture, and this
they have translated *Holy Scripture* . . .
                    Mr Jefferson

and they continue this error.

115   "Bonaparte . . . knowing nothing of commerce . . . .
       . . . or paupers, who are about one fifth of the whole . . .
           (on the state of England in 1814).

                    Hic Explicit Cantus

from CANTO XXXVI

A LADY asks me
        I speak in season
        She seeks reason for an affect, wild often
        That is so proud he hath Love for a name
5   Who denys it can hear the truth now
Wherefore I speak to the present knowers
Having no hope that low-hearted
            Can bring sight to such reason
Be there not natural demonstration
10   I have no will to try proof-bringing
Or say where it hath birth
What is its virtu and power
Its being and every moving
Or delight whereby 'tis called "to love"
15 Or if man can show it to sight.

W here memory liveth,
            it takes its state
Formed like a diafan from light on shade
Which shadow cometh of Mars and remaineth
20 Created, having a name sensate,
Custom of the soul,
            will from the heart;
Cometh from a seen form which being understood
Taketh locus and remaining in the intellect possible
25 Wherein hath he neither weight nor still-standing,
Descendeth not by quality but shineth out
Himself his own effect unendingly
Not in delight but in the being aware
Nor can he leave his true likeness otherwhere.

30 H e is not vertu but cometh of that perfection
    Which is so postulate not by the reason
But 'tis felt, I say.
Beyond salvation, holdeth his judging force
Deeming intention to be reason's peer and mate,
35 Poor in discernment, being thus weakness' friend
Often his power cometh on death in the end,
Be it withstayed

and so swinging counterweight.
Not that it were natural opposite, but only
40 Wry'd a bit from the perfect,
Let no man say love cometh from chance
Or hath not established lordship
Holding his power even though
        Memory hath him no more.

45 Cometh he to be
        when the will
From overplus
Twisteth out of natural measure,
Never adorned with rest   Moveth he changing colour
50 Either to laugh or weep
Contorting the face with fear
        resteth but a little
Yet shall ye see of him That he is most often
With folk who deserve him
55 And his strange quality sets sighs to move
Willing man look into that forméd trace in his mind
And with such uneasiness as rouseth the flame.
Unskilled can not form his image,
He himself moveth not, drawing all to his stillness,
60 Neither turneth about to seek his delight
Nor yet to seek out proving
Be it so great or so small.

He draweth likeness and hue from like nature
        So making pleasure more certain in seeming
65 Nor can stand hid in such nearness,
Beautys be darts tho' not savage
Skilled from such fear a man follows
Deserving spirit, that pierceth.
Nor is he known from his face
70 But taken in the white light that is allness
Toucheth his aim
Who heareth, seeth not form
But is led by its emanation.
Being divided, set out from colour,
75 Disjunct in mid darkness
Grazeth the light, one moving by other,

Being divided, divided from all falsity
Worthy of trust
From him alone mercy proceedeth.

80   Go, song, surely thou mayest
       Whither it please thee
For so art thou ornate that thy reasons
Shall be praised from thy understanders,
With others hast thou no will to make company.

.   .   .

CANTO XXXVIII

*il duol che sopra Senna
Induce, falseggiando la moneta.*
            Paradiso XIX, 118.

AN' that year Metevsky went over to America del Sud
            (and the Pope's manners were so like Mr. Joyce's,
            got that way in the Vatican, weren't like that before)
            Marconi knelt in the ancient manner
5   like Jimmy Walker sayin' his prayers.
His Holiness expressed a polite curiosity
            as to how His Excellency had chased those
electric shakes through the a'mosphere.
            Lucrezia
10 Wanted a rabbit's foot,
            and he, Metevsky said to the one side
(three children, five abortions and died of the last)
            he said: the other boys got more munitions
(thus cigar-makers whose work is highly repetitive
15 can perform the necessary operations almost automatically
and at the same time listen to readers who are hired
for the purpose of providing mental entertainment while they
work; Dexter Kimball 1929.)

Don't buy until you can get ours.
20 And he went over the border
            and he said to the other side:
The *other* side has more munitions. Don't buy
            until you can get ours.
And Akers made a large profit and imported gold into England
25 Thus increasing gold imports.
            The gentle reader has heard this before.
And that year Mr Whitney
Said how useful short sellin' was,
            We suppose he meant to the brokers
30 And no one called him a liar.
And two Afghans came to Geneva
To see if they cd. get some guns cheap,
As they had heard about someone's disarming.
And the secretary of the something

35   Made some money from oil wells
                 (In the name of God the Most Glorious Mr D'Arcy
    is empowered to scratch through the sub-soil of Persia
    until fifty years from this date...)
    Mr Mellon went over to England
40   and that year Mr Wilson had prostatitis
    And there was talk of a new Messiah
    (that must have been a bit sooner)
    And Her Ladyship cut down Jenny's allowance
    Because of that bitch Agot Ipswich
45   And that year (that wd. be 20 or 18 years sooner)
    They begin to kill 'em by millions
    Because of a louse in Berlin
              and a greasy basturd in Ausstria
    By name François Giuseppe.

50   "Will there be war?" "No, Miss Wi'let,
    "On account of bizschniz relations."
              Said the soap and bones dealer in May 1914
    And Mr Gandhi thought:
              if we don't buy any cotton
55   And at the same time don't buy any guns......
    Monsieur Untel was not found at the Jockey Club
    ...but was, later, found in Japan
    And So-and-So had shares in Mitsui.
    "The wood (walnut) will always be wanted for gunstocks"
60   and they put up a watch factory outside Muscou
    And the watches kept time....Italian marshes
    been waiting since Tiberius' time...
    "Marry" said Beebe, "how do the fish live in the sea."
    Rivera, the Spanish dictator, dictated that the
65   Infante was physically unfit to inherit...
              gothic type still used in Vienna
    because the old folks are used that that type.
                    And Schlossmann
    suggested that I stay there in Vienna
70   As stool-pigeon against the Anschluss
              Because the Ausstrians needed a Buddha
    (Seay, brother, I leev et tuh yew!)
    The white man who made the tempest in Baluba
    Der im Baluba das Gewitter gemacht hat...

75   they spell words with a drum beat,
   "The country is overbrained" said the hungarian nobleman
   in 1923. Kosouth (Ku' shoot) used, I understand
   To sit in a café—all done by conversation—
   It was all done by conversation,
80   possibly because one repeats the point when conversing:
   "Vienna contains a mixture of races."
      wd. I stay and be Bhudd-ha?
   "They are accustomed to having an Emperor. They must have
   Something to worship. (1927)"
85   But their humour about losing the Tyrol?
   Their humour is not quite so broad.
   The ragged arab spoke with Frobenius and told him
   The names of 3000 plants.
      Bruhl found some languages full of detail
90   Words that half mimic action; but
   generalization is beyond them, a white dog is
   not, let us say, a dog like a black dog.
   Do not happen, Romeo and Juliet...unhappily
   I have lost the cutting but apparently
95   such things do still happen, he
   suicided outside her door while
   the family was preparing her body for burial,
   and she knew that this was the case.

   Green, black, December. Said Mr Blodgett:
100 "Sewing machines will never come into general use.

   "I have of course never said that the cash is constant
   (Douglas) and in fact the population (Britain 1914)
   was left with 800 millions of *"deposits"*
   after all the cash had been drawn, and
105 these deposits were satisfied by the
      printing of treasury notes.
   A factory
   has also another aspect, which we call the financial aspect
   It gives people the power to buy (wages, dividends
110 which are power to buy) but it is also the cause of prices
   or values, financial, I mean financial values
   It pays workers, and pays *for* material.
   What it pays in wages and dividends

stays fluid, as power to buy, and this power is less,
115   per forza, damn blast your intellex, is less
than the total payments made by the factory
(as wages, dividends AND payments for raw material
bank charges, etcetera)
and all, that is the whole, that is the total
120   of these is added into the total of prices
caused by that factory, any damn factory
and there is and must be therefore a clog
and the power to purchase can never
(under the present system) catch up with
125   prices at large,

          and the light became so bright and so blindin'
in this layer of paradise
       that the mind of man was bewildered.
Said Herr Krupp (1842): guns are a merchandise
130   I approach them from the industrial end,
I approach them from the technical side,
1847 orders from Paris and Egypt....
        orders from Crimea,
Order of Pietro il Grande,
135   and a Command in the Legion of Honour...
500 to St Petersburg and 300 to Napolean Barbiche
from Creusot. At Sadowa
      Austria had some Krupp cannon;
      Prussia had some Krupp cannon.
140   "The Emperor ('68) is deeply in'erested in yr. catalogue
and in yr. services to humanity"
                  (signed) Leboeuf
who was a relative of Monsieur Schneider
1900 fifty thousand operai,
145   53 thousand cannon, about half for his country,
Bohlem und Halbach,
      Herr Schneider of Creusot
Twin arse with one belly.
Eugene, Adolf and Alfred "more money from guns than from tractiles"
150   Eugene was sent to the deputies;
      (Soane et Loire) to the Deputies, minister;
Later rose to be minister,
      "guns coming from anywhere,

but appropriations from the Chambers of Parliaments"
155   In 1874 recd. license for free exportation
Adopted by 22 nations
1885/1900 produced ten thousand cannon
to 1914, 34 thousand
one half of them sent out of the country
160   always in the chamber of deputies, always a conservative,
Schools, churches, orspitals fer the workin' man
Sand piles fer the children.
Opposite the Palace of the Schneiders
        Arose the monument to Herr Henri
165   Chantiers de la Gironde, Bank of the Paris Union,
The franco-japanese bank
        François de Wendel, Robert Protot
To friends and enemies of tomorrow
"the most powerful union is doubtless
170   that of the Comité des Forges,"
"And God take your living" said Hawkwood
15 million: Journal des Débats
30 million paid to Le Temps
Eleven for the Echo de Paris
175   Polloks on Schneider patents
Our bank has bought us
        a lot of shares in Mitsui
Who arm 50 divisions, who keep up the Japanese army
and they are destined to have a large future
180   "faire passer ces affaires
        avant ceux de la nation."

CANTO XLV

WITH *Usura*

With usura hath no man a house of good stone
each block cut smooth and well fitting
that design might cover their face,
5   with usura
hath no man a painted paradise on his church wall
harpes et luz
or where virgin receiveth message
and halo projects from incision,
10   with usura
seeth no man Gonzaga his heirs and his concubines
no picture is made to endure nor to live with
but it is made to sell and sell quickly
with usura, sin against nature,
15   is thy bread ever more of stale rags
is thy bread dry as paper,
with no mountain wheat, no strong flour
with usura the line grows thick
with usura is no clear demarcation
20   and no man can find site for his dwelling.
Stonecutter is kept from his stone
weaver is kept from his loom
WITH USURA
wool comes not to market
25   sheep bringeth no gain with usura
Usura is a murrain, usura
blunteth the needle in the maid's hand
and stoppeth the spinner's cunning. Pietro Lombardo
came not by usura
30   Duccio came not by usura
nor Pier della Francesca; Zuan Bellin' not by usura
nor was 'La Calunnia' painted.
Came not by usura Angelico; came not Ambrogio Praedis,
Came no church of cut stone signed: *Adamo me fecit.*
35   Not by usura St Trophime
Not by usura Saint Hilaire,
Usura rusteth the chisel
It rusteth the craft and the craftsman

It gnaweth the thread in the loom
40   None learneth to weave gold in her pattern;
Azure hath a canker by usura; cramoisi is unbroidered
Emerald findeth no Memling
Usura slayeth the child in the womb
It stayeth the young man's courting
45   It hath brought palsey to bed, lyeth
between the young bride and her bridegroom
                    CONTRA NATURAM
They have brought whores for Eleusis
Corpses are set to banquet
50   at behest of usura.

N.B. Usury: A charge for the use of purchasing power, levied without regard to pro-
duction; often without regard to the possibilities of production. (Hence the failure of
the Medici bank.)

CANTO XLVII

WHO even dead, yet hath his mind entire!
This sound came in the dark
First must thou go the road
to hell

5   And to the bower of Ceres' daughter Proserpine,
Through overhanging dark, to see Tiresias,
Eyeless that was, a shade, that is in hell
So full of knowing that the beefy men know less than he,
Ere thou come to thy road's end.
10   Knowledge the shade of a shade,
Yet must thou sail after knowledge
Knowing less than drugged beasts. *phtheggometha
thasson*
φθεγγώμεθα θᾶσσον
15   The small lamps drift in the bay
And the sea's claw gathers them.
Neptunus drinks after neap-tide.
Tamuz! Tamuz!!
The red flame going seaward.
20   By this gate art thou measured.
From the long boats they have set lights in the water,
The sea's claw gathers them outward.
Scilla's dogs snarl at the cliff's base,
The white teeth gnaw in under the crag,
25   But in the pale night the small lamps float seaward
                              Τυ Διώνα
                        TU DIONA

Και Μοῖραι' Αδονιν
KAI MOIRAI' ADONIN
30   The sea is streaked red with Adonis,
The lights flicker red in small jars.
Wheat shoots rise new by the altar,
              flower from the swift seed.
Two span, two span to a woman,
35   Beyond that she believes not. Nothing is of any importance.
To that is she bent, her intention
To that art thou called ever turning intention,
Whether by night the owl-call, whether by sap in shoot,
Never idle, by no means by no wiles intermittent
40   Moth is called over mountain

The bull runs blind on the sword, *naturans*
To the cave art thou called, Odysseus,
By Molü hast thou respite for a little,
By Molü art thou freed from the one bed
45   that thou may'st return to another
The stars are not in her counting,
          To her they are but wandering holes.
Begin thy plowing
When the Pleiades go down to their rest,
50   Begin thy plowing
40 days are they under seabord,
Thus do in fields by seabord
And in valleys winding down toward the sea.
When the cranes fly high
55   think of plowing.
By this gate art thou measured
Thy day is between a door and a door
Two oxen are yoked for plowing
Or six in the hill field
60   White bulk under olives, a score for drawing down stone,
Here the mules are gabled with slate on the hill road.
Thus was it in time.
And the small stars now fall from the olive branch,
Forked shadow falls dark on the terrace
65   More black than the floating martin
          that has no care for your presence,
His wing-print is black on the roof tiles
And the print is gone with his cry.
So light is thy weight on Tellus
70   Thy notch no deeper indented
Thy weight less than the shadow
Yet hast thou gnawed through the mountain,
          Scylla's white teeth less sharp.
Hast thou found a nest softer than cunnus
75   Or hast thou found better rest
Hast'ou a deeper planting, doth thy death year
Bring swifter shoot?
Hast thou entered more deeply the mountain?

The light has entered the cave. Io! Io!
80   The light has gone down into the cave,
Splendour on splendour!

By prong have I entered these hills:
That the grass grow from my body,
That I hear the roots speaking together,

85 The air is new on my leaf,
The forked boughs shake with the wind.
Is Zephyrus more light on the bough, Apeliota
more light on the almond branch?
By this door have I entered the hill.

90 Falleth,
Adonis falleth.
Fruit cometh after. The small lights drift out with the tide,
sea's claw has gathered them outward,
Four banners to every flower

95 The sea's claw draws the lamps outward.
Think thus of thy plowing
When the seven stars go down to their rest
Forty days for their rest, by seabord
And in valleys that wind down toward the sea

100   Καὶ Μοῖραι' Ἀδονιν
        KAI MOIRAI' ADONIN

When the almond bough puts forth its flame,
When the new shoots are brought to the altar,
        Τυ Διώνα, Καὶ Μοῖραι

105   TU DIONA, KAI MOIRAI

Καὶ Μοῖραι' Ἀδονιν
KAI MOIRAI' ADONIN
        that hath the gift of healing,
that hath the power over wild beasts.

CANTO XLIX

FOR the seven lakes, and by no man these verses:
Rain; empty river; a voyage,
Fire from frozen cloud, heavy rain in the twilight
Under the cabin roof was one lantern.
5   The reeds are heavy; bent;
and the bamboos speak as if weeping.

Autumn moon; hills rise about lakes
against sunset
Evening is like a curtain of cloud,
10   a blurr above ripples; and through it
sharp long spikes of the cinnamon,
a cold tune amid reeds.
Behind hill the monk's bell
borne on the wind.
15   Sail passed here in April; may return in October
Boat fades in silver; slowly;
Sun blaze alone on the river.

Where wine flag catches the sunset
Sparse chimneys smoke in the cross light

20   Comes then snow scur on the river
And a world is covered with jade
Small boat floats like a lanthorn,
The flowing water clots as with cold. And at San Yin
they are a people of leisure.
25   Wild geese swoop to the sand-bar,
Clouds gather about the hole of the window
Broad water; geese line out with the autumn
Rooks clatter over the fishermen's lanthorns,
A light moves on the north sky line;
30   where the young boys prod stones for shrimp.
In seventeen hundred came Tsing to these hill lakes.
A light moves on the south sky line.

State by creating riches shd. thereby get into debt?
This is infamy; this is Geryon.
35   This canal goes still to TenShi
though the old king built it for pleasure

K E I	M E N	R A N	K E I
K I U	M A N	M A N	K E I
JITSU	GETSU	K O	K W A
T A N	F U K U	T A N	K A I

40

Sun up; work
sundown; to rest
dig well and drink of the water
dig field; eat of the grain

45   Imperial power is? and to us what is it?

The fourth; the dimension of stillness.
And the power over wild beasts.

from CANTO LII

. . .

50   Know then:
           Toward summer when the sun is in Hyades
  Sovran is Lord of the Fire
        to this month are birds.
  with bitter smell and with the odour of burning
55   To the hearth god, lungs of the victim
          The green frog lifts up his voice
         and the white latex is in flower
  In red car with jewels incarnadine
         to welcome the summer
60   In this month no destruction
         no tree shall be cut at this time
  Wild beasts are driven from field
         in this month are simples gathered.
  The empress offers cocoons to the Son of Heaven
65   Then goes the sun into Gemini
  Virgo in mid heaven at sunset
         indigo must not be cut
  No wood burnt into charcoal
        gates are all open, no tax on the booths.
70   Now mares go to grazing,
          tie up the stallions
  Post up the horsebreeding notices
          Month of the longest days
  Life and death are now equal
75   Strife is between light and darkness
  Wise man stays in his house
        Stag droppeth antlers
  Grasshopper is loud,
        leave no fire open to southward.
80   Now the sun enters Hydra, this is the third moon of summer
  Antares of Scorpio stands mid heaven at sunset
  Andromeda is with sunrise
        Lord of the fire is dominant
  To this month is SEVEN,
85   with bitter smell, with odour of burning
  Offer to gods of the hearth
          the lungs of the victims

Warm wind is rising, cricket bideth in wall
Young goshawk is learning his labour
90   dead grass breedeth glow-worms.
In Ming T'ang HE bideth
         in the west wing of that house
Red car and the sorrel horses
         his banner incarnadine.
95   The fish ward now goes against crocodiles
To take all great lizards, turtles, for divination,
sea terrapin.
The lake warden to gather rushes
         to take grain for the *manes*
100   to take grain for the beasts you will sacrifice
to the Lords of the Mountains
          To the Lords of great rivers
Inspector of dye-works, inspector of colour and broideries
see that the white, black, green be in order
105   let no false colour exist here
black, yellow, green be of quality
          This month are trees in full sap
Rain has now drenched all the earth
         dead weeds enrich it, as if boil'd in a bouillon.
110   Sweet savour, the heart of the victim
yellow flag over Emperor's chariot
         yellow stones in his girdle,
Sagittarius in mid-course at sunset
         cold wind is beginning. Dew whitens.
115   Now is cicada's time,
         the sparrow hawk offers birds to the spirits.
Emperor goes out in war car, he is drawn by white horses,
white banner, white stones in his girdle
eats dog and the dish is deep.
120   This month is the reign of Autumn
Heaven is active in metals, now gather millet
         and finish the flood-walls
Orion at sunrise.
         Horses now with black manes.
125   Eat dog meat. This is the month of ramparts.
Beans are the tribute, September is end of thunder
The hibernants go into their caves.
         Tolls lowered, now sparrows, they say, turn into oysters

The wolf now offers his sacrifice.
130   Men hunt with five weapons,
They cut wood for charcoal.
            New rice with your dog meat.
First month of winter is now
         sun is in Scorpio's tail
135 at sunrise in Hydra, ice starting
The pheasant plunges into Houai (great water)
         and turns to an oyster
Rainbow is hidden awhile.
         Heaven's Son feeds on roast pork and millet,
140 Steel gray are stallion.
         This month winter ruleth.
The sun is in archer's shoulder
         in crow's head at sunrise
Ice thickens. Earth cracks. And the tigers now move to mating.
145 Cut trees at solstice, and arrow shafts of bamboo.
Third month, wild geese go north,
         magpie starts building,
Pheasant lifteth his voice to the Spirit of Mountains
The fishing season is open,
150   rivers and lakes frozen deep
Put now ice in your ice-house,
         the great concert of winds
Call things by the names. Good sovereign by distribution
Evil king is known by his imposts.
155 Begin where you are said Lord Palmerston
         began draining swamps in Sligo
Fought smoke nuisance in London. Dredged harbour in Sligo.

chih[3]

from CANTO LIII

Yᴇᴏᴜ taught men to break branches
       Seu Gin set up the stage and taught barter,
          taught the knotting of cords
       Fou Hi taught men to grow barley
5   2837 ante Christum
and they know still where his tomb is
by the high cypress between the strong walls,
the FIVE grains, said Chin Nong, that are
          wheat, rice, millet, *gros blé* and chick peas
10   and made a plough that is used five thousand years
Moved his court then to Kio-feau-hien
held market at mid-day
'bring what we have not here', wrote an herbal
Souan yen bagged fifteen tigers
15   made signs out of bird tracks
Hoang Ti contrived the making of bricks
and his wife started working the silk worms,
          money was in days of Hoang Ti.
He measured the length of Syrinx
20   of the tubes to make tune for song
Twenty-six (that was) eleven ante Christum
          had four wives and 25 males of his making
His tomb is today in Kiao-Chan
Ti Ko set his scholars to fitting words to their music
25   is buried in Tung Kieou
This was in the twenty fifth century a.c.
          YAO like the sun and rain,
saw what star is at solstice
saw what star marks mid summer
30   YU, leader of waters,
          black earth is fertile, wild silk still is from Shantung
Ammassi, to the provinces,
          let his men pay tithes in kind.
'Siu-tcheou province to pay in earth of five colours
35   Pheasant plumes from Yu-chan of mountains
Yu-chan to pay sycamores
          of this wood are lutes made
Ringing stones from Se-choui river
and grass that is called Tsing-mo' or μῶλυ,

40 Chun to the spirit Chang Ti, of heaven
  moving the sun and stars
        que vos vers expriment vos intentions,
        et que la musique conforme

YAO

45 CHUN

YU

KAO-YAO

                    abundance.
  Then an Empress fled with Chao Kang in her belly.
50 Fou-hi by virtue of wood;
  Chin-nong, of fire; Hoang Ti ruled by the earth,
  Chan by metal.
  Tchuen was lord, as is water.
  CHUN, govern
55 YU, cultivate,
  The surface is not enough,

from Chang Ti nothing is hidden.
For years no waters came, no rain fell
      for the Emperor Tching Tang
60   grain scarce, prices rising
so that in 1760 Tching Tang opened the copper mine (ante
                            Christum)

made discs with square holes in their middles
      and gave these to the people
65   wherewith they might buy grain
                  where there was grain
The silos were emptied
7 years of sterility
         der im Baluba das Gewitter gemacht hat
70   Tching prayed on the mountain and
      wrote MAKE IT NEW
on his bath tub
      Day by day make it new
cut underbrush,
75   pile the logs
keep it growing.
Died Tching aged years an hundred,
in the 13th of his reign.
      'We are up, Hia is down.'
80   Immoderate love of women
Immoderate love of riches,
Card for parades and huntin'.
      Chang Ti above alone rules.
Tang not stinting of praise:
85   Consider their sweats, the people's
If you wd/ sit calm on throne.

 hsin[1]

 jih[4]

jih[4]

 hsin[1]

         . . .

175   Thus came Kang to be Emperor/.
White horses with sorrel manes in the court yard.
      'I am pro-Tcheou' said Confucius
      'I am' said Confutzius 'pro-Tcheou in politics'
Wen-wang and Wu-wang had, sage men, strong as bears
180   Said young Kang-wang:
             Help me to keep the peace!
Your ancestors have come one by one under our rule
                for our rule.

Honour to Chao-Kong the surveyor.
185   Let his name last 3000 years
Gave each man land for his labour
                not by plough-land alone
But for keeping of silk-worms
                Reforested the mulberry groves
190   Set periodical markets
Exchange brought abundance, the prisons were empty.
'Yao and Chun have returned'
                sang the farmers
'Peace and abundance bring virtue.' I am
195   'pro-Tcheou' said Confucius five centuries later.
With his mind on this age.

                        .   .   .

        Never were so many eclipses.
Then Kungfutseu was made minister and moved promptly
350   against C. T. Mao
        and had him beheaded
that was false and crafty of heart
        a tough tongue that flowed with deceit
A man who remembered evil and was complacent in doing it.
355   LOU rose. Tsi sent girls to destroy it
                Kungfutseu retired
At Tching someone said:
                there is man with Yao's forehead
Cao's neck and the shoulders of Tsé Tchin
360   A man tall as Yu, and he wanders about in front of the
                                        East gate
        like a dog that has lost his owner.
Wrong, said Confucius, in what he says of those Emperors
        but as to the lost dog, quite correct.
365   He was seven days foodless in Tchin
        the rest sick and Kung making music
'sang even more than was usual'
Honour to Yng P the bastard
Tchin and Tsai cut off Kung in the desert
370   and Tcheou troops alone got him out
                Tsao fell after 25 generations
And Kung cut 3000 odes to 300

Comet from Yng star to Sin star, that is two degrees long
in the 40th year of King Ouang

375 Died Kung aged 73   *b.c. 479*

.   .   .

Thus of Kung or Confucius, and of 'Hillock' his father

395 when he was attacking a city
his men had passed under the drop gate
And the warders then dropped it, so Hillock caught
the whole weight on his shoulder, and held till his
last man had got out.

400   Of such stock was Kungfutseu.

Chou

CANTO LXX

'**M**Y situation almost the only one in the world
where firmness and patience are useless'
J. A. vice president and president of the senate
1791
5 Will the french refuse to receive Mr Pinckney?
idea of leading Mr Adams . . .
Blount (senator) has been speculating with the English . . .
surrounded by projecters and swindlers, you will be, Gerry,
Friendship, Marshall a plain man and the frogs
10 countenance only enemies of our constitution.
set our seamen ashore at St Jago de Cuba
till our ships arm . . . office of Secretary as rival of president
in aim to have quintuple directory . . . . Vervennes' friends
dislike the facts laid to his charge.
15 Hamilton no command,
too much intrigue. McHenry was secretary for war, in 98
We shd/ have frigates, no European peace can be lasting.
expedient to recommend war against France?
(presupposing they shall not have declared war against us
20 (thus to Pickering.) 'Talleyrand
affects utter ignorance, Mr Gerry has communicated, although
knowing that Talleyrand had much greater acquaintance with the
said X, Y, Z than has Mr Gerry.
(Signed Gerry)
25 Hague 1st July '98
peculators, cd/ they be aroused to drive out the French . . .
Vans M/ exhausted all things in enormous bribes' (ciphered)
Talleyrand, leaving however reserves for chicanery,
and Murray not yet removed from the Hague
30 about 'peace'
shortly ago were howling for war with Britain,
peace, war
aimed at elections. My appointment of Murray
has at least laid open characters to me
35 'you are hereby discharged'
John Adams, President of the United States
to Tim Pickering
to execute office so far as to affix seal to enclosed commission
John Marshal of Virginia, to be Chief Justice

40   and certify your own name *pro hac vice*
Hamilton's total ignorance (or whatever)
     of practice and usage of nations.
eternal neutrality in all wars of Europe.
          I leave the state with its coffers full
45   Dec 28th 1800
73 for Jefferson
73 for Burr
a few foreign liars, no Americans in America
our federalists no more American than were the antis
50 And in the mirror of memory, *formato loco*
My compliments to Mrs Warren
          as to the sea nymphs
Hyson, Congo, Bohea, and a few lesser divinities
Sirens shd/ be got into it somehow.
55   Tories were never so affable
          Tories were never so affable.
We shall oscillate like a pendulum.
slow starvation, a conclave, a divan,
          what shall we do when we get there
60 (first congress of Philadelphy) a nursery
          for American statesmen
treasons, felonies, new praemunires
Virginia has sown wheat instead of tobacco
          never happy in large and promiscuous companies
65 Quincy's knowledge of Boston harbour, 2 million issued in bills
old to bind young unconsenting, what right?
why exclude women from franchise?
          power follows balance of land
been months here, and never on horseback.
70   fountain head of Justinian,
deep, Bracton, Domat, Ayliffe and Taylor
          from '61 here in Braintree
was aversion to paper, they preferred to do business by barter
you are right, Rush, our trouble is iggurunce
75   of money especially
are still stockjobbers to believe English reports
          'No extravagance is too great
Ten thousand of General Washington's army
gone over to Clinton. Count D'Estaing making procession through
80 Boston with the Host, and seizing a meeting house

for a chapel and the devil knows what.'
      40,000 Russians about to go through
more solicitation as to means of obtaining it, than as to
                      amount of
85   my salary
At any rate send me the *news*.
        quails, partridges, squirrels
God willing, I will not go to Vermont
I must be
90   (whole of french policy)
within scent of
        (merely to string us along to keep us from)
the sea
        (sinking entirely, to have us strong enough for their
95 purpose, but not strong enough for our own, to prevent us
from obtaining consideration in Europe. Hence my pleasure
        in having set up a standard in Holland.
populariser, dépopulariser
        to popularize Mr Jefferson
100 and *dépopulariser* General Washington, all on system.
        were our interest the same as theirs
we might better trust them, yet not entirely
for they do not understand even their own.
        I have hitherto paid the Dutch interest out of capital.
105   (London '85 to Art Lee)
Court as putrid as Amsterdam, divine science of politics.
sale of six million acres to diminish the national debt —
and the society of a few men of letters.
left at New England Coffee House, London
110 will be brought me by some Boston sea captain
        I shall call my brook, Hollis Brook
After generous contest for liberty, Americans forgot
        what it consists of
after 20 years of the struggle *meminisse juvebit*
115 'seeks information from all quarters and judges more
independently than any man I ever met'
              J. A. on G. Washington
that there were Americans indifferent to fisheries
        and even some inclined to give them away
120   this was my strongest motive
        for twice going to Europe.

fish boxes were rec'd in my absence.
'Their constitution, experiment, I KNOW
that France can not be long governed by it.'

125   To Price, 19 April 1790
aim of my life has been to be useful, how small in
any nation the number who comprehend ANY
system of constitution or administration
                          and these few do not unite.
130 Americans more rapidly disposed to corruption in elections
                          than I thought in '74
fraudulent use of words monarchy and republic

I am for balance

and know not how it is but mankind have an aversion
135   to any study of government
Thames a mere rivulet in comparison to the Hudson river
73 to Jefferson, to Mr. Burr 73
                          UM SÞIRO
nec lupo committere agnum
140   so they are against any rational theory.
                          UM SÞIRO AMO

from CANTO LXXIV

THE enormous tragedy of the dream in the peasant's bent
    shoulders
    Manes! Manes was tanned and stuffed,
    Thus Ben and la Clara *a Milano*
5   by the heels at Milano
That maggots shd/ eat the dead bullock
DIGONOS, Δίγονος, but the twice crucified
          where in history will you find it?
yet say this to the Possum: a bang, not a whimper,
10   with a bang not with a whimper,
To build the city of Dioce whose terraces are the colour of stars.
The suave eyes, quiet, not scornful,
          rain also is of the process.
What you depart from is not the way
15 and olive tree blown white in the wind
washed in the Kiang and Han
what whiteness will you add to this whiteness
          what candor?

       . . .

120 and there was a smell of mint under the tent flaps
especially after the rain
      and a white ox on the road toward Pisa
        as if facing the tower,
dark sheep in the drill field and on wet days were clouds
125 in the mountain as if under the guard roosts.
      A lizard upheld me
      the wild birds wd not eat the white bread
      from Mt Taishan to the sunset
From Carrara stone to the tower
130   and this day the air was made open
      for Kuanon of all delights,
Linus, Cletus, Clement
          whose prayers,
the great scarab is bowed at the altar
135 the green light gleams in his shell

plowed in the sacred field and unwound the silk worms early
in tensile 顯

in the light of light is the *virtù*
"sunt lumina" said Erigena Scotus

140   as of Shun on Mt Taishan
and in the hall of the forebears
as from the beginning of wonders
the paraclete that was present in Yao, the precision
in Shun the compassionate

145   in Yu the guider of waters

4 giants at the 4 corners
three young men at the door
and they digged a ditch round about me
lest the damp gnaw thru my bones

150   to redeem Zion with justice
sd/ Isaiah. Not out on interest said David rex
the prime s.o.b.
Light tensile immaculata
the sun's cord unspotted

155   "sunt lumina" said the Oirishman to King Carolus,
"OMNIA,
all things that are are lights"
and they dug him up out of sepulture
soi disantly looking for Manichaeans.

160   Les Albigeois, a problem of history,
and the fleet at Salamis made with money lent by the state to the
shipwrights
Tempus tacendi, tempus loquendi.
Never inside the country to raise the standard of living

165   but always abroad to increase the profits of usurers,
dixit Lenin,
and gun sales lead to more gun sales
they do not clutter the market for gunnery
there is no saturation

170   Pisa, in the 23rd year of the effort in sight of the tower
and Till was hung yesterday
for murder and rape with trimmings   plus Cholkis
plus mythology, thought he was Zeus ram or another one
Hey Snag wots in the bibl'?

175   wot are the books ov the bible?

Name 'em, don't bullshit ME.

 OỶ TIΣ

a man on whom the sun has gone down

.   .   .

under the gray cliff in periplum
    the sun dragging her stars
        a man on whom the sun has gone down
and the wind came as hamadryas under the sun-beat
220   Vai soli
                     are never alone
amid the slaves learning slavery
    and the dull driven back toward the jungle
    are never alone ʽΗΛΙΟΝ ΠΕΡΙ ʽΗΛΙΟΝ
225   as the light sucks up vapor
            and the tides follow Lucina
    that had been a hard man in some ways
        a day as a thousand years
as the leopard sat by his water dish;
230   hast killed the urochs and the bison sd/ Bunting
          doing six months after that war was over
as pacifist tempted with chicken but declined to approve
of war "Redimiculum Metellorum"
                     privately printed
235   to the shame of various critics
nevertheless the state can lend money
        and the fleet that went out to Salamis
        was built by state loan to the builders
           hence the attack on classical studies
240   and in this war were Joe Gould, Bunting and cummings
as against thickness and fatness

black that die in captivity
        night green of his pupil, as grape flesh and sea wave
undying luminous and translucent

245   Est consummatum, Ite;

    surrounded by herds and by cohorts looked on Mt Taishan

.   .   .

nor is it for nothing that the chrysalids mate in the air
265   color di luce
green splendour and as the sun thru pale fingers
Lordly men are to earth o'ergiven
                 these the companions:
Fordie that wrote of giants
270   and William who dreamed of nobility
                 and Jim the comedian singing:
                       "Blarrney castle me darlin'
                       you're nothing now but a StOWne"
and Plarr talking of mathematics
275   or Jepson lover of jade
Maurie who wrote historical novels
                 and Newbolt who looked twice bathed
                       are to earth o'ergiven.
                 And this day the sun was clouded

.   .   .

and Mr Edwards superb green and brown
                 in ward No 4 a jacent benignity,
of the Baluba mask: "doan you tell no one
320   I made you that table"
                       methenamine eases the urine
and the greatest is charity
to be found among those who have not observed
                              regulations
325   not of course that we advocate —
           and yet petty larceny
           in a regime based on grand larceny
           might rank as conformity nient' altro
           with justice shall be redeemed
330 who putteth not out his money on interest
           "in meteyard in weight or in measure"
                 XIX Leviticus   or
First Thessalonians 4, 11
300 years culture at the mercy of a tack hammer
335   thrown thru the roof
Cloud over mountain, mountain over the cloud

I surrender neither the empire nor the temples
                                        plural
nor the constitution nor yet the city of Dioce
340 each one in his god's name
as by Terracina rose from the sea Zephyr behind her
                        and from her manner of walking
                                        as had Anchises
        till the shrine be again white with marble
345   till the stone eyes look again seaward
                                The wind is part of the process
                                The rain is part of the process
and the Pleiades set in her mirror
Kuanon, this stone bringeth sleep;
350   offered the wine bowl
                                        grass nowhere out of place
χθόνια γέα, Μήτηρ,
        by thy herbs menthe thyme and basilicum,
                from whom and to whom,
355   will never be more now than at present
being given a new green katydid of a Sunday
emerald, paler than emerald,
                        minus its right propeller
        this tent is to me and ΤΙΘΩΝΩΙ
360 eater of grape pulp
        in coitu inluminatio
Manet painted the bar at La Cigale or at Les Folies in that year
        she did her hair in small ringlets, à la 1880 it might have been,
red, and the dress she wore Drecol or Lanvin
365   a great goddess, Aeneas knew her forthwith
by paint immortal as no other age is immortal
                la France dixneuvième
Degas Manet Guys unforgettable
a great brute sweating paint said Vanderpyl 40 years later
370   of Vlaminick
                for this stone giveth sleep
                staria senza più scosse
                        and eucalyptus that is for memory

. . .

    I don't know how humanity stands it
390   with a painted paradise at the end of it
        without a painted paradise at the end of it
    the dwarf morning-glory twines round the grass blade
    magna NOX animae   with Barabbas and 2 thieves beside me,
        the wards like a slave ship,
395   Mr Edwards, Hudson, Henry *comes miseriae*
                Comites Kernes, Green and Tom Wilson
          God's messenger Whiteside
    and the guards op/ of the . . .
        was lower than that of the prisoners
400   "all them g.d. m.f. generals c.s. all of 'em fascists"
    "fer a bag o' Dukes"
            "the things I saye an' dooo"
      ac ego harum
    so lay men in Circe's swine-sty;
405   ivi in harum *ego* ac vidi cadavers animae
       "c'mon small fry" sd/ the little coon to the big black;
    of the slaver as seen between decks
        and all the presidents
    Washington Adams Monroe Polk Tyler
410   plus Carrol (of Carrolton) Crawford
    Robbing the public for private individual's gain ΘΈΛΓΈΙΝ
    every bank of discount is downright iniquity
        robbing the public for private individual's gain
        nec benecomata Kirkê, mah! κακὰ φάργακ' ἔδωκεν
415   neither with lions nor leopards attended
    but poison, veneno
        in all the veins of the commonweal

. . .

    nox animae magna from the tent under Taishan
    amid what was termed the a.h. of the army
    the guards holding opinions. As it were to dream of
    morticians' daughters raddled but amorous
435   To study with the white wings of time passing
        is not that our delight
    to have friends come from far countries

is not that pleasure
nor to care that we are untrumpeted?
440   filial, fraternal affection is the root of humaneness
            the root of the process
nor are elaborate speeches and slick alacrity.
        employ men in proper season
           not when they are at harvest
445   E al Triedro, Cunizza
         e l'altra: "Io son' la Luna."
dry friable earth going from dust to more dust
     grass worn from its root-hold
     is it blacker? was it blacker? Νύξ animae?
450   is there a blacker or was it merely San Juan with a belly ache
                writing ad posteros
     in short shall we look for a deeper or is this the bottom?

                    .   .   .

Time is not, Time is the evil, beloved
Beloved the hours βροδοδάκτυλος
       as against the half-light of the window
660   with the sea beyond making horizon
le contre-jour the line of the cameo
profile "to carve Achaia"
      a dream passing over the face in the half-light
      Venere, Cytherea "aut Rhodon"
665   vento ligure, veni
"beauty is difficult" sd/ Mr Beardsley

                    .   .   .

Beauty is difficult . . . . the plain ground
                  precedes the colours
740 and this grass or whatever here under the tentflaps
     is, indubitably, bambooiform
representative brush strokes wd/ be similar
. . . . cheek bone, by verbal manifestation,
      her eyes as in "La Nascita"
745   whereas the child's face
is at Capoquadri in the fresco square over the doorway
      centre background

the form beached under Helios
                                   funge la purezza,
750   and that certain images be formed in the mind
                              to remain there
                                             formato locho
           Arachne mi porta fortuna
        to remain there, resurgent ΕΙΚΟΝΕΣ
755   and still in Trastevere
        for the deification of emperors
        and the medallions
                              to forge Achaia

                                    .   .   .

        Serenely in the crystal jet
                    as the bright ball that the fountain tosses
        (Verlaine) as diamond clearness
                    How soft the wind under Taishan
830   where the sea is remembered
                    out of hell, the pit
                    out of the dust and glare evil
                    Zephyrus / Apeliota
        This liquid is certainly a
835   property of the mind
        nec accidens est   but an element
                                    in the mind's make-up
        est agens and functions   dust to a fountain pan otherwise
                    Hast 'ou seen the rose in the steel dust
840   (or swansdown ever?)
        so light is the urging, so ordered the dark petals of iron
        we who have passed over Lethe.

from CANTO LXXVI

. . .

l'ara sul rostro
20 years of the dream
    and the clouds near to Pisa
        are as good as any in Italy
140 said the young Mozart: if you will take a *prise*
        or following Ponce ("Ponthe")
          to the fountain in Florida
de Leon alla fuente florida
        or Anchises that laid hold of her flanks of air
145 drawing her to him
                Cythera potens, Κύθηρα δεινά
no cloud, but the crystal body
        the tangent formed in the hand's cup
      as live wind in the beech grove
150   as strong air amid cypress

Κόρη, Δελιά δεινά / et libidinis expers
the sphere moving crystal, fluid,
      none therein carrying rancor
Death, insanity / suicide degeneration
155 that is, just getting stupider as they get older
πολλά παθεῖν,

             nothing matters but the quality
of the affection —
in the end — that had carved the trace in the mind
160 dove sta memoria

and if theft be the main principle in government
    (every bank of discount J. Adams remarked)
there will be larceny on a minor pattern
a few camions, a stray packet of sugar
165   and the effect of the movies
      the guard did not think that the Führer had started it
Sergeant XL thought that excess population
         demanded slaughter at intervals
      (as to the by whom . . .) Known as 'The ripper.'

170   Lay in soft grass by the cliff's edge
with the sea 30 metres below this
      and at hand's span, at cubit's reach moving,
the crystalline, as inverse of water,
      clear over rock-bed

175   ac feræ familiares
the gemmed field *a destra* with fawn, with panther,
      corn flower, thistle and sword-flower
      to a half metre grass growth,
lay on the cliff's edge
180   . . . nor is this yet *atasal*
      nor are here souls, nec personæ
      neither here in hypostasis, this land is of Dione
and under her planet
      to Helia the long meadow with poplars
185   to   Κύπρις
      the mountain and shut garden of pear trees in flower
here rested.

                   .   .   .

      and the spring of their squeak-doll is broken
and Bracken is out and the B.B.C. can lie
205   but at least a different bilge will come out of it
      at least for a little, as is its nature
can continue, that is, to lie.

       As a lone ant from a broken ant-hill
from the wreckage of Europe, ego scriptor.
210   The rain has fallen, the wind coming down
      out of the mountain
      Lucca, Forti dei Marmi, Berchthold after the other one . . .
parts reassembled.
      . . . and within the crystal, went up swift as Thetis
215 in colour rose-blue before sunset
and carmine and amber,

spiriti questi? personæ?
       tangibility by no means *atasal*
       but the crystal can be weighed in the hand

220 formal and passing within the sphere: Thetis,
Maya, Αφροδίτη,

                    no overstroke
               no dolphin faster in moving
                    nor the flying azure of the wing'd fish under Zoagli
225   when he comes out into the air, living arrow.
and the clouds over the Pisan meadows
                    are indubitably as fine as any to be seen
from the peninsula
                    οἱ βάρβαροι have not destroyed them
230   as they have Sigismundo's Temple
          Divae Ixottae (and as to her effigy that was in Pisa?)
          Ladder at swing jump as for a descent from the cross
O white-chested martin, God damn it,
                    as no one else will carry a message,
235   say to La Cara: amo.

          Her bed-posts are of sapphire
               for this stone giveth sleep.

               and in spite of hoi barbaroi
               pervenche and a sort of dwarf morning-glory
240   that knots in the grass, and a sort of buttercup
et sequelae

Le Paradis n'est pas artificiel
          States of mind are inexplicable to us.
          δακρύων   δακρύων   δακρύων
245   L.   P.   gli onesti
               J' ai eu pitié des autres
probablement pas assez, and at moments that suited my own convenience
               Le paradis n'est pas artificiel,
                         l'enfer non plus.

250 Came Eurus as comforter
and at sunset la pastorella dei suini
               driving the pigs home, benecomata dea

               under the two-winged cloud
               as of less and more than a day
                    .   .   .

from CANTO LXXIX

. . .

The moon has a swollen cheek
and when the morning sun lit up the shelves and battalions
of the West, cloud over cloud
165   Old Ez folded his blankets
Neither Eos nor Hesperus has suffered wrong at my hands

                    O Lynx, wake Silenus and Casey
                    shake the castagnettes of the bassarids,
the mountain forest is full of light
170   the tree-comb red-gilded
Who sleeps in the field of lynxes
          in the orchard of Maelids?
(with great blue marble eyes
          "because he likes to," the cossak)
175 Salazar, Scott, Dawley on sick call
          Polk, Tyler, half the presidents and Calhoun
"Retaliate on the capitalists" sd/ Calhoun " of the North"
ah yes, when the ideas were clearer
          debts to people in N. Y. city
180   and on the hill of the Maelids
in the close garden of Venus
          asleep amid serried lynxes
set wreathes on Priapus Ιακχος, Io! Κύθηρα, Io!
                    having root in the equities
185 Io!
          and you can make 5000 dollars a year
all you have to do is to make one trip up country
then come back to Shanghai
                    and send in an annual report
190 as to the number of converts
                    Sweetland on sick call
                    'ελέησον   Kyrie Eleison
          each under his fig tree
          or with the smell of fig leaves burning
195 so shd/ be fire in winter
with fig wood, with cedar, and pine burrs

O Lynx keep watch on my fire.

So Astafieva had conserved the tradition
From Byzance and before then
200   Manitou remember this fire
O lynx, keep the phylloxera from my grape vines
Ιακχε, Ιακχε, Χαῖρε, AOI
           "Eat of it not in the under world"
           See that the sun or the moon bless thy eating
205 Κόρη, Κόρη, for the six seeds of an error
or that the stars bless thy eating

         O Lynx, guard this orchard,
         Keep from Demeter's furrow

This fruit has a fire within it,
210   Pomona, Pomona
No glass is clearer than are the globes of this flame
what sea is clearer than the pomegranate body
         holding the flame?
            Pomona, Pomona,

215   Lynx, keep watch on this orchard
           That is named Melagrana
or the Pomegranate field
           The sea is not clearer in azure
           Nor the Heliads bringing light

220   Here are lynxes   Here are lynxes,
      Is there a sound in the forest
           of pard or of bassarid
    or crotale   or of leaves moving?

         Cythera, here are lynxes
225 Will the scrub-oak burst into flower?
     There is a rose vine in this underbrush
Red? white? No, but a colour between them
     When the pomegranate is open and the light falls
half thru it

230   Lynx, beware of these vine-thorns
         O Lynx, γλαυκῶπις coming up from the olive yards,

Kuthera, here are Lynxes and the clicking of crotales
There is a stir of dust from old leaves
Will you trade roses for acorns
235   Will lynxes eat thorn leaves?
What have you in that wine jar?
ἰχώρ, for lynxes?

Maelid and bassarid among lynxes;
how many? There are more under the oak trees,
240 We are here waiting the sun-rise
and the next sunrise
for three nights amid lynxes. For three nights
of the oak-wood
and the vines are thick in their branches
245   no vine lacking flower,
no lynx lacking a flower rope
no Maelid minus a wine jar
this forest is named Melagrana

O lynx, keep the edge on my cider
250   Keep it clear without cloud

We have lain here amid kalicanthus and sword-flower
The heliads are caught in wild rose vine
The smell of pine mingles with rose leaves
O lynx, be many
255   of spotted fur and sharp ears.
O lynx, have your eyes gone yellow,
with spotted fur and sharp ears?

Therein is the dance of the bassarids
Therein are centaurs
260 And now Priapus with Faunus
The Graces have brought Ἀφροδίτην
Her cell is drawn by ten leopards

O lynx, guard my vineyard
As the grape swells under vine leaf
265   Ἥλιος is come to our mountain
there is a red glow in the carpet of pine spikes

O lynx, guard my vineyard
As the grape swells under vine leaf

This Goddess was born of sea-foam
270   She is lighter than air under Hesperus
δεινὰ εἶ, Κύθηρα
terrible in resistance
Κόρη καὶ Δήλια καὶ Μαῖα
trine as praeludio
275   Κύπρις Αφρόδιτη
a petal lighter than sea-foam
Κύθηρα

aram

nemus

280   vult

O puma, sacred to Hermes, Cimbica servant of Helios.

from CANTO LXXX

. . .

180   "Hot hole hep cat"
  or words of similar volume
    to be recognized by the god-damned
       or man-damned trainee
  Prowling night-puss leave my hard squares alone
185   they are in no case cat food
      if you had sense
  you wd / come here at meal time
     when meat is superabundant
  you can neither eat manuscript nor Confucius
190   nor even the hebrew scriptures
    get out of that bacon box
    contract W, 11 oh oh 9 oh
  now used as a wardrobe
       ex 53 pounds gross weight
195 the cat-faced eucalyptus nib
     is where you cannot get at it
    Tune: kitten on the keys
     radio steam Calliope
  following the Battle Hymn of the Republic
200   where the honey-wagon cease from stinking
       and the nose be at peace
  "mi-hine eyes hev"
     well yes they *have*
  seen a good deal of it
205   there is a good deal to be seen
  fairly tough and unblastable
    and the hymn . . .
  well in contrast to the *god*-damned crooning
    put me down for temporis acti
210   ΟΥ ΤΙΣ
    ἄχρονος
  now there are no more days

. . .

  Nancy where art thou?
  Whither go all the vair and the cisclatons

and the wave pattern runs in the stone
585   on the high parapet (Excideuil)
Mt Segur and the city of Dioce
Que tous les mois avons nouvelle lune
What the deuce has Herbiet (Christian)
            done with his painting?
590   Fritz still roaring at treize rue Gay de Lussac
with his stone head still on the balcony?
Orage, Fordie, Crevel too quickly taken

        de mis soledades vengan

lay there till Rossetti found it remaindered
595   at about two pence
(Cythera, in the moon's barge whither?
            how hast thou the crescent for car?

or did they fall because of their loose taste in music
            "Here! none of that mathematical music!"
600   Said the Kommandant when Münch offered Bach to the regiment
or Spewcini the all too human
            beloved in the eyetalian peninsula
for quite explicable reasons
            so that even I can now tolerate
605   man seht but with the loss of criteria
and the wandering almost-tenor explained to me:
            well the operas in the usual repertoire
have been sifted out, there's a reason

Les hommes ont je ne sais quelle peur étrange,
610   said Monsieur Whoosis, de la beauté

La beauté, "Beauty is difficult, Yeats" said Aubrey Beardsley
            when Yeats asked why he drew horrors
            or at least not Burne-Jones
            and Beardsley knew he was dying and had to
615   make his hit quickly

hence no more B-J in his product.

So very difficult, Yeats, beauty so difficult.

"I am the torch" wrote Arthur "she saith"
in the moon barge βροδοδάκτυλος Ηώς

620   with the veil of faint cloud before her
                Κύθηρα δεινὰ as a leaf borne in the current
        pale eyes as if without fire

        all that Sandro knew, and Jacopo
                and that Velásquez never suspected
625   lost in the brown meat of Rembrandt
                and the raw meat of Rubens and Jordaens

                                    .   .   .

                        Favonus, vento benigno
660   Je suis au bout de mes forces/
        That from the gates of death,
                    that from the gates of death: Whitman or Lovelace
                        found on the jo-house seat at that
        in a cheap edition! [and thanks to Professor Speare]
665   hast'ou swum in a sea of air strip
                through an æon of nothingness,
        when the raft broke and the waters went over me,

        Immaculata, Introibo
                for those who drink of the bitterness
670   Perpetua, Agatha, Anastasia
                            saeculorum

        repos donnez à cils
                senza termine funge   Immaculata Regina
                        Les larmes que j'ai creées m'inondent
675   Tard, très tard je t'ai connue, la Tristesse,
        I have been hard as youth sixty years

                if calm be after tempest
        that the ants seem to wobble
                as the morning sun catches their shadows
680   Nadasky, Duett, McAllister,
                also Comfort K.P. special mention
                on sick call Penrieth, Turner, Toth hieri

(no fortune and with a name to come)
Bankers, Seitz, Hildebrand and Cornelison
685   Armstrong special mention K.P.
White gratia Bedell gratia
Wiseman (not William) africanus.
with a smoky torch thru the unending
labyrinth of the souterrain
690 or remembering Carleton let him celebrate Christ in the grain
and if the corn cat be beaten
Demeter has lain in my furrow
This wind is lighter than swansdown
the day moves not at all
695 (Zupp, Bufford, and Bohon)

men of no fortune and with a name to come

his helmet is used for a pisspot
this helmet is used for my footbath
Elpenor can count the shingle under Zoagli
700 Pepitone was waiting toothwash
as I lay by the drain hole
the guard's opinion is lower than that of the
prisoners

o.   t.   a.

705 Oh to be in England now that Winston's out
Now that there's room for doubt
And the bank may be the nation's
And the long years of patience
And labour's vacillations
710 May have let the bacon come home,
To watch how they'll slip and slide
watch how they'll try to hide
the real portent
To watch a while from the tower
715 where dead flies lie thick over the old charter
forgotten, oh quite forgotten
but confirming John's first one,
and still there if you climb over attic rafters;
to look at the fields; are they tilled?

720   is the old terrace alive as it might be
with a whole colony
                    if money be free again?
Chesterton's England of has-been and why-not,
or is it all rust, ruin, death duties and mortgages
725   and the great carriage yard empty
                    and more pictures gone to pay taxes

        When a dog is tall but
        not so tall as all that
        that dog is a Talbot
730   (a bit long in the pasterns?)
When a butt is ½ as tall as a whole butt
That butt is a small butt
                Let backe and side go bare
and the old kitchen left as the monks had left it
735   and the rest as time has cleft it.

        [Only shadows enter my tent
                    as men pass between me and the sunset,]
        beyond the eastern barbed wire
                a sow with nine boneen
740   matronly as any duchess at Claridge's

and for that Christmas at Maurie Hewlett's
Going out from Southampton
they passed the car by the dozen
            who would not have shown weight on a scale
745   riding, riding
                                for Noel the green holly
            Noel, Noel, the green holly
            A dark night for the holly

That would have been Salisbury plain, and I have not thought of
750   the Lady Anne for this twelve years
                Nor of Le Portel
How tiny the panelled room where they stabbed him
                In her lap, almost, La Stuarda
                Si tuit li dolh ehl planh el marrimen
755   for the leopards and broom plants

Tudor indeed is gone and every rose,
Blood-red, blanch-white that in the sunset glows
Cries: "Blood,   Blood,   Blood!" against the gothic stone
Of England, as the Howard or Boleyn knows.

760   Nor seeks the carmine petal to infer;
Nor is the white bud Time's inquistor
Probing to know if its new-gnarled root
Twists from York's head or belly of Lancaster;

Or if a rational soul should stir, perchance,
765   Within the stem or summer shoot to advance
Contrition's utmost throw, seeking in thee
But oblivion, not thy forgiveness, FRANCE.

as the young lizard extends his leopard spots
along the grass-blade seeking the green midge half an ant-size
770   and the Serpentine will look just the same
and the gulls be as neat on the pond
and the sunken garden unchanged
and God knows what else is left of our London
my London, your London
775   and if her green elegance
remains on this side of my rain ditch
puss lizard will lunch on some other T-bone

sunset grand couturier.

from CANTO LXXXI

. . .

AOI!
95   a leaf in the current
             at my grates no Althea

libretto Yet
       Ere the season died a-cold
       Borne upon a zephyr's shoulder
100   I rose through the aureate sky
             Lawes and Jenkyns guard they rest
             Dolmetsch ever be thy guest,
       Has he tempered the viol's wood
       To enforce   both the grave   and the acute?
105   Has he curved us the bowl of the lute?
             Lawes and Jenkyns guard thy rest
             Dolmetsch ever be thy guest
       Has 'ou fashioned so airy a mood
          To draw up leaf from the root?
110   Has'ou found   a cloud   so light
          As seemed neither mist nor shade?

             Then resolve me, tell me aright
             If Waller sang or Dowland played.

         Your eyen two wol sleye me sodenly
115   I may the beauté of hem nat susteyne

And for 180 years almost nothing.

Ed ascoltando al leggier mormorio
       there came new subtlety of eyes into my tent,
whether of spirit or hypostasis,
120   but what the blindfold hides
or at carneval
             nor any pair showed anger
       Saw but the eyes and stance between the eyes,
colour, diastasis,
125   careless or unaware it had not the

whole tent's room
nor was place for the full Εἰδὼς
interpass, penetrate
    casting but shade beyond the other lights
130   sky's clear
        night's sea
        green of the mountain pool
        shone from the unmasked eyes in half-mask's space.
What thou lovest well remains,
135   the rest is dross
What thou lov'st well shall not be reft from thee
What thou lov'st well is thy true heritage
Whose world, or mine or theirs
                or is it of none?
140 First came the seen, then thus the palpable
    Elysium, though it were in the halls of hell,
What thou lovest well is thy true heritage
What thou lov'st well shall not be reft from thee

The ant's a centaur in his dragon world.
145 Pull down thy vanity, it is not man
Made courage, or made order, or made grace,
    Pull down thy vanity, I say pull down.
Learn of the green world what can be thy place
In scaled invention or true artistry,
150 Pull down thy vanity,
                Paquin pull down!
The green casque has outdone your elegance.

"Master thyself, then others shall thee beare"
    Pull down thy vanity
155 Thou art a beaten dog beneath the hail,
A swollen magpie in a fitful sun,
Half black half white
Nor knowst'ou wing from tail
Pull down thy vanity
160   How mean thy hates
Fostered in falsity,
        Pull down thy vanity,
Rathe to destroy, niggard in charity,
Pull down thy vanity,

165   I say pull down.
         But to have done instead of not doing
                    this is not vanity
         To have, with decency, knocked
         That a Blunt should open
170   To have gathered from the air a live tradition
         or from a fine old eye the unconquered flame
         This is not vanity.
              Here error is all in the not done,
         all in the diffidence that faltered . . .

from CANTO LXXXIII

· · ·

Δρυάς, your eyes are like clouds

65   Nor can who has passed a month in the death cells
                believe in capital punishment
        No man who has passed a month in the death cells
                believes in cages for beasts

        Δρυάς, your eyes are like the clouds over Taishan
70   When some of the rain has fallen
                and half remains yet to fall

        The roots go down to the river's edge
                and the hidden city moves upward
                        white ivory under the bark

75   With clouds over Taishan-Chocorua
                when the blackberry ripens
        and now the new moon faces Taishan
        one must count by the dawn star
                Dryad, thy peace is like water
80   There is September sun on the pools

        Plura diafana
                Heliads lift the mist from the young willows
        there is no base seen under Taishan
                but the brightness of 'udor   ὕδωρ
85   the poplar tips float in brightness
        only the stockade posts stand

        And now the ants seem to stagger
                as the dawn sun has trapped their shadows,
        this breath wholly covers the mountains
90   it shines and divides
        it nourishes by its rectitude
        does no injury
        overstanding the earth it fills the nine fields
                        to heaven

95   Boon companion to equity
            it joins with the process
                 lacking it, there is inanition

       When the equities are gathered together
       as birds alighting
100   it springeth up vital

       If deeds be not ensheaved and garnered in the heart
       there is inanition

                                        .   .   .

            and Brother Wasp is building a very neat house
            of four rooms, one shaped like a squat indian bottle
            La vespa, *la* vespa, mud, swallow system
130   so that dreaming of Bracelonde and of Perugia
       and the great fountain in the Piazza
         or of old Bulagaio's cat that with a well timed leap
            could turn the lever-shaped door handle
       It comes over me that Mr. Walls must be a ten-strike
135   with the signorinas
       and in the warmnth after chill sunrise
       an infant, green as new grass,
       has stuck its head or tip
       out of Madame La Vespa's bottle

140   mint springs up again
                 in spite of Jones' rodents
       as had the clover by the gorilla cage
            with a four-leaf

       When the mind swings by a grass-blade
145   an ant's forefoot shall save you
       the clover leaf smells and tastes as its flower

            The infant has descended,
            from mud on the tent roof to Tellus,
       like to like colour he goes amid grass-blades
150   greeting them that dwell under ΧΤΗΟΝΟΣ   ΧΘΟΝΟΣ
       ΟΙ ΧΘΟΝΙΟΙ;   to carry our news

εἰς χθονίους   to them that dwell under the earth,
begotten of air, that shall sing in the bower
        of Kore,   Περσεφόνεια
155   and have speech with Tiresias, Thebae

        Cristo Re, Dio Sole

in about ½ a day she has made her adobe
(la vespa) the tiny mud-flask

        and that day I wrote no further

160   There is fatigue deep as the grave.
        The Kakemono grows in flat land out of mist
                sun rises lop-sided over the mountain
                        so that I recalled the noise in the chimney
        as it were the wind in the chimney
165   but was in reality Uncle William
        downstairs composing
        that had made a great Peeeeacock
                in the proide ov his oiye
                        had made a great peeeeeeecock in the . . .
170   made a great peacock
                    in the proide of his oyyee

        proide ov his oy-ee
        as indeed he had, and perdurable

        a great peacock aere perennius
175   or as in the advice to the young man to
        breed and get married (or not)
                        as you choose to regard it

        at Stone Cottage in Sussex by the waste moor
        (or whatever) and the holly bush
180   who would not eat ham for dinner
        because peasants eat ham for dinner
                despite the excellent quality
        and the pleasure of having it hot

well those days are gone forever
185   and the traveling rug with the coon-skin tabs
and his hearing nearly all Wordsworth
        for the sake of his conscience but
preferring Ennemosor on Witches

did we ever get to the end of Doughty:
190   The Dawn in Britain?
                                perhaps not
        Summons withdrawn, sir.)
(bein' aliens in prohibited area)
clouds lift their small mountains
195   before the elder hills

A fat moon rises lop-sided over the mountain
The eyes, this time my world,
        But pass and look *from* mine
            between my lids
200   sea, sky, and pool
            alternate
            pool, sky, sea,

morning moon against sunrise
like a bit of the best antient greek coinage

                    .   .   .

CANTO XC

Animus humanus amor non est,
sed ab ipso amor procedit, et
ideo seipso non diligit, sed amore
qui seipso procedit.

"FROM the colour the nature
& by the nature the sign!"
Beatific spirits welding together
as in one ash-tree in Ygdrasail.
5   Baucis, Philemon.
Castalia is the name of that fount in the hill's fold,
the sea below,
narrow beach.
Templum aedificans, not yet marble,
10   "Amphion!"

And from the San Ku 三

to the room in Poitiers where one can stand
casting no shadow,
15 That is Sagetrieb,
that is tradition.
Builders had kept the proportion,
did Jacques de Molay
know these porportions?
20 and was Erigena ours?
Moon's barge over milk-blue water
Kuthera δεινά
Kuthera sempiterna
Ubi amor, ibi oculus.
25 Vae qui cogitatis inutile.
quam in nobis similitudine divinae
reperetur imago.
"Mother Earth in thy lap"
said Randolph
30   ἠγάπησεν πολύ
liberavit masnatos.

Castalia like the moonlight
   and the waves rise and fall,
Evita, beer-halls, semina motuum,
35   to parched grass, now is rain
not arrogant from habit,
  but furious from perception,
       Sibylla,
from under the rubble heap
40   m'elevasti
from the dulled edge beyond pain,
     m'elevasti
out of Erebus, the deep-lying
  from the wind under the earth,
45   m'elevasti
from the dulled air and the dust,
     m'elevasti
by the great flight,
    m'elevasti
50   Isis Kuanon
  from the cusp of the moon,
     m'elevasti
the viper stirs in the dust,
     the blue serpent
55 glides from the rock pool
  And they take lights now down to the water
the lamps float from the rowers
  the sea's claw drawing them outward.
"De fondo" said Juan Ramon,
60   like a mermaid, upward,
but the light perpendicular, upward
and to Castalia,
    water jets from the rock
and in the flat pool as Arethusa's
65   a hush in papyri.
Grove hath its altar
  under elms, in that temple, in silence
a lone nymph by the pool.
   Wei and Han rushing together
70 two rivers together
  bright fish and flotsam
torn bough in the flood

and the waters clear with the flowing
Out of heaviness where no mind moves at all
75   "birds for the mind" said Richardus,
"beasts as to body, for know-how"
Gaio! Gaio!
             To Zeus with the six seraphs before him
The architect from the painter,
80   the stone under elm
Taking form now,
        the rilievi,
      the curled stone at the marge
Faunus, sirenes,
85   the stone taking form in the air
      ac ferae,
           cervi,
                the great cats approaching.
Pardus, leopardi, Bagheera
90   drawn hither from woodland,
woodland ἐπὶ χθονί
        the trees rise
      and there is a wide sward between them
οἱ χθόνιοι myrrh and olibanum on the altar stone
95 giving perfume,
            and where was nothing
  now is furry assemblage
         and in the boughs now are voices
grey wing, black wing, black wing shot with crimson
100 and the umbrella pines
              as in Palatine,
as in pineta. χελιδών, χελιδών
For the procession of Corpus
          come now banners
105 comes flute tone
        οἱ χθόνιοι
to new forest,
      thick smoke, purple, rising
bright flame now on the altar
110   the crystal funnel of air
out of Erebus, the delivered,
      Tyro, Alcmene, free now, ascending
e i cavalieri,

                    ascending,
115   no shades more,
                         lights among them, enkindled,
         and the dark shade of courage
                              Ηλέκτρα
                  bowed still with the wrongs of Aegisthus.
120   Trees die & the dream remains
                         Not love but that love flows from it
                         ex animo
                         & cannot ergo delight in itself
                         but only in the love flowing from it.
         UBI AMOR IBI OCULUS EST.

from CANTO XCI

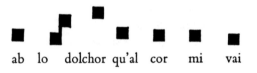

ab lo dolchor qu'al cor mi vai

AB LO DOLCHOR QU'AL COR MI   VAI

5   that the body of light come forth
                 from the body of fire
     And that your eyes come to the surface
                 from the deep wherein they were sunken,
     Reina—for 300 years,
10   and now sunken
     That your eyes come forth from their caves
            & light then
                  as the holly-leaf
              qui laborat, orat
15   Thus Undine came to the rock,
                 by Circeo
     and the stone eyes again looking seaward
       Thus Apollonius
              (if it was Apollonius)
20   & Helen of Tyre
           by Pithagoras
           by Ocellus
     (pilot-fish, et libidinis expers, of Tyre;
     Justinian, Theodora
25   from brown leaf and twig
     The GREAT CRYSTAL
               doubling the pine, and to cloud.
           pensar di lieis m'es ripaus
     Miss Tudor moved them with galleons
30   from deep eye, versus armada
     from the green deep
             he saw it,
     in the green deep of an eye:

Crystal waves weaving together toward the gt/
35   healing
Light *compenetrans* of the spirits
The Princess Ra-Set has climbed
                to the great knees of stone,
She enters protection,
40   the great cloud is about her,
She has entered the protection of crystal
                                convien che si mova
                                la mente, amando
                                                XXVI, 34

45   Light & the flowing crystal
            never gin in cut glass had such clarity
     That Drake saw the splendour and wreckage
                in that clarity
     Gods moving in crystal
50   ichor, amor
     Secretary of Nature, J. Heydon.
                Here Apollonius, Heydon
                hither Ocellus
                        "to this khan."
55   The golden sun boat
                        by oar, not by sail
     Love moving the stars παρὰ βώμιον
     by the altar slope
                "Tamuz!   Tamuz!"
60   They set lights now in the sea
            and the sea's claw gathers them outward.
     The peasant wives hide cocoons now
                                under their aprons
                                for Tamuz
65   That the sun's silk

          hsien   顯   tensile

                        be clear

     Ελέναυς That Drake saw the armada
                & sea caves
70   Ra-Set over crystal

moving

in the Queen's eye the reflection

& sea-wrack—

> green deep of the sea-cave

75 ne quaesaris.

> > He asked not

nor wavered, seeing, nor had fear of the wood-queen, Artemis

> > that is Diana

nor had killed save by the hunting rite,

80 > > > sanctus.

Thus sang it:

> Leafdi Diana, leove Diana

> Heye Diana, help me to neode

Witte me thurh crafte

85 > whuder ich maei lidhan

> to wonsom londe.

> > > Rome th'ilke tyme was noght.

So that he spread a deer-hide near the altar,

Now Lear in Janus' temple is laid

90 > > timing the thunder

震 . . .

from CANTO XCII

·   ·   ·

"And if I see her not,
         no sight is worth the beauty of my thought."
Then knelt with the sphere of crystal
50   That she should touch with her hands,
                  Coeli Regina,
The four altars at the four coigns of that place,
But in the great love, bewildered
         farfalla in tempesta
55   under rain in the dark:
                        many wings fragile
Nymphalidae, basilarch, and lycaena,
Ausonides, euchloe, and erynnis
And from far
60   il tremolar della marina
chh   chh
      the pebbles turn with the wave
chh   ch'u
            "fui chiamat'
65   e qui refulgo"
Le Paradis n'est pas artificiel
                        but is jagged,
For a flash,
            for an hour.
70   Then agony,
            then an hour,
                        then agony,
Hilary stumbles, but the Divine Mind is abundant
                  unceasing
75   *improvisatore*
Omniformis
            unstill

·   ·   ·

from CANTO XCIII

. . .

The autumn leaves blow from my hand,
   agitante calescemus . . .
   and the wind cools toward autumn.
Lux in diafana,
    Creatrix,
150   oro.
Ursula benedetta,
     oro
By the hours of passion,
      per dilettevole ore,
155   guide your successor,
Ysolt, Ydone,
    have compassion,
Picarda,
    compassion
160 By the wing'd head,
    by the caduceus,
       compassion;
By the horns of Isis-Luna,
       compassion.
165 The black panther lies under his rose-tree.
J'ai eu pitié des autres.
    Pas assez! Pas assez!
For me nothing. But that the child
   walk in peace in her basilica,
170 The light there almost solid.

力 li⁴

行 hsing²

近 chin⁴

平 hu¹ 2154

175 仁 jên²

holding that energy is near to benevolence,
Au bois dormant,

            not yet . . . ! Not yet!
            do not awaken.

180   The trees sleep, and the stags, and the grass;
The boughs sleep unmoving.
"Krr! Krr!" from the starling:
            "mai tardi . . .
"per l'ignoto"

185   and the soul's job? (Ocellus)
           "Renew
as on the T'ang tub:
            Renew

        jih   日

190

        hsin   新

        renew

Plus the luminous eye   見   chien⁴

            . . .

from CANTO XCIX

. . .

And if your kids don't study, that's your fault.
330   Tell 'em. Don't kid yourself, and don't lie.
In statement, answer; in conversation
         not with sissified fussiness (chiao¹)
       always want your own way.
Let 'em ask before taking action;
335   That there be no slovenly sloppiness
         between goodman & wife.
Gt. is gt. . Little is little;
With friends one is one
         2 is 2
340   Not to lie out of heedlessness
        let alone out of trickery
Fitting the tone to their words
        as water goes over the mill-wheel.
Dress'em in folderols
345   and feed 'em with dainties,
In the end they will sell out the homestead.
Taxes, for public utility,
        a share of a product,
People have bodies
350   ergo they sow and reap,
Soldiers also have bodies,
        take care of the body as implement,
It is useful,
To shield you from floods and rascality.

355   Born of the blue sky and a wild cat
        Cloud in thunder and rain,
Basalt, the stone gong
     "if," as Yao said: "you can keep these two lovelies
     in order!"
360   You forget the timing of budgets
        that is to say you probably don't even know that
Officials exist in time. You are fairly unconscious
      Hsiang i hsiang

but in muddle and incomprehension   14.5
365   the contemplation of outlay
            hsiao⁴
tsou (four) memorial
the k'ao ch'eng is according to harvest,
the tax as a share of something produced.

370   You can waste more on tips and wangles
          (Thiers a progress from Talleyrand,
less brain and more morals)
      PANURGIA? SOPHIA:
         what will *not* do,
375   Are distinguished by what they will not—
Cannibals wd/ resist canneries, Ersatz
     a given state of enlightenment, scienza
           XIV
Thru the ten voices of the tradition
380   the land has been ploughed
           t'ien² ti⁴
& there have been taxes in kind, and by (liang²) measure
This is important
     as to the scope of such taxes
385   all Courts have levied them
       the right pattern of levy is yang⁴ cheng¹
           id est: for use
not a fountain of folderols
for top poppinjays.
390   Wranglings won't get you out of it
High & low, top & under
       INCORPORATE
& one body.
The ups are not malevolent,
395   you might consider their complications;
Dykes for flood-water,
        someone must build 'em;
        must plan 'em,
By the ten mouths of the tradition:
           have peace
400 Meaning get rid of criminality. Catch 'em!

Ancestral spring making breed, a pattern

Yong (2. 2. 3)
"12 inches, guinea an inch!" said Elkin Mathews
405   in regard to Courtney's review.
The State is corporate
                    as with pulse in its body
& with Chou rite at the root of it
The root is thru all of it,
410   a tone in all public teaching:
This is not a work of fiction
                    nor yet of one man:
The six kinds of action, filial, reciprocal,
Sincerity from of old until now,
415   holding together
Not shallow in verbal usage
                    nor in dissociations;
Shallow prides, feeble dissociations,
And spend their time slanting rumours;
420   keep things off center slander and blabber-mouth;
Rail; scold and ructions; *manesco*
               and the whole family suffers.
The whole tribe is from one man's body,
               what other way can you think of it?
425 The surname, and the 9 arts.
               The father's word is compassion;
               The son's, filiality.
               The brother's word: mutuality;
               The younger's word: deference.
430 Small birds sing in chorus,
Harmony is in the proportion of branches
               as clarity (chao¹).
Compassion, tree's root and water-spring;
               The state: order, inside a boundary;
435   Law: reciprocity.
What is statute save reciprocity?
One village in order,
               one valley will reach the four seas.

CHÊN, *yo el Rey,* wish you to think of this EDICT.
440   4.
Having heard that provisions are the root of the people
                    (logistica)

nung

     sang

445   To sprout in season

        and have trees for your silk-worms,

One big chap not plow,

        one female not weave

Can mean shortage,

450   From of old the sovereign likes plowing

& the Empress tends trees with reverence;

      Nor shrink from the heat of labour

兆   an omen

The plan is in nature

455   rooted

Coming from earth, times (ch'ang²) respected

Their powers converging

       (chu four assemble

There is a must at the root of it

460   not one man's mere power,

Thru high-low, parch and dampness

High, dry for panicled millet

Damp, low for rice (non-glutinous) and paddy

     wu² mu ch'i² ying² pei⁴ li⁴

465   (interest)

not for a quick buck at high interest

the legal rate does not exhaust things

     (Byzance did better)

Don't burn to abandon production and go into trading,

470   Dig up root to chase branches

vide Michelet & Ambrose "De Tobia"

      The rate in Byzance was lower,

as can continuous far

       (que ça doure)

475   Established that everybody got some education

AND you had literate Confucians

         in the burocracy,

Focus of men of ability solidified our good customs.

Shut out graceful bigots

480   and moderate thundering phalloi

      (this is a mistranslation)

Strong, weak, to one coöperation,

           our SAGE FOREBEAR examined to
                     stimulate anagogico
and more especially magnified schools—
485   everything that wd/ bring up esprit de corps

                en[1] 恩

trained his officers not to slant government
490   and to be ready for anything.
1st/ the basic in his own practice,
           then village usage
             to see what style for the casting
Filiality and fraternity are the root,
495   Talents to be considered as branches.
Precise terminology is the first implement,
                 dish and container,
After that the 9 arts.
AND study the classic books,
500   the straight history
                   all of it candid.
Be friends with straight officers
             chiao[1] communicate,
They *are* your communications,
505   a hasty chirrp may raise ruin.
You, soldiers, civilians,
           are not headed to be professors.
The basis is man,
           and the rectification of officers
510   But the four TUAN
             are from nature
        jen, i, li, chih
Not from descriptions in the school house;
They are the scholar's job,
           the gentleman's and the officer's.
515

There is worship in plowing
           and equity in the weeding hoe,
A field marshal can be literate.
           Might we see it again in our day!

520   7

All I want is a generous spirit in customs
　　　　ist/ honest man's heart demands sane curricula
　　　　　　(no, that is not textual)
Let him analyze the trick programs
　　　　　　　and fake foundations
The fu jen receives heaven, earth, middle
　　　　　　and grows

　　　　　　　　　　.　.　.

FROM CANTO CXII

. . . owl, and wagtail
and huo³-hu², the fire-fox
Amṛta, that is nectar
          white wind, white dew
5   Here from the beginning, we have been here
             from the beginning
From her breath were the goddesses
          ²La ²mu<u>n</u> ³mi
If we did not perform ²Ndaw ¹bpö
10   nothing is solid
without ²Mùa<u>n</u> ¹bpö
         no reality
Agility, that is from the juniper,
rice grows and the land is invisible
15   By the pomegranate water,
           in the clear air
             over Li Chiang
The firm voice amid pine wood,
          many springs are at the foot of
20   Hsiang Shan
By the temple pool, Lung Wang's
         the clear discourse
          as Jade stream

玉 Yü⁴

河 ho²

Artemisia
Arundinaria
Winnowed in fate's tray

 neath
30   luna ☽

CANTO CXIII

Thru the 12 Houses of Heaven
　　　　seeing the just and the unjust,
　　　　　tasting the sweet and the sorry,
Pater Helios turning.
5　　"Mortal praise has no sound in her ears"
　　　　　　　　(Fortuna's)
θρῆνος
And who no longer make gods out of beauty
θρῆνος　　　this is a dying.
10　Yet to walk with Mozart, Agassiz and Linnaeus
　　　　'neath overhanging air under sun-beat
Here take thy mind's space
And to this garden, Marcella, ever seeking by petal, by leaf-vein
　　　　out of dark, and toward half-light

15　And over Li Chiang, the snow range is turquoise
Rock's world that he saved us for memory
　　　　　a thin trace in high air
And with them Paré (Ambroise) and the Men against Death
Tweddel, Donnelly,
20　　　　　　　old Pumpelly crossed Gobi
"no horse, no dog, and no goat."

"I'd eat his liver, told that son of . . .
and now bigod I have done it"
　　　　　　17 Maggio,
25　　　　　　　　　why not spirits?
But for the sun and serenitas
　　　　(19th May '59)
H.D. once said "serenitas"
　　　　　　(Atthis, etc.)
30　　　at Dieudonné's
　　　　　　in pre-history,
No dog, no horse, and no goat,
The long flank, the firm breast
　　　　and to know beauty and death and despair
35　and to think that what has been shall be,
　　　　　flowing, ever unstill.

Then a partridge-shaped cloud over dust storm.
The hells move in cycles,
                    No man can see his own end.
40 The Gods have not returned. "They have never left us."
                    They have not returned.
Cloud's processional and the air moves with their living.
Pride, jealousy and possessiveness
                    3 pains of hell
45 and a clear wind over garofani
                    over Portofino 3 lights in triangulation
Or apples from Hesperides fall in their lap
                    from phantom trees.
The old Countess remembered (say 1928)
50   that ball in St. Petersburg
and as to how Stef got out of Poland . . .
                    Sir Ian told 'em help
                            would come via the sea
(the black one, the Black Sea)
55   Pétain warned 'em
And the road under apple-boughs
                    mostly grass-covered
And the olives to windward
                    Kalenda Maja.
60 Li Sao, Li Sao, for sorrow

          but there is something intelligent in the cherry-stone
Canals, bridges, and house walls
          orange in sunlight
But to hitch sensibility to efficiency?
65   grass versus granite,
For the little light and more harmony
Oh God of all men, none excluded
and howls for Schwundgeld in the Convention
                            (our Constitutional
70   17 . . . whichwhat)
Nothing new but their ignorance,
                    ever perennial
Parsley used in the sacrifice
          and (calling Paul Peter) 12%
75   does not mean one, oh, four, 104%

Error of chaos. Justification is from kindness of heart
    and from her hands floweth mercy.
As for who demand belief rather than justice.
And the host of Egypt, the pyramid builder,
80   waiting there to be born.
No more the pseudo-gothic sprawled house
    out over the bridge there
        (Washington Bridge, N.Y.C.)
    but everything boxed for economy.
85   That the body is inside the soul —
    the lifting and folding brightness
    the darkness shattered,
      the fragment.
That Yeats noted the symbol over that portico
90   (Paris).
And the bull by the force that is in him —
    not lord of it,
      mastered.
And to know interest from usura
95 (Sac. Cairoli, prezzo giusto)
    In this sphere is Giustizia.
In mountain air the grass frozen emerald
    and with the mind set on that light
    saffron, emerald,
100   seeping.
"but that kind of ignorance" said the old priest to Yeats
    (in a railway train) "is spreading every day from the schools"
to say nothing of other varieties.
Article X for example — put over, and 100 years to get back
105   to the awareness of
    (what's his name in that Convention)
And in thy mind beauty.
    O Artemis.
As to sin, they invented it — eh?
110   to implement domination
eh? largely.
    There remains grumpiness,
    malvagità
Sea, over roofs, but still the sea and the headland.
115 And in every woman, somewhere in the snarl is a tenderness,
    A blue light under stars.

The ruined orchards, trees rotting. Empty frames at Limone.
And for a little magnanimity somewhere,
And to know the share from the charge
120   (scala altrui)
God's eye art 'ou, do not surrender perception.

And in thy mind beauty, O Artemis
        Daphne afoot in vain speed.
When the Syrian onyx is broken.
125   Out of dark, thou, Father Helios, leadest,
but the mind as Ixion, unstill, ever turning.

FROM CANTO CXV

The scientists are in terror
>and the European mind stops
Wyndham Lewis chose blindness
>rather than have his mind stop.
5 Night under wind mid garofani,
>the petals are almost still
Mozart, Linnaeus, Sulmona,
When one's friends hate each other
>how can there be peace in the world?
10 Their asperities diverted me in my green time.
A blown husk that is finished
>but the light sings eternal
a pale flare over marshes
>where the salt hay whispers to tide's change
15 Time, space,
>neither life nor death is the answer.
And of man seeking good,
>doing evil.
In meiner Heimat
20 >where the dead walked
>and the living were made of cardboard.

CANTO CXVI

Came Neptunus
            his mind leaping
                  like dolphins,
These concepts the human mind has attained.
5   To make Cosmos —
To achieve the possible —
Muss., wrecked for an error,
But the record
            the palimpsest —
10   a little light
                  in great darkness —
cuniculi —
An old "crank" dead in Virginia.
Unprepared young burdened with records,
15   The vision of the Madonna
                  above the cigar butts
                        and over the portal.
"Have made a mass of laws"
                        (mucchio di leggi)
20   Litterae nihil sanantes
                        Justinian's,
a tangle of works unfinished.

I have brought the great ball of crystal;
                  who can lift it?
25   Can you enter the great acorn of light?
                  But the beauty is not the madness
Tho' my errors and wrecks lie about me.
And I am not a demigod,
I cannot make it cohere.
30   If love be not in the house there is nothing.
The voice of famine unheard.
How came beauty against this blackness,
Twice beauty under the elms —
                  To be saved by squirrels and bluejays?
35   "plus j'aime le chien"
Ariadne.
            Disney against the metaphysicals,
and Laforgue more than they thought in him,

Spire thanked me in proposito
40 And I have learned more from Jules
                              (Jules Laforgue) since then
deeps in him,
              and Linnaeus.
                          chi crescerà i nostri —
45 but about that terzo
              third heaven,
                          that Venere,
again is all "paradiso"
              a nice quiet paradise
50   over the shambles,
and some climbing
              before the take-off,
to "see again,"
the verb is "see," not "walk on"
55 i.e. it coheres all right
                          even if my notes do not cohere.
Many errors,
              a little rightness,
to excuse his hell
60   and my paradiso,
And as to why they go wrong,
                          thinking of rightness
And as to who will copy this palimpsest?
              al poco giorno
65   ed al gran cerchio d'ombra
But to affirm the gold thread in the pattern
                          (Torcello)
al Vicolo d'oro
              (Tigullio).
70 To confess wrong without losing rightness:
Charity I have had sometimes,
              I cannot make it flow thru.
A little light, like a rushlight
              to lead back to splendour.

NOTES FOR CXVII ET SEQ.

For the blue flash and the moments
                benedetta
the young for the old
              that is tragedy
5   And for one beautiful day there was peace.
         Brancusi's bird
                  in the hollow of pine trunks
or when the snow was like sea foam
           Twilit sky leaded with elm boughs.
10 Under the Rupe Tarpeia
           weep out your jealousies—
To make a church
          or an altar to Zagreus Ζαγρεύς
Son of Semele Σεμέλη\
15 Without jealousy
          like the double arch of a window
Or some great colonnade.

M'amour, m'amour
           what do I love and
              where are you?
That I lost my center
5   fighting the world.
The dreams clash
           and are shattered—
and that I tried to make a paradiso
               terrestre.

I have tried to write Paradise

Do not move
  Let the wind speak
    that is paradise.

5 Let the Gods forgive what I
    have made
Let those I love try to forgive
    what I have made.

La faillite de François Bernouard, Paris
or a field of larks at Allègre,
  "es laissa cader"
so high toward the sun and then falling,
5 "de joi sas alas"
to set here the roads of France.

Two mice and a moth my guides—
To have heard the farfalla gasping
  as toward a bridge over worlds.
10 That the kings meet in their island,
    where no food is after flight from the pole.
Milkweed the sustenance
  as to enter arcanum.

To be men not destroyers.

Translations 1954–1964

from THE CLASSIC ANTHOLOGY
DEFINED BY CONFUCIUS (1954)

"Hid! Hid!"

"Hid! Hid!" the fish-hawk saith,
by isle in Ho the fish-hawk saith:
    "Dark and clear,
    Dark and clear,
5   So shall be the prince's fere."

Clear as the stream her modesty;
As neath dark boughs her secrecy,
    reed against reed
    tall on slight
10   as the stream moves left and right,
    dark and clear,
    dark and clear.
To seek and not find
as a dream in his mind,
15   think how her robe should be,
    distantly, to toss and turn,
    to toss and turn.

HIgh reed caught in *ts'ai* grass
    so deep her secrecy;
20   lute sound in lute sound is caught,
    touching, passing, left and right.
Bang the gong of her delight.

"Lies a dead deer"

Lies a dead deer on younder plain
whom white grass covers,
A melancholy maid in spring
                is luck
5   for
                lovers.

Where the scrub elm skirts the wood,
be it not in white mat bound,
as a jewel flawless found,
10   dead as doe is maidenhood.

Hark!
Unhand my girdle-knot,
            stay, stay, stay
            or the dog
15   may
            bark.

"Rabbit goes soft-foot"

Rabbit goes soft-foot, pheasant's caught,
I began life with too much élan.
Troubles come to a bustling man.
            "Down Oh, and give me a bed!"

5   Rabbit soft-foot, pheasant's in trap,
I began life with a flip and flap,
Then a thousand troubles fell on my head,
            "If I could only sleep like the dead!"

Rabbit goes soft-foot, pheasant gets caught.
10   A youngster was always rushin' round,
Troubles crush me to the ground.
            I wish I could sleep and not hear a sound.

ALITER

Ole Brer Rabbit watchin' his feet,
15   Rabbit net's got the pheasant beat;
            When I was young and a-startin' life
            I kept away from trouble an' strife
But then, as life went on,
Did I meet trouble?
20   Aye, my son;
Wish I could sleep till life was done.

"Hep-Cat Chung"

Hep-Cat Chung, 'ware my town,
don't break my willows down.
The trees don't matter
but father's tongue, mother's tongue
5   Have a heart, Chung,
                    it's awful.

Hep-Cat Chung, don't jump my wall
nor strip my mulberry boughs,
The boughs don't matter
10   But my brothers' clatter!
          Have a heart, Chung,
                    it's awful.

Hep-Cat Chung, that is *my* garden wall,
Don't break my sandalwood tree.
15   The tree don't matter
But the subsequent chatter!
          Have a heart, Chung,
                    it's awful.

Je Bois dans Mon Verre

Garden peach, in a dish ere long (my own)
as my worry goes into song.
Strangers say: "The scholar is proud.
Others fit in. Why's he so loud?"
5   Those who know me, plumb not my thought.

Garden blackberry (my own) made to eat,
a heart worries for the state of the State;
Strangers find me utterly wrong
because "other men get along."
10   Friends, finding me distraught,
Plumb not my thought.

(Who can plumb another man's thought?)

"Lonely pear tree"

At the road's bend
dare say he'd make a
nice gentleman-friend.

Lonely pear tree by the way side,
How shall I for my true-love provide?

Dare say he'd agree, but how feed him?

Russet pear at bend of the way,
5   Dare say he'd come play, but . . .

True love won't feed him.

"Chariots, rank on rank"

Chariots, rank on rank
with white-fronted horses;
You'd see Milord?
            Eunuchs are bosses.

5   Terebinth on the hill, chestnuts in valley;
Once you're inside, there are lutes in each alley.
            Delight, delight
            and the long night
                        coming.

10   Mulberries on the crest,
willows in marsh-land valley,
            drum-beat and shamisan,
                        dally, dally,
            Death's up the alley.

"Pick a fern"

Pick a fern, pick a fern, ferns are high,
"Home," I'll say: home, the year's gone by,
no house, no roof, these huns on the hoof.
Work, work, work, that's how it runs,
5   We are here because of these huns.

Pick a fern, pick a fern, soft as they come,
I'll say "Home."
Hungry all of us, thirsty here,
no home news for nearly a year.

10   Pick a fern, pick a fern, if they scratch,
I'll say "Home," what's the catch?
I'll say "Go home," now October's come.
King wants us to give it all,
no rest, spring, summer, winter, fall,
15   Sorrow to us, sorrow to you.
We won't get out of here till we're through.

When it's cherry-time with you,
we'll see the captain's car go thru,
four big horses to pull that load.
20   That's what comes along our road,
What do you call three fights a month,
and won 'em all?

Four car-horses strong and tall
and the boss who can drive 'em all
25   as we slog along beside his car,
ivory bow-tips and shagreen case
to say nothing of what we face
sloggin' along in the Hien-yün war.

Willows were green when we set out,
30   it's blowin' an' snowin' as we go
down this road, muddy and slow,
hungry and thirsty and blue as doubt
(no one feels half of what we know).

Huang Niao

Yaller bird, let my corn alone,
Yaller bird, let my crawps alone,
These folks here won't let me eat,
I wanna go back whaar I can meet
5   the folks I used to know at home,
        I got a home an' I wanna' git goin'.

Yalla' bird, let my trees alone,
Let them berries stay whaar they'z growin',
These folks here ain't got no sense,
10   can't tell 'em nawthin' without offence,
Yalla' bird, lemme, le'mme go home.
        I gotta home an' I wanna' git goin'.

Yalla' bird, you stay outa dem oaks,
Yalla' bird, let them crawps alone,
15   I just can't live with these here folks,
        I gotta home and I want to git goin'
        To whaar my dad's folks still is a-growin'.

"Flies, blue flies"

Flies, blue flies on a fence rail,
should a prince swallow lies wholesale?

Flies, blue flies on a jujube tree,
slander brings states to misery.

5   Flies, blue flies on a hazel bough
even we two in slanderers' row
        B'zz, b'zz, hear them now.

"Folk worn out"

Folk worn out, workin' so late,
Kind rule at centre hauls on a state.
Pitch out the slimers and scare off worse,
Thieves and thugs see a light and curse;
5   Easy on far men, do with what's near,
And the king can sit quiet the rest of the year.

2

Folk worn out need support,
Men gather round a kindly court;
Throw out the punks who falsify your news,
10   scare off the block heads, thugs, thieves and screws.
Don't shove it off on the working man,
But keep on doing what you can
                for the king's support.

3

Folk worked out need time for breath,
15   Kindness in capital
draws on the four coigns withal;
Sweep out the fakes and scare the obsequious
thugs, thieves and screws
and don't promote the snots to sin on sly.
20   Respect men who respect the right
and your own honesty may heave into sight.

4

Folk burnt out need a vacation,
Kind court alleviates people's vexation;
Throw out the flattering fakes,
25   scare blighters and crushers,
Don't ruin folk pretending it's government,
tho' you're mere babes in this business
and the job bigger than you can guess.

5

Folk burnt out need a little peace,
30   Kindness in middle causes no injuries.
Turn out the oily tongues and parasites,

thieves, squeezing governors; don't upset honest men.
The king wants jewels and females,
I therefore lift up these wails.

Attributed to the Earl of Fan

Compassionate heaven, O thou autumnal sky
hasty to awe, famine is here, now surely death draws nigh,
Folk die and flow to exile in the waste,
dead homes and stables are hidden beneath wild grass.

2

5   Heaven has let down a drag-net of ill-doing,
the locusts have gnawed us with word-work,
they have hollowed our speech,
Perverse alliances and continuing crookedness have divided us,
evil men are set above us, in ease.

3

10   Amid slanders and vain disputations
they see themselves flawless,
they know not their errors
they count on their not being seen,
emulous, ostentatious, cantankerous in their ostentation
15   by long disorder
the high offices are brought down.

4

As grass in a drought year
with nothing to water its shoots,
as cress in dry tree fork, dry as a bird's nest
20   so in this state
there is none not given to sabotage.

5

Former prosperity stood not on a chance of weather,
nor does calamity now.
They have dredged up their rice,
25   why don't they retire from office,
and the older ones first?

6

Pool dry without inflow,
Fountain dry without inner spring,
they have overflowed wide with their injuring,
they have engrossed and expanded their functions,
may they not overwhelm me.

7

When the king (Süan) got the Decree here before you
he had a Duke of Shao to uphold him
who brought the state an hundred *li* in one day;
Today they lose daily similar holding,
and as to the nature of sorrow
there are men who do not strive to grasp the antique.

"Great Hand"

Great	hand	King	Wu
vied	not,	made	heat.
He	drew	not as	sun
rest	from	work	done.
Shang-	Ti	(over	sky)
king'd	our	Ch'eng and	K'ang;
bound	all	four	coigns;
hacked	clear	their	light.
Gong,	drum,	sound	out,
stone,	flute,	clear in	tone
ring	in	strong	grain;
bring	here	hard	ears.
Work,	true,	shall	pay.
As we've	drunk	we are	full,
Luck	ever	is and	shall
Come	with	new	grain.

Choruses from Sophokles'
WOMEN OF TRACHIS

(1)

KHOROS: *Str. I (accompaniment strings, mainly cellos)*:
PHOEBUS, Phoebus, ere thou slay
and lay flaked Night upon her blazing pyre,
Say, ere the last star shimmer is run:
5   Where lies Alkmene's son, apart from me?
Aye, thou art keen, as is the lightning blaze,
Land way, sea ways,
in these some slit hath he
found to escape thy scrutiny?

10   *Ant. I*
DAYSAIR is left alone,
    so sorry a bird,
For whom, afore, so many suitors tried.
And shall I ask what thing is heart's desire,
15   Or how love fall to sleep with tearless eye,
So worn by fear away, of dangerous road,
A manless bride to mourn in vacant room,
Expecting ever the worse,
    of dooms to come?

20   *Str. 2*
NORTH WIND or South, so bloweth tireless
wave over wave to flood.
Cretan of Cadmus' blood, Orcus' shafts err not.
What home hast' ou now,
25   an some God stir not?

    Ant. 2
PARDON if I reprove thee, Lady,
To save thee false hopes delayed.
Thinkst thou that man who dies,
30   Shall from King Chronos take
    unvaried happiness?
Nor yet's all pain.

(*drums, quietly added to music*)
The shifty Night delays not,
35 Nor fates of men, nor yet rich goods and spoil.
Be swift to enjoy, what thou art swift to lose.
Let not the Queen choose despair.
Hath Zeus no eye (who saith it?)
     watching his progeny?

(2)

KHOROS: *Str.*
KUPRIS bears trophies away.
Kronos' Son, Dis and Poseidon,
There is no one
5   shaker unshaken.
Into dust go they all.
Neath Her they must
          give way.

Ant.
10 TWO gods fought for a girl,
Battle and dust!
Might of a River with horns
               crashing.
Four bulls together
15   Shall no man tether,
Akheloös neither,
          lashing through Oneudai
As bow is bent
          The Theban Cub,
20 Bacchus' own, spiked is his club,
HE is God's Son.
          Hurled to one bed,
Might of waters like a charge of bulls crashing.
Get a dowsing rod.
25 Kupris decides
To whom brides
          fall.

ROCK and wrack,
Horns into back,
30 Slug, grunt and groan,

Grip through to bone.

Crash and thud
Bows against blood
Grip and grind

35 Bull's head and horn.

BUT the wide-eyed girl on the hill,
Out of it all,
frail,

Who shall have her?
40 To stave her and prove her,
Cowless calf lost,
Hurtled away,
prized for a day?

[*Music in this Khoros fifes, kettle drums, oboes, etc., with flute solo or clarinet.*]

(3)

KHOROS: *Str. I*
SAFE the port, rocky the narrows,
Streams warm to a glaze on Oeta's hill,
Malis' pool and Dian's beach
5 Neath her golden-shafted arrows
Ye who live here and disdeign

All greek towns less than the Pelean,

Ant. I (fifes, flute & grosse caisse)
SOON shall hear the skirl and din
10 Of flutes' loud cackle shrill return,
Dear to Holy Muses as
Phoebus' lyre ever was.
From the valours of his wars

Comes now the God, Alkmene's son
15 Bearing battle booty home.

Str. 2 (clarinette, bassoon)
TWELVE moons passing,
night long, and day.

Exile, exile
20 Knowing never, to come? to stay?
Tears, tears, till grief
Hath wrecked her heart away,

Ere mad Mars should end him
    his working day.

25   *Ant. I (cello, low register)*
TO PORT, to port.
Boat is still now;
The many oars move not.
    By island shrine ere he come to the town
30   Day long, day long
If the charm of the gown prove not?
'Tis dipped, aye in the unguent
drenched through it, in every fold.
Told, told,
35   in all as she had been told.

(4)

    KHOROS *(low cello merely sustaining the voice): Str. I*
OYEZ:
Things foretold and forecast:
Toil and moil.
5   God's Son from turmoil shall
    — when twelve seed-crops be past —
be loosed with the last,
            his own.
Twining together, godword found good,
10   Spoken of old,
    as the wind blew, truth's in the flood.
We and his brood see in swift combine,
    here and at last that:
Amid the dead is no servitude
15   nor do they labour.

    (contrabassi & drums muffled) Ant. I
LO, beneath deadly cloud
Fate and the Centaur's curse, black venom spread.
Dank Hydra's blood
20   Boils now through every vein, goad after goad
from spotted snake to pierce the holy side,
nor shall he last to see a new day's light,
Black shaggy night descends
          as Nessus bade.

25   *Str. 2*
WHAT MOURNFUL case
  who feared great ills to come,
New haste in mating threatening her home,
Who hark'd to reason in a foreign voice
30   Entangling her in ravage out of choice.
Tears green the cheek with bright dews
                           pouring down;
Who mourns apart, alone
Oncoming swiftness in o'erlowering fate
35   To show what wreck is nested in deceit.

     Ant. 2
LET the tears flow.
  Ne'er had bright Herakles in his shining
Need of pity till now
40   whom fell disease burns out.
How swift on Oechal's height
  to take a bride.
Black pointed shaft that shielded her in flight,
Attest
45   That
Kupris stood by and never said a word,
Who now flares here the contriver
manifest . . .
and indifferent.

                     (5)
    KHOROS (*declaimed*): *Str. I*
TORN between griefs, which grief shall I lament,
which first? Which last, in heavy argument?
One wretchedness to me in double load.

5   *Ant. I*
DEATH'S in the house,
    and death comes by the road.

    (*sung*) *Str. 2*
THAT WIND might bear away my grief and me,
10   Sprung from the hearth-stone, let it bear me away.
God's Son is dead,

    that was so brave and strong,
And I am craven to behold such death
    Swift on the eye,
15 Pain hard to uproot,
    and this so vast
A splendour of ruin.

    Ant. 2
THAT NOW is here.
20 As Progne shrill upon the weeping air,
'tis no great sound.
    These strangers lift him home,
with shuffling feet, and love that keeps them still.
The great weight silent
25   for no man can say
If sleep but feign
    or Death reign instantly.

CABARET VERT
from Rimbaud

Wearing out my shoes, 8th day
On the bad roads, I got into Charleroi.
Bread, butter, at the Green Cabaret
And the ham half cold.

5 Got my legs stretched out
And was looking at the simple tapestries,
Very nice when the gal with the big bubs
And lively eyes,

Not one to be scared of a kiss and more,
10 Brought the butter and bread with a grin
And the luke-warm ham on a colored plate,

Pink ham, white fat and a sprig
Of garlic, and a great chope of foamy beer
Gilt by the sun in that atmosphere.

COMEDY IN THREE CARESSES
from Rimbaud

She hadn't much left on, and the big trees,
With no discretion, swished
Their leaves over the window-pane
Teasingly, so near, so near.

5   Half naked in my big chair,
She put her hands together
And her little toes tickled the floor,
Quivering comfortably, and so small.

I watched a little sprouting flush,
10   The color of wax, flutter
Like a smile over her neat breasts:
Fly on a rose bush.

I kissed her traced ankles
And she smiled a longish smile, bad sign
15   That shattered out into clear trills,
Crystalline.

Her little feet scampered under her shift:
"Will you *stop* now!!"
After the first permitted boldness,
20   The smile pretending coldness?

Her poor eyelids fluttered under my lips
As I kissed her eyes
And she threw back her weakling head:
"That's better now," she said.

25   "But I have something still to . . ."
I chucked the rest between her breasts
In a caress that brought a kindly smile,
Benevolence, all of it.

She hadn't much left on, and the big trees
30   Swished their leaves over the window-pane
At ease, teasingly, and so near.

ANADYOMENE
from Rimbaud

As it might have been from under a green tin coffin-lid,
A woman's head with brown over-oiled hair
Rises out of a theatre box, slow and stupid
With ravages in rather poor repair.

5   Then ups the fat grey neck and bulgy shoulder-blades,
The shortish back going out and in
And the fat, in clumsy slabs under the skin,
Seems ready to emerge without further aids.

LICE-HUNTERS
from Rimbaud

When the kid's forehead is full of red torments
Imploring swarms of dreams with vague contents,
Two large and charming sisters come
With wafty fingers and silvery nails, to his bedroom.

5   They set the kid by a wide-open window where
A tangle of flowers bathes in the blue air
And run fine, alluring, terrible
Fingers through his thick dew-matted hair.

He hears the rustling of their timid breath
10   Flowered with the long pinkish vegetable honies underneath
Or broken anon, sibilant, the saliva's hiss
Drawn from a lip, or a desire to kiss.

He hears their black eyelashes beat in that quietude
And "Crack!" to break his inebriated indolences
15   Neath their electric and so soft fingers death assails
The little lice beneath their regal nails.

And Lo! there mounts within him Wine of Laziness—a squiffer's sigh
Might bring delirium—and the kid feels
Neath the slowness of their caresses, constantly
20   Wane and fade a desire to cry.

from CONVERSATIONS IN COURTSHIP
*from Boris de Rachewiltz's Italian versions of
Egyptian hieroglyphic texts*

HE SAYS:
Darling, you only, there is no duplicate,
More lovely than all other womanhood,
    luminous, perfect,
5   A star coming over the sky-line at new year,
    a good year,
Splendid in colors,
    with allure in the eye's turn.
Her lips are enchantment,
10   her neck the right length
       and her breasts a marvel;
Her hair lapislazuli in its glitter,
    her arms more splendid than gold.
Her fingers make me see petals,
15   the lotus' are like that.
Her flancs are modeled as should be,
    her legs beyond all other beauty.
Noble her walking
    (vera incessu)
20 My heart would be a slave should she enfold me.
Every neck turns — that is her fault —
    to look at her.
Fortune's who can utterly embrace her;
    he would stand first among all young lovers.
25 Deo mi par esse
    Every eye keeps following her
    even after she has stepped out of range.
A single goddess,
    uniquely.

          • • •

30 SHE SAYS:
My heart runs out if I think how I love him,
    I can't just act like anyone else.
It, my heart, is all out of place
    It won't let me choose a dress

35   or hide back of my fan.
I can't put on my eye make-up
                    or pick a perfume.

"Don't stop, come into the house,"
     That's what my heart said, one time,
40   And does, every time I think of my beloved.
          Don't play the fool with me, oh heart.
               Why *are* you such an idiot?
Sit quiet! keep calm
                and he'll come to you.
45   And my alertness won't let people say:
     This girl is unhinged with love.
When you remember him
     stand firm and solid,
               don't escape me.

50   HE SAYS:
I adore the gold-gleaming Goddess,
               Hathor the dominant,
                    and I praise her.
I exalt the Lady of Heaven,
55   I give thanks to the Patron.
She hears my invocation
     and has fated me to my lady,
Who has come here, herself, to find me.
     What felicity came in with her!
60   I rise exultant
          in hilarity
                    and triumph when I have said:
                         Now,
And behold her.
65   Look at it!
               The young fellows fall at her feet.
Love is breathed into them.

I make vows to my Goddess,
     because she has given me this girl for my own.
70   I have been praying three days,
          calling her name.
For five days she has abandoned me.

. . .

HE SAYS:
Yesterday. Seven days and I have not seen her.
75   My malady increases;
                  limbs heavy!
                        I know not myself any more.
High priest is no medicine, exorcism is useless:
          a disease beyond recognition.

80   I said: She will make me live,
          her name will rouse me,
Her messages are the life of my heart
          coming and going.
My beloved is the best of medicine,
85   more than all pharmacopoeia.
My health is in her coming,
          I shall be cured at the sight of her.
Let her open my eyes
          and my limbs are alive again;
90   Let her speak and my strength returns.
Embracing her will drive out my malady.
          Seven days and
                        she has abandoned me.

CATULLUS: XXVI

This villa is raked of winds from fore and aft,
All Boreas' sons in bluster and yet more
Against it is this TWO HUNDRED THOUSAND sesterces,
All out against it, oh my God:
                        some draft.

CATULLUS: LXXXV

I hate and love. Why? You may ask but
It beats me. I feel it done to me, and ache.

"ASK NOT UNGAINLY"
from Horace

Ask not ungainly askings of the end
Gods send us, me and thee, Leucothoë
Nor juggle with the risks of Babylon,
     Better to take whatever,
5   Several, or last, Jove sends us. Winter is winter,
Gnawing the Tyrrhene cliffs with the sea's tooth.

Take note of flavors, and clarity's in the wine's manifest.
Cut loose long hope for a time.
We talk. Time runs in envy of us,
10   Holding our day more firm in unbelief.

(*Odes*, Book I, II)

"BY THE FLAT CUP"
from Horace

By the flat cup and the splash of new vintage
What, specifically, does the diviner ask of Apollo? Not
Thick Sardinian corn-yield nor pleasant
Ox-herds under the summer sun in Calabria, nor
5   Ivory nor gold out of India, nor
Land where Liris crumbles her bank in silence
Though the water seems not to move.

Let him to whom Fortune's book
Gives vines in Oporto, ply pruning hook, to the
10   Profit of some seller that he, the seller,
May drain Syra from gold out-size basins, a
Drink even the Gods must pay for, since he found
It is merchandise, looking back three times,
Four times a year, unwrecked from Atlantic trade-routes.

15   Olives feed me, and endives and mallow roots.
Delight had I healthily in what lay handy provided.

Grant me now, Latoe:
> Full wit in my cleanly age,
Nor lyre lack me, to tune the page.

(*Odes*, Book I, 31)

"THIS MONUMENT WILL OUTLAST"
from Horace

This monument will outlast metal and I made it
More durable than the king's seat, higher than pyramids.
Gnaw of the wind and rain?
> Impotent
5   The flow of the years to break it, however many.

Bits of me, many bits, will dodge all funeral,
O Libitina-Persephone and, after that,
Sprout new praise. As long as
Pontifex and the quiet girl pace the Capitol
10   I shall be spoken where the wild flood Aufidus
Lashes, and Daunus ruled the parched farmland:

Power from lowliness: "First brought Aeolic song to Italian
> fashion" —
Wear pride, work's gain! O Muse Melpomene,
15   By your will bind the laurel.
> My hair, Delphic laurel.

(*Odes*, Book III. 30)

AIR: SENTIR AVEC ARDEUR
La Marquise de Boufflers
(1711–1786)

Say what you will in two
Words and get thru.
Long, frilly
Palaver is silly.

5   Know how to read? you MUST
Before you can write. An idiot
Will always
Talk a lot.

You need not always narrate;
10   cite; date,
But listen a while and not say: "I! I!"
Want to know why?

The ME is tyrannical;
       academical.
15   Early, late
Boredom's cognate mate
       in step at his side
And I with a ME, I fear,
              yet again!

20   Say what you will in two
Words and get thru!
Long, frilly
Palaver is silly.

NOTES

Unless otherwise indicated, Pound's *Collected Early Poems*, edited by Michael King (New York: New Directions, 1979) provides the setting text for the poems selected from *A Lume Spento* (1908), *A Quinzaine for this Yule* (1908), *Personæ* (1909), *Exultations* (1909), *Canzoni* (1911), and *Ripostes* (1912). The selections from *Lustra* follow the 1917 Knopf edition. In addition, the following first book printings have been consulted: *Cathay* (London: Elkin Mathews, 1915), *Quia Pauper Amavi* (London: The Egoist Press, 1919), *Hugh Selwyn Mauberley* (London: The Ovid Press, 1920), *Personæ* (New York, 1926). The selections from *The Cantos* are based on the thirteenth printing of the New Directions complete edition of 1995. Cantos are referred to in the notes by their Roman numerals and by line, thus: Canto XXX.10. Chinese ideograms are identified by their numbers in the Mathews Chinese-English Dictionary (e.g. M1504). Their pronunciation is given in pinyin, followed (where relevant) by their traditional Wade-Giles romanization in parenthesis.

POEMS 1908–1912

THE TREE

A Lume Spento (Venice, 1908). Chosen by Pound to open his collected poems, *Personæ* (New York, 1926). Originally included in "Hilda's Book," a hand-bound book of poems written between 1905 and 1907 and dedicated to his early muse, Hilda Doolittle (1886–1961), better known under her pen name H.D.

3   *Daphne*: Cf. Ovid, *Metamorphoses*, I, where Daphne is turned into a tree to escape Apollo.
4   *that god-feasting couple old*: Philemon and Baucis, see *Metamorphoses*, VIII.

LA FRAISNE

First poem in *A Lume Spento* (1908), where it was preceded by a pastiche of the biographical *vidas* or *razos* of the troubadours recounting the story of the fictitious poet Miraut de Garzelas, whose madness is compared to the (real) Piere Vidal's: "'The Legend thus: 'Miraut de Garzelas, after the pains he bore a-loving Riles de Calidorn and that to none avail, ran mad in the forest. Yea even as Piere Vidal ran as a wolf for her of Penautier tho some say that twas folly . . . so was he ever by the Ash Tree.' Hear ye his speaking: (low, slowly he speaketh it, as one drawn apart, reflecting) (égaré)."

TITLE   *La Fraisne*: Ash-tree.
SUBTITLE   *Malvern*: Forest in Worcestershire.
13   *Mar-nan-otha*: The biblical place name "Maranantha" transformed into a Yeatsian Celtic form.

CINO

A Lume Spento (1908).

TITLE   Cino da Pistoia (1270–1337) was a friend of Dante who in his *De Vulgari Eloquentia* ranked him beside the troubadours Arnaut Daniel, Bertan de Born, and Giraut de Borneil as a leading poet of love. Pound adopted his name as an early pseudonym.
SUBTITLE   *Campagna*: Countryside. Cino was exiled from his native Pistoia in 1303.
25   *Cino Polnesi*: Cino the Bolognese.
42   *'Pollo Phoibee*: Phoebus Apollo.

NA AUDIART

A Lume Spento (1908).

TITLE *Na Audiart:* Lady Aldigart of Malemort.

EPIGRAPH *Que be-m vols mal:* "Though thou wish me ill," adapted from "Dompna pois de me no'us cal," the so-called "song of the borrowed lady" by the Provençal poet Bertran de Born (1140–1215)

31 *Aultaforte:* Bertran's castle at Hautefort. Cf. "Sestina: Altaforte," p. 10.

HISTRION

A Quinzaine for this Yule (London, 1908). Pound's first poem to be published in England, in the *Evening Standard & St. James Gazette,* October 1908.

TITLE *Histrion:* Actor.

14 *the Florentine:* Dante.

IN DURANCE

Personæ (London, 1909).

TITLE *Durance:* Forced confinement, imprisonment. Alludes to Samuel Butler's *Hudibras* (II,i), "And though I'm now in durance fast."

20 *"Quasi KALOUN."*: See S. T. Coleridge, "On the Principles of Genial Criticism": "the Greeks called a beautiful object καλόν quasi καλοῦν, i.e., *calling on* the soul, which receives it instantly, and welcomes it as something connatural."

40 *"Veltro"*: Greyhound.

SESTINA: ALTAFORTE

Exultations (London, 1909). *English Review* (London), June 1909.

TITLE Also known as the "Bloody Sestina" to Pound's circle in London, who admired his vigorous performances of this poem. Based on Bertran de Born's poem in praise of war ("B'em platz lo gais temps de pascor"). Pound later remarked of this sestina that "technically it is one of my best, though a poem on such a theme could never be very important." In *Inferno* XXVIII, 118–123, Dante placed Bertran de Born (holding his own severed head) in Malebolge among the sowers of discord for setting Prince Henry against his brother Richard and their father Henry II.

NOTE *Loquitur:* "He speaks." *En:* Sir. *Eccovi:* "Here you are!"

PIERE VIDAL OLD

Exultations (1909).

TITLE Among several early poems inspired by the life and works of the "wolfman" troubadour Piere Vidal (1175–1215). In Canto IV, Pound rhymes Vidal's metamorphosis with the myth of Actaeon pursued by the huntress Diana.

BALLAD OF THE GOODLY FERE

Exultations (1909). *English Review* (London), October 1909.

TITLE "Made very angry by a certain sort of cheap irreverence" in a Soho café, Pound claimed to have written this poem at a single sitting in the British Museum Reading Room the following morning, "with scarcely any erasures." A ballad in the style of Kipling and Masefield, "The Goodly Fere" was by far Pound's best received poem among contemporary British reviewers (and a favorite of T. E. Lawrence's). Feeling that it had "much greater popularity than it deserves" T. S. Eliot pointedly omitted this paean to muscular Christianity from his 1928 edition of Pound's *Selected Poems.* The epigraph's Simon Zelotes (as in zealot) was an apostle of Christ (Luke 6:15).

7   *let these go*: Cf. John 18:8.
11   *Why took ye not me*: Cf. Luke: 22:53.
13   *we drank*: Cf. Matthew 26:27.
17   *I ha' seen him drive*: Cf. Matthew 21:12–13.
45–48   *Like the sea . . . suddenly*: Cf. Mark 6:47–53. *Genseret*: Gennesaret.

PLANH FOR THE YOUNG ENGLISH KING

Exultations (1909).
TITLE   *Planh*: Lament. An adaptation of the second of two poems written by Bertran de Born
on the death of Prince Henry (called "the Young King" because he was crowned in 1170
before the death of his father, King Henry II, in 1189). Its first line, given at the outset of
the poem, literally translates as "If all the griefs and laments and pain."

SONNET: CHI È QUESTA?

Canzoni (London, 1911).
TITLE   *Chi è questa*: An imitation of a sonnet by Guido Cavalcanti (c.1255–1300) entitled "Chi
è questa che vien, ch'ogni uom la mira" (translated in Pound's 1912 *Sonnets and Ballate of
Guido Cavalcanti* as "Who is she coming, drawing all men's gaze").

BLANDULLA, TENULLA, VAGULA

Canzoni (1911).
TITLE   *Blandulla, Tenulla, Vagula*: Cf. the emperor Hadrian's dying address to his soul: "Animula,
vagula, blandula,/hospes, comesque, corporis/quae nunc abibis in loca,/pallida, rigida,
nudula?/nec ut soles dabis iocos!" ("Little soul, wandering, gentle guest and companion
of the body, into what places will you now go, pale stiff, and naked, no longer sporting as
you did!"). The adjective "tenulla" ("tender") is an interpolation from Flaminius.
5   *at Sirmio*: Catullus's father owned a villa at Sirmio (now Sirmione), a town on the south
shore of Lake Garda in northern Italy. Catullus XXXI praises Sirmio, "bright eye of pen-
insulas and islands," as a happy place of rest following arduous travels. Pound spent the
spring of 1910 in Sirmione working on his Cavalcanti translations.
15   *peak of Riva*: The lower Italian Alps rise up behind Riva, a town on the northernmost
part of the Lago di Garda.

ERAT HORA

Canzoni (1911).
TITLE   *Erat Hora*: "It Was the Hour."

ROME

Canzoni (1911).
TITLE   *du Bellay*: A translation of the sonnet "Nouveau venu qui cherches Rome en Rome"
from Joachim du Bellay's *Antiquetez de Rome* (1558). *"Troica Roma resurges"*: "Trojan Ro-
man shall arise" (Propertius, *Elegies* IV, 1, 87).

TRANSLATIONS FROM HEINE

Canzoni (1911).
Among Pound's first experiments in the kind of modern irony he would later define as
"logopoeia." The sources in Heine's works are as follows: I: *Die Heimkehr (The Homecom-
ing*, 1826), LXXVI ("Bist du wirklich mir so feindlich"); II: *Lyrisches Intermezzo* (Lyrical
Intermezzo, 1827), XXI ("So hast du ganz und gar vergessen"); III: *Die Heimkehr*, LXX–
VIII ("Sag', wo ist dein schönes Liebchen"); IV: *Die Heimkehr*, LXVI ("Mir traümt: ich

bin der liebe Gott"); V: *Die Heimkehr,* LXXIX ("Doch die Kastraten klagten"); VI, *Die Heimkehr,* LXV ("Diesen liebenwürd'gen Jüngling").

THE FLAME

Canzoni (1911). Section eight of a sequence of poems entitled "Und Drang" (as in "Sturm und Drang," Storm and Stress).

9   *Oisin:* Cf. Yeats's *The Wanderings of Oisin* (1889).

21   *"of days and nights":* Cf. Arthur Symons's *Days and Nights* (1889), where he observes that since art's true subject is "man with trouble born to death," the poet's "song is less of Days than Nights."

29   *Benacus:* Lake Garda.

AU SALON

Canzoni (1911). Section eleven of "Und Drang."

15   *Roger de Coverley's:* Imaginary country gentleman created by Joseph Addison.

17   *sic crescit . . . :* "Thus the glory of the world increases," ironic adaptation of "Sic transit gloria mundi" ("So the glory of the world passes away").

21   *aegrum vulgus:* Diseased rabble.

25   *cari laresques, penates:* Dear family and household gods.

THE SEAFARER

Ripostes (London, 1912; Boston, 1913). Sent to its initial publisher (Swift and Company) in March 1912, but not officially published by Elkin Matthews until October of that year (Swift having in the meantime gone bankrupt), *Ripostes of Ezra Pound* also featured as an appendix, "The Complete Poetical Works of T. E. Hulme" with a "Prefatory Note" by Pound referring to Hulme as the "forerunner" of *"Les Imagistes"* — Pound's first reference in print to this (at that point more or less imaginary) new school of poetry. According to John Berryman, *Ripostes* is "the volume with which modern poetry in English may be felt to have begun."

TITLE   First published as part of Pound's "I Gather the Limbs of Osiris" (a series of essays outlining his "new method in scholarship") in the London weekly *The New Age* in November 1911. Later reprinted in *Cathay* (London, 1915) between "Exile's Letter" and "Four Poems of Departure" as a cross-cultural eighth-century rhyme. In 1912, when challenged about the liberties he had taken with this Old English poem from the Exeter Book, Pound defended his version as "nearly literal, I think, as any translation can be," thus opening himself up to attacks by academic specialists. In a note to *Umbra* (London, 1920), Pound described "The Seafarer" along with the "Exile's Letter" (and *Cathay* in general) and *Homage to Sextus Propertius* as belonging to his "major personae."

THE PLUNGE

Ripostes (1912).

1   *"I would bathe myself":* Possible allusion to the final lines of Baudelaire's "Le Voyage."

N.Y.

Ripostes (1912). The version in *Umbra* (1920) includes the note: "Madison Ave. 1910."

A GIRL

Ripostes (1912).

THE PICTURE
Ripostes (1912).

PORTRAIT D'UNE FEMME
Ripostes (1912). Rejected by the North American Review in January 1912, according to Pound, on the grounds that "I had used the letter 'r' three times in the first line, and that it was very difficult to pronounce."

TITLE Portrait d'une femme: May allude to Henry James's novel The Portrait of a Lady (1881). Pound first met James in London in February 1912 and later characterized his 1920 poem Hugh Selwyn Mauberley as "an attempt to condense the James novel." One of the models for this portrait may have been Yeats's friend and collaborator, the actress and composer Florence Farr (1860–1917).

SUB MARE
Ripostes (1912). Poetry Review (London), February 1912.

TITLE Sub Mare: Under the sea.

Δώρια
Ripostes (1912). Poetry Review, February 1912. Later included in Pound's anthology Des Imagistes (New York, 1914).

TITLE Δώρια (Dôria). Echoes the Greek word for gift while also evoking Victor Plarr's book of poems, In the Dorian Mood (1896). Biographers have also heard the name of his wife-to-be, Dorothy.

10 Orcus: Roman god of the underworld; by extension, the land of the dead.

APPARUIT
Ripostes (1912). English Review (London), June 1912. Written in Sapphics, the poem represents a Swinburne-inspired experiment in applying classical quantitative meters to English verse.

TITLE Apparuit: Cf. Dante's Vita nuova, when he first sees Beatrice: "At that moment the animate spirit, which dwelleth in the lofty chamber whither all the senses carry their perception, was filled with wonder, and speaking more especially unto the spirits of the eyes, said these words: Apparuit iam beatitude vestra ['Your beatitude hath now been made manifest unto you']" (trans. D. G. Rossetti).

THE RETURN
Ripostes (1912). English Review, June 1912. Reprinted in Des Imagistes. W. B. Yeats considered this "the most beautiful poem that has been written in the free form, one of the few in which I find real organic rhythm," as if Pound "were translating at sight from an unknown Greek masterpiece." While visiting Paris in the Spring of 1913, Pound read the poem into the phonoscope of the abbé Jean Pierre Rousselot, who was investigating the sound profiles of the new vers libre which in this particular poem are defined by the recurrence of the rhythmic figure –˘ ˘–.

TO WHISTLER, AMERICAN
Poetry, October 1912. Pound's first publication in the Chicago-based magazine of verse edited by Harriet Monroe, of which he soon would become Foreign Editor.

TITLE On the loan: July–October 1912.

POEMS 1913–1915

In the fall of 1916, Pound collected most of the poems he had published over the past four years (including the poems of *Ripostes* and *Cathay*) into the sprawling omnium gatherum entitled *Lustra*. Two British editions (one unabridged, the other bowdlerized) appeared in London in 1916 under the imprint of Elkin Matthews; the following year, a private edition, followed by a trade edition by Alfred A. Knopf, appeared in New York. With three exceptions, all the poems between 1912 and 1916 in our selection were initially published in these editions of *Lustra*. Wherever possible, however, they have been grouped according to the sequence of their first magazine publications. Pound glossed the title *Lustra* as follows: "LUSTRUM: an offering for the sins of the whole people, made by the censors at the expiration of their five years of office, etc. Elementary Latin Dictionary of Charlton T. Lewis."

TENZONE

This and the following seven poems were among the twelve gathered under the title of "Contemporania" in the April 1913 issue of *Poetry*, where Pound's manifesto, "A Few Don'ts by an Imagiste" had appeared the previous month.

TITLE   *Tenzone*: Troubadour poetic genre consisting of a verbal exchange largely in the form of invective.

THE GARRET

Poetry, April 1913.

7   *Pavlova*: Anna Pavlova (1885–1931), star ballerina who visited London with the Russian ballet in 1910.

THE GARDEN

Poetry, April 1913.

EPIGRAPH   *En robe de parade*: From the prefatory poem to *Au Jardin de l'Infante* (1893) by French poet Albert-Victor Samain (1858–1900), which reads "Mon âme est une infante en robe de parade" ("My soul is an Infanta in fancy dress").

ORTUS

Poetry, April 1913.

TITLE   *Ortus*: Origin, birth. Generally believed to concern "H.D., Imagiste," three of whose poems had appeared in the January 1913 issue of *Poetry* at Pound's recommendation.

SALUTATION THE SECOND

Poetry, April 1913.

25   *"The Spectator"*: English periodical lampooned by Pound for its mediocrity and prudery; from 1898 to 1925 it editor was John St. Loe Strachey (1860–1927), mentioned later in the poem.

29   *Cybele*: Fertility goddess of Asia Minor, whose cult spread to Greece in the fifth century B.C.E. She was praised with music and ecstatic dancing.

COMMISSION

Poetry, April 1913

A PACT

Poetry, April 1913.

IN A STATION OF THE METRO
Poetry, April 1913. The spacing and punctuation of the poem's first magazine publication are retained here.

TITLE *Metro*: Pound described the genesis of this poem in his 1913 essay, "How I Began": "Three years ago in Paris I got out of a 'metro' train at La Concorde, and saw suddenly a beautiful face, and then another and another, and then a beautiful child's face, and then another beautiful woman, and I tried all that day to find words for what this had meant to me, and I could not find any words that seemed to me worthy, or as lovely as that sudden emotion. And that evening, as I went home along the Rue Raynouard, I was still trying, and I found, suddenly, the expression. I do not mean that I found words, but there came an equation... not in speech, but in little splotches of colour. It was just that—a 'pattern,' or hardly a pattern, if by 'pattern' you mean something with a 'repeat' in it. But it was a word, the beginning, for me, of a language in colour.... Colour was, in that instance, the 'primary pigment': I mean that it was the first adequate equation that came into consciousness.... The 'one image poem' is a form of super-position, that is to say, it is one idea set on top of another. I found it useful in getting out of the impasse in which I had been left by my metro emotion, I wrote a thirty-line poem, and destroyed it because it was what we call work of 'second intensity.' Six months later I made a poem half that length; a year later I made the following *hokku*-like sentence [quotes 'In a Station of the Metro'].... In a poem of this sort one is trying to record the precise instant when a thing outward and objective transforms itself, or darts into a thing inward and subjective."

APRIL
Poetry, November 1913.

EPIGRAPH *Nympharum disjecta membra*: "The scattered limbs of the nymphs," from Ovid's description of the dismembering of Pentheus (Metamorphoses III, 723–724). Cf. Canto II.59.

GENTILDONNA
Poetry, November 1913.

TITLE *Gentildonna*: Gentlewoman. Imagist reprise of Cavalcanti's "Chi è questa."

THE REST
Poetry, November 1913. Initially printed as "Lustra I" and subsequently retitled "The Rest" when republished in *Lustra* (1916).

LES MILLWIN
Poetry, November 1913. "Lustra II," then "Les Millwin" in *Lustra* (1916).

6 *"Slade"*: The Slade School of Fine Art, Gower Street, London.

9 *futuristic*: The first Futurist Exhibition in London was held at the Sackville Gallery in March 1912.

10 *Cleopatra*: Diaghilev's one-act ballet *Cléopâtre* was first performed by the Ballets Russes in Paris in 1909.

ALBA, THE BATH TUB, ARIDES, THE ENCOUNTER, SIMULACRA
All originally published as part of an eleven-poem sequence entitled "Zenia" [from "Xenia," the epigrams of Martial] in the American magazine *Smart Set*, December 1913.

COITUS
Poetry and Drama (London), March 1914.

1 *phaloi*: Helmet ridges.

5   *Giulio Romano*: Italian painter (1499–1546) responsible for the erotic frescoes of the gods in the Palazzo del Te in Mantua.

7   *Dione*: Greek earth goddess, consort of Zeus and mother of Aphrodite, presiding deity over the "Pervigilium Veneris" (or "Vigil of Venus"), an archaic rite of spring.

LIU CH'E

Published with "Fan-Piece" and "Ts'ai Chi'h" below in Pound's anthology, *Des Imagistes* in March 1914. Derived from the translation of H. A. Giles in his *History of Chinese Literature* (1901).

TITLE   *Liu Ch'e*: Liu Zhe, also known as Wudi (156–87 B.C.E.), became sixth emperor of the Han dynasty in 140 B.C.E.

FAN-PIECE, FOR HER IMPERIAL LORD

Reprinted in *Poetry and Drama*, June 1914.

TITLE   *Fan-Piece*: Based on Giles's account of an incident in the life of Ban Jieyu, a favorite concubine of the Han emperor Cheng.

TS'AI CHI'H

Reprinted in *Poetry and Drama*, June 1914

TITLE   *Ts'ai Chi'h:* Cao Zhi (192–232 C.E.), poet of Eastern Han Dynasty.

EPITAPHS

Blast (London), June 1914.

TITLE   *Fu-I*: Chinese poet (555–639). Pound's note in Blast: "This is his epitaph very much as he wrote it."

TITLE   *Li Po*: Chinese poet (701–62) whom Pound translates in Cathay under his Japanese name Rihaku. The anecdote was found in Giles.

"IONE, DEAD THE LONG YEAR"

Poetry and Drama, December 1914, under the title "Dead Iònè."

TITLE   *Ione*: Perhaps the French dancer Jeanne Heyse, who used the stage name "Ione de Forest" and committed suicide at age 19 in August 1912. "Ione" was also the name of a muse of the English poet Walter Savage Landor (1775–1864).

PAPYRUS

First published in *Lustra* (1916), where it formed part of a series with "Ione" (above) and " Ιμερρω" (below). The poem is based on a papyrus scrap of Sappho first published in Berlin in 1902.

Ιμερρω

Poetry, September 1916. Originally entitled "O Atthis," in reference to Saphho's beloved.

TITLE   Ιμερρω: "Imerrô" ("too long"), from Sappho, LXXXVI.

PROVINCIA DESERTA

Poetry, March 1915. This and the following five poems from this issue of *Poetry* constitute a mosaic that offers the first preview of Pound's *Cantos* to come. The same issue also included his translation of Li Po's "Exile's Letter," published the following month in *Cathay* (see below).

TITLE   *Provincia Deserta*: Alludes to C. M. Doughty's *Travels in Arabia Deserta* (1888). The place names in this poem map the itinerary of Pound's peregrinations through southern France in the early summer of 1912 in search of the traces of the troubadours. Rochechouart, Chalais, Montaignac, and Hautefort are all associated with Bertran de Born. Mareuil and Ribeyrac were the homes of, respectively, the troubadours Arnaut de Mareuil and Arnaut Daniel; Chalus is where Richard Coeur de Lion was killed; Excideuil is the birthplace of the troubadour Giraut de Borneil. The "Dorata" is the church of La Daurade in Toulouse.

63 *Riquier! Guido*: Guiraut de Riquier (c.1230–1292), one of the last of the Provençal troubadours, and Italian poet Guido Cavalcanti, one of the first of the Italian *stil novisti* (i.e. poets in the new style). Pound speculated that the two might have met in Toulouse, thus making possible the direct personal transmission of the troubadour tradition from Provence to Tuscany.

66 *Two men tossing a coin*: After their coin toss, Austors de Maensac received the castle and Pieire de Maensac the poetry — with which he then seduced the wife of Bernart de Tierci and abducted her. Pound returns to this "second Troy" in the Auvergne in Canto V.

IMAGE FROM D'ORLÉANS
Poetry, March 1915.
TITLE *d'Orleans*: The French poet Charles d'Orléans (1394–1465). From his *Chansons*, LXXIII ("Jennes amoureux nouveaulx,/En la nouvelle saison,/Par les rues, sans raison,/Chevauchent, faisans les saulx.")

THE SPRING
Poetry, March 1915.
TITLE *The Spring*: An adaptation of a poem by the Greek poet Ibycus (sixth century B.C.E.); when the poem was collected in *Personæ* (1926), Pound added the Greek poem's first line as an epigraph: Ηρι μὲν αἴ τε κυδώνιαι: ("In Spring the Cydonian quinces"). Cydonia was a town in Crete.
2 *Mælids*: Pound's coinage for a fruit-tree nymph.

THE COMING OF WAR: ACTAEON
Poetry, March 1915.
TITLE *Actaeon*: In Greek mythology, Actaeon inadvertently wanders into a grove where Artemis and her nymphs are bathing. The enraged goddess splashes him with water, transforming him into a stag, and his own hounds pursue him and tear him to pieces. See Ovid, *Metamorphoses*, III and Canto IV.33.

THE GYPSY
Poetry, March 1915.
TITLE *Gypsy*: The poems records an encounter toward the end of Pound's walking tour through southern France in mid-July 1912 near Clermont-Ferrand. Previous stops on this journey had included Arles, Beaucaire, Rodez, and Gourdon, where he had witnessed the festivities of St. John's Eve on June 23.

THE GAME OF CHESS
Poetry, March 1915. Reprinted in *Blast* 2, July 1915.
TITLE *Game of Chess*. Pound was an avid chess-player (in Paris in the early twenties he even played chess with Marcel Duchamp). The vectors of medieval warfare here evolve into the abstract "planes in relation" of Vorticist painting.

ANCIENT MUSIC

Blast 2, July 1915.

TITLE *Ancient Music*: A riff on the Middle English lyric (ca. 1260), beginning "Sumer is icumen in." The "Dr. Ker" of the note is the noted scholar and essayist William Paton Ker (1855–1923) who had underscored the continuities between medieval Latin and the emergence of lyric in the vernacular.

ET FAIM SAILLIR LES LOUPS DES BOYS

Blast 2, July 1915.

TITLE *From François Villon's Testament*, XXI: "And hunger makes the wolves leap forth from the woods."

9 *Lewis*: Wyndham Lewis (1882–1957), English painter and novelist, one of the prime movers of Vorticism, together with the sculptors Jacob Epstein (1880–1959) and Henri Gaudier-Brzeska (1891–1915) and the painter Edward Wadsworth (1889–1949).

THE TEA SHOP, PHYLLIDULA, SHOP GIRL, ANOTHER MAN'S WIFE

First published as a part of a sequence in *Others: A Magazine of the New Verse* (Ridgefield, New Jersey), November 1915.

POEM ABBREVIATED FROM THE CONVERSATION OF T. E. H.

First appeared in *Catholic Anthology* 1914–1915, edited by Pound and published by Elkin Mathews in London in 1915. Including poems by W. B. Yeats, Edgar Lee Masters, William Carlos Williams and others, the volume was also notable for the first publication of T. S. Eliot's "The Love Song of J. Alfred Prufrock" in book form. Reprinted in *Umbra* (London, 1920).

TITLE T. E. H.: Thomas Ernest Hulme (1883–1917), English philosopher and poet killed by a shell at Oostduinkerke in World War I.

CATHAY (1915)

Cathay: Translations by Ezra Pound for the most part from the Chinese of Rihaku, from the notes of the late Ernest Fenollosa, and the decipherings of the professors Mori and Ariga was published in London by Elkin Mathews in April 1915. Pound had met Mary Fenollosa, widow of the American scholar of Far Eastern literature Ernest Fenollosa (1853–1908) in London in 1912. Impressed by the "Oriental quality" of the poems that Pound had published in *Poetry* (notably "In a Station of the Metro"), she presented him with seventeen notebooks and other manuscripts belonging to her late husband in 1913. From these Pound would quarry *Cathay* as well as *"Noh" or Accomplishment* (London, 1919) and "The Chinese Written Character as a Medium for Poetry" (in *Instigations*, New York, 1919). Fenollosa's notebook texts (compiled in Tokyo in 1896–1899 with the help of the Japanese scholars Hirai, Shida, Mori, and Ariga) contained the Chinese characters for the original poems, followed interlinearly by their Japanese pronunciations and rough translations. Pound's choice of Japanese names for Chinese poets (e.g. "Rihaku" for Li Po) signals the cultural mediations at work in his versions. The 1915 edition of *Cathay* (in whose heavy tan wrappers some have seen an allusion to the military apparel of World War I) contained eleven poems, with Pound's early translation of the eighth-century Anglo-Saxon "The Seafarer" intercalated between "Exile's Letter" and "Four Poems of Departure" in order to emphasize the simultaneity of the Tang Dynasty and Anglo-Saxon versions of exile. When published as a section of *Lustra* in 1916, the four following poems from the Fenollosa notebooks (included here) were added to *Cathay*: "Sennin Poem by Kakuhaku," "A Ballad of the Mulberry Road," "Old Idea of Choan by Rosoriu," and "To-Em-Mei's 'The Unmoving Cloud.'" With the *vers libre* of *Cathay*, T. S. Eliot famously observed, Pound had become "the inventor of Chinese poetry for our time."

SONG OF THE BOWMEN OF SHU

26   *By Kutsugen:* Footnote in the original 1915 printing corrected in all editions from *Lustra* onward: "By Bunno, reputedly 1100 B.C." Bunno is Japanese for the Chinese Zhou ruler Wen Wang. Cf. Pound's later translation of this same poem ("Hid! Hid!") in his *The Classic Anthology Defined by Confucius* (Cambridge, Mass., 1954), on p. 259 of this selection. When Pound sent this poem together with "Lament of the Frontier Guard" and "South-Folk in Cold Country" to his friend the sculptor Henri Gaudier-Brzeska who was stationed at the French front, the latter wrote back: "The poems depict our situation in a wonderful way. We do not yet eat the young nor old fern shoots, but we cannot be over-victualled where we stand."

THE BEAUTIFUL TOILET

10   *Mei Sheng:* No longer attributed to Mei Sheng; one of the "Nineteen Old Poems," probably composed in the Han dynasty.

THE RIVER SONG

A translation of two separate poems by Li Po (701–762). Apparently confused by the pagination of Fenollosa's notebook, Pound conflated these poems into a single work.

1   *shato-wood:* Spice wood.
6   *Sennin:* Pound remarked in a letter that "Sennin [xian ren] are the Chinese spirits of nature or of the air. I don't see that they are any worse than Celtic Sidhe."
9   *Kutsu:* The Chinese minister Qu Yuan. Cf. "After Ch'u Yuan."
18   *Han:* The Han river flows from north-east central China into the Yangtze.
30   *"Kwan, Kuan":* onomatopoeia for birdsong.
34   *Ko:* Chinese Hao, capital of kings Wen and Wu of the Zhou dynasty.

THE RIVER-MERCHANT'S WIFE: A LETTER

2   *I:* In his essay "Chinese Poetry" (*To-Day*, May 1918), Pound compares this first-person poem to Ovid's *Heroides* (fictitious letters written by mythological women to lovers who have abandoned them) and to Browning's dramatic monologues.
5   *Chokan:* Chinese Changgan, near Nanjing.
16   *Ku-to-yen:* Chinese Qu Tang, river known for its dangerous rocks. The word "Kiang" ("Jiang" in Chinese) in l. 26 below is the word for river.
29   *Cho-fu-Sa:* Chinese Chang-feng-sha ("long wind sand"), a beach several hundred miles upriver fron Nanjing.

POEM BY THE BRIDGE AT TEN-SHIN

TITLE   *Ten-Shin:* Chinese Tianjin ("Heavenly Ford").
11   *Sei-go-yo:* Chinese Xi Shangyang ("Shangyang Palace").
29   *Riokushu:* Chinese Lu Zhu, concubine of Shi Chong of the Western Jin dynasty. When Shi Chong refused to give Lu Zhu to General Sun Xiu, the General sent troops to seize her, whereupon she jumped off a balcony and killed herself.
31   *Han Rei:* Chinese minister Fan Li.

293

THE JEWEL STAIRS' GRIEVANCE

NOTE   In a further commentary on this poem in his essay "Chinese Poetry" (see above) Pound observed: "I have never found any occidental who could 'make much' [of it] at one reading. Yet upon careful examination we find that everything is there, not merely by 'suggestion' but by a sort of mathematical process of reduction. Let us consider what circumstances would be needed to produce just the words of this poem. You can play Conan Doyle if you like."

LAMENT OF THE FRONTIER GUARD

23   *Riboku*: Li Mu, famous general who died defending China against the Tartars in 223 B.C.E.

EXILE'S LETTER

Poetry, March 1915, where it was preceded by the note: "From the Chinese of Rihaku (Li Po), usually considered the greatest poet of China: written by him while in exile about 760 A.D., to the Hereditary War-Councillor of Sho, 'recollecting former companionship.'"

1   So-Kin of Rakuyo: Dong Caojiu of Loyang, a military official.
12   South Wei: Huainan, south of the Huai River.
17   Sen-Go: City of Immortals ("Xian Cheng"), name of a mountain.
23   Kan: A state south of the Han River.
24   "True man": Daoist hermit.
26   San-ko: Tower of Feasting Mist ("cang-xia").
66   Layu: Yang Xiong, author who sought promotion by offering a rhymeprose in praise of the Choyo (Chang-Yang) Palace.

FOUR POEMS OF DEPARTURE

EPIGRAPH   *Rihaku or Omakitsu*: The poem is in fact by "Omakitsu," i.e. Wang Wei (699–759), whom Pound described as "the real modern — even Parisian — of VIII cent. China."

SEPARATION ON THE RIVER KIANG

1   *Ko-jin*: Chinese "gu ren ("old friend"). In this case refers to poet Meng Haoran. *Ko-kaku-ro*: Huang He Lou (Yellow Crane Tower).

LEAVE-TAKING NEAR SHOKU

TITLE   *Shoku*: Ancient state of Shu, also called Cancong ("Sanso") after Can Cong, the legendary inventor of sericulture. Shu was invaded by the state of Qin ("Shin" in l. 6 and poems below) in the third century B.C.E.

THE CITY OF CHOAN

TITLE   *Choan*: Chang'an, the ancient capital of more than ten Chinese dynasties; today's Xi'an.
5   *dynastic house of the Go*: The Wu dynasty (222–265).

SOUTH-FOLK IN COLD COUNTRY

1   *Dai . . . Etsu*: Chinese "Tai" (north) and "Yüeh" (south). In his essay on "Chinese Poetry" Pound underscores the referential exactitude of the poem's geography: "The writer expects his hearers to know that Dai and Etsu are in the south, that En is a bleak north country, and that the 'Wild Goose Gate' is in the far northeast, and the 'Dragon Pen' is in the very opposite corner of the great empire, and probably that the Mongols are attacking the borders of China. Given these geographical facts the poem is forthright in its manner. . . . You have no mellifluous circumlocution, no sentimentalizing of men who have never seen a battlefield and who wouldn't fight if they had to. You have war, cam-

paigning as it has always been, tragedy, hardship, no illusions." He adds that the poem has "a directness and realism such as we find only in early Saxon verse and in the *Poema del Cid*, and in Homer."

12   *Rishogu:* I.e. Rishogun ("shogun" being the Japanese title of a commander-in-chief). Alludes to General Li Guang (d. 119 B.C.E.), known as "the Winged General" who fought, according to Fenollosa, "more than 74 battles with the northern barbarians."

SENNIN POEM BY KAKUHAKU

TITLE   *Sennin:* In his "Chinese Poetry" piece, Pound noted of these "sennin" or nature spirits: "Chinese poetry is full of fairies and fairy lore. Their lore is 'quite Celtic' ... The desire to be taken away by the fairies, the idea of souls flying with the sea-birds, and many other things recently made familiar to us by the Celtic school crop up in one's Chinese reading."

OLD IDEA OF CHOAN BY ROSORIU

TITLE   *Rosoriu:* Chinese Lu Zhaolin (c.637–689), one of the Four Eminences of early Tang poetry.

28   *Butei of Kan:* Possibly the Emperor Wudi (156–87 B.C.E.).

TO-EM-MEI'S "THE UNMOVING CLOUD"

TITLE   *To-Em-Mei:* the Chinese poet Tao Qian (365–427), known early in life as Tao Yuanming.

POEMS 1915–1918

NEAR PERIGORD

Poetry, December 1915.

EPIGRAPH   *A Perigord . . . ab malh:* In *The Spirit of Romance* (1910), Pound translated these lines of Bertran de Born as: "At Perigord near the wall, / Aye, within a mace throw of it." "Perigord" is the town of Périgueux in old Aquitaine. The composition of this poem, which explores the resistance of the past to conventional discourses of historical "truth," is contemporary with that of the original "Three Cantos" first published in *Poetry* in the summer of 1917.

2   *Cino:* See the poem "Cino," p. 5.

3   *Uc St. Circ:* Attributed author of commentary to some of Bertran de Born's poems (fl. 1217–1253)

4   *Solve me the riddle:* In the summer of 1912, Pound closely inspected the topography around Bertran de Born's castle of Altafort (Hautefort), attempting to determine whether the poet's canzone "Dompna pois de me no'us cal" (see "Na Audiart," p. 6) was merely a lover's attempt to regain Lady Maent's favor or instead a warrior's ploy to infiltrate neighboring castles and thus consolidate his power over rival barons.

23   *"that made its head a lamp":* Cf. Dante, *Inferno* XXVIII, 121–22.

27   *"counterpass":* Laws of divine justice. Cf. *Inferno* XXXVIII, 142.

51   *The Talleyrands:* Also referred to later in the poem as "Tairirin." One of the most ancient and powerful families in the Périgord. Its descendant Charles Maurice de Talleyrand-Perigord, the wily nineteenth-century politician and diplomat, appears frequently in Pound's late Cantos.

69   *Papiol:* Bertran's jongleur.

86–87   *(St. Leider . . . hidden):* As Pound explained in "Troubadours: Their Sorts and Conditions" (1913): "If you wish to make love to women in public, and out loud, you must resort to subterfuge; and Guillaume St. Leider even went so far as to get the husband of his lady [the Viscount of Polhanac] to do the seductive singing." Cf. Canto IV.

90 "Et albirar ab lor bordon": In "Troubadours: Their Sorts and Conditions," Pound translated this line by Gaston Phoebus, Count of Foix (1331–91): "And sing not all they have in mind."

100 al and ochaisos: Rhyming words used in Bertran's "Dompna pois de me no'us cal."

104 his "magnet" singer, i.e. Papiol, Bertran's "aziman."

140 trobar clus: A hermetic style practiced by some Provençal poets, notably by Arnaut Daniel.

141 "best craftsman": In Purgatorio XXVI, 117, Dante calls Arnaut Daniel the "better craftsman" ("miglior fabbro")—a compliment T. S. Eliot would later pay to Pound in the dedication of The Waste Land.

163–68 Surely I saw . . . counterpart: Cf. Inferno XXVIII, 118–23, 139–42.

170 Ed eran due . . . : "And they were two in one and one in two."

VILLANELLE: THE PSYCHOLOGICAL HOUR

Poetry, December 1915. The later Lustra version is given here.

TITLE Vilanelle: Form used in light verse, consisting of five tercets (ABA) and a final quatrain (ABBA) using only two rhymes; the first and the third line of the first tercet are repeated as a refrain through the poem and form the final two lines of the quatrain. Pound uses the form rather loosely here, primarily interested as he was in using the recurrence of theme as a vehicle for the psychological analysis of a "modern subject." As he explained, "the refrains are an emotional fact, which the intellect, in the various gyrations of the poem, tries in vain and in vain to escape." Appearing a month after Pound's thirtieth birthday, the poem would seem to be based on his first meetings with the sculptor Henri Gaudier and Sophie Brzeska (whom Gaudier called his "sister") in 1913.

FISH AND THE SHADOW

Poetry, September 1916. Part of a six-page tapestry entitled "Poems Old and New."

16–17 Qu'ieu. . . sai: "That I am handsome, I know," from a poem by Arnaut de Mareuil (fl. 1170–1200).

PAGANI'S, NOVEMBER 8

Poetry, September 1916.

TITLE Pagani's: London restaurant, in Great Portland Place.

THE LAKE ISLE

Poetry, September 1916.

TITLE Innisfree: An affectionate parody of W. B. Yeats's "The Lake Isle of Innisfree" (The Rose, 1893). Excluded from the private and trade editions of Lustra in London, the British printers having refused to print the poem "in any form whatever." But Knopf allowed it to stand in the American edition.

IMPRESSIONS OF FRANÇOIS-MARIE AROUET (DE VOLTAIRE)

Poetry, September 1916. Pound's adaptations omit many lines from Voltaire's poems. I: based on "Epître connue sous le nom des Vous et des Tu." II: based on Stances. III. based on Stances, "A Madame Lullin de Genève."

PHYLLIDULA AND THE SPOILS OF GOUVERNET

TITLE Phyllidula: a mock-classical name substituted by Pound for Voltaire's "Philis." Gouvernet: Jean-Frédéric de La Tour du Pin Gouvernet (1727–1794), French nobleman and politician.

TO MADAME DU CHATELET

TITLE   *Madame du Châtelet*: Voltaire's mistress during the 1730s and 1740s.

TO MADAME LULLIN

TITLE   *Madame Lullin*: Poem accompanying a bouquet of flowers sent to Mme. Lullin on her one-hundreth birthday.

CANTICO DEL SOLE

Little Review (New York), March 1918. Reprinted in *Instigations* (New York, 1920).

TITLE   *Cantico*: Alludes to St. Francis's "Cantico del Sole," translated by Pound in his *Spirit of Romance* (1910).

9   *Nunc dimittis*: Luke 2:29, from the Vulgate: "Now lettest thou thy servant depart in peace."

L'AURA AMARA

As early as 1913, Pound had compiled a book-length collection of his translations of *The Canzoni of Arnaut Daniel,* which he unsuccessfully attempted to place with a Chicago publisher. Returning to these translations in 1917, he extensively revised the entire manuscript. One of these newly revised versions appeared in the *Little Review* in November 1918; four more, including this one, were included in *Umbra* (1920). In the course of his revisions, Pound came across the work of Gavin Douglas (1472–1522), translator of the *Aeneid.* Most of the deliberate archaisms in these Arnaut Daniel translations of 1917–18 can be traced to Douglas's Middle Scots idiom

TITLE   *L'Aura Amara*: "The Bitter Air." In a note reproduced in his volume of collected *Translations* (New York, 1953), Pound observes: "In this poem we have the chatter of birds in autumn, the onomatopoeia obviously depends upon the '-utz, -etz, -ences, and -ortz' of the rhyme scheme, 17 of the 68 syllables of each strophe therein included . . . I have not been able to make more than a map of the relative positions in this canzo."

35   *yare*: Without delay.
42   *dree*: Endure.
59   *apertly*: Openly.
65   *raik*: Hasten.
83   *Dome*: [Pound's note in *Translations*]: "Our Lady of Poi [Puy] de Dome? No definite solution of this reference yet found. H. and B. say: 'town of Périgord'. The same?" According to Canello, an allusion to the monks of the town of Domme in the Périgord."
94   *cates*: Choice viands or delicacies.
103   *mirk*: Murk.
109   *mearing*: Not bounded by. "Dante cites this poem in the second book of *De Vulgari Eloquio* with poems of his own, De Born's, and Cino Pistoija's" [Pound's note in *Translations*].

ALBA

Little Review (New York), May 1918. The epigraph to a five-poem sequence of translations from the Provençal, collectively entitled "Homage à la Langue d'Oc." The following poem "Avril" was the second poem in the sequence. Reprinted in *Quia Pauper Amavi* (London, 1919).

TITLE   *Alba*: A dawn song, or "aubade." Pound had previously translated this anonymous song ("Quan lo rossinhols escria") into prose in *The Spirit of Romance* (1910).

AVRIL

Little Review, May 1918.

TITLE   Avril: April. From a poem by Guillaume de Poitiers (Guilhem de Peitieu, 1071–1126), considered to be the founder of the art of troubadour poetry.

19   gesning: Hospitality.

MŒURS CONTEMPORAINES

Little Review, May 1918. Reprinted in *Quia Pauper Amavi*. The eight following poems are gathered under this title (which translates as "contemporary manners and morals").

TITLE/V   "*Nodier raconte*. . .": Cf. the first line of Théophile Gautier's poem "Inès de la Sierras": "Nodier raconte qu'en Espagne . . . ." ("Nodier recounts that in Spain. . .")

TITLE/VI   *Stele*: Funerary monument.

4–5   *poluphloisboious*: "loud roaring," a Homeric epithet. The line in Greek that follows translates as "To the shore of the loud-roaring sea" (*Iliad* I, 34).

6   *SISTE VIATOR*: "Stay, traveler."

TITLE/VII   *I Vecchi*: "The Old Men."

3   *Il était* . . . *garçon*: "He was like a very little boy."

6   "*Con gli occhi* . . . *tardi*": "With slow eyes and grave." Cf. Dante, *Purgatorio* VI, 63 and Canto VII.26.

10   *Great Mary*: The novelist Mrs. Humphrey Ward (1851–1920).

13   *my bust by Gaudier*: Pound's friend, the sculptor Henri Gaudier-Brzeska, completed his white-marble "Hieratic Head of Ezra Pound" in 1915.

TITLE/VIII   Ritratto: Portrait.

2   *Lowell*: James Russell Lowell (1819–1891), poet and man of letters, was the American ambassador to Italy from 1880 to 1885.

HOMAGE TO SEXTUS PROPERTIUS (1918/19)

"Poems from the Propertius Series" was first published in Chicago in the March 1919 issue of *Poetry*; selections from it were also published in London in *The New Age* the same year. It was subsequently collected in *Quia Pauper Amavi* (London, 1919), *Poems 1918–21* (New York, 1921,) *Personæ* (New York, 1926), and printed separately as a book by Faber in 1934. The version reproduced here is the one given in Baechler and Litz's revised edition of *Personæ* (New York, 1990).

   Described by Pound as a "major persona" (or mask), *Homage to Sextus Propertius* is at once a tribute, a translation, and, as T. S. Eliot observed, a "criticism" of the first-century Roman poet "which in a most interesting way insists upon an element of humour, of irony and mockery in Propertius which Mackail and other interpreters have missed" — an element which Pound himself defined as *logopoeia*, "the dance of the intellect among words," a technique that "employs words not only for their direct meaning, but takes count in a special way of habits of usage, of the context we *expect* to find with the words, its usual concomitants, of its known acceptances, and of ironical play." Pound's tonal strategy in this "homage" is deliberately anachronistic, for while attempting to capture "the spirit of the young man of the Augustan Age, hating rhetoric and undeceived by imperial hog-wash," he also sought (as he wrote in 1931) to present "certain emotions as vital to me in 1917, faced with the infinite and ineffable imbecility of the British Empire, as they were to Propertius some centuries earlier, when faced with the infinite and ineffable imbecility of the Roman Empire." When a considerably truncated version of the poem ("the left foot, knee, thigh and right ear," according to Pound) was published in *Poetry* in March 1919, it immediately aroused the ire of University of Chicago classicist William Gardner Hale, who attacked its numerous errors and "howlers" in the April issue of the magazine. "Mr. Pound is incredibly ignorant of Latin. . . . For sheer magnificence of blundering, this is unsurpassable. . . . If Mr. Pound were a professor of Latin, there would be nothing left for him but suicide." Pound retorted: "No, I have not done a translation of Propertius. That fool in Chicago took the *Homage* for a translation, despite the mention of Wordsworth and the parodied line from Yeats." His real purpose, he explained, was less to "translate" Propertius than "to bring a dead man to life."

EPIGRAPH   *Orfeo*: Orpheus (*Inferno* IV, 140)? *Quia pauper amavi*: From Ovid, *Ars amatoria* II, 165: "Pauperibus vates ego sum, quia pauper amavi" ("I am the poet for the poor because I loved as a pauper").

TITLE   *Homage*: Pound later explained that he was following Debussy's usage of the term in "Homage à Rameau," i.e. "a piece of music recalling Rameau's manner." Thomas Hardy in 1922 told Pound that the entire poem would be clearer if entitled (in the fashion of Browning) "Propertius Soliloquizes." In later editions, the title is followed by the date "1917." Pound's sources in Propertius's *Elegies* are as follows: 1: from III.i; 2: from III.iii; 3, from II.xvi; 4: from III.vi; 5: from II.x; II.i; 6: from II.xiiiA; III.v; III.iv; II.viiiA; 7: from II.xv; 8: from II.xxviii; 9: from II.xxviii; I.xxviiiA; 10: from II.xxix; I.xxxixA; II.xxx; I.xxxii; II.xxx; II.xxxii; II.xxx; II.xxxii; II.xxiv; 12: from II.xxxiv.

1.1   *Callimachus*: Greek poet and critic (280–245 B.C.E.) from Cyrene. *Philetas*: Poet and grammarian (c.300 B.C.E.) from Cos, an island in the Aegean Sea.

1.33   *Oetian*: Hercules died on Mt. Oeta.

1.40   *devirginated young ladies*: The most celebrated "howler" in Pound's version. Propertius's Latin reads: "Gaudeo in solita tacta puella sono" ("Let my girl be touched by the sound of a familiar music and rejoice in it"). Pound reads "tacta" as the opposite of "intacta" (untouched virgin).

1.51   *Taenarian columns*: Columns made of black marble quarried at Taenarus, Sparta.

1.59   *wine jars*: In *Personæ* (1926), Pound added the radically anachronistic line "nor is it equipped with a frigidaire patent."

II.2   *Bellerophon's horse*: Pegasus, who according to legend made the water of the Hippocrene (a spring on Mount Helicon) flow when he stamped on the mountain. The spring gave inspiration to those who drank from it. Pegasus sprang into being from the blood of the Medusa.

II.8   *Curian brothers*: Three Curian brothers fought against the Horatii, three Roman brothers, to decide the conflict between Alva and Rome.

II.10   *Q. H. Flaccus'*: Horace's.

II.11   *Amelia . . . raft*: Aemillius Paulus celebrated his defeat of the Macedonians in 168 B.C.E. with a spectacular processional in Rome.

II.12   *victorious delay of Fabius*: Against Hannibal's forces as they advanced on Rome.

II.13   *battle at Cannae*: In which the Roman forces suffered heavy losses at the hands of Hannibal's army.

II.14   *lares*: Spirits guarding Rome.

II.17   *Jove protected by geese*: Cf. Livy, V, 47, which recounts how the noise of geese alerted the outnumbered Roman garrison guarding the Capitoline hill of an imminent attack by the Gauls in 387 B.C.E.

II.18   *Castalian*: Castalia, a sacred spring on Mount Parnassus.

II.31   *Silenus*: A satyr.

II.33   *small birds . . . mother*: In conventional depictions small doves draw Aphrodite's chariot.

II.34   *Gorgon's lake*: The Hippocrene.

II.49   *Suevi*: The Suebi were defeated by the Romans in 29 B.C.E.

II.51   *Night dogs*: Another celebrated "howler." The original reads "Nocturnaeque canes ebria signa fugae ("you will sing of the tokens of drunken flight through the dark").

III.27 *Cypris*: Aphrodite.

TITLE   *Lygdamus*: Propertius's slave.

V.2   *Emathian*: Macedonian.

V.14   *Pierides!*: The Muses.

V.41–42   *Ossa . . . Olympus*: Pelios and Ossa were the mountains that the Aloade, two giants, piled on Mount Olympus in an attempt to scale heaven and overthrow the gods.

V.56   *ore rotundas*: With round mouth. Horace, *Ars Poetica*, 323.

VI.70 *Jugurtha*: King of Numidia, captured and slain by Gaiius Marius.

VI.91 *Syrian onyx*: Syrian unguents used in embalming were kept in onyx boxes.

VII.14   *Endymion's . . . Diana*: The Moon (Diana) descended to visit Endymion, a handsome shepherd of Mount Latmos, and fell love with him while he slept.

VIII.19–20 *Io . . . Nile water*: Io, a priestess of Hera, was beloved of Zeus, who changed her into a heifer to conceal her from his wife. She was restored to her original form in Egypt after long wandering, and was worshipped there as Isis.

VIII.21   *Ino*: Fleeing her Theban husband, Ino was transformed into the goddess Leucothea when she entered the sea.

VIII.22   *Andromeda . . . Perseus*: Perseus rescued Andromeda from a sea monster sent by Poseidon.

VIII.24   *Callisto*: Transformed by Juno into a bear after she bore a child by Zeus.

VIII.30–31   *danger . . . Semele's*: When Zeus appeared to Semele in his full majesty, she was burned to ashes.

IX.16 *Iope, and Tyro, and Pasiphae*: Cassiope, wife of Ethiopian King Cepheas and mother of Andromeda. *Tyro*: Seduced by Poseidon in the shape of a river god, Tyro gave birth to the twin Neleus and Pelias. *Pasiphae*: Wife of Cretan King Minos, Pasiphae was made by Poseidon to fall in love with a bull; the Minotaur was the result of their union.

X.41   *Vesta*: Goddess of the hearth.

XII.8   *That woman in Colchis*: Medea.

XII.9 *Lynceus*: A rival poet who seeks Cynthia's affections.

XII.50   *Hamadryads*: Tree nymphs.

XII.51   *Ascraeus'*: Hesiod's.

XII.67   *Varro . . . expedition*: In his translation of *Argonautica*, by Apollonius of Rhodes.

XII.68   *His great passion . . . parchment*: Varro's love poems have not survived.

XII. 71–73   *Calvus . . . Lycoris*: Neither the poems of Calvus (82–46 B.C.E.) on his wife Quintilla nor that of Gallus (b. 70 B.C.E.) to his mistress Lycoris have survived.

HUGH SELWYN MAUBERLEY (1919)

Published in an edition of 200 copies by the Ovid Press in London in June 1919 as *Hugh Selwyn Mauberley / By E.P.* A slightly revised version of the entire poem was included in *Poems 1918–1921* (New York, 1921) and in *Personæ* (New York, 1926), where it was accompanied by this note by Pound: "The sequence is so distinctly a farewell to London that the reader who chooses to regard this as an exclusively American edition may as well omit it and turn at once to [*Homage to Sextus Propertius*]." The version reproduced here is the one given in Baechler and Litz's revised edition of *Personæ* (New York, 1990).

Pound himself described the poem in a letter as "a study in form, an attempt to condense the James novel." In a series of articles on the work of Henry James that Pound had published the previous year in the *Little Review*, he praised the recently deceased novelist not only for his acute portraiture of modern states of consciousness (particularly "his perennial theme of the unlived life"), but also for his social criticism of the class-bound small-mindedness of England and America. The quatrain stanza used throughout *Hugh Selwyn Mauberley* is adapted from

Théophile Gautier's *Emaux et Camées* (1852), a formalist reaction to what Pound termed "the dilutation of vers libre" and "general floppiness" of much contemporary verse. Though often read as an autobiographical satire of the fin-de-siècle aestheticism of his early work, Pound himself asserted that the poem was merely another ironic mask: "I'm no more Mauberley than Eliot is Prufrock." In his introduction to his Faber edition of Pound's *Selected Poems* (London, 1928 — see Appendix), T. S. Eliot influentially pronounced *Mauberley* to be a "great poem" and Pound's major achievement to date — an opinion echoed by F. R. Leavis in his *New Bearings in English Poetry* (1932) and by many New Critics thereafter.

EPIGRAPH   *Vocat . . . umbram*: "The heat calls us into the shade," the shepherd Mopsus calling out to his beloved, Meroe, to come hither; from the fourth Eclogue of Nemesianus (fl. 283).

TITLE   *(Contacts and Life)*: In its first printings, the subtitle was "Life and Contacts," but when republished with *Homage to Sextus Propertius* in *Diptych Rome-London* (New York, 1958), it was reversed to read "Contacts and Life," Pound having informed his publisher James Laughlin, "Note inversion in subtitle of *Mauberley*, NOT Life and Contacts but the actual order of the subject matter."

E. P. ODE POUR L'ÉLECTION DE SON SÉPULCHRE

TITLE   *E. P.*: Pound's standard signature — in other words, a "persona" or "character" of his proper name. He later commented, "*Mauberley* buries E.P. in the first poem; gets rid of all his troublesome energies." *Ode . . . Sépulchre*: "Ode for the Selection of His Tomb," an adaptation of an ode by Pierre Ronsard (1524–1584).

8   *Capaneus*: One of the seven warriors dispatched from Argos to attack Thebes. Appears in Dante's *Inferno*, XIV, as an embodiment of defiant hubris and unabated rage.

9   ἴδμεν γάρ τοι πάνθ', ὅσ' ἐνὶ Τροίη: *Odyssey* XII 189, from the sirens' song: "For we know all the toils that are in wide Troy."

18–19   *l'an . . . eage*: "In the thirty-first year of his life"; adapted from the opening of *Le Testament* by François Villon (1431–c.1463). Pound himself had turned 31 in October 1916.

II

11   *kinema*: From the Greek *kineou*, to move, set in motion, hence "cinema."

III

2   *mousseline of Cos*: Muslin cloth from the Greek island of Cos used for the draperies of ancient dress.

4   *barbitos*: Seven-stringed instrument resembling the lyre.

15   τὸ καλόν: "To kalon" ("The beautiful"). "To Kalon" was an American brand of port wine around the turn of the century.

22   *Pisistratus*: Tyrant of Athens (605?–527 B.C.E.)

26   τίν' ἄνδρα, τίν' ἥρωα, τίνα θεόν: From the Tin-Pan Alley cadence of the opening of Pindar's Second *Olympian*: "What god, what hero, aye, and what man shall we loudly praise."

IV

3   *pro domo*: For home.

11   *pro patria . . . "et decor"*: "For the fatherland, neither sweetly nor gloriously." Adaptation of Horace, *Odes* III.ii.13: "dulce et decorum est pro patria mori" ("it is sweet and glorious to die for one's fatherland").

YEUX GLAUQUES

TITLE   "Glaucous eyes," phrase used by Gautier to evoke the dull grayish green or grayish blue gaze common in Pre-Raphaelite portraits of women.

2–3 *When John . . . Treasuries:* "Of Kings' Treasuries" was the opening chapter in Ruskin's *Sesame and Lilies* (1865).

5 *Foetid Buchanan:* Robert W. Buchanan castigated the Pre-Raphaelite poets in "The Fleshly School of Poetry" (1871). Dante Gabriel Rossetti's poem "Jenny" (mentioned below) was signaled out for attack.

9 *Burne-Jones:* Edward Burne-Jones's painting *King Cophetua and the Beggar Maid* entered the Tate Gallery's collection in 1919.

15 *The English Rubaiyat:* Edward Fitzgerald's 1859 version of *The Rubaiyat of Omar Khayyam* was virtually unknown until the discovery of its remaindered first edition by Rossetti and the Pre-Raphaelites.

"SIENA MI FE', DISFECEMI MAREMMA"

TITLE "Siena made me; Maremma undid me": Dante, *Purgatorio* V, 134.

5 *Gallifet:* French general (1830–1930) who led a cavalry charge at Sedan during the Franco-Prussian War. Cf. Canto XVI. 74.

6 *Rhymers' Club:* Group founded in the 1890s, various members of which are mentioned in this section: "Verog," i.e. Victor Plarr (1863–1929), author of *In the Dorian Mood* (1896), Ernest Dowson (1867–1900), Lionel Johnson (1867–1902, and Selwyn Image (1849–1930).

12 *Newman:* Cardinal John Henry Newman (1801–1890), major figure in the Oxford Movement to bring the Church of England back to its Catholic roots.

14 *Headlam:* Christian socialist minister Stewart D. Headlam (1847–1924), speaker at working-men's clubs.

BRENNBAUM

5 *Horeb, Sinai:* The mountains, respectively where Moses saw the burning bush and was given the Ten Commandments.

8 *The Impeccable:* May allude to "The Incomparable" Max Beerbohm (1872–1956), a later neighbor of Pound's in Rapallo, Italy.

MR. NIXON

2 *Mr. Nixon:* Resembles the commercially successful English man of letters, Arnold Bennett (1867–1931).

21 *friend of Blougram's:* Gigadibs, literary hack in Browning's poem "Bishop Blougram's Apology" (1855).

X

2 *The stylist has taken shelter:* As did Ford Madox Ford (1873–1939) in the English countryside in 1919.

XI

1 *"Conservatrix of Milésien":* The phrase, adapted from Remy de Gourmont's short story "Stratagèmes" (1894), was later glossed by Pound as "Woman, the conservator [i.e. of the erotic folklore of the bawdy Milesian tales], inheritor of past gestures."

XII

1–2 *Daphne . . . hands:* Translation of lines from Théophile Gautier's "Le Château du souvenir" (1852).

22 *"Which the highest cultures have nourished":* Translation of the first line of Jules Laforgue's "Complainte des pianos" (1885).

28   *Pierian roses*: The muses were worshipped at Pieria. Cf. Swinburne, "Anactoria": "For never Muse has bound above thine hair / The high Pierian flower whose graft outgrows / All summer kinship of the mortal rose."

ENVOI (1919)

2   *Lawes*: Henry Lawes (1596–1662) set to music "Goe lovely Rose" and other poems by Edmund Waller (1607–1687), the figure who, according to Edmund Gosse's *From Shakespeare to Pope* (1885), was single-handedly responsible for the classical revival in seventeenth-century English poetry. Cf. Canto LXXXI.101.

MAUBERLEY (1920)

EPIGRAPH   Added in the 1926 *Personæ* version, from Ovid, *Metamorphoses* VII, 786: "Vacuos exercet aera morsus" ("His empty mouth snaps at the air"), picked up below at II, 34.

I

1–2   *"eau-forte . . . Jaquemart"*: Jules Jacquemart (1837–1880) engraved the frontispiece for the 1881 edition of Gautier's *Emaux et Camées*.
4   *Messalina*: Lubricious wife of Roman emperor Claudius; her head appeared on coins struck in his reign.
14   Pier Francesca: Italian painter (1420–92).
15   Pisanello: Antonio (or Vittore) Pisano (c. 1397–1455), praised as an engraver of medals in Reinach's *Apollo* (cf. "Medallion" below). Created a medallion of Sigismondo Malatesta.

II

EPIGRAPH   *Qu'est ce qu'ils savent . . . CAID ALI*: "What do they know of love, and what can they understand? If they cannot understand poetry, if they have no feeling for music, what can they understand of this passion, in comparison with which the rose is coarse and the perfume of violets a clap of thunder?" "Caid Ali" is a pseudonym for Pound, here sounding much like his mentor Remy de Gourmont.
1   *diabolus in the scale*: medieval music theorists called the augmented fourth the "devil in music."
3   *ANANGKE*: Necessity.
7   *NUKTOS AGALMA*: 'Jewel of the Night." From the Greek pastoral poet Bion's address to the Evening Star. [All editions previous to the 1958 *Diptych Rome-London* read *NUKTIS*.]
17   *TO AGATHON*: The good.
29   *diastasis*: Literally, "spaced apart" — or "dilated." Cf. Canto LXXXI.124.

"THE AGE DEMANDED"

4   *The Cytheræan*: Aphrodite, born from the sea, her chariot drawn by doves and swans.
39   *apathein*: Impassivity, indifference, much prized by the Parnassian aesthetic of Flaubert and Gautier.

IV

20–21   *on an oar/Read this*: Cf. Canto I.54–57, where the shade of Elpenor asks to be remembered by an inscription on his oar, reading "a man of no fortune, and with a name to come."
25   *An hedonist*: In *Blast* I (June 1914), Pound defined hedonism as "the vacant place of the Vortex, without force, deprived of past and future." Cf. the Lotus-Eaters of Canto XX.153.

MEDALLION

1   *Luini*: The Lombard painter Bernardino Luini (ca. 1480–1582).

7   *Anadyomene*: Foam-born (epithet of Aphrodite).

8   *Reinach*: Salomon Reinach (1858–1932), French art historian; his *Apollo: An Illustrated Manual of Art throughout the Ages* was published in English in 1907.

THE CANTOS (1925–1969)

After *Hugh Selwyn Mauberley*, Pound would publish virtually no more isolated poems, instead devoting himself to his lifelong work-in-progress, *The Cantos*, the first installment of which appeared in early 1925 (after many delays) under the title *A Draft of XVI. Cantos of Ezra Pound for the Beginning of a Poem of Some Length now first made into a Book* (Paris, Three Mountains Press). The composition of Pound's modern epic (or "poem including history") dated back to 1915. The initial "Three Cantos" (sometimes called the "Ur-Cantos") were published in *Poetry* in the summer of 1917, but Pound revised the entire opening of the work over the following six years and, no doubt influenced by his reading of James Joyce's *Ulysses* in manuscript form, made Book XI of the *Odyssey* his new point of departure. The other major first editions of *The Cantos* include: *A Draft of XXX Cantos* (Paris, Hours Press, 1930); *Eleven New Cantos XXXI–XLI* (New York, Farrar & Rinehart, 1934); *The Fifth Decad of the Canto* (London, Faber & Faber, 1937); *Cantos LII–LXXI* (London, Faber & Faber, 1940); *The Pisan Cantos* (New York, New Directions, 1948); *Section: Rock-Drill 85–95 de los cantares* (Milan, Scheiwiller, 1955); *Thrones: 96–109 de los cantares* (Milan, Scheiwiller, 1959); *Drafts and Fragments of Cantos CX–CXVII* (New York, New Directions, 1969). Editorial ellipses within *The Cantos* are indicated by three centered dots.

from A DRAFT OF XXX CANTOS (1930)

CANTO I

Originally published as the second portion of "Canto 3" in *Poetry*, August 1917, and subsequently included in the American edition of *Lustra* (1917). The Canto consists of a translation of Book XI of the Odyssey into the alliterative Anglo-Saxon meter of *The Seafarer*—Homer's Greek here also refracted through its Latin translation by the Renaissance scholar Andreas Divus. In this book of the *Odyssey*, sometimes referred to as the *nekuia* (or "descent"), Odysseus, having spent a year on Circe's island, and having been directed by her to seek out Tiresias in the "house of Hades," sails toward the mistenshrouded lands of the Cimmerians, beaches his ship, and prepares to receive instructions from the prophet on how to return home to Ithaca. Pound felt that this moment of descent, with its sacrificial offering of blood to make the shades of the underworld appear (an apt metaphor for his own act of translation), constituted the most archaic portion, the "hinter-time," as it were, of Homer's epic: "the Nekuia shouts aloud that it is *older* than the rest," he observed in a 1935 letter.

21   *pitkin*: Pound's invention: a little pit.

28   *fosse*: Ditch.

33   *dreory*: Anglo-Saxon, "blood-dripping".

42   *Elpenor*: One of Odysseus's companions who had drunkenly fallen to his death from Circe's roof, his absence unremarked by the crew until this moment.

50   *ingle*: Inglenook, from the Scots "chimney corner" (via Gavin Douglas).

58   *Anticlea*: Odysseus's dead mother.

62   *bever*: Drink.

69   *In officina Wecheli*: "At the workshop of Wechelus," printer's information on the title page of the Andreas Divus Latin translation of the *Odyssey* (Paris, 1538) which Pound discovered in a bookstall on the quais of the Seine during one of his earliest visits to the city.

72–74   *Venerandam . . . est*: "Worthy of veneration, golden-crowned and beautiful, whose dominion is the walled cities of all sea-set Cyprus" (Loeb). From the "Cretan" Georgius Dartona's Latin version of the second Homeric Hymn to Aphrodite, bound into Pound's copy of Andreas Divus.

74   *orichalchi*: Of copper, used by Dartona with reference to Aphrodite's earrings.

76   *Argicida*: Either "Slayer of the Greeks," a reference to Aphrodite's favoring the Trojans (and especially her son Aeneas) over the Greeks; or "slayer of Argus," an epithet for Hermes, messenger of the gods and conductor of souls to the underworld. *A golden bough* enabled Aeneas to traverse the Styx and enter Hades.

CANTO II

First published as the "Eighth Canto" in the *Dial* (New York), May 1922, then moved forward in *A Draft of XVI Cantos* (1925).

1   *Hang it all*: The original "Three Cantos" published in *Poetry* in 1917 opened with this line.

2   *the one "Sordello"*: Pound read *Sordello*, Robert Browning's 1840 semi-fictionalized verse biography of the thirteenth-century Lombard troubadour, in 1915, declaring it "the best long poem in English since Chaucer."

4   *Lo Sordels*: "Sordello was from Mantua," a fragment of a Provençal *vida* of the poet.

5   *So-Shu*: Corruption of Shiba-shōjo, the Japanese name for the Chinese Han dynasty poet Sima Xiangru; from the Fenollosa papers.

7   *Lir*: Celtic sea-god.

11   *Eleanor . . . ἑλέπτολις!*: Eleanor of Aquitaine (1122–1204), wife of King Louis VII of France and subsequently of Henry II of England; said to have sown discord between the English king and his sons and to have been the cause of the Hundred Years War. Cf. Canto VII.1–2. Ἑλέναυς: *elenaus*: Aeschylus, *Agammemnon* (l. 689), a punning reference to Helen of Troy as "ship-destroying" (*helenaus*) and "city-destroying" (*heleptolis*) and "man-destroying" (*helandros*).

12–13   *Homer . . . sea-surge*: "Of Homer," Pound wrote in 1918, "two qualities remain untranslated: the magnificent onomatopoeia, as of the rush of the waves on the sea-beach and their recession in *para thina poluphloisboio thalasses*, untranslated and untranslatable; and secondly, the authentic cadence of speech."

14   *"Let her go. . ."*: *Iliad* III, 139–160, the old men on the walls discussing Helen (during the teichoscopia).

19   *Schoeney's daughters*: Pound declared that Arthur Golding's 1567 translation of Ovid's *Metamophoses* was "possibly the most beautiful book in our language." In his translation of VIII, 427–35, Golding refers to Atalanta as "one / Of Schoenyes daughters."

23–27   *Tyro*: The first of the beautiful female shades to appear to Odysseus in Hades in Book XI of the *Odyssey*. She was loved by the sea god Poseidon who in the form of the river Enipeus caused a great wave to envelop and conceal them.

34–35   *Scios. . . Naxos*: Golding's spelling of the Greek island of Chios, said to have been the birthplace of Homer. The nearby island of Naxos was a center of Dionysian worship.

40–118   *The ship landed*: The story of the kidnapping of the young Dionysus and his revenge on his captors is told in *Metamorphoses* III, 597–691.

46   *I*: The speaker is Acoetes, the captain of the ship taking Dionysus to Naxos; the only member of the crew to believe in the god, so his life was spared.

59   *Pentheus*: King of Thebes who attempted to arrest Dionysus; later torn to pieces by the Maenads, led by his own mother. Here being addressed by Acoetes as he narrates the

tale of Dionysus's abduction.

95   *Lyæus*: Name for the wine-god Dionysus: "he who unties," "deliverer from care."

100   *Olibanum*: Frankincense used in the rites of Dionysus.

104   *Lycabs*: The pirate Lycabas of 47, turned into a porpoise by Dionysus.

113   *Medon*: Another member of the pirate crew.

115   *Tiresias*: In *Metamorphoses* III, 511–527, the Theban prophet foretells the coming of Diony-
sus and the dismemberment of Pentheus. *Cadmus*: Founder of Thebes, who also warns
his grandson Pentheus about Dionysus.

124   *Ileuthyeria*: Sea-nymph transformed into coral (as Daphne was changed into a laurel); name
invented by Pound, modelled on Eleutherios ("the liberator"), an epithet of Dionysus.

153   *Proteus*: In Homer, "the old man of the sea" and traditional incarnation of the power of
metamorphosis, the subject of this Canto.

CANTO III

Some of the material in this Canto originally appeared in the first of "Three Cantos" in
Poetry in 1917.

1   *I sat on the Dogana's steps*: Pound remembering himself on the steps of the customs-house
in Venice in 1908, in a line that recalls Browning's *Sordello* III, 676–77: "I muse this on a
ruined palace-step / At Venice."

3   *"those girls"*: Browning's description of peasant girls journeying to market by gondola in
Sordello III, 699.

4   *Buccentoro . . . "Stretti'*: The Bucentoro was a Venetian rowing club that took its name
from the ship used by the Doge to celebrate the symbolic marriage between Venice and
the Adriatic Sea by casting a ring into the water. "*Stretti*": Title of a popular Italian song
("In Close Embrace").

5   *Morosoni*: The palazzo Morosini in Venice.

6   *And peacocks in Koré's house*: Koré is Persephone, daughter of Demeter. A translation of
a line from Gabriel D'Annunzio's *Notturno* (1920), referring to the neglected grounds of
a palazzo that had become a rookery.

10–11   *Panisks . . . dryas . . . maelid*: Little Pan-gods, tree-nymphs, and apple-tree nymphs.

13   *the lake*: Lake Garda, cf. "Blandulla, Tenulla, Vagula" (p. 18).

17   *Poggio*: Gian Francesco Poggio Bracciolini (1380–1459), Papal secretary and humanist.

20–25   *My Cid*: Paraphrase of the opening of the twelfth-century Spanish epic, *Poema del Cid*,
which Pound praised for its "swift narration, its vigor, the humanness of its characters"
in his 1910 *Spirit of Romance*. "My Cid" ("My Lord") is Rodrigo Diaz de Bivar, the soldier
of fortune and hero of the epic. Burgos is the Castilian city in which he lived and died.

23   *Una niña*: "A nine-year-old girl," the only person in Burgos who dared to tell the banished
Ruy Diaz of King Alfonso's threat to severely punish anyone who came to Diaz's assis-
tance.

25   *voce tinnula*: "With a ringing voice," from Catullus, LXI.

34   *Raquel and Vidas*: Jewish moneylenders tricked by Ruy Diaz, who instead of offering them
two chests of gold as security as he had promised, gave them chests filled with sand.

36   *menie*: Private army.

37   *Valencia*: Captured and ruled by Diaz from 1094–99.

38   *Ignez da Castro*: Castillian noblewoman (c.1320–1355) secretly married to Pedro, heir to
the throne of Portugal and stabbed to death by King Alfonso IV. When Pedro succeeded
him, he had her body exhumed and placed on a throne by his side, demanding that the
court pay necrophilic homage to the dead queen by kissing her hand. The story is told
in Camões's sixteenth-century Portuguese epic, *Os Lusiades*, summarized by Pound in
The Spirit of Romance.

41 Mantegna: Andrea Mantegna (1431–1506), Italian painter who executed frescoes for the Gonzaga family in Mantua.

42 *Nec Spe Nec Metu*: "With neither hope nor fear," a motto in the rooms of Isabelle D'Este Gonzaga (1474–1539) in the ducal palace at Mantua.

CANTO IV

First published in an edition of forty copies by John Rodker in London in October 1919, then reprinted in *The Dial* (New York), June 1920.

1 *Palace in smoky light*: Burning Troy, via the *Aeneid* II, 309–310.

3 *ANAXIFORMINGES*: "Lords of the Lyre," from the opening of Pindar's *Olympian* II. *Aurunculeia!*: Bride praised in Catullus, *Epithalamium* LXI, 86–87.

4 *Cadmus of Golden Prows*: Left his native Phoenicia to found the city of Thebes.

10 *Choros nympharum*: Chorus of nymphs.

16 *Ityn*: Itys was the son of Procne, the wife of Tereus, king of Thrace. Tereus raped Philomela, Procne's sister, and cut out her tongue. In revenge Procne killed Itys and served his flesh to Tereus (Ovid, *Metamorphoses* VI).

17 *et ter flebiliter*: "And thrice with tears," via Horace, *Odes* IV, xii.

21 *Cabestan's heart*: Guillem de Cabestany (1181–96), Provençal troubadour and lover of the lady Soremonda. Her husband, Raimond of Castle Rossillon, killed the singer, had his heart cooked, and served it to Soremonda for her infidelity. She vowed to eat no more food and in her grief committed suicide.

29 *Rhodez*: Earlier spelling of Rodez, France.

53 *Vidal*: See "Piere Vidal Old" (p. 12), the Actaeon-like victim of Lady Loba.

66–67 *Pergusa . . . Salmacis*: Pergusa: lake in Ovid, Metamorphoses V, 386; *Gargaphia*: spring in which Artemis was surprised by Acteaon while bathing (*Metamorphoses* III, 156); *Salmacis*: spring belonging to the water-nymph Salmacis who unsuccessfully attempted to rape the boy Hermaphroditos (*Metamorphoses* IV, 285–388).

69 *e lo soleills plovil*: "Thus the sun rains," from Arnaut Daniel.

74–75 *Takasago*: Title of Japanese Noh play, based on the Philemon and Baucis-like legend of a couple growing old together, symbolized by two pines, one on Takasago Bay, the other other at Sumiyoshi (which Pound confuses with Isé).

77 *Tree of Visages*: Fenollosa's mistranslation of the "trees of life" in the Noh play *Takasago*.

84 *Gourdon*: Town in southern France visited by Pound during his walking tour of 1912.

86–87 *Hymenaeus Io*: "Hymen, hail! Hymen, Hymen." Catullus, LXI, cf. l. 3 above.

89–99 *Sō-Gyokyu*: Japanese form of the Chinese poet Song Yu, fourth-century B.C.E. author of "Rhymprose on the Wind," which includes a dialogue between King Xiang of Chu and the poet on the various kinds of winds, quoted here from the Fenollosa notebooks.

101 *Ecbatan*: Capital of the Medes, founded in the sixth century B.C.E. by their legendary first king, Deioces. This ideal city recurs in Canto LXXIV as "The city of Dioce whose terraces are the color of stars."

102 *Danaë*: Daughter of Acrisius, King of Argos, and mother of Perseus by Zeus. Having been informed by an oracle that his daughter's son would kill him, Acrisius imprisoned Danaë at the top of a bronze tower, where Zeus descended upon her as a golden shower pouring onto her lap.

111 *Père Henri Jacques*: Example of the French Jesuit priests in China who were among the first Westerners to study its culture. *Sennin*: cf. "Sennin Poem" in *Cathay* (p. 65).

113–14 *Polhonac . . . Gyges*. Héracle III, Viscount of Polignac, unwitting accomplice in his own cuckoldry when he agreed to sing a love song to his wife composed by the troubadour Guillems de San Leidier. Here rhymed with the story of King Candaules who secretly introduced his bodyguard Gyges in his bedroom so that he could admire the naked beauty of his wife. Discovering the latter's presence, the offended queen persuaded Gyges to kill Candaules and marry her.

119–23 *Saave*: "Hail! . . . hail Queen," memory of religious procession witnessed by Pound in Toulouse (near the river Garonne) in 1919.

124–25 *Stefano*: Stefano da Verona (c.1374–1451), painter of the "Madonna in hortulo" ("Madonna in the Little Garden"), located in Verona (through which the Adige river flows). Confused by Pound with the Madonna of San Michele in Orto (in Florence) evoked in Cavalcanti's Sonnet 35.

128 arena: The arena at Verona, visited by Pound and Eliot in the summer of 1919.

CANTO VII

First published in *The Dial*, August 1921. Sometimes referred to as the Paris Canto.

1–2 Eleanor: Cf. Canto II.11–13.

8–10 *Marble . . . execute*: From Ovid's *Ars amatoria* I, 133–142; 149–51, recommending that the reader pick out a comely girl as she is about to enter a theater and follow her to a seat where they will be forced to sit in close proximity. Then "if a speck of dust should fall into your lady's lap, flick it off with your fingers; if there be no speck of dust, well, flick it off anyway."

11–13 *file . . . armatz*: Medieval evocations of religious processions and battles. *E li mestiers ecoutes*: "and hearken to the mysteries [or crafts]"; *y cavals armatz*: "and horses in armor" (from Bertran de Born, cf. "Sestina: Altaforte" (p. 10)).

15 *And Dante's "ciocco"*: "log," From *Paradiso* XVIII, 100, where spirits are described as ascending from the heaven of Mars to that of Jupiter like the innumerable sparks that leap forth when burning logs are struck.

16–18 *Un peu moisi . . . baromètre*: "A bit mildewed, the floor lower than the garden. Against the wainscoting, a wicker armchair, an old piano, and beneath the barometer." From the opening description of Mme. Aubain's house in Flaubert's story *Un Coeur simple* (1877).

19–30 *The old men's voices . . . endless sentence*: After the descriptive realism of Flaubert, the atmospherics of Henry James. *Con gli occhi onesti et tardi*: "With eyes honest and slow" (*Purgatorio* VI, 63), Dante's description of Sordello, here applied to Henry James. *Grave incessu*: "grave in movement" (*Inferno* IV, 112).

43–44 *Ione*: See "Ione, Dead the Long Year" (p. 44) and "Liu Ch'e" (p. 43).

46 *The Elysée*: Pound (and later Joyce) briefly resided at the Hotel de l'Elysée in Paris, an echo of Elysium, home of the blessed dead.

48 *the Erard*: Famous French piano make.

52 *Fritz*: Fritz-René Vanderpyl (1876–?), Dutch writer, friend of Pound's and Joyce's in Paris.

55 *Smaragdos, chrysolithos*: Emeralds, topazes (from Sextus Propertius, *Elegies* II, xvi, 43–46, describing Cynthia's finery). *De Gama*: Vasco da Gama (c.1469–1524), as described by Camões in the *Lusiads* II, xcviii, 3–4.

57 *Le vieux commode*: The old mahogany chest, mahogany being, according to Pound, the most bourgeois and least workable of woods.

63 *The scarlet curtain*: From Golding's Ovid, describing Atalanta's blush (*Metamorphoses* X, 694–95).

64 *Lamplight . . . remir*: Arnaut Daniel loved the wife of Guillem de Bouvila. *E quel remir* ("and that I may gaze upon her"), from his poem "Doutz brais et critz."

66 *Nicea*: Perhaps the dancer Ione of 43, likened to the Nike of Samothrace in the Louvre.

80 *"Toc"*: French for sham or ersatz.

95 *O voi che siete*: *Paradiso* II, 1, translated by Pound in Canto XCIII as "Oh you, in the dinghy astern there."

96–98 *Dido . . . new Eros*: While still grieving for her husband Sychaeus, murdered by h brother Pygmalion, Dido became the lover of Aeneas (her "new Eros"?) in Carthage, *Aeneid* I, 341–356.

115 *Lorenzaccio*: Derogatory diminutive for Lorenzo de Medici (1449–1492).

117 *Ma se morisse*: "But if he should die, believed killed by himself," Lorenzo's words as reported in the *Storia Fiorentina* of Benedetto Varchi (1503–1565), one of Pound's major sources for Renaissance Italian history.

122 *Alessandro*: Tyrannical duke of Florence, assassinated by his cousin Lorenzo de Medici in 1587.

126 *E biondo*: "He is blond" (*Inferno* XII, 110), Dante evoking the blond head of Obizzo d'Este (d. 1293), one of the most homicidal tyrants of Italy, in the first round of the seventh circle of Hell.

CANTO IX

First published as part of the "Malatesta Cantos," *Criterion* (London), July 1923. Cantos VIII–XI, Hemingway's favorites, deal with the martial exploits, political intrigues, and patronage of the arts of Sigismondo Pandolfo Malatesta (1417–68), lord of Rimini and professional soldier of fortune. Pound later wrote in *Guide to Kulchur* (1938): "If you consider . . . Sigismundo a failure, he was at all events a failure worth all the successes of his age. He had in Rimini, Pisanello, Pier della Francesca. . . . If the Tempio is a jumble and junk shop, it nevertheless registers a concept. There is no other single man's effort equally registered."

10 *Astorre Manfredi of Faenza*: Hereditary enemy of Sigismondo who set dogs upon him in a marsh as he was crossing his territory.

14 *Fano*: Town in the Marches south of Rimini which Sigismondo inherited in 1431 and later lost to the Pope.

16 *Emperor*: Sigismund V (1368–1437), Holy Roman Emperor; knighted Sigismondo and his brother Domenico in Rome in 1433.

18 *Basinio*: Basinio de Basanii (1427–57), Sigismondo's court poet; in 1456, he defeated Porcellio Pandeone (the "anti-Hellene") in a public literary debate in which the latter argued that it was unnecessary to have studied Greek to write good Latin verse.

23 *Madame Ginevra*: (1418–40); became Sigismondo's first wife when she was 16 and he 17. The son she bore him lived only a year and she died at 22, with Pope Pius II later accusing her husband of having poisoned her.

26 *Rocca*: La Rocca, Sigismondo's fortress in Rimini, considered one of the engineering marvels of Italy.

29–41 *old Sforza. . . Pesaro*: Francesco Sforza (1401–66), ruler of Lombardy (referred to as "Wattle-wattle" at ll. 64 and 107 because of his loose, fleshy neck). He finagled a deal with Sigismondo's arch-rival, Federigo d'Urbino (also referred to as "Feddy" several times below) and with Sigismondo's cousin, Galeazzo Malatesta ("Geleaz") in which the city of Pesaro would go to his brother Alessandro Sforza through the arranged marriage between Galeazzo and Alessandro's granddaughter — with Federigo receiving the town of Fossombrone in the same swap.

39 *bestialmente*: "In a beastly manner."

40 *per capitoli*: "By the chapters."

46–55 *King o' Ragona*: Alfonso, King of Aragon. Sigismondo broke the contract by which he had agreed to fight as a mercenary for Alfonso and instead sided with the Florentines, encouraged in "haec traditio" ("this treachery") by his secretary and engineer, Roberto Valturio.

52 *old bladder . . . saluavit*: Pope Pius II (1458–1462), who noted in his Commentaries "there is no doubt that Sigismondo's treachery saved their [i.e. the Florentines'] cause."

56 *TEMPIO*: The unfinished Tempio Malatestiano in Rimini, largely built between 1446 and 1465 in honor of Isotta degli Atti, Sigismondo's beloved third wife, and featuring frescoes by Piero della Francesca and carvings and sculptures by Agostino di Duccio.

57 *Polixena*: Polissena Sforza, Sigismondo's second wife; died in 1449 amid accusations that she, too, had, been poisoned.

67 *old Foscari*: Francesco Foscari, Doge of Venice from 1423–57. *Caro mio*: my dear.

72 *Classe*: The Byzantine basilica of S. Apollinare in Classe in Ravenna, from which Sigismondo stole the marble for the building of his Tempio.

73 *Casus est talis*: "This is the case." The citizens of Ravenna had complained to the Doge of Venice about Sigismondo's spoilation of their cathedral.

77–92 *Filippo*: F. Calandrini, Cardinal of Bologna, commendatory of the Abbey ("abbazia") of S. Apollinare. The Tempio was built over the Church of Santa Maria in Trivio. *Plaustra*: the oxcarts in which the marble was carted away under the cover of night.

93 *that German-Burgundian female*: Another accusation levied at Sigismondo by Pope Pius II in his *Commentaries*: that he had raped and killed a German noblewoman on her way to Rome in 1450. The accusation cost him the support of the Venetians (see l. 104).

94–95 *Poliorcetes*: Greek epithet ("taker of cities") applied to Sigismondo by Pisanello on the medals he made bearing his likeness. *POLUMETIS*: Homer's standard epithet for Odysseus ("of many wiles").

102 *Broglio*: Gaspare Broglio, a soldier in the service of Sigismondo and author of the *Cronaca* detailing Malatesta's life and campaigns in Rimini, one of Pound's sources.

103 *m'l'ha calata*: "He double-crossed me."

106 *the silk war*: Conflict between Venice and Ragusa, two rival centers of silk production.

117–24 *Pitigliano*: Malatesta had been engaged by Siena to attack the Count of Pitigliano, whose castle of Sorano he besieged in 1454. Having finally made a breach in the fortifications, Sigismondo made a truce with the count and, suspected of treachery by his employers, barely escaped arrest, leaving behind him a postbag containing about fifty letters. The Sienese authorities would have discovered in these letters little evidence of secret machinations, but merely the record of his concern with domestic matters and his plans for the construction of the Tempio. By providing extracts from eight of these letters, which were rediscovered in the Archives of Siena in the nineteenth century and reproduced in Yriarte's *Un Condottiere au XVe siècle* (Paris, 1882), Pound moves his "poem including history" into the realm of the documentary.

124–30 *in the post-bag*: This is the first letter in Malatesta's post-bag: from the architect Matteo Nutti, invited to interpret Alberti's plans for the Tempio when the latter was called back to Rome. *Ex Ariminio . . .* : "From Rimini the 20th of December / 'My most excellent lord, magnificent and powerful.'" *Alwidge*: Luigi Alvise, overseer of carpenters on the Tempio (cf. l. 136).

132–38 *Magnifico exso*: "Magnificent most excellent." *Signor mio*: "My lord." Excerpt from a letter by Giovane, son of the overseer Alvise, writing at his father's dictation. *Genare*: Sigismondo's secretary.

139 *Sagramoro*: Sigismondo's secretary, in a postscript to the second letter, saying that he had examined all the works.

140–45 *Illustre. . .* : "My excellent lord." The third letter, addressed to the architect Leon Battista Alberti (1404–1472) and signed by Pietro di Genari and Matteo da Pasti, listing materials needed to construct the Tempio.

146–59 *MONSEIGNEUR*: Fourth letter, to Sigismondo from "De de M." writing on behalf of his wife-to-be Isotta, who bore him two sons before their marriage, Sallustio (cf. ll. 163, 180, 195) and Valerio. *Sr. Galeazzo's daughter*: a girl reputedly seduced by Malatesta. *Mi pare . . .* : "It seems to me that he has said everything." *Madame Lucrezia*: one of

Sigismondo's other five illegitimate children.

160   *sagramoro*: Continues l. 139 above.

162–75   *MAGNFICENT LORD*: Fifth letter, from Lunardo de Palla, tutor of Sigismondo's and Isotta's son Sallustio (1448–1470), later murdered at the behest of his half-brother Roberto Malatesta. Rambottom: Giorgi Ranbutino, stonemason at the Tempio.

178   *Magnifice ac potens*: cf. l. 126.

180–99 *Malatesta de Malatestis . . .* : "Malatesta of the Malatestas to his Magnificent Lord and Father." Sixth letter, from Sallustio to Sigismondo, here addressed as "Most excellent lord and lord without lord Sigismondo, son of Pandolfo, Captain General of the Malatestas."

200–201   *"Illustrious Prince"*: Seventh letter, an excerpt from a message from Trachulo, Sigismondo's court poet, written toward the end of the siege of Sorano, advising his master ("Hannibal") to take over the city of Siena itself — just the smoking gun that the Sienese authorities might have been looking for in the post-bag.

202–34 *"Magnifice ac potens . . ."*: "To the magnificent and powerful lord, my most excellent lord, a humble advice be permitted." Eighth letter, from Pietro Genari, Sigismondo's secretary, dealing with the construction of the Tempio.

221   *the aliofants*: The columns of the Tempio rested on sculpted elephant heads made of black porphyry.

227   *Octavian*: Painter who illustrated the papal bull authorizing the church.

231   *Messire Agostino*: Agostino di Duccio (1418–1481), Florentine sculptor who worked on the sarcophagus dedicated to Sigismondo's ancestors and on the bas-reliefs of the Tempio. Cf. Canto XLV.30: "Duccio came not by usura / nor Pier della Francesca."

238–43   "et amava . . . decus": "And he loved Isotta degli Atti to distraction and she was worthy of it constant in purpose / She delighted the eye of the prince / lovely to look / at pleasing to the people (and ornament of Italy)." Tribute to Isotta assembled from Pope Pius's *Commentaries*, Horace's *Odes* III,iii, and Broglio's chronicle of Rimini.

246   *Past ruin'd Latium*: Echoes "Past ruined Ilion Helen lives," from W. S. Landor's poem "To Ianthe."

250   *San Vitale*: Byzantine church in Ravenna dating back to the sixth century.

CANTO XIII

First published in the *Transatlantic Review* (Paris), January 1924. Pound considered this Canto to be the "announcement of the backbone moral of the *Cantos*." His primary source here is M. G. Pauthier's *Doctrine de Confucius: Les Quatre livres de philosophie morale et politique de la Chine* (Paris, 1841), which contains the "Four Books" of the classical Confucian canon, whose titles (in the French Romanization) run: *Lun-Yu* (or *The Analects*), *Ta Hio* (or *The Great Digest*), *Tchoung-Young* (translated by Pound as *The Unwobbling Pivot*), and *Meng Tzeu* (or *Mencius*). Pound published a separate translation (from Pauthier's French) of the *Ta Hio* in 1928; further English translations of *The Unwobbling Pivot* and *The Analects* followed in 1947 and 1950.

1   *Kung*: Kong Fuzi (K'ung-fu-tzu), i.e. Confucius (551–479 B.C.E.). In Canto LII, Pound noted that his epic moved between the ethics of KUNG and the mystery rites of ELEUSIS.

5–30 Largely a paraphrase of *The Analects* II, xxv, 1–8. Pound follows Pauthier's French spellings of the Chinese names (most of which refer to disciples of Confucius).

7–9   *The Analects* 9, ii, 2.

31–37   *The Analects* 14, xlvi.

38–42   *The Analects* 9, xxii.

45–51   *The Great Digest*, chapters 8 and 9.

56–58   *The Unwobbling Pivot* I, 3–4. Cf. *Analects* II, xv.

59–62   *The Analects* 13, xviii.

63–66   *The Analects* 5, i.

67   *Wang*: Wu Wang, ruled as the first emperor of the Zhou dynasty (c.1046–221 B.C.E.).

69–72   *The Analects* 15, xxv.

73–75   *The Analects* 16, xiii; 17, ix–xi. *The Odes*, i.e. the *Shi Jing* (Book of Songs), composed of 305 poems and traditionally thought to have been compiled by Confucius. Pound translated them as *The Classic Anthology Defined by Confucius* in 1954.

CANTO XIV

A Draft of XVI Cantos (1925). After Canto XIII's glimpse of the earthly paradise made possible by the ethics of Confucius, Cantos XIV and XV, drafted in England in 1919, constitute contemporary Hell Cantos. Pound wrote in his "Postscript to *The Natural Philosophy of Love* by Remy de Gourmont" (1922): "Three channels, hell, purgatory, heaven, if one wants to follow yet another terminology: digestive excretion, incarnation, freedom in the imagination." In 1918–1919, while reading *Ulysses* in manuscript, he was struck by the "excremental" emphasis of Joycean satire, later noting in *Guide to Kulchur* that with *Ulysses* "the sticky, molasses-covered filth of current print, all the fuggs, all the foetors, the whole boil of the European mind, had been lanced" — an apt characterization of the scatological intent of these Hell Cantos.

1   *Io venni* . . . . : "I came to a place mute of all light," *Inferno* V, 28.

3   . . . . *e*: In the original 1925 edition, the number of dots was meant to give a clue to the names that had been elided ("my point being that not even the first but only the last letters of their names had resisted corruption"). Hence, Lloyd George and Wilson here.

22   . . . . *f*: Basil Zaharoff (1849–1936), Turkish-born French arms dealer, director of the Vickers munitions firm during WWI.

41   ΕΙΚΩΝ ΓΗΣ: "Eikôn Gês" ("The Image of the Earth").

49–50   *Pearse and MacDonagh*: Patrick Henry Pearse (1879–1916) and Thomas MacDonagh (1878–1916), leaders of the Irish uprising of 1916, both executed by the British. Cf. Yeats's memorial tribute, "Easter, 1916." *Captain H*: Captain J. Bowen-Colthurst, British officer arrested in Ireland in 1916 for his cold-blooded shooting of political prisoners; eventually court-martialed and confined to Broadmoor Criminal Asylum.

51   *Verres*: Gaius Verres (c.120–43 B.C.E.), Roman administrator notorious for his corruption.

52   *Calvin . . . Alexandria*: Pound considered the Protestant theologian John Calvin (1509–1564) and the early Christian theologian St. Clement of Alexandria (c.150–c.220) exemplars of narrowly puritanical, repressive morality.

74   *usurers*: Dante placed usurers in the seventh circle of Hell (*Inferno*, XVII).

75   *pets-de-loup*: Wolf-farts (or the name for dusty mushrooms, hence French slang for doddering professors).

82   *Invidia*: Envy.

86   *without dignity, without tragedy*: Commenting on this line in his *After Strange Gods* (1934), T. S. Eliot observed: "Mr. Pound's Hell, for all its horrors, is a perfectly comfortable one for the modern mind to contemplate, and disturbing to no one's complacency: it is a Hell for the *other people*, the people we read about in the newspapers, not for oneself and one's friends."

CANTO XVI

A Draft of XVI Cantos (1925). Between Hell and Purgatory.

1   *hell mouth*: Laboring back upwards from the depths of the Inferno at the center of the earth, Dante and Virgil approach the mouth of Hell and the foot of Mount Purgatory just before dawn on Easter Sunday.

9   *Blake*: The early Pound shared W. B. Yeats's interest in William Blake, who illustrated

Dante's *Divine Comedy* in the 1820s.

20 *Peire Cardinal*: anticlerical Provençal troubadour (c.1185–1275) of whom Pound noted in the *Spirit of Romance*: "Peire Cardinal's fable of the sane man in the city gone mad is a weaker equation for what Dante presents as a living man amongst the dead."

21 *Il Fiorentino*: i.e. Dante, who as he left Hell could see Satan, as in a mirror, only backward or "upside down" (*Inferno* XXXIV, 103ff.)

23 *Sordels*: Sordello, see Canto II.4 and *Purgatorio* VI, 58–75.

25 *Augustine*: Mentioned in *Paradiso* X, 120; XII,130; XXXII, 35.

30 *crimen est actio*: "Crime is action."

35 *Palux Laerna*: The swamp of Lerna where Hercules killed Hydra, the poisonous snake.

36 *aqua morta*: Dead water.

57 *patet terra*: "The earth lies open."

62 *Malatesta Novello*: Domenico Malatesta (1418–1465), younger brother of Sigismondo.

71 *Prone in that grass*: Dante, having fainted at Beatrice's reproaches, in *Purgatorio* XXI, 85–90; or, alternately, Rimbaud's sleeping (i.e. dead) soldier of the Franco-Prussian War in his poem "Le Dormeur du val."

72 *et j'entendis des voix . . .* : "and I heard voices." Switch of scene to the hell/purgatory of contemporary warfare for the remainder of the Canto: the Franco-Prussian War of 1870, the Silk War between Venice and Ragusa (see Canto IX.106), World War I, and the Russian Revolution.

74 *Gallifet*: See *Hugh Selwyn Mauberley*, I, vi ("Siena Mi Fe'"), where Monsieur Verog, i.e. the poet Victor Plarr (1863–1929), whose family settled in England after the Franco-Prussian war, told stories about the conflict: "For two hours he talked of Gallifet." In this Canto, Plarr is again recalled as reminiscing about the heroism of the French general Gaston de Gallifet (1830–1909) who, after distinguishing himself in the colonial conquest of Algeria, led the doomed charge of the Chasseurs d'Afrique against the Prussians in the battle of Sedan in September 1870.

84 *Brother Percy*: Algernon Percy (1792–1865), 4th Duke of Northumberland, British naval officer and first lord of the Admiralty, 1852–53.

88 *Ragusa*: Dalmatian port (today's Dubrovnik), Venice's rival in the fifteenth-century Silk War.

107 *Franz Josef*: Emperor of Austria (1830–1916) whose policies contributed to the outbreak of World War I after the assassination of the Austrian archduke Franz Ferdinand in Sarajevo in 1914.

108 *Napoléon Barbiche*: Louis Bonaparte (1808–1873) wore a trademark goatee (barbiche) and was foolhardy enough to declare war on Prussia in July 1870; captured at Sedan in September of that year.

109 *Aldington*: Richard Aldington (1892–1962), member of Pound's Imagiste circle and, from 1913–1919, husband of Pound's early muse, Hilda Doolittle (H.D.); on active military service from 1916–1918. His embittered *Death of a Hero* (1929) is considered one of the finest British WWI novels.

117 *Henri Gaudier*: The French sculptor Henri Gaudier-Brzeska (1891–1915) died in combat at Neuville St. Vaast in June, 1915. Pound published his memorial tribute to him, *Gaudier-Brzeska: A Memoir*, in 1916.

120 *T. E. H.*: Thomas Earnest Hulme (1883–1917), see "Poem Abbreviated from the Conversation of Mr. T. E. H." (p. 52).

129 *Wyndham Lewis*: Percy Wyndham Lewis (1884–1957), Canadian-born British writer and painter and one of the original members of the Vorticist group, served as second lieutenant in the Royal Artillery. After the Third Battle of Ypres in 1917, he was appointed official war artist for the Canadian and British governments.

136 *Windeler*: B. Cyril Windeler, mysterious author of *Elimus*, published by William Bird's
Three Mountains Press in 1923 with designs by Pound's wife Dorothy Shakespear.

144 *Captain Baker*: early Faber editions of the Cantos read "Captain Cochoran."

149 *Fletcher*: Early Faber editions read "Bimmy."

155 *Ernie Hemingway*: Hemingway (1899–1961) served in the Red Cross Ambulance Corps and
experienced the Italian Front. Early Faber editions read "Cyril Hammerton."

158–203 *Et ma foi*: The voice relaying this long narrative of the travails of the French soldiers
(or poilus) on the front in World War I is probably that of Pound's Paris acquaintance,
the painter Fernand Léger (1881–1955), who was mobilized in 1914 and then gassed and
hospitalized in 1917. The demotic French recalls Henri Barbusse's First World War clas-
sic *Le Feu (Under Fire)* of 1916. Translation: "Well, you know, / everybody so skittish. No /
There's a limit; animals, animals ain't / Cut out for this, a horse just don't have what it
takes. / 34-year-old men down on all fours / screaming 'mamma.' But the tough ones /
Out there, over at Verdun, nothing but these big guys / And saw the whole thing com-
ing. / What are they worth, generals, the lieutenant, / they weigh nothing in the balance, /
blockheads all of 'em, / Our captain, about as stuffy as they get / military academy type,
but solid, / Head screwed on straight. You know, out there, / Everything works just right,
and the thieves, every vice, / But the vultures, / there were three of them in our com-
pany, all killed. / They used to go out and just pick the corpses clean, / they would just
go out and do it. / And the Jerries, everything you can imagine, / militarists, et caetera, et
caetera. / All that, but, BUT, / the Frenchman only fights once he has eaten. / But these
poor guys / In the end went on the attack just to eat, / Without orders, wild animals, then
taken / Prisoners; those who spoke French would say: / 'Why? Well, I guess we attacked
just to get some food.' / It's the fa-aa-at, the fat, / trains lurching along at three kilometers
an hour, / creaking and screeching, you could hear them five kilometers away. / (It's what
finished the war.) / Official list of the dead: 5,000,000. / He sez to you, waal, it all stank
of petrol. / No way! I gave him a piece of my mind. / I said to him: You're a damn fool!
You've missed out on the war. / O sure! All the fine gentleman, you've got to admit, / All
of 'em in the rear. / But a fellow like you! / He's a man, a type like that! / The beating he
could have taken! / He was in a factory. / What, burying squad, navvies, with their heads /
thrown back, casting looks like that / Risking one's life for a shovelful, / Get it nice and
square, just right . . ."

205 *Trotzsk*: Leon Trotsky (1879–1940), principal negotiator of the Treaty of Brest-Litovsk of
March 1918, in which humiliating concessions were made to the Central Powers so that
the Bolsheviks would be free to promote the revolution at home.

228 *Come to the bolsheviki*: In October 1922 in Paris, Pound attended (with rapt attention) a lec-
ture by the American journalist Lincoln Steffens on the Russian Revolution. The "man
talking" at l. 222 is Lenin who, according to Steffens's *Autobiography* (1931) had said: "when
you want a government that will do socialism, then — come to the Bolsheviki."

232 *"Pojalouista"*: Russian for "if you please." From Steffens.

236 *Nevsky*: Broad avenue in St. Petersburg that leads into a large square near the train sta-
tion; site of the March 1917 bread riots.

253 *Haig*: Douglas Haig (1861–1928), Commander in Chief of the expeditionary forces in
France and Flanders 1915–1919.

CANTO XVII

Composed 1924, the year that Pound left Paris to settle in Rapallo, Italy. Published in
This Quarter (Paris), Autumn / Winter 1925 / 26. Has sometimes been read as a celebration
of his love for Olga Rudge, whom he met in Paris in late 1922 and with whom he had a
daughter in 1925.

1   *So that*: Cf. Canto I.76.

6   *Io Zagreus!*: Hail, Dionysus!

9   *goddess of the fair knees*: Artemis/Diana.

20   *Chrysophrase*: I.e chrysoprase: brilliant to light green, slightly darker than sea foam.

24   *Nerea*: Pound's amalgamation of Thetis, daughter of Nereus, whose sea-cave was in Thessaly, and Aphrodite/Venus, born of the sea-foam and carried ashore (in Botticelli's "Birth of Venus") on a giant scallop-shell.

46   *choros nympharum*: Chorus of nymphs. Cf. Canto IV.10.

51   *sylva nympharum*: Wood of nymphs.

57   *Memnons*: The statue of Memnon at Thebes, said to respond with a musical tone when struck by the morning light.

73   *Borso . . . i vitrei*: Borso d'Este (1431–71), lord of Ferrara, patron of the arts, peacemaker between Sigismondo Malatesta and Federigo d'Urbino (see Canto IX); *Francesco da Carmagnola* (1380–1431): soldier of fortune in the military service of the Venetian doge, who eventually had him executed for treason. *i vitrei*: Venetian glass makers.

85   *Now supine*: Cf. Odysseus washed up on the beach of Phaiakia (*Odyssey* V, 470–93).

88   *Zothar*: an invented name, like the "Aletha" of l. 91.

95   *Koré*: Persephone, daughter of Demeter.

97   *brother of Circe*: Aeëtes, king of Colchis, from whom Jason retrieved the golden fleece.

CANTO XX

First sixty lines published in *Contact Collection of Contemporary Writers* (Paris, 1925), then as "Part of Canto XX," *Exile* (Paris), Spring 1927.

1   *quasi tinnula*: "As if ringing" [of wedding bells], from Catullus, LXI; cf. Canto IV.3.

2–3 *Ligur' aoide*: "Clear sweet song" (*Odyssey* XII, 183: "[The sirens] raised their clear-toned song"). "*Si no'us . . .*": "If I don't see you, Lady, for whom I must burn,/Even not seeing you cannot match my beautiful thought of you," from Benart de Ventadorn's poem "Can par la flors."

6   *s'adora*: "She [or he] is adored," from Cavalcanti, Sonnet 35.

7–8 *Possum . . .* : "Can I not remember your nature?," from Propertius II, xx, 28, addressing Cynthia. *Qui son . . .* : "Here are Propertius and Ovid."

12–33 *And that year I went up to Freiburg*: In the spring of 1911, Pound visited the Ambrosian Library in Milan, where he had photographs made of the MsR71 superiore, the sole manuscript containing the actual musical notation for two of Arnaut Daniel's poems. He then traveled to Freiburg in Breisgau to show the copy of this manuscript to Emil Lévy (1855–1918), one of the premier German Romance philologists of the day, recommended to him by his undergraduate professor of Romance Languages at the University of Pennsylvania, Hugh Rennert (1858–1927).

28   *noigandres*: A celebrated philological crux in the Canello edition of Arnaut Daniel's poetry (1883), where the thirteenth canzone reads "E jois lo grans, e l'olors de noigandres." Lévy emended the manuscript to read "d'enoi gandres" (see ll. 46–47 below), i.e. "wards off boredom." The Brazilian avant-garde school of poets of the 1950s known as Noigandres took its name from this line.

38   *Agostino . . . Boccata*: Agostino di Duccio, Italian sculptor who executed the bas reliefs for Sigismondo Malatesta's Tempio. Cf. Canto IX. 231. Jacopo Sellaio (1422–1493), Florentine painter. Giovanni Boccata (c.1435–c.1480), Umbrian painter.

43   *Sandro*: Sandro Botticelli (1444–1510), Florentine painter.

55   *remir*: "I gaze." Cf. Canto VII.64.

58   *Parisina*: Cousin of Sigismondo Malatesta; married Niccolò d'Este of Ferrara (1384–1441) in a Malatesta family power play; when the latter discovered Parisina was having an affair

with his natural son Ugo he had them both beheaded.

59–60   *E'l Marchese... pazzo*: "And the Marquis [i.e. Niccolò d'Este] was about to go crazy." In a 1927 letter to his father Pound explained this entire passage as follows: "Nic[c]olo d'Este in a sort of delirium after the execution of Parisina and Ugo ... in the delirium Nic[c]olo remembers or thinks he is watching death of Roland, Elvira on wall or Toro (subject-rhyme with Helen on Wall). . . . The whole reminiscence jumbled or 'candied' in Nic[c]olo's delirium. Take that as a sort of bounding surface from which one gives the subject of the Canto, the lotophagoi: lotus eaters, or respectable dope smokers, and general paradiso."

64   *condit Atesten*: "Founded Este" (referring to the legendary founding of the d'Este family).

65   *Borso*: Third son of Niccolò d'Este, figure of the peace-maker. Cf. Canto XVII.74.

67   *Ganelon*: Prompted by envy, he betrayed the presence of Roland's rear-guard forces to the Saracens in *The Song of Roland*.

73   *l'olofans*: from the Old French for elephant, referring to Roland's ivory horn, which he used to bash in the head of the Saracen.

74   *Tan mare fustes*: "You are ill-starred."

78   *Toro, las almenas*: The battlements of Toro. Scenes that follow are based on Lope de Vega's seventeenth-century play *Las Almenas de Toro* (*The Battlements of Toro*), featuring the characters Elvira, Sancho and Alfonso.

81   *Epi purgo*: "On the wall;" cf. the teichoscopia of *Iliad* III, 153. *Peur de la hasle*: "fear of sunburn," from Hugues Salel's sixteenth-century French translation of the *Odyssey*.

84   *telo rigido*: "With rigid rod."

85   *Ancures*: King Sancho's companion in the Lope de Vega play.

86   *Alf*: Alfonso, brother of King Sancho.

91   *arras*: Painting of Paola and Francesca, Dante's adulterous lovers: a subject rhyme with Parisina and Ugo.

102   *Zoe... Zothar*: Zoë: Byzantine empress (d. 1050) who poisoned her husband, Romanus III, took the throne and married Michael the Paphlagonian. *Marozia*: (d. 945?), wife of Alberic I, prince of Rome, and mistress of Pope Sergius III. *Zothar*: see Canto XVII.88.

105–6   *HO BIOS . . . cosi Elena*: "Life." "Thus I saw Helena" (*Inferno* V, 64).

133–35   *Nel fuoco . . . mi mise*: Pound's gloss from the above-quoted letter: "The 'nel fuoco' is from St. Francis's "Cantico [del sol]": 'My new spouse placeth me in the flame of love.' Then the remarks of the opium smoker about the men who sailed under Ulysses."

135   *croceo*: Saffron-colored.

152   *lotophagoi*: Lotus-eaters. See *Odyssey* IX, 82–104.

155   *silver spilla*: The stalk of the opium plant.

158   *Voce-profondo*: "In a deep voice."

170   *Elpenor*: See Canto I.42.

184   *neson amumona*: "Noble island" (according to Pound: "bullfield where Apollo's cattle were kept").

190   *Khan's hunting leopard*: Unidentified khan who may have sent a leopard to Sigismondo Malatesta. *young Sallustio*: Son of Sigismondo Malatesta and Isotta. Cf. Canto IX.162.

192   *Ac ferae familiars*: "And domesticated wild animals."

194   *Somnus*: Roman god of sleep.

206   *chiostri*: Cloisters.

211   *le donne e i cavalieri*: "The ladies and the knights" (*Purgatorio* XIV, 109, describing the past glory of Romany).

212   *hennin*: High cone-shaped headdress with a thin veil worn by women in the fifteenth century.

216   *Cramoisi and diaspre*: Crimson cloth; jasper.

221   *Vanoka*: An invented name.

from CANTO XXX

Hound and Horn (Cambridge, Mass.), April/June, 1930.

1 *Compleynt:* Cf. Chaucer's "Compleynt unto Pity." Pound comments in *The Spirit of Romance* on Dante's *Inferno*, XX: "When Dante weeps in pity for the sorcerers and diviners, Virgil shows classic stoicism: 'Art thou, too, like the other fools? Here liveth pity when it were well dead. Who is more impious than he who sorrows at divine judgment?" But compare the references to pity in Cantos LXXVI.246 and XCIII.166.

19 *Paphos:* Town on island of Cyprus sacred to Aphrodite.

27–35 *Pedro . . . beside her:* Reprise of Ignez de Castro story. Cf. Cantos III.38 and XLV.49.

from ELEVEN NEW CANTOS XXXI–XLI (1934)

The first thirty Cantos end amid the violence and corruption of the Italian Renaissance, the ambiguous theater of the "rebirth" of Antiquity into Modernity. Cantos XXXI–XLI, which Pound referred to as the "Jefferson/Nuevo Mondo" section of the poem, look to the New World for another, more revolutionary model of the translation of past into present. Cantos XXXI–XXXII are composed of extracts from the letters of Thomas Jefferson and John Adams, architects of the new Republic and its second and third presidents. Canto XXXIII continues with the Adams/Jefferson correspondence, then modulates into nineteenth-century documents (including Marx) illustrative of the dehumanizing evils of industrial capitalism, and closes with quotations that lay bare the corruption of the banking and financial sectors. Canto XXXIV distills the diary of John Quincy Adams, U.S. President from 1825 to 1829, around the time of the outbreak of the so-called Bank War involving Andrew Jackson. Canto XXXV sometimes called the Mitteleuropa Canto, offers a scathing (and occasionally anti-Semitic) satire of the mental and financial state of Vienna in the late 20s. Canto XXXVI is a translation of Cavalcanti's great and cryptic canzone on "the generation of light." Canto XXXVII deals with the Presidency of Martin Van Buren (1837–41), a further chapter in the Republic's battle against the manipulation of monetary supply and value by private banking interests. Canto XXXVIII, where radio broadcasting makes its official entrance, is devoted to the military-industrial-financial complex that abetted the wars of the late 19th and 20th centuries, and that threatens to bring about another one all too soon; Major Douglas's "A + B Theorem" is presented as a nostrum against the economic maladies of the current world-wide depression. Canto XXXIX returns to Book X of the *Odyssey*, with Odysseus enjoying an erotic sojourn on Circe's island before leaving to consult Tiresias in Hades about the way back home, the subject of Canto I. Canto XL returns to the financial conspiracies of the nineteenth century and concludes with a vision of an escape into Elsewhere: Hanno the Catharginian's fourth-century-B.C.E. expedition through the straits of Gibraltar. Canto XLI concludes this section of the poem: in it, Pound records an audience with Mussolini in early 1933 in which Il Duce is quoted as saying of the poet's *Cantos*, "Ma qvesto è divertente," ("How amusing this is"), thus, according their author, "catching the point before the aesthetes had got there." Pound's prose accompaniment to this block of Cantos may be found in his *Jefferson and/or Mussolini* (1935).

CANTO XXXI

Pound's source for these American analects is Andrew Lipscomb and Albert Bergh, eds., *The Writings of Thomas Jefferson*, V, VI, X, XIII, XIV (Washington, D.C., 1905). Cf. also Pound's 1937 essay, "The Jefferson-Adams Letters as a Shrine and a Monument."

1–2 *Tempus loquendi . . . tacendi:* A time to speak, a time to be silent. Inscribed by Sigismondo on the tomb of his wife Isotta, reversing the Vulgate's "'Tempus tacendi, et tempus loquendi" (Ecclesiastes 3:7).

5   *modern dress*: In response to arguments as to whether the statue of George Washington should be done in classical garb or in modern dress.

6   *Congress*: The so-called Congress of the Confederation (1781–1788), which sat at Annapolis.

20   *Bushnell*: Fellow inventor David Bushnell (c.1742–1824), noted for his invention of a submarine.

23–32   *Tom Paine*: In 1801, Paine (1737–1809) was preparing to return to America from his long residence in Europe at Jefferson's invitation.

33   *English papers*: From a Jefferson letter to James Monroe (Paris, August, 1785).

44   *Maison Quarrée*: The Maison Carée in Nîmes, France, a Corinthian temple restored in 1789, the model for Jefferson's new Capitol in Richmond, Virginia.

45   *Madison writing*: From *The Letters and Other Writings of James Madison* (Philadelphia, 1865); President Madison criticizing the performance of his secretary of state Robert Smith (1757–1842).

50   *that country*: i.e. Holland; Jefferson here proposing to John Adams that he borrow money from Holland to pay the U.S. debts to France.

56   *Beaumarchais*: Pierre Augustin Caron de Beaumarchais (1732–1799), French playwright and man of affairs; acting as a secret agent of the French king, he provided arms, ammunition, and supplies for the American Revolution.

63   *Cul de Sac*: Jefferson leased a townhouse situated on the Tête-bout cul-de-sac while in Paris from Oct.1784–Oct. 1785.

71   *Monticello*: Jefferson's residence near Charlottesville, Virginia. The correspondence cited in the rest of this Canto was written during his retirement there after 1809.

72   *Mr Barlow*: Joel Barlow (1754–1812), American diplomat; dispatched to France in 1811 to negotiate a commercial treaty with Napoleon.

73   *Gallatin*: Abraham Alfonse Albert Gallatin (1761–1849), Swiss-born American statesman and financier.

74   *Adair*: James Adair (c.1709–1783), author of *The History of the American Indians* (1775).

81   *Eppes*: John Wayles Eppes (1773–1832), Jefferson's nephew and son-in-law; Jefferson here complaining about a bill in Congress to raise the public debt.

97   *Gosindi*: From a letter of Jefferson's praising the Syntagma of the doctrines of Epicurus by the French materialist philosopher Pierre Gassendi (1592–1655) as "the most rational system remaining of the philosophy of the ancients."

107   *D. Carr*: Dabney Carr (1773–1837), Jefferson's nephew; the five lines of the letter concern the controversy about who exactly proposed the "Committees of Correspondence" as a channel of communication among the colonies before the Revolution.

108   *church of St. Peter*: John Adams to Jefferson (February 1816) referring to "that stupendous monument of human hypocrisy and fanaticism, the church of St. Peter at Rome."

111   *A tiel . . . scripture*: "According to such laws, in old handwriting." Jefferson criticizing an error of translation from the old French in which the "ancient handwriting" (of common law) was mistaken for Holy Scripture.

115   *Bonaparte*: Jefferson's critique (to John Adams) of Napoleon: "a lion in the field only; in civil life, a cold-blooded . . . usurper, without a virtue; no statesman, knowing nothing of commerce, political economy, or civil government."

118   *Hic Explicit Cantus*: Here the Canto ends.

from CANTO XXXVI

First published as "Donna mi Prega by Guido Cavalcanti with Traduction and Commentary by Ezra Pound" in the *Dial*, July 1928; then included in Pound's bilingual Italian-English edition of *Guido Cavalcanti Rime* (Genoa, 1932); further revised in this *Cantos* version of 1934. By this point Pound had been studying the work of the Tuscan poet Guido Cavalcanti

(1255–1300) for some twenty-five years. His bilingual edition of the *Sonnets and Ballate* of 1912 moved the pre-Raphaelite sonneteer of Rossetti's *Early Italian Poets* (1861) into a mode at once more literal and more baroque, while his discovery of the neglected Canzone d'Amore, "Donna mi prega," in the mid-twenties led to a far more "philosophical" reading of Cavalcanti as an "experimental" thinker and "natural philosopher" in the (Arabic) Aristotelian tradition of Avicenna and Averroes, whose meditative focus lay on Love as a form of erotic intellection. Pound's Cavalcanti (compared to his Dante) is a proto-modernist *philosophe*: a mystical materialist whose "light philosophy" provides an opening onto that lost *duecento* "radiant world where one thought cuts through another with clean edge, a world of moving energies," a " 'harmony of the sentient,' where the thought has its demarcation, the substance its *virtù*." In addition to this version of the Canzone, in 1931–32 Pound further "translated" Cavalcanti into a B.B.C.-commissioned radio opera, *Cavalcanti: A Sung Dramedy in 3 Acts*, for which he wrote both the music and the libretto (never produced in his lifetime). Pound's disciple, the "Objectivist" Louis Zukofsky rewrote the Cavalcanti of this Canto into the Marx half of his "A-9" (1940). The two sizes of initial caps indicate Pound's articulation of the strophic structure of Cavalcanti's original.

3   *reason for an affect*: Guido's original reads "accidente," i.e. "accident" (as in medieval philosophy's scholastic distinction between "essence" [permanent] and "accident" [contingent]). Pound explains that he deliberately chose the English word "affect" in order to avoid the distracting confusion between an (injurious) "accident" and the local "accident" (i.e. lived instance) of absolute Love within an alert heart and mind. Pound compared Cavalcanti's philosophy of Love to the Amour Fou of the French surrealists. In his commentary he further observed that Cavalcanti's "definition of 'L'accidente,' i.e. the whole poem, is a scholastic definition in form, it is as clear and definite as the prose treatises of the period, it shows an equal acuteness of thought. It seems to me that the whole of it is a sort of metaphor for the generation of light."

12   *virtu*: Pound comments: "*La virtù* . . . is the potency, the efficient property of a substance or person."

16–17   *Where memory liveth / it takes its state*: Cavalcanti's original here reads: "In quella parte / dove sta memoria." Cf. Canto LXXVI.160.

18   *Formed like a diafan*: Pound translated this line with the treatise *De Luce* by the English thirteenth-century philosopher Robert Grosseteste in mind; one of its passages speaks of things or events as transiting "per plura diphana" ("through more things diaphanous"). The "diaphane" is the medium of visibility, just as the Chinese character is the "medium" for poetry, or a pound a "medium" of exchange.

23   *Cometh from a seen form*: In his notes to the poem, Pound cites Spinoza's "The intellectual love of thing consists in the understanding of its perfections."

56   *that formèd trace in his mind*: From Pound's commentary on Cavalcanti's "formato locho": "Determined locus or habitat . . . As to 'form'; you may here add the whole of medieval philosophy by way of footnote. Form. Gestalt, every spiritual form sets in movement the bodies in which (or among which) it finds itself." Cf. Canto LXXVI.157: "nothing matters but the quality / of the affection— / in the end— that has carved the trace in the mind / dove sta memoria."

CANTO XXXVIII

New English Weekly (London), Sept. 1933.

EPIGRAPH   *"il duol . . . moneta"*: "the woe brought upon the Seine [Paris] / by falsifying the coinage." Dante commenting on Philip the Fair's having debased the value of coinage by a third to finance his Flemish campaigns in 1302.

1   *Metevsky*: Sir Zenos Metevsky, Pound's pseudonym for Sir Basil Zaharoff (1849–1936) the

European munitions magnate, director of Vickers and shareholder in Schneider-Creusot (see l. 137 below). Already placed in Hell in XIV.22. *America del Sud*: South America.

2   *the Pope's*: Pound probably first met Achille Ratti, who served as Pope Pius XI between 1922 and 1939, while the latter was assigned to the Ambrosian Library in Milan in 1911 (see Canto XX.24)—his manners here compared to the Jesuit courtliness of James Joyce.

4–8   *Marconi . . .a'mosphere*: Gugliemo Marconi (1874–1937), the perfector of wireless telegraphy, devised the Vatican's radio station; inaugurated in 1931, its "electric shakes" enabled Pope Pius XI to speak on the world's first transnational broadcasting system. Jimmy Walker: mayor of New York (1926–32).

9   Lucrezia: Lucrezia Borgia(1480–1519), daughter of Pope Alexander IV and sister of Cesare Borgia. May have wanted the rabbit's foot as a charm against conception (see l. 12).

14–18   *thus cigar-makers*: From Dexter Kimball, *Industrial Economics* (1929) on the Cuban practice of having readers in cigar factories who (in pre-radio days) read newspapers and novels aloud to the rollers while they were working.

24   *Akers*: Probably Vickers Ltd., the British armament manufacturer.

27   *Mr Whitney*: Richard Whitney (1888–1974), banker-president of the New York Stock Exchange, credited with attempting to halt the Wall Street panic of 1929.

31   *two Afghans*: Amanullah Khan (1892–1960), then emir of Afghanistan, was one of the five Afghans who traveled to Europe in 1921 to make treaties with Russia and Great Britain to restore their country's right to import munitions through India.

36   *Mr D'Arcy*: William Knox D'Arcy (1849–1917), one of the principal founders of the petrochemical industry in Persia; awarded a sixty-year concession to explore for oil in the region in 1901. Zaharoff later invested in his Anglo-Persian Oil Company.

39   *Mr Mellon*: Andrew Mellow (1855–1937), American financier, named ambassador to Great Britain by President Hoover in 1932.

40   *Mr Wilson*: Thomas Woodrow Wilson (1856–1924), thought by some to be the New Messiah of Peace, suffered from various nervous and physical illnesses after the Treaty of Versailles (1919).

43–44   *And Her Ladyship*: The upper crust: Lady Maud "Emerald" Cunard (1872–1948), mother of "Jenny," i.e. Nancy Cunard (1896–1965), who published the first edition of *A Draft of XXX Cantos* in Paris in 1930. *Agot Ipswich* may be the London hostess Margot Asquith (1864–1945); early Faber editions read "Minny Humbolt."

46   *They begin to kill 'em*: In August, 1914, at the outbreak of WWI, thanks to Kaiser Wilhelm II (1859–1941), Emperor of Germany and Franz Joseph (1830–1916), Emperor of Austria.

53   *Mr Gandhi*: Mohandas Karamchand Gandhi (1869–1948) on ways of peacefully (and economically) resisting British rule over India.

56–58   *Monsieur Untel*: Mister So-and-So did not frequent Paris's most snobbish social club. *Mitsui*: Central bank in Japan and name of Japanese holding company associated with Vickers.

59   *The wood*: From the *Diary of John Quincy Adams*, observing the military uses of nature's bounty.

60–62   *watch factory . . . Tiberius' time*: Revolutionary progress: watch factories outside Moscow; Mussolini draining and reclaiming the Pontine marshes. *Tiberius*: the second Roman emperor (42 B.C.E.–37).

63   *Beebe*: Charles William Beebe (1877–1962), author of *Beneath the Tropic Seas: A Record of Diving among the Coral Reefs of Haiti* (1928).

64–65   *Rivera*: Miguel Primo de Rivera (1870–1930), dictator of Spain (1923–1930). *Infante*: probably the eldest son of the last king of Spain, Alfonso XIII.

68–70   *Schlossmann*: A figure Pound met during his Spring 1928 stay in Vienna. *Anschluss*: German annexation of Austria (1938).

73–75 *white man . . . drum beat*: Leo Frobenius (1878–1938), German anthropologist and Africanist, whose Frankfurt Research Institute for the Morphology of Culture Pound first visited in 1930. In the fifth volume of his *Erlebte Erteile* (1925–1929), Frobenius recounts how the Babunda tribesman in Biembe (mistakenly identified as "Baluba" by Pound), although initially hostile, subsequently welcomed him after the occurrence of a thunderstorm which they credited to his powers. He was thereafter referred to in messages conveyed in their local drumbeat language as "the white man who made the tempest in Biembe" — an African example of radio-like communication over the airwaves. Pound tells the story in his contribution to Nancy Cunard's *Negro Anthology* (London, 1934) and again in *The Pisan Cantos.*

77 *Kosouth*: Ferencz Kossuth (1841–1914), Hungarian noble and leader of the (anti-Austrian) Party of Independence.

85 *the Tyrol*: The South Tyrol, Austrian territory transferred to Italy by the 1919 Treaty of Versailles.

89 *Bruhl*: Lucien Lévy-Bruhl (1857–1939), French anthropologist best known in translation for his *Primitive Mentality* (1923) and *How Natives Think* (1926).

99 *Mr Blodgett*: Lorin Blodget, author of *The Textile Industries of Philadelphia* (1880).

102–25 *Douglas*: Major Clifford Hugh Douglas (1879–1952), British economist and exponent of the theory of Social Credit, under whose sway Pound came in 1919. He here quotes Douglas's "A + B Theorem" (the lynchpin of his critique of capitalism) in *Economic Democracy* (1920). The total of wages, profits, and production costs is divided into two parts: "A" represents payments to individuals in the form of wages or dividends; "B" payments for the cost of raw materials, bank charges, and other overhead. Logically, the price of any commodity should be the sum of "A" plus "B" but because "B" takes money out of circulation (in the form of bank charges, etc.), the money made available as purchasing power can never catch up with prices, resulting in under-consumption.

129–81 *Herr Krupp*: Alfred Krupp (1812–1887), founder of the German munitions dynasty, who made his fortune by selling cannons to both sides of armed conflicts: Britain and Russia during the Crimean War, or France and Prussia during the Franco-Prussian War. The remainder of this Canto deals with the cozy financial arrangements between the French steel industry (Schneider-Creusot), the armaments industry, the banking industry (such as the Schneider-Creusot and Zaharoff-controlled Bank of the Paris Union of l. 166), corrupt politicians (associated with the Comité des Forges in l. 167) and newspapers (ll. 173–75), often in collusion with the German Krupps (or their successors, Gustave von Bohlen und Halbach of l. 146). Pound drew his information about this military-industrial-financial complex from the works of such muckrakers as Robert Pinot (*Le Comité des forges de France au service de la nation*, 1919), Richard Lewinsohn (*A la conquête de la richesse*, 1928), and Fenner Brockway (*The Bloody Traffic*, 1933).

180–81 *"faire passer . . . la nation"*: "Put business interests before those of the nation."

from THE FIFTH DECAD OF CANTOS (1937)

Section entitled "Siena/The Leopoldine Reforms" in Pound's *Selected Cantos* (1967). Cantos XLII and XLIII explore the early seventeenth-century establishment of the Sienese bank, the Monte dei Paschi (Mountain of the Pastures), the oldest surviving bank in the world and for Pound the model of a financial institution whose funds were literally grounded in the revenues from its grazing rights to nearby sheep pastures: "The lesson is the very basis of solid banking. The CREDIT rests in ultimate on the ABUNDANCE OF NATURE, on the growing grass that can nourish the living sheep." Canto XLIV pursues Sienese history into the eighteenth century, with the political, financial, and agrarian reforms instituted by the enlightened Pietro Leopoldo, Grand Duke of Tuscany (1765–1790). Canto XLV contains Pound's celebrated denunciation of Usury. Canto XLVI, which he considered the "turning point" of his poem because he had at last discovered the inception of the *ex nihilo* creation of money, is devoted to the establishment of the Bank of England in 1694, a bank that (in marked contrast to the Sienese Monte dei Paschi), according to its founder William Paterson, "*Hath benefit of interest on all/the moneys, which it, the bank, creates out of nothing.*" Canto XLVII rehearses an erotic descent into the Underworld (cf. Canto I), based in part on the Adonis myth described in Frazer's *Golden Bough*. After Canto XLVIII, a miscellany of reminiscences past and present, Canto XLIX, known as the Seven Lakes Canto and translated from the Chinese, moves into "the fourth; the dimension of stillness." Canto L juxtaposes the Leopoldine Reforms in eighteenth-century Tuscany with the new political and philosophical mindset that led to the American Revolution; Napoleon's defeat at Waterloo is seen as the end of this Enlightenment interlude in European history. Canto LI restates the imprecations against Usury of Canto XLV.

CANTO XLV

First published as "Canto — 'with Usura'" in the English monetary reform journal *Prosperity* (London), February 1936. In a 1938 review in *Poetry*, Delmore Schwartz observed: "It is interesting to observe in passing that in this particular Canto the attack on usury as a poetic statement can be separated from its connection with a particular economic theory by the mere device of substituting another three-syllable word with the same accents, for example, 'capital.'" In a note dated July 4, 1972, to his publisher on the occasion of the gathering of his *Selected Prose* by William Cookson, Pound wrote: "re USURY: I was out of focus, taking a symptom for a cause. / The cause is AVARICE."

6–7 *hath no man a painted paradise . . . harpes et luz*: From the "Ballade pour prier Nôtre Dame" in François Villon's *Testament*, in which "a pitiful old women" speaks of looking at the "painted paradise on the church wall" filled with "harps and lutes."

11 *Gonzaga*: See Canto III.41. Alludes to Mantegna's fresco painting "Gonzaga, His Heirs and His Concubines" in the Palace of the Dukes in Mantua.

18 *with usura the line grows thick*: Pound observes in *Guide to Kulchur* that "finer and future critics of art will be able to tell from the quality of painting the degree of tolerance or intolerance of usury in the age and milieu that produced it."

26 *murrain*: Plague, pestilence.

28 *Pietro Lombardo*: Italian sculptor (1435–1515) who ornamented Dante's tomb at Ravenna and carved the mermaids at the church of Santa Maria dei Miracoli in Venice.

30 *Duccio*: Agostino di Duccio, sculptor of the bas-reliefs in Sigismondo Malatesta's Tempio. Cf. Canto IX.231.

31 *Pier della Francesca . . . Bellin'*: Two more contributors to Malatesta's Tempio: Piero della Francesca (c.1416–92) with his fresco "Sigismondo Malatesta Before St. Sigismund" and Giovanni Bellini (1430–1576) with his painting of the "Pietà."

32 *'La Calunnia'*: "Calumny," a painting by Sandro Botticelli (1445–1510) in the Uffizi Gallery, Florence.

33 *Angelico . . . Praedis*: Fra Angelico (c.1400–1455), Florentine painter; Ambrogio Praedis (c.1455–c.1506), Milanese portrait painter.

34 *Adamo mi fecit*: "Adam made me," the sculptor's signature on a hand-made column in the Church of San Zeno in Verona

35–36 *St Trophime . . . Saint Hilaire*: Churches in Arles and Toulouse visited by Pound in 1919.

41 *cramoisi*: Crimson cloth.

42 *Memling*: Hans Memling (c.1430–1495), painter of the Flemish school.

47 *CONTRA NATURAM*: Against Nature. Cf. Book I of Aristotle's *Politics* (the basis of the

condemnation of usury by Catholic Canon Law), where the distinction is made between "natural" transactions, related to the satisfaction of needs and yielding wealth that is limited in quantity by the purpose it serves, and "unnatural" transactions, aimed merely at monetary gain and yielding wealth that is potentially without limits. Usury is condemned as "of all forms the most contrary to nature," given that "money is intended to be used in exchange, not to increase at interest" (I,10).

48   *Eleusis*: Town in Attica where the Eleusinian mysteries in celebration of Demeter were performed; understood by Pound as a place of sacramental coition.

49   *Corpses . . . banquet*: Cf. the necrophile reification of the dead queen Ignez de Castro in Cantos III.38 and XXX.27–33, here rhymed with commodity fetishism.

NOTE   *Medici bank*: The bank in Florence established by Cosimo de Medici (1389–1464) failed, Pound claimed in Canto XCIV, "from accepting too many deposits." Not in the original Canto XLV, this note was added in all New Directions editions from 1970 onward.

CANTO XLVII

1   *Who even dead*: Description of Tiresias (*Odyssey* X, 493) and, for Pound, emblematic of the "Greek honor of human intelligence."

3–9   *First must thou . . .road's end*: Adaption of Circe's instructions to Odysseus (*Odyssey* X, 490–95).

5   *Ceres*: Latin name of Demeter, goddess of the harvest and central figure in the Eleusinian Mysteries (interpolated by Pound into the *Odyssey* passage).

12–13   *phtheggometha thasson*: Let us raise our voices without delay (the crew before the palace of Circe, *Odyssey* X, 228).

15–19   *The small lamps*: During the July festival of the Montallegre Madonna in Rapallo, local women would set votive lights adrift in the Tigullian Gulf—a pagan practice here rhymed with the vegetation rites held to celebrate the death of the Syrian Tammuz/Greek Adonis, the yearly slain, whose blood caused the rivers to run red to the sea, causing the shore to be fringed with crimson. See James George Frazer, *The Golden Bough* (1890). Cf. Canto XCI.59–64.

23   *Scilla*: Scylla, a sea monster with six heads, each with a triple row of teeth, and a bark like a dog, lived in a cave opposite Charybdis (*Odyssey* XII, 80–100).

26–29   *Tu Diona . . . Adonin*: You Dione (i.e. Aphrodite). *Kai Morai' Adonin*: From Bion's "Lament for Adonis," ("The fates [cry over] Adonis").

41   *naturans*: obeying its nature. This and the other examples of nature's drives are taken from Remy de Gourmont's *Natural Philosophy of Love*, translated by Pound in 1922. Cf. Canto CXIII.91.

43   *Molü*: Herb given to Odysseus by Hermes to resist Circe's drugs (*Odyssey* X, 302–335).

50–61   *Begin thy plowing . . . hill road*: Adapted from Hesiod's *Works and Days*, 383–91.

69   *Tellus*: Roman goddess of the earth.

74   *cunnus*: Cunt.

79   *Io!*: Hail.

87   *Zephyrus*: West wind. *Apeliota*: East wind.

CANTO XLIX

Known as The Seven Lakes Canto. Based on an old Japanese manuscript book (entitled *Sho-Sho Hakkei* [The River + Eight Classes of Scenery]) owned by Pound's parents, which contained eight Chinese and eight Japanese poems illustrated by paintings. Pound initially translated the poems with the help of a Chinese visitor to Rapallo in the spring of 1928. The Chinese poems evoking famous scenes in the lake region of Hunan have been rearranged into the following lines of this Canto: 2–6; 7–17; 18–19; 20–24; 25–28; 29–32.

31   *Tsing*: Pound's addition. Probably Kangxi, the third Qing emperor (ruled 1661–1712). His reign is the subject of Cantos LVIII–LXI and his *Sacred Edict* lies at the core of Cantos XCVIII–XCIX.

34   *Geryon*: In *Inferno*, XVII, monstrous guardian of the eighth circle of Hell and symbol of Fraud; for Pound, Geryon is "twin with usura."

37–40   *KEI . . . KAI*: From the Fenollosa notebooks (see headnote to *Cathay*). Japanese transcription of an ancient poem ascribed to Emperor Shun (c.2255–2205 B.C.E.). Translated by Pound in 1958 as: "Gate, gate of gleaming,/knotting, dispersing,/flower of sun, flower of moon/day's dawn after day's dawn new fire."

41–45   *Sun up . . . what is it?*: From Fenollosa. Translation of ancient Chinese folk song ("Chi-yang ko" or "Beating sod song") dating from the time of Shun's predecessor, Emperor Yao.

from CANTOS LII–LXXI (1940)

Cantos LII–LXI, known as the Chinese History Cantos, provide a continuous chronological sweep of the Middle Kingdom's history from its legendary beginnings in the Xia dynasty (c.2205 B.C.E.) through the reign of the Qianlong emperor (1736–1795). Cantos LXII–LXXI cut from eighteenth-century China to the synchronous American colonies to record the origins and development of the Adams Dynasty and with it, that of the Republic. Pound's source for his Chinese History Cantos was *Histoire générale de la Chine, ou Annales de cet empire* (Paris, 1777–83) by the Jesuit missionary Joseph-Anne-Marie de Moyriac de Mailla. He follows de Mailla's French spellings of the Chinese throughout.

from CANTO LII
After a page of incoherent anti-Semitic vituperation which required that five complete lines and two references to the Rothschilds (replaced by "Stinkschuld" in later printings) be blacked out by dark lines in the original 1940 Faber and New Directions editions, the Canto moves into the orderly civic empyrean of Confucian China.

50–154   *Know then . . . his imposts*: Adapted from the *Book of Rites* (or *Li Ji*), one of the five foundational classics of the Confucian canon. Describing the social forms, the governmental system and the ceremonial rites of the early Zhou Dynasty (c.1050–256 B.C.E.), its original text was believed to have been compiled by Confucius himself. The term *Li* literally means "rites," but refers more broadly to those traditional rules of conduct that harmonize the ethics of good government and social etiquette with the order of nature. Pound here works from *Li Ki, ou mémoires sur les bienséances et les cérémonies, Texte chinois avec une double traduction en français et en latin* (Ho Kien Fou, 1913) by the French sinologist Seraphin Couvreur (1835–1919).

64   *Son of Heaven*: Traditional title of the Chinese Emperor.

91   *Ming T'ang*: The Temple of Light (or Wisdom) where the imperial family of China worshipped its ancestors.

99   *manes*: Spirits of the dead.

155   *Lord Palmerston*: Henry John Temple Palmerston (1784–1865), British statesman, belonging to the Irish peerage; sought to reclaim the marshes and improve the living conditions of the tenants on his estates in Sligo.

[IDEOGRAM]: zhi (chih³) [M939] ("to stop").

from CANTO LIII
Covers, via De Mailla, early Chinese history from the great factive emperors of the first (Xia), second (Shang), and third (Zhou) dynasties through the days of Confucius (551–479 B.C.E.).

1   *Yeou*: Mythical ruler You Chaoshi taught his people to build bird-nest-like huts out of branches.

2–3 *Seu Gin*: You's successor Sui Rensi's innovations are listed here.

4   *Fou Hi*: Fu Xi, first of the Three Sovereigns.

8   *Chin Nong*: Shen Nong (2838–2698 B.C.E.), the third of the Three Sovereigns, known as the Prince of Cereals for his introduction of wheat, rice, millet, barley and peas.

14 *Souan Yen*: First of the Legendary Emperors, ruled under the name of Huang Di or "Yellow Emperor" (c.2698–2597 B.C.E.)

24 *Ti Ko*: Di Ku, great grandson of the Yellow Emperor, ruled c.2436–2366 B.C.E.

27 *YAO*: Model sage-king who ruled c.2356–2258 B.C.E.

30 *YU*: Founder of the Xia dynasty, ruled c.2205–2197 B.C.E.

32 *Ammassi*: System of grain stores instituted by Mussolini to facilitate distribution.

39 *Tsing-mo*: Sacrificial herb compared to *moly*, the magical herb Hermes gave Odysseus to protect him from Circe's spell.

40 *Chun*: Shun, successor to Yao, ruled c.2255–2205 B.C.E. *Chang Ti*: the Great Spirit.

42–43 *que vos vers . . . conforme*: "That your verses express your intentions / and that the music conform."

44 *YAO*: Corresponding ideogram of his name [M7295] means "eminent."

45 *CHUN*: His ideogram [M5936] means "wise."

46 *YU*: His ideogram [M7620] means "insect" or "reptile."

47 *KAO-YAO*: The ideograms [M3285, M6156] mean "bless kiln."

59 *Tching Tang*: Cheng Tang, founder of the Shang dynasty, ruled c.1766–1753 B.C.E.

69 *der im Baluba*: See Canto XXXVIII.74. Frobenius's reputed powers to induce thunderstorms here rhymed with Cheng Tang's sacrificial offering of himself to the gods on a mountain in order to bring seven years of drought to an end.

71–73 *MAKE IT NEW*: Cheng Tang inscribed these words on his bathtub to commemorate the end of the drought effected by his act of sacrifice. The ideograms xin (hsin¹) [M2737] and ri (jih⁴) [M3124], according to Pound, show 1) an axe (to the right) clearing the underbrush (to the left) and 2) the light of day.

79 *Hia is down*: Xia, the first dynasty (2205–1766 B.C.E.) was followed by the Shang dynasty (c.1766–1121 B.C.E.) founded by Cheng Tang.

175 *Kang*: Kang Wang, third emperor of the Zhou dynasty, ruled 1078–1052 B.C.E.

177 *Tcheou*: The Zhou dynasty (c.1134–256 B.C.E.); its respect for tradition is celebrated in Confucius's *Book of Rites*, summarized in Canto LII.

179 *Wen-wang and Wu-wang*: Duke of Zhou and his son, the first emperor of the Zhou dynasty.

184 *Chao-kong*: Duke of Shao, brother of Wu Wang, counselor to Kang Wang.

349 *Kungfutseu*: I.e. Confucius.

350 *C. T. Mao*: Corrupt official whose execution Confucius made a condition for his serving as minister for the state of Lu.

355 *Tsi*: To counter Confucius's influence in Lu, the prince of Qi (Tsi) sent singing girls to corrupt its prince; Confucius reacted by retiring from his position and moving to the neighboring state of Wei.

357–64 *At Tching . . . quite correct*: Description of Confucius, the latter modestly only admitting his resemblance to a "lost dog."

369–70 *Tchin and Tsai*: The princes of these states intercepted Confucius on his way to visit the Prince of Zhou in 489 b.c.e. and drove him into the desert, where he was rescued by Zhou's troops.

371 *Tsao*: Small state in Shandong that lasted from c.1122 to 501 B.C.E.

372 *Kung cut*: Upon his retirement at age sixty-eight in 493 B.C.E., Confucius set to editing the Odes.

373–75   *Comet . . . 479:* Confucius's death coincided with a comet in the fortieth year of the reign of Qing Wang, twenty-fifth Emperor of the Zhou dynasty.

394–99   *Hillock:* Nickname of Confucius, not (as Pound believed) of his father, who is the subject of the following anecdote: as an officer in Lu's army, he bravely held up a portcullis so that his besieged troops could escape. The Canto ends with the Chinese ideogram for the dynasty Zhou (Chou) [M1293].

CANTO LXX

The next to last of the Adams Cantos. Pound's source of quotations is Charles Francis Adams, ed., *The Works of John Adams* (Boston, 1850), VIII, IX.

1–4   *My situation . . . 1791:* Adams served as George Washington's vice-president from 1789 to 1797, a largely honorific position in which he often felt frustrated.

5   *Mr Pinckney:* On assuming the Presidency, Adams became embroiled in what came to be known as the "XYZ Affair" (l. 24). In early 1797 a commission was dispatched to France to meet with foreign minister Talleyrand (1754–1838) in order to iron out a number of disagreements that had developed between the two former allies as a result of John Jay's favorable treaty with England in 1794 and Adams and his Federalist Party's criticisms of the increasingly undemocratic and expansionist course that French policies were taking. The members of the American commission to France mentioned below were Charles Pinckney (1746–1825), Elbridge Gerry (1744–1814), and John Marshall (1755–1825). The three reported back that the French agents X, Y, and Z (later revealed to be Conrad Hottinguer, a Swiss banker; Pierre Bellamy; and Lucien Hauteval), set the following conditions for negotiations: a $250,000 bribe for Talleyrand, a twelve million dollar loan to the French to help defray the cost of their current wars, and a public apology from Adams. Adams refused, but the XYZ Affair provided further fodder for the pro-English faction of the Federalists, led by Alexander Hamilton, who wanted war with France. The Democrat-Republicans, led by Jefferson, were in turn pro-France and antiwar. Although Adams continued to look for diplomatic maneuverability, the conflict erupted into what was dubbed the Quasi-War: between 1798 and 1800 American and French warships fought battles in the Caribbean (cf. l. 11) and off the East Coast of the U.S. The Adams administration eventually negotiated an end to the hostilities with the 1800 Treaty of Mortefontaine. Adams not only wanted to chart a course avoiding the extremes of either the pro-French or pro-English factions, but, more importantly, wanted to avoid involving the U.S. in any European conflicts: "eternal neutrality in all wars of Europe" (l. 44) — which prefigures Pound's own American isolationist position on World War II.

7   *Blount:* William Blount (1749–1800), expelled from the Senate in 1797 for plotting to aid the British in getting control of Spanish Florida and French Louisiana.

12   *office of Secretary:* Adams suspected arch-rival Hamilton of wanting to establish a Secretary of the Treasury whose powers would rival that of the President.

13   *Vervennes:* Charles Gravier comte de Vergennes (1717–1787), French statesman and supporter of the American War of Independence under Louis XVI.

15–16   *Hamilton . . . intrigue:* Refers to Hamilton's intrigues to be named second-in-command under Washington in the newly re-organized American military during the Quasi-War.

20   *Pickering:* Timothy Pickering (1745–1829) Adams's Secretary of State until dismissed in 1800 for his pro-Hamilton and pro-war policies (l. 35–37).

27   *Vans M/:* William Vans Murray (1760–1803), Appointed by Adams as minister to The Hague in 1797 and later vital in the negotiations with France that led to 1800 peace accords.

40   *pro hac vice:* "In return."

44   *I leave the state:* Upon learning that he had been defeated for reelection in Dec. 28, 1800, Adams wrote in a letter: "I shall leave the State with its coffers full, and the fair prospects

of a peace with all the world smiling in its face." The following lines give the tied elec-
toral votes for Thomas Jefferson and Aaron Burr (with Jefferson eventually being chosen
by the House to succeed Adams).

50 *formato loco*: Formed space. From Calvacanti' "Donna mi prega," translated in Canto
XXXVI.56 as "forméd trace."

51–54 *My compliments . . . somehow*: These lines and the remainder of the Canto return to events
in Adams's life from 1773 to his first years as vice-president. In a letter to James Warren he
suggested in a spirit of jest that the recent events of the Boston Tea Party (Dec. 16, 1773) be
retold in a mythological form, with the various kinds of tea (Hyson, Congo, and Bohea)
appearing as sea-nymphs and goddesses.

55–58 *Tories . . . slow starvation*: From an early 1774 letter to Warren, Adams's musings on the
current political climate.

58–61 *a conclave . . . statesmen*: Adams's thoughts after being selected to the first Congress at
Philadelphia in June, 1774.

62 *treasons . . . praemunires*: Fears of British duplicity.

63 *Virginia . . . tobacco*: As a way of reducing its economic dependence on Britain.

66–68 *old to bind . . . balance of land*: From a long meditation on majority vs. minority rights
in a government by and of the people.

70–71 *Justinian . . . Taylor*: From a letter on the "beauties" of the law: Justinian, Byzantine em-
peror (r.527–565) who completely revised Roman law into the Corpus Juris Civilis; Henry
de Bracton (d.1268), author of the first systematic treatise of law in England; Jean Domat
(1625–1696), French jurist, John Ayliffe (1676–1732), English jurist, John Taylor (1703–1766),
English jurist.

74 *you are right, Rush*: From a 1778 letter to Benjamin Rush, warning of regulation of prices.

76–82 *are still stockjobbers . . . to go through*: False rumors spread by the British about dissen-
sions among the Americans or between the Americans and their French allies, including
rumors that there were Russians ready to go to war.

87–97 *quails . . . Holland*: Splicing of two Adams letters, one written from The Hague in June
1782, the other from Paris in November 1782.

98–100 *populariser . . . system*: Vice-president Adams in 1797, still as suspicious of French
motives as he was fifteen years earlier; here, they are seen to be backing Jefferson to un-
dermine Adams's Federalist party.

104 *Dutch interest*: In 1782, Adams had negotiated a five-million guilder loan to the United
States by the Dutch.

114 *meminisse juvebit*: "It will be pleasing to recall."

118–22 *that there were Americans . . . in my absence*: In the commercial treaty he negotiated
with Britain in 1782, Adams was especially determined that the right of the United States
to the fisheries along the Atlantic coast be recognized.

133 [IDEOGRAM]: The ideogram zhong (chung¹) [M1504], "middle." Part of the title of one
of the Confucian Classics that Pound translated: the *Chung Yung*, or *Unwobbling Pivot*.

138 *Dum Spiro*: "While I breathe" (from a 1790 Adams letter). Pound added the "Amo" to
make it "While I breathe I love."

139 *nec lupo . . .* : "nor entrust a lamb to wolf" (Adams's "fundamental maxim of government").

from THE PISAN CANTOS (1948)

First published in 1948 by New Directions, under a title chosen by its publisher, James Laugh-
lin. The Faber edition, delayed by potential libel issues, appeared a year later. The Fellows in
American Literature of the Library of Congress (which included the 1948 Nobel Prize winner

T. S. Eliot, Conrad Aiken, W. H. Auden, Louise Bogan, Robert Lowell, Katherine Anne Por-
ter, Karl Shapiro, Allen Tate, and Robert Penn Warren) voted to award the book the first an-
nual Bollingen Prize of $10,000. When the prize was made public in early 1949, considerable
controversy ensued; the New York Times headline read "Pound, In Mental Clinic, Wins Prize
for Poetry Penned in Treason Cell." As a result of the negative publicity, Congress barred the
Library from giving any further awards or prizes in the future.

On July 26, 1943, the U.S. Department of Justice had officially indicted Pound for treason
for his broadcasts over Radio Rome; he replied to the Attorney General that his radio work
was merely an exercise of his constitutionally guaranteed right to free speech. When the war
ended in northern Italy in early May 1945, Pound was arrested at his home in Sant'Ambrogio
in the hills above Rapallo by local partisans and briefly detained. Upon his release, he turned
himself over to the American Counter Intelligence Center in Genoa, where he remained for
the next three weeks, undergoing interrogation by an FBI agent. On May 24, he was transferred
to the U.S. Army's Disciplinary Training Center in Pisa, a military prison camp for American
soldiers, where he was placed in a maximum-security cage. After three weeks in solitary con-
finement, Pound suffered a mental breakdown and was transferred to an officer's tent in the
medical compound area, where he began composing Cantos in late June or early July, shifting
the poem back into contemporary English after the two previous Cantos (LXXII and LXXIII),
which were written entirely in Italian and published in Fascist newspapers in early 1945. Apart
from the Chinese dictionary and the edition of the Confucian Classics he had brought with
him from Sant'Ambrogio, the only reading materials mentioned in the The Pisan Cantos are
a Bible, a Catholic Prayer Book, stray issues of Time magazine, and The Pocket Book of Verse.
Writing in the expectation of his imminent execution for treason, Pound modeled his prison
poem after François Villon's Le Testament — a last will and testament in which the memories of
his personal odyssey through the twentieth century are transmitted to posterity as a gift and a
warning. On November 17, after nearly five months of incarceration at the DTC, Pound was
flown back to Washington, D.C., to stand trial. In late December of 1945, he was committed to
St. Elizabeths Hospital, a federal mental institution in Washington, there to remain until 1958.

from CANTO LXXIV

3   Manes: Third-century Persian founder of the Manicheans, murdered for his heretical
     teachings by the Zoroastrians.

4–6 Thus Ben . . . dead bullock: After Benito Mussolini and his mistress Claretta Petacci were
     captured and summarily executed by partisans on April 28, 1945, their bodies were brought
     to Milan and strung up by the heels in the Piazzale Loreto, thus "twice crucified." As a
     sacrificial victim, Mussolini (whose unofficial title, Il Duce, is often translated by Pound
     as "the Boss") evokes the symbolic slaying of Dionysus in the form of a bull (*bos* in Latin).

7   DIGONOS: "Twice-born," Greek epithet for Dionysus, born once from his mother,
     Semele, and then from the thighs of his father, Zeus.

9–10 Possum: Pound's nickname for T. S. Eliot, whose poem the "Hollow Men" sees the
     world as ending "Not with a bang but a whimper."

11   Dioce: Deïoces, the first great ruler of the Medes, built the city of Ectabana in the 6th
     century B.C.E.; according to Herodotus it was encircled by seven rising concentric walls
     in a variety of colors. Cf. Canto IV.101.

12   The suave eyes: Canto LXIV originally began here, before Pound revised the poem in
     October, appending the previous 11 lines, written on a sheet of toilet paper and perhaps
     withheld, given their explicitly pro-Mussolini tenor.

14   the way: I.e. the Confucian Way or Truth: dao (tao⁴).

14–18 Citations from the Confucian Classics, The Unwobbling Pivot I, 1 and Mencius III, 4, xiii,
     later translated by Pound: "After Confucius's death, when there was talk of regrouping,

Tsang declined, saying: 'Washed in the Keang and Han, bleached in the autumn sun's-slope, what whiteness can one add to that whiteness, what candour?'"

128   *Mt Taishan*: Tai Shan, or Great Mountain, a sacred site in China's Shantung province, here visually rhymed with one of the mountains in the Apuan Alps to the northeast of the DTC.

129   *Carrara stone*: Marble from the nearby quarry of Carrara was used in the construction of the leaning tower of Pisa.

131   *Kuanon*: Japanese form of Guanyin (Kuan-yin), the Chinese bodhisattva, goddess of mercy.

132–35   *Linus...shell*: Bishops of Rome in the first century, among the list of Apostles and Martyrs invoked in the Catholic Prayer Book. The design on the back of the priest's chasuble at a mass held at the DTC may have suggested the image of the scarab at the altar.

137–38   [IDEOGRAM]: Xian (hsien³) [M2692], "manifest, display, be illustrious." Contains the radicals for sun and moon and is sometimes translated by Pound as "tensile light descending."

138   *virtù*: "Virtue," glossed by Pound in his Confucian translations as "The *virtù*, i.e. this self-knowledge [looking straight into the heart and acting hence] is the root."

139   *sunt lumina*: "Are lights." From the Latin of the medieval Neoplatonic philosopher (and heretic) John Scotus Erigena (c.810–c.877): "Omnia, quae sunt, lumina sunt." Cf. ll. 155–57 below: "all things that are are lights."

140–45   *Shun...Yao...Yu*: Three legendary early rulers of China, often referred to in the Confucian classics as paragons of virtuous statecraft.

146   *4 giants*: Guard towers at the four corners of the DTC stockade. Cf. *Inferno* XXXI, 41–44.

150–51   *to redeem Zion*: Cf. Isaiah 1:27: "Zion shall be redeemed by justice, and those in her who repent, by righteousness." As opposed, presumably, to the policies of "David rex," i.e. King David ("the prime s.o.b." omitted from the 1949 Faber edition).

155   *the Oirishman*: The Irishman is Scotus Erigena and "King Carolus," the Holy Roman Emperor Charles II, grandson of Charlemagne.

158–60   *and they dug him up*: The body of Erigena was supposedly ("soi disantly") exhumed as part of a witch-hunt against Manichean heretics — although there is no record of this (it was the bones of his disciple, Amaury de Bène, that were dug up and scattered in 1210). "Les Albigeois," or Albigensians, were persecuted and eventually destroyed in a crusade against heresy launched by Simon de Montfort in the thirteenth century.

161–69   *and the fleet at Salamis*: Themistocles won the battle of Salamis in ships built by money loaned by the state of Athens and not by private banks — an early example of Social Credit. The Soviet statesman Lenin is quoted ("dixit Lenin") attacking the war-profiteering of the international arms industry.

163   *Tempus tacendi...*: "A time to be silent, a time to speak." Malatesta's motto, inscribed on Isotta's tomb in the Tempio. Cf. Canto XXXI.1.

170   *23rd year of the effort*: Pound observed the Italian Fascist calendar, in which all events were dated from Mussolini's March on Rome in 1922. 1945 was thus year 23.

171–73   *and Till was hung*: Louis Till, an African American trainee at the DTC executed on July 24, 1945, here mythologically associated with Zeus's ram, whose golden fleece Jason and the Argonauts hunted in the kingdom of Colchis. Till was the father of Emmet Till, whose cold-blooded murder at age fourteen by two white men in Mississippi in 1955 sparked the Civil Rights Movement in the South.

176–77   [IDEOGRAM]: in Pound's hand: mo⁴ [M4557], "not, no," echoing the Greek "No man" ("ou tis") and visually evoking "a man on whom the sun has gone down." The Greek "ou tis" (or "nobody") often adopted by Pound to refer to himself in the Pisans, was the name Odysseus gave to himself to trick the Cyclops Polyphemus.

216 *in periplum*: From the Latin "periplus," a circumnavigation defined in Canto LIX as "peri-plum, not as the land looks on a map/but as sea bord seen by men sailing."

219 *hamadryas*: Hamadryad, or tree nymph.

220 *Vai soli*: I.e. "vae soli," from Ecclesiastes 4:10 ("Woe to him who is alone"), via Pound's translation of Jules Laforgue's "Pierrots: Scène courte mais typique."

224 'ΗΛΙΟΝ ΠΕΡΙ 'ΗΛΙΟΝ: "HELION PERI HELION" ("The sun around the sun").

226 *Lucina*: Epithet of Diana, the moon goddess; also the name of the Roman Goddess of childbirth.

230–35 *Bunting*: Basil Bunting (1900–1985), jailed as conscientious objector in 1918, conducted a hunger-strike in prison. His collection of poems, *Redimiculum Matellarum* ("A Garland of Chamberpots"), was published in 1930.

240 *Joe Gould . . . cummings*: Joe Gould (1889–1957), Greenwich Village bohemian, author of the apocryphal *Oral History of Our Times*. Edward Estlin Cummings (1894–1962), impris-oned by the French army at the end of WWI, as recounted in *The Enormous Room* (1922).

245 *Est consummatum, Ite*: "It is finished, Go," Latin formula used at the end of Mass, derived from Christ's final words on the cross.

265 *color di luce*: "Color of light."

267 *Lordly men*: From Pound's translation of the Anglo-Saxon poem *The Seafarer*: "Grey-haired he groaneth, knows gone companions,/Lordly men are to earth o'ergiven."

268–76 *these the companions*: An enumeration of shades: Ford Madox [Hueffer] Ford (1873–1939), English novelist, poet, and editor; William Butler Yeats (1865–1939), Irish poet; James Joyce (1882–1939), Irish novelist; Victor Plarr (1863–1929), British poet; Edgar Jepson (1863–1938), English novelist; Maurice Hewlett (1861–1923), English novelist and poet; Sir Henry Newbolt (1862–1938), English poet.

317–20 *Mr Edwards*: Henry Hudson Edwards, the G.I. who made a writing table for Pound out of a packing box; his African American features are associated with the Baluba (i.e. Biembe) masks from the Congo studied by Frobenius.

328 *nient' altro*: "Nothing else."

331–33 *in meteyard . . .* : "Ye shall do no unrighteousness in judgment, in meteyard, in weight, or in measure" (Leviticus 19.35). "And that ye study to be quiet, and to do your business, and to work with your own hands, as we commanded you" (First Thessalonians 4.11).

340 *each one in his god's name*: "For all people will walk every one in the name of his god" (Micah 4.5).

341–45 *Terracina*: Terracina, site on Italy's western seacoast associated with the birth of Venus and, Pound dreamt, locus of a future shrine reestablished in her honor. Virgil's *Aeneid* I, 404 records that Anchises, father of Aeneas, recognized Aphrodite from her gait when she approached him in human guise.

348 *Pleiades*: A cluster of stars said to be composed of the seven daughters of Atlas.

352 χθόνια γέα, Μήτηρ: "Chthonia gea, Mêtêr" ("nether earth, Mother").

359 ΤΙΘΩΝΩΙ: "TITHONOI." The goddess Eos transformed Tithonos into a grasshop-per (or katydid) so that she might hear her lover's song forever.

361 *in coitu inluminatio*: "In coitus illumination."

362–70 *Manet painted*: Aphrodite-like Olga Rudge, henna-haired, dressed in the latest fashions of Drecol or Lanvin, like a figure out of Manet's painting of the bar at the Folies-Bergère — the painterly tradition of nineteenth-century France ("la France dixneuvième") repre-sented by Edouard Manet (1832–83), Edgar Degas (1834–1917) and Constantin Guys (1802–92) continuing on into the fauviste work of Maurice Vlaminck (1876–1958), according to the Dutch writer Fritz Vanderpyl (1876–?).

372 *staria senza più scosse*: "It would rest without further tossing" (*Inferno* XXVII, 63).

373 *eucalyptus*: When seized by the partisans at his house at Sant'Ambrogio above Rapallo

(overlooking the Tyrrhenian Sea), Pound picked up a eucalyptus pip along the hill path which he kept with him at Pisa as a talismanic mnemonic device.

390 *with a painted paradise*: From Villon's "Paradis peint où sont harpes et luths" ("Painted paradise where are harps and luths") in "Ballade pour prier Nôtre Dame." Cf. Canto XLV.6.

393 *magna NOX animae*: "Great NIGHT of the soul."

395 *comes miseriae*: "Companion[s] of misery," referring to Pound's fellow-prisoners, here listed by name.

401 *fer a bag o' Dukes*: Dukes mixture, the name of the tobacco ration allotted to the trainees, bags of which served as the unit of exchange in commercial transaction among the prisoners.

403 *ac ego in harum . . .* : "And I too in the pig-sty," referring to Circe's transformation of Odysseus's crew into swine in Book X of the *Odyssey*.

405 *ivi in harum*: "I went into the pig-sty and saw corpses of souls."

410 *plus Carrol*: Carrol Crawford, a fellow-prisoner, named after the revolutionary leader Charles Carroll of Carrollton (1737–1832), just as many other African American trainees in the DTC bore the names of early American presidents.

411 ΘΕΛΓΕΙΝ: "THELGEIN" ("to enchant, betwitch, cheat").

414 *nec benecomata . . .*: "Nor fair-tressed Circe, well!, 'kaka phargak edôken' ('she had given them bad drugs')."

416 *veneno*: Probably a misprint for *veleno*, "poison."

435–44 *To study with the white wings*: Snippets from the Confucian *Analects*.

445–46 *E al Triedro, Cunizza*: "And at the crossing of the three roads, Cunizza/and the other woman: 'I am the Moon.'" Reminiscence of a visionary encounter recorded in the drafts of the Italian Cantos LXXIV–LXXV composed by Pound in January/February 1945, and later abandoned. Standing at the triedro ("trihedron') or symbolic crossing of three paths near Sant'Ambrogio, Basinio Basini (1425–57), the court poet of Sigismundo Malatesta and persona of Pound, sees the apparition of Cunizza da Romano (1198–1279), lover of the troubadour poet Sordello and, because she freed her brother's slaves, symbol of Kuanon-like compassion. Dante places her in the Third Heaven of Love.

449–50 Νύξ *animae*: "Night of the soul," here associated with the wisdom addressed to posterity ("ad posteros") by the Spanish mystic St. John of the Cross (1542–91).

658 βροδοδάκτυλος: "Brododactylus," Aeolic form (via Sappho) of Homer's "rosy-fingered" dawn.

661 *le contre-jour*: "Against the light." Evokes a photograph of Olga Rudge.

662 *to carve Achaia*: Cf. "Pisanello lacking the skill/To forge Achaia" [i.e. to recreate Greece] in Pound's poem *Hugh Selwyn Mauberley*.

664 *Venere*: "Venus, Cythera, or Rhodes" (cf. Horace, *Odes* I, vii).

665 *vento ligure, veni*: "Ligurian wind, come."

666 *Beardsley*: Aubrey Beardsley (1872–98), English illustrator, associated with the symbolists and decadents.

744 *"La Nascita"*: "The Birth of Venus," by Botticelli.

746–48 *Capoquadri*: The Palazzo Capoquadri, Olga Rudge's residence in Siena during the thirties, contains a panel painting with a child's face which reminded Pound of his daughter Mary.

749 *funge la purezza*: From Pound's 1945 Italian translation of *L'Asse che non vacilla*. His 1947 English version (*The Unwobbling Pivot*, X) runs: "The unmixed functions [in time and space] without bourne."

752 *formato locho*: "In a prepared place," from Calvacanti's "Donna mi prega," also translated by Pound as "in a sacred place" or "the formèd trace." Cf. XXXVI.56.

753 *Arachne mi porta fortuna*: "Spider brings me good luck."

754 ΕΙΚΟΝΕΣ: "*EIKONES*," pictures, images, icons.

827-28 *crystal jet . . . tosses*: Lines refracting the poems "Clair de Lune" and "Fountain Court (à Arthur Symons)" by the symbolist Paul Verlaine (1844–96).

833 *Zephyrus /Apeliota*: West and east winds.

836-38 *nec accidens . . . est agens*: "And is not an accident. . . it is an agent." Medieval scholastic distinctions found in commentaries on Cavalcanti's "Donna mi prega." See note to Canto XXXVI.3 for Pound's discussion of "accident" (vs. "essence").

839 *rose in the steel dust*: Pound observes in his commentary on Cavalcanti that the rose form made by the magnet in iron filings is a perfect example of energy realizing itself as pattern.

839-40 *Hast 'ou seen*: Cf. Ben Jonson's poem "Her Triumph" (in his 1624 *Celebration of Charis*): "Ha' you felt the wool of beaver/Or swan's down ever?/Or have smelt o' the bud o' the briar?/Or the nard in the fire?"

842 *Lethe*: The river of forgetfulness in Hades; in Dante's sacred geography, however, it is placed at the summit of Purgatory, on the near side of Paradise (*Purgatory*, XXI).

from CANTO LXXVI

136 *l'ara sul rostro*: "The altar on the rostrum."

140 *Mozart*: Insulted by an arrogant patrician, the young Mozart challenged him to a battle of snuff-powder, suggesting in the end that the aristocrats could get a better pinch ("prise") by licking his ass.

143 *alla fuente florida*: "To the flowery fountain" (of youth) sought by Ponce de Léon (c.1474–1521) in Florida.

146 *Cythera*: Aphrodite (whose epithets are given in Latin and Greek, "Kuthêra deina," "powerful (or fearsome) Cythera") appeared in human guise to Anchises, father of Aeneas.

151 Κόρη, Δελιά δεινά: "Korê, Delia deina" ("Daughter [Persephone], fearsome Delia/to whom passion is unknown"). The virgin huntress Artemis/Diana, sister of the Delian Apollo.

156 πολλά παθεῖν: "Polla pathein" ("to suffer much"), cf. *Odyssey* I, 4: "and his heart experienced many sufferings upon the sea."

160 *dove sta memoria*: "Where memory liveth," from Pound's translation of Cavalanti's "Donna mi prega." Cf. Canto XXXVI.16.

162 *J. Adams*: Cf. John Adams's grumblings about banks, Canto LXX.75.

175-76 *ac ferae familiares*: "And domesticated wild animals." *a destra*: "To the right."

180 *atasal*: I.e. *ittisal* (transliteration from the Arabic) "Union with the divine," a Sufi term used by Avicenna, elsewhere defined by Pound as "contemplation, the identification of the consciousness WITH the object."

181 *nec personæ*: "Nor [flesh-and-blood] people."

182 *hypostasis*: The technical philosophical term "hypostasis" occurs in Pound's commentaries on Cavalcanti's "Donna mi prega" and is defined by the O.E.D. as "That which subsists, or underlies anything: a) as opposed to qualities, attributes, or 'accidents'; b) as distinguished from what is unsubstantial, as a shadow or reflection." Cf. "nec accidens," Canto LXXIV.836.

182-83 *Dione*: Dione, mother of Aphrodite, sometimes confused with Aphrodite herself. Her planet would therefore be Venus.

184-85 *Helia*: Probably a misprint for Delia (cf. l. 151 above). Κύπρις: *Kupris*, i.e. Cypris, home of Aphrodite.

203-7 *their squeak-doll*: As reported in *Time* magazine of August 6, 1945 (to which Pound had access at the DTC), Winston Churchill ("their squeak-doll") was swept out of office by the unexpected victory of Clement Attlee's Labour Party; Brendan Bracken was Churchill's Minister of Information.

209 *ego scriptor*: "I the writer."

212 *Lucca, Forti dei Marmi*: Two towns to the north of Pisa. Graf Leopold von Berchtold (1863–1942), war-mongering Austro-Hungarian foreign minister (rhymed with Churchill?), visitor to Rapallo.

214 *Thetis*: A nereid, wife of Peleus and mother of Achilles.

217 *spiriti questi? personæ?*: "Are these spirits? [real] people?"

221 *Maya*: The Kalenda Maya, or May Day fertility rites celebrated by the troubadours, juxtaposed with Aphrodite.

224 *Zoagli*: A town just south of Rapallo.

229–31 οἱ βάρβαροι: "Hoi barbaroi," the barbarians (i.e. the Allies) whose bombs had damaged the façade of Tempio Malatestiano in Rimini containing images of the "Divine Isotta."

235 *La Cara: amo*: "The Beloved: I love." Pound's term of endearment for Olga Rudge.

239 *pervenche*: Periwinkle.

241 *et sequelae*: "And all that follow."

242 *Le Paradis . . . artificiel*: "Paradise is not artificial," unlike, say, Baudelaire's 1858 study of opium and hashish, *Les Paradis artificiels*.

244 δακρύων: "Dakruôn" ("weeping" or "of tears").

245 *L . . . P . . .*: "L[aval]. P[étain]. the honest [or honorable] ones." Time magazine of August 13 featured a photo of Pierre Laval (1883–1945), former head of the Vichy government, testifying at the trial for treason of Henri Philippe Pétain (1865–1951), Chief of State of the collaborationist Vichy regime.

246–47 *J'ai eu pitié . . .* : "I have had pity for others,/probably not enough."

248 *Le paradis . . non plus*: "Paradise is not artificial/nor is Hell."

250 *Eurus*: The East or Southeast Wind. The Catholic Prayer Book includes "Come, Holy Ghost": "O Comforter! to Thee we cry,/Thou heavenly gift of God Most High."

251–52 *la pastorella . . . dea*: "The little swineherd." "The fair-tressed goddess" (Circe).

from CANTO LXXIX

165 *Old Ez*: Pound was known at the DTC as "Uncle Ez." The is the only appearance of his name in *The Pisan Cantos*.

166 *Eos. . .Hesperus*: The Morning and Evening stars.

167–72 *Lynx*: Sacred to the wine-god Dionysus and traditional emblem of keen-sightedness, the lynx figured in the private feline mythology Pound shared with his wife Dorothy, for whose birthday on September 24 he composed the choruses of this Canto. *Silenus*: Companion of Dionysus. *Casey*: corporal at the DTC. *Bassarids*: Thracian maenads. *Maelids*: tree nymphs.

177 *Calhoun*: John Calhoun (1782–1850), senator from South Carolina, champion of the Confederate cause.

183 *Priapus*: God of fertility, son of of Dionysus and Aphrodite. *"Iakchos, Io! Cythera, Io!"* ("Hail Dionysus! Hail Aphrodite").

192 ἐλέησον: "Lord, have mercy."

198 *Astafieva*: Serafima Astafieva (1876–1934), Russian dancer and director of a ballet school in London.

201 *phylloxera*: Species of small insects devastating to grape crops.

202 Ιακχε, Ιακχε, Χαῖρε: "Iakche, Iakche, Chaîre" ("Dionysus, Dionysus, Hail").

203 *Eat of it not*: Because Persephone (also known as "Kore," the "daughter" of Demeter) ate the pomegranate seed that Dis gave her, Zeus condemned her to return to Hades for four months each year.

210 *Pomona*: Roman goddess of fruit trees.

219 *Heliads*: Daughters of Helios, the sun.

223   *crotale*: Rattle, castanet.

231   γλαυκῶπις: "Glaukôpis" ("glare-eyed"), Homeric epithet for Athena.

237   ἰχώρ: "Ichôr," the juice that courses in the veins of gods.

240–43   *We are here waiting*: Alludes to the three nights of festivities evoked in the Pervigilium Veneris, the feast of Venus Genetrix, whose May Day rites Pound located at the source of troubadour song.

260–81   Αφροδίτην: "Aphrodite." Ἥλιος: "Helios." δεινὰ ει, Κύθηρα: "Deina ei, Cythera" ("You are fearsome, Cythera [Aphrodite]"). Κόρη καὶ Δήλια καὶ Μαῖα: "Korê kai Dêlia kai Maia" ("Kore [the daughter] and Delia [Artemis/Diana] and Maia [mother of Hermes]"). *trine as praeludio*: "Threefold [i.e. in Trinity] as prelude." Κύπρις Ἀφρόδιτη: "Cyprus Aphroditê." Κύθηρα: "Cythera." *aram/nemus/vult*: "The grove needs an altar." *Cimbica*: "C[h]imbica," a South American puma and, according to W. H. Hudson, "friend of man, the most loyal of wildcats."

from CANTO LXXX

180   *Hot hole hep cat*: The chants of the trainees doing forced drills late in the evening?

202   *"mi-hine eyes hev"*: From "The Battle Hymn of the Republic."

209–14   *temporis acti*: "Bygone days" (Horace, *Ars poetica*). ΟΥ ΤΙΣ: "OU TIS" ("noman"). ἄχρονος: "Achronos" ("without (or beyond) time").

582   *Nancy*: Nancy Cunard, who shared Pound's love for the Dordogne. Cf. Canto XXXVIII.44.

583   *Whither go. . .*: From Andrew Lang's translation of *Aucassin and Nicolette*. Aucassin evokes the fair ladies in squirrel-fur ("vair") and rich silk gowns ("cisclatons") whom he would gladly follow into Hell—just as Pound was briefly tempted by the affluent charms of Nancy Cunard in the 1920s?

585–86   *Excideuil*: The castle of Excideuil, birthplace of the troubadour Giraut de Bornelh, the stonework of whose parapets contains "wave patterns," here associated with the solar temple of Montségur, visited in 1919, and the paradisal city of Dioce (cf. Canto LXXIV.11).

587   *Que tous les mois. . .*: "That every month we have a new moon," from a rondeau by Jean Froissart (c.1337–c.1404).

588–90   *Herbiet . . .Fritz*: Georges Herbiet (1895–1969), painter and early French translator of Pound. Fritz Vanderpyl, cf. Canto VII.52.

592   *Orage . . . Crevel*: Alfred Richard Orage (1873–1934), English editor of *The New Age*, Pound's major journalistic outlet 1913–1920; Ford Madox Ford (1873–1939); René Crevel (1900–35), French surrealist and suicide.

593   *de mis soledades . . .*: "Out of my solitude let them come," from a poem by Lope de Vega.

594   *till Rossetti found it*: Fitzgerald's *Rubaiyat*, remaindered copies of which were discovered in a bookshop by pre-Raphaelite poet and painter Dante Gabriel Rossetti (1828–82).

601–5   *Spewcini*: I.e. Puccini. *Man seht*: "One sees."

609–15   *Les hommes . . . beauté*: "Men have I know not what strange fear . . . of beauty." Aubrey Beardsley (1872–98), English aesthete and illustrator, died of tuberculosis. Sir Edward Burne-Jones (1833–98), English pre-Raphaelite painter. "Modern Beauty," by Arthur Symons includes the lines: "I am the torch, she saith, and what to me/If the moth die of me? I am the flame/of Beauty, and I burn that all may see."

619–21   βροδοδάκτυλος Ηώς: "Brododaktulos Eôs" ("Rosy-fingered dawn"), cf. Canto LXXIV. 658. Κύθηρα δεινὰ: "Cythera deina" ("fearsome Cythera"), Aphrodite or, here, the planet Venus.

623–26   *all that Sandro knew*: Painters of Venus: Sandro Botticelli (c. 1444–1510), Jacopo da Sellaio (c. 1440–93), Velázquez (1599–1660), Rembrandt (1606–69), Rubens (1577–1640), Jordaens (1593–1678).

659–60   *Favonus, vento benigno*: "West Wind, kindly breeze." *Je suis au bout de mes forces*: "I am at the end of my tether."

661–65   *thanks to Professor Speare*: *The Pocket Book of Verse: Great English and American Poems*, edited by M.E. Speare, Ph.D. (New York, 1940), discovered in the DTC's latrine, contains 18 pages of Whitman as well as Richard Lovelace's "To Althea, from Prison," and selections from the King James version of the Bible, including the Book of Job, chap. 38: "Have the gates of death been revealed unto thee? / Or hast thou seen the gates of the shadow of death?"

665–67   *when the raft broke*: Cf. *Odyssey* V, 365ff. where Odysseus's raft is destroyed by a storm created by Poseidon and he is saved from drowning by Ino, daughter of Cadmus, transformed into Leucothea. The "air strip" refers to the steel mats (used to construct temporary airplane runways) which were installed to reinforce the cage in which Odysseus-Pound spent his first three weeks at Pisa before his "raft broke" and he was transferred to a tent in the medical compound.

668–71   *Immaculata . . .* : From the Catholic Prayer Book: "Immaculate, I shall go [unto the altar of God]" (preparation for Mass). Three martyred saints recalled in the "Memento for the Dead" prayer; their names mean "Eternal, "Good," and "Reborn." *Per omnia saecula saeculorum*: "world without end," from the Latin mass.

672–75   *repos donnez à cils*: Echoes the liturgical "Repos eternel donne a cil" ("Grant him eternal rest") from the "Epitaphe et Rondeau" of Villon's *Testament*. Pound's French, however, literally translates as "give rest to eyelashes." *Senza termine funge*: "It acts without end," from Pound's Italian translation of the *Chung Yung*, which in his English reads: "The unmixed functions without bourne. This unmixed is the tensile light, the Immaculata. There is no end to its action." During his first three weeks at Pisa, there was indeed no end to the light's action, for in his "death cell" Pound was exposed to the sun all day and to electric reflector lamps all night, causing considerable eye problems. *Les larmes. . . Tristesse*: "The tears I have created flood me / Late, very late, have I known you, Sadness" (cf. Saint Augustine, *Confessions* X, 27, "Sero ti amavi": "Late have I loved you, Beauty so old and so new! Late have I loved you!")

682–83   *hieri*: Yesterday. *no fortune and with a name to come*: for the Elpenor tag, cf. Canto I.56.

686–87   *gratia*: "With thanks to." The black trainee Wiseman ("from Africa"), as opposed to William Wiseman, ex-head of British Intelligence and international financier with the New York firm of Kuhn, Loeb & Company.

689   *the souterrain*: The underground (i.e. a locus of initiatory descent).

690–92   *remembering Carleton*: Mark Alfred Carleton (1866–1925), American agronomist who developed new and hardier strains of wheat, oats, and barley, here associated with Demeter, goddess of grain.

699   *Zoagli*: Beach south of Rapallo.

704   *o.t.a.*: "O[f] t[he] a[rmy]?"

705   *Oh to be in England*: Imitation of Browning's "Home-Thoughts from Abroad" (in Speare's *Pocket Book of Verse*): "Oh, to be in England / Now that April's there."

714–18   *the tower*: The tower attic at Lacock Abbey in Salisbury Plain containing a copy of the 1225 Magna Carta, which "confirmed" the 1100 Charter presented to King John by his barons.

723   *Chesterton's England*: Gilbert Keith Chesteron (1874–1936), Catholic writer and eminent Edwardian.

729   *that dog is a Talbot*: Charles Talbot, cousin of Pound's wife Dorothy, inheritor of Lacock Abbey. The Talbots' family emblem was a dog.

733   *Let backe and side go bare*: From John Still (1543–1608), "Jolly Good Ale and Old," in Speare.

740   *Claridge's*: Posh London hotel.

741–49   *Maurie Hewlett*: Hewlett (cf. Canto LXXIV.276) lived in Salisbury, where Pound visited him on Christmas Eve, 1911. "Heigh ho! sing, heigh ho! unto the green holly," from Shakespeare's *As You Like It*, in Speare.

750   *Lady Anne*: Lady Anne Blunt, wife of W. S. Blunt (cf. Canto LXXXI.169), née Anne Isabella King-Noel.

751–53   *Le Portel*: French fishing port associated by Pound with Swinburne, author of a play dealing with Mary Stuart ("La Stuarda").

754   *Si tuit . . .marrimen*: "If all the griefs and laments and pain," from Bertran de Born's funeral lament for the young King Henry. See "Planh for the Young English King," p. 16.

756–67   *Tudor indeed is gone*: Tudor, the royal family that ruled England from the beginning of Henry VII's reign in 1485 to the death of Elizabeth in 1603. The War of the Roses opposed the House of York (White) and the House of Lancaster (Red). Catherine Howard (c.1521–42), fifth wife of Henry VIII, beheaded for her immoral conduct. Anne Boleyn (c.1507–36), second wife of Henry VIII and mother of Queen Elizabeth, also beheaded. The three stanzas imitate the strophic forms of Fitzgerald's *Rubaiyat of Omar Khayyam*, anthologized in Speare.

770   *the Serpentine*: A curved pond in Hyde Park, near Pound's pre-war lodgings in Kensington.

from CANTO LXXXI

94   *AOI!*: In Pound's translation of the Noh play *Kinuta*, this cry of grief is uttered first by the wife (and then by her ghost and by the chorus) when she realizes she has been abandoned by her husband.

96   *at my grates no Althea*: From Richard Lovelace's "To Althea , From Prison" ("When Love with unconfinèd wings/Hovers within my gates,/And my divine Althea brings/To whisper at the grates"), in Speare.

101–2   *Lawes and Jenkyns*: Henry Lawes (1596–1662), English composer who set Waller's poem "Go, lovely Rose" (in Speare). John Jenkins (1592–1678), English composer and musician. Arnold Dolmetsch (1858–1940), pioneer of the Early Music movement and maker of renaissance stringed and key instruments.

113   *Waller . . . Dowland*: Edmund Waller (1606–87), cf. l. 100 above; John Dowland (1563–1626), Irish composer and lutist.

114–16   *Your eyen two*: From Chaucer's "Merciless Beaute," a triple roundel thought to be composed around 1380, thus roughly 180 years before Shakespeare's birth.

117   *Ed ascoltando . . .* : "And listening to the gentle murmur," perhaps a trace of Pound's Italian Cantos of Jan./Feb., 1945. Cf. Canto LXXIV.445.

119   *hypostasis*: See note to Canto LXXVI.182.

120–21   *what the blindfold hides*: In one of the drafts of the Italian Cantos LXXIV–LXXV, Pound-Basinio's glimpse of Cunizza on the hillside near Sant'Ambrogio modulates into a larger vision of a theatrical troupe whose women are dressed for carnival (cf. the "half-mask's space" below).

124   *diastasis*: From the Greek, "set apart," or displaced (as opposed to "hypostasis," i.e. "set beneath," as of a foundation or base?). Can also refer to the dilation of the pupils, as in *Hugh Selwyn Mauberley* ("inconscient, full gaze,/The wide-banded irides/And botticellian sprays implied/in their diastasis").

127   Ειδὼς: "Eidôs," participial form of the Greek verb for knowing or seeing. Cf. Canto LXXVI.180, "nor is this yet atasal."

134   *What thou lovest well remains*: A pointed reply, on one level, to the famous axiom of Oscar Wilde's prison poem, "The Ballad of Reading Gaol" (in Speare): "And all men kill the thing they love."

145 *Pull down thy vanity*: "Vanity of vanities, saith the Preacher; all is vanity," from Ecclesiastes (in Speare).

151 *Paquin*: Jeanne Paquin (1869–1936), French fashion designer, known as the queen of Paris Couture at the turn of the century.

153 *Master thyself*: Refracts a line from Chaucer's "Ballade of Good Counsel" ("Subdue thyself, and others thee shall hear"), in Speare.

155 *Thou art a beaten dog*: Cf. Pound's musical setting of "L'Epitaphe de Villon" ("Ballade des pendus"): "La pluie nous a bués et lavés. / Et le soleil dessechés et noircis; / Pies, corbeaux, nous ont les yeux cavés, / Et arrachée la barbe et les sourcils." ("The rain has washed and cleansed us / And the sun dried and blackened us, / Magpies and crows have pecked out our eyes / And plucked off our beards and brows.")

169 *Blunt*: Pound's memory of Wilfrid Scawen Blunt (1840–1922) was perhaps jogged by his double sonnet, "With Esther," included in Speare (and containing the lines "Till I too learn'd what dole of vanity / Will serve a human soul for daily bread"). A poet and political activist, jailed by the British for two months in Ireland as a political prisoner, Blunt was the author of *The Shame of the Nineteenth Century* (1900), a scathing indictment of British imperialism, hence his "unconquered flame." In January 1914, Pound organized a visit of six poets (including Yeats and Sturge Moore) to Blunt's country estate in Essex, where they presented him with a Gaudier-Breszka sculpture in his honor.

from CANTO LXXXIII

64 Δρυάς: "Dryas," tree nymph. "Dryad" was Pound's name for his first muse, the poet Hilda Doolittle (H.D.), whose September 10 birthday this passage may celebrate.

81 *Plura diafana*: "More things diaphanous," from *De Luce*, the treatise on light by the mediediafaval philosopher Robert Grosseteste (c.1175–1253). Cf. Canto XXXVI.18.

90–102 *it shines and divides . . . inanition*: Paraphrase of *Mencius*, II.i.2.13–15, 190.

129–30 *La vespa*: "The wasp." *Bracelonde*: Brocéliande, the enchanted forest of Arthurian romance?

141 *Jones' rodents*: Trainees assigned to weeding the grass at the DTC by Lt. Jones, provost officer of the camp.

152 εἰς χθονίους: "Eis chthonious" ("to those beneath the earth"), here the Underworld of Persephone and Tiresias.

156 *Cristo Re . . . .* : "Christ the King, God the Sun."

159 *and that day*: Cf. the Paolo and Francesca episode of *Inferno* V, 138: "quel giorno più non vi leggemmo avante" ("that day we read no farther in it").

160 *fatigue deep as the grave*: Cf. Swinburne's "A Forsaken Garden" (in Speare): "What love was ever as deep as a grave?"

161 *Kakemono*: Painted scroll.

163–92 *so that I recalled*: Pound spent the winters of 1913 through 1915 serving as Yeats's secretary at the latter's country home, Stone Cottage, in Coleman's Hatch, Sussex. Near the coast, the area was considered a "prohibited area" by British military authorities during WWI, and Pound and his wife were accordingly served a summons (later withdrawn) for their illegal presence there. Among the works Pound read aloud to Yeats (whose eyes were weak): seven volumes of Wordsworth, *The History of Magic* (1854) by Joseph Ennemoser, and Charles Doughty's epic poem, *The Dawn in Britain* (1906). Yeats's 1914 poem "The Peacock," memorializing the roast peacock dinner Blunt had offered Yeats, Pound and company on the occasion of their January 1914 visit (cf. Canto LXXXI.169) runs: "What's riches to him / That has made a great peacock / With the pride of his eye?" *aere perennius*: ([a work of art] "more enduring than bronze"), Horace, *Odes*, III.

from SECTION: ROCK-DRILL 85–95 DE LOS CANTARES (1955)

First published by Vanni Scheiwiller in Milan in 1955, then by New Directions and Faber and Faber in 1956 and 1957, respectively. The title alludes to Jacob Epstein's 1913 sculpture, "Rock Drill," a plaster figure of a man straddling an actual pneumatic drill. Reviewing the recently published *Letters of Ezra Pound* (1950), Wyndham Lewis of *Blast* days remembered Pound's early dealings with Harriet Monroe, the editor of *Poetry* (Chicago): "His rock-drill action is impressive: he blasts away tirelessly, prodding and coaxing its mulish editress." Pound's first years of psychiatric internment in the Chestnut Ward of St. Elizabeths Hospital in Washington, D.C., were largely devoted to translation: *Confucius: The Unwobbling Pivot and Great Digest* (1947), *Elektra* (1951), *Women of Trachis* (1953), *The Classic Anthology Defined by Confucius* (1954). Nine years after the trauma of Pisa and his trial, he returned to the *Cantos* in earnest in 1954, elaborating a vision of Paradise pitched against the ongoing purgatorial nightmare of History. The pages of Cantos LXXXV–LXXXVII are radiant with ideograms drawn from the *Shu Jing*, or the *Classic of History* (or of *Documents*), written in the sixth century B.C.E., and China's first continuous narrative of its history from 2357 to 631 B.C.E. The Confucian ethos of the Middle Kingdom's exemplary rulers is contrasted with the moral turpitude of the modern West in matters military and economic. Cantos LXXXVIII–LXXXIX return to the early years of the American Republic, with a narration of the 1824 duel between Virginia representative John Roanoke and Henry Clay, President John Quincy Adams's Secretary of State—according to Thomas Hart Benton, "the last high-toned duel I have witnessed." These Cold War Cantos reexamine the "Bank War" during the Jackson Era, an epic battle already introduced in Canto XXXVII. In addition to Benton, President Martin Van Buren, the economic historian Alexander Del Mar, and the explorer John Frémont make their appearance. Cantos XC–XCV shift from the historical to the meditative and represent Pound's most sustained effort to "write Paradise," a move "into the light and 'fra i maestri di color che sanno' ['among the masters of those who know']" that was already in the planning in 1940 before the disaster of WWII intervened. Governed by the practice of "contemplation" (defined by Richard of St. Victor as the highest act of the mind, in which it is unified with its object), Pound's quirky blend of neo-Confucianism and neo-Platonism invites into its philosophical ambit such mystics as Pythagoras, Apollonius of Tyana, John Scotus Erigena, Avicenna, Richard of St. Victor, and John Heydon, while the Egyptian hieroglyphs that begin to enter the poem come from the work of his son-in-law, the Egyptologist Boris de Rachewiltz (1926–1997). Dante's *Paradiso*, especially its third heaven, remains the central model for Pound's vision of a place "above civic order, l'AMOR."

CANTO XC

EPIGRAPH   *Animus . . . procedit:* "The human soul is not love, but love flows from it, and it delights not in the idea of itself but in the love which flows from it." From Richard of St. Victor (d. 1173), one of the most important mystical theologians of twelfth-century Paris. Pound explained to his publisher James Laughlin that the theme of Canto XC was "the domination of benevolence."

1–2   *From the colour . . . the sign:* From the doctrine of signatures of the English alchemist and astrologer John Heydon (1629–1667).

4   *Ygdrasail:* i.e. Yggdrasil, great ash tree of Nordic mythology whose roots reached the center of the earth and whose branches supported the sky.

5   *Baucis, Philemon:* Old couple transformed into two intertwined trees to acknowledge their generosity to the gods. Cf. Canto IV.74 and "The Tree," p. 3.

6   *Castalia:* Fountain dedicated to Apollo on Mt. Parnassus at Delphi.

9–10 *Templum aedificans:* "Building the temple." *Amphion:* Legendary king of Thebes who caused the stones to build themselves into a wall at the sound of his lyre.

11–12   *San Ku*: An inner council in ancient China, associated by Pound with Eluesinian traditions and the Order of the Templars. [IDEOGRAMS]: San [M5415] "three," gu (ku) [M3470], "alone."

13   *the room in Poitiers*: Room in the Hôtel de Ville in Poitiers (France); associated with the first known troubadour, William IX of Acquitaine.

15   *Sagetrieb*: Pound's coinage, from the German (*Sage*: legend, saga; *Trieb*: compulsion, drive) understood as the instinct to "pass on (oral) tradition."

18   *Jacques de Molay*: (c.1250–1314), last Grand Master of the Knights Templars, burned at the stake for heresy.

20   *Erigena*: Medieval neo-Platonic (and heretical) philosopher. Cf. Canto LXXIV.139,158–60.

22–23   *Kuthera . . . semipterna*: "Aphrodite fear-inspiring," "Aphrodite everlasting."

24   *Ubi amor, ibi oculus*: "Where love lies, there lies the eye." From the *Benjamin Minor* of Richard St. Victor.

25–27   *Vae qui cogitates . . . imago*: Inspired by Richard of St. Victor: "Woe to you who think without purpose." "[The good things of will,] through which an image of the divine likeness will be found in us."

29   *Randolph*: John Randolph "of Roanoke" (1773–1833), Virginian member of the House and the Senate and colorful gadfly. Included in his will a provision to free his slaves after his death.

30–31   ἠγάπησεν πολύ: *êgapêsen polu* ("She loved much"—from Luke 7:47). Probably refers to Cunizza da Romano (1198–1279), who briefly eloped with the court poet Sordello (cf. Canto II.4); Dante places her in the *terzo cielo* or third sphere of Love in *Paradiso* IX, 13–65. *Liberavit masnatos*: "she freed her slaves." Cunizza freed her brother Ezzelino da Romano's slaves after the latter's death, an unusual act of manumission that parallels Randolph of Roanoke's.

34   *Evita*: Pound's German translator Eva Hesse (1925–), a resident of Munich. *semina motuum*: "The seeds of motion."

38   *Sibylla*: Priestess of the oracle at Delphi. May also refer to Pound's muse at St. Elizabeths, Sheri Martinelli (1918–1996), for whom he wrote an introduction to a book of her paintings in 1956.

40   *m'elevasti*: "You lifted me up," adapted from *Paradiso* I, 75.

50   *Isis Kuanon*: Composite Egyptian and Chinese goddess of compassion. Cf. Canto LXXIV.131.

54   *blue serpent*: The uraeus or blue cobra, emblem of the sacred serpent in the headdress of Egyptian divinities; subject of a Sheri Martinelli painting.

56–58   *they take lights now down to the water . . .*: Cf. Canto XLVII.15–19.

59   *"De fondo"*: From the poem "Soy animal da fondo" (1949) by Spanish poet Juan Ramón Jiménez (1881–1958).

64–68   *Arethusa*: Water-nymph in the service of Diana. Scene remembered from Ovid, *Metamorphoses* V, 600ff.

69   *Wei and Han*: Two Chinese rivers that join, like the fountain of Arethusa with the water-god Alpheus.

75–76   *"birds for the mind . . . for know-how"*: From Richard of St. Victor, translated by Pound in the compilation of St. Victor's quotes he published in 1956 as "Watch birds to understand how spiritual things move, animals to understand physical motion."

82   *rilievi*: Sculptural reliefs.

84   *Faunus, sirenes*: Pan, sirens.

86–87   *ac ferae*: "And wild beasts." Cf. Canto XX.192. *cervi*: "deer."

89   *Pardus . . . Bagheera*: "Panther," "leopards." *Bagheera*: the black panther in Kipling's *Jungle Book* who educates Mowgli.

91 ἐπὶ χθονί: "epi chthoni" ("around [or on] the earth").

94 οἱ χθόνιοι: "hoi chthonioi" ("spirits of the underworld").

101–2 *Palatine*: One of the seven hills of Rome. pineta: "pinewood."

102 χελιδών: "chelidôn" ("swallow"). Echoes l. 429 of *The Waste Land* and IV.31.

103 *procession of Corpus*: On Corpus Christi day, the first Thursday after Trinity Sunday.

112–13 *Tyro, Alcmene*: Tyro: cf. II.23–27. Alcmene: Wife of Jupiter and mother of Hercules. *e i cavalieri*: "and the chevaliers."

118–19 Ἠλέκτρα: Elektra, whose mother Clytemnestra became the lover of Aegisthus while her husband Agamemnon was at Troy. Pound translated Sophocles' *Elektra* (with Rudd Fleming) in 1951.

122 *ex animo*: "From the soul."

from CANTO XCI

1–4 *Ab lo dolchor*: The blocky musical neumes recall the melodies in the medieval channson-niers (or song-books) of the troubadours that Pound studied at the Bibliothèque Natio-nale and at the Ambrosian Library in Milan in 1911–1912. Cf. Canto XX.12–33. Pound's lyr-ics splice two Provençal poems together: William of Aquitaine's: "*Ab lo dochor* del temps novel" ("*With the joy* of the new season") and Bernart de Ventadorn's "per la doussor c'al cor li vai" ("through the sweetness *that comes into his heart*") from his poem about larks on wing (cf. Canto CXX.3–5).

9 *Reina*: A Canto of queens: Helen of Troy, or of Tyre, or of Aquitaine, Princess Ra-Set. If the same as the "Miss Tudor" of l. 29, then this Reina would be Queen Elizabeth I (1533–1603). The 300 "sunken" years could thus either be 1603–1903 or 1233–1533.

14 *qui laborat, orat*: "Who works, prays," attributed to St. Augustine.

15 *Undine*: Water-sprite; Pound's name for muse Sheri Martinelli.

16–17 *Circeo . . . seaward*: Monte Circeo, isolated promontory on southwest coast of Italy. Cf. Canto LXXIV.341–45. In a 1930 "Credo" Pound wrote: "Given the material means I would replace the statue of Venus on the cliffs of Terracina. I would erect a temple to Artemis in Park Land. I believe that a light from Eleusis persisted throughout the middle ages and set beauty in the song of Provence and Italy."

18 *Apollonius*: First-century Pythagorean philosopher and wandering mystic portrayed in Philostratus's *Life of Apollonius of Tyana* as a rival to his contemporary, Jesus Christ. Ar-rested and tried for treason by Emperor Domitian.

20 *Helen of Tyre*: Refers to the legend of Helen of Tyre, said to be a reincarnation of Helen of Troy, discovered by Simon Magus in a brothel of Tyre and redeemed by what Pound saw as his "chivalric love" for her.

21–22 *Pithagoras . . . Ocellus*: the Greek philosopher Pythagoras (c.580–497 B.C.E.) is one of othe pervasive presences throughout the *Rock-Drill* section: his education in Egypt, his silent, ascetic life, his theory of musical intervals and of numbers, his doctrine of metempsychosis all make him the chosen philosopher of Pound's Paradiso. Ocellus of Lucanus, said to be a student of Pythagoras himself, is credited by Pound with the phrase "to build light" in Canto LXXXVII and may be the "pilot-fish" who guided Simon to Helen of Tyre.

23 *et libidinis expers*: "untouched by lust." Cf. Canto LXXVI.151 in reference to Artemis/Diana.

24 *Justinian, Theodora*: Justinian I (483–565), Byzantine emperor and law-giver. A former prostitute (like Helen of Tyre), Theodora became one of the most powerful figures in the Empire when Justinian made her his wife.

28 *pensar di lieis . . .*: "To think of her is my rest," from Arnaut Daniel's "En breu brisaral temps braus."

29–33 *Miss Tudor*: Elizabeth I (see l. 9 above). The "he" of l. 32 is usually read as referring to

Sir Francis Drake (c.1540–1596) mentioned at l. 47, admiral of the English fleet victorious over the Spanish armada in 1588 and, as legend has it, knighted by the Virgin Queen herself aboard the *Golden Hinde.*

36   *compenetrans:* "Interpenetrating."

37   *Princess Ra-Set:* Fusion of two Egyptian deities, Ra (the sun-god) and Set (the water-god).

42   *convien che si mova:* "It is fitting that the mind be drawn by love," from *Paradiso* XXVI, 34–35.

50   *ichor, amor:* "ichor," Greek for the for life-sap that runs in the veins of gods; "amor," Latin for love.

51   *J. Heydon:* Cf. Canto XC.2. Pound recommended Heydon's *Holy Guide* (1662) for its account of "the joys of pure form. . . inorganic geometrical form." Another Pythagorean.

57   *Love moving the stars:* Cf. the very last line of Dante's *Paradiso:* "The Love that moves the sun and the other stars." παρὰ βώμιον: "para bômion" ("beside the altar").

59–64   *Tamuz:* Cf. Canto XLVII.15–19.

66   [IDEOGRAM]: xian (hsien³) [M2692], translated by Pound as the "tensile light" (an ideogram with silk to the left and sun to the right).

68   Ἐλέναυς: [Helen] "destroyer of ships." Cf. Canto II.11. Queen Elizabeth?

75   *ne quaesaris:* "he asked not." From Horace *Carmen* I, 11, 1.

82–87   *Leafdi Diana. . . londe:* Part of a ritual incantation to Diana sung by Brutus in Layamon's *Brut* (c.1215), a history of England in verse. Brutus had come to an island empty except for wild deer, where his men found a marble temple sacred to Diana, at whose altar he proceeded to sacrifice, singing: "Lady Diana, dear Diana / High Diana, help me in my need, / Teach me through skill / where I might go / to a winsome land." *Rome th'ilke tyme . . . :* "Rome at this time was not [inhabited]."

89   *Lear:* King Leir in Layamon's *Brut* (c.1215).

90   [IDEOGRAM]: zhen (chên⁴) [M315], to "terrify, shake, or excite."

from CANTO XCII

47   *And if I see her not:* From Bernart de Ventadorn's "Can par la flors." Cf. Canto XX.3.

51   *Coeli Regina:* Queen of Heaven.

54–58   *farfalla in tempesta. . . :* "Butterfly in storm," from *Purgatorio* X, 125 where the soul (psyche, or butterfly) in search of beatific vision is compared to the worm seeking to realize itself as an "angelic butterfly." The scientific names of the butterflies in the family of nymphalidae follow, a rhyme with Canto XC.99 and an anticipation of Canto CXX.8.

60   *il tremolar della marina:* "The trembling of the sea," *Purgatorio* I,116–17, a dawn scene marking the first sight of light after the pilgrim's ascent from Hell. Cf. Canto XVI.1.

64–65   *fui chiamat' . . . refulgo:* "I was called and here I glow," *Paradiso* IX, 32, Cunizza da Romana speaking in the third heaven of Venus.

66   *Le Paradis . . . artificiel:* "Paradise is not artificial." Cf. Canto LXXXVI.242.

73   *Hilary:* Hilary (c.300–368), Bishop of Poitiers and Doctor of the Church.

75–76   *improvisatore:* "Improviser." *Omniformis:* "every shape."

from CANTO XCIII

146   *agitante calescemus:* From Ovid, *Fasti* VI, 15 ("A god dwells within us; when he stirs we are enkindled").

148   *Lux in diafana:* "Light in the diaphane." Cf. Canto XXVI.18.

149–54   *Creatrix . . . ore:* "Creatress, / I beseech." "Blessed Ursula, I beseech." "By the hours of delight."

156   *Ysolt, Ydone:* Isolde, of the legend of Tristan and Isolde; *Ydoine,* of the legend of Amadis and Ydoine.

158 *Picarda*: Piccarda dei Donati, kidnapped from her convent by her brother and forced into marriage, tells her story in *Paradiso* II, 34–125.

166–67 *J'ai eu pitié . . . Pas assez*: "I had pity of others. Not enough! Not enough!" Cf. Canto LXXVI.246.

168 *But that the child*: Perhaps Pound's daughter Mary.

171–75 [IDEOGRAMS]: Five characters from *The Unwobbling Pivot*: li (li⁴) [M3920], "power" or "energy," xing (hsing²) [M2754]), "walk" or "act," jin (chin⁴) [M1061], "near to," hu (hu¹) [M2154], "to or "at," ren (jen²) [M3099], "benevolence." Translated by Pound as "energy is near to benevolence."

177 *Au bois dormant*: "La Belle au bois dormant" is Charles Perrault's French for Sleeping Beauty.

183–84 *mai tardi . . .* : "It's never too late [to attempt] the unknown," from Gabriele D'Annunzio's 1908 play, *La Nave*.

185–91 *Ocellus . . . renew*. The Pythagorean "builder of light" here rhymed with the Cheng Tang emperor who inscribed "Make it New" on his bathtub. Cf. Canto LIII.71–73.

193 chien⁴: jian, the ideogram "to see" [M860]—construed by Pound as running legs beneath an eyeball.

from THRONES 96–109 DE LOS CANTARES (1959)

First published by Scheiwiller in Milan in 1959, then by New Directions and Faber and Faber. Pound explained in a 1960 *Paris Review* interview: "The thrones in Dante's *Paradiso* are for the spirits of the people who have been responsible for good government. The thrones in the *Cantos* are an attempt to move out from egoism and to establish some definition of an order possible or at any rate conceivable on earth. . . . *Thrones* concerns the states of mind of people responsible for something more than their personal conduct." This section of the poem is dominated by the figure of the enlightened law-giver: Leo the Wise (866–912), the Eastern Roman Emperor, whose *Edict*, a series of ordinances addressed to the eparch (roughly, governor) of Byzantium, regulated the social and economic life of the city (with particular emphasis on interest rates and the quality of the coinage in circulation), occupies Canto XCVI. The Kangxi Emperor's late seventeenth-century *Sacred Edict*, which proposed a similar series of neo-Confucian principles to inform local legislation and administration, is translated in Cantos XCVIII and XCIX. The *Institutes* of Sir Edward Coke (1552–1634) are excerpted in Cantos CVII–CIX. Coke, much admired by lawyer John Adams, was charged with treason by King James I for his defense of Common Law, the rights of Parliament, and the authority of the Magna Carta. From the Tables (or Thrones) of the Law, anthropologist Pound moves onto local Custom, introducing in Canto CI the Tibetan religious practices of the Naxi tribe of Southwest China as described in Joseph Rock's *The Ancient Na-khi Kingdom* (1947). Pound is above all interested in the propitiatory rites devised to purify the wandering spirits of young lovers who chose to commit suicide rather than submit to the pre-arranged marriages demanded by (Confucian) custom—an uncanny anticipation of the suicide motif in *Drafts and Fragments*.

from CANTO XCIX

In 1670 the Manchu Emperor, Kangxi, wishing to revive Confucianism, issued a Hortatory Edict made up of sixteen maxims (each containing seven characters) which were to be read aloud twice a month in every village and town of the land. His son, the Yongzheng Emperor, expanded this *Sacred Edict* in 1724, adding a long commentary (the so-called Wen Li edition). Soon thereafter, the imperial Salt Commissioner of Shanxi, Wang

Youpu, wanting to "take the sense down the people," rewrote the *Edict* in colloquial language, further interspersing it with proverbs and homely sayings. To compose this Canto, Pound used the bilingual version of this latter text published by the American missionary F. W. Baller as *The Sacred Edict* (Shanghai: China Inland Mission, 1924). Analyzing the components of its characters in order to devise his own idiosyncratic translation cum commentary, Pound here speaks in the voice of the Salt Commissioner, addressing his precepts on statecraft and householding (*oikos*) in part to his daughter Mary and her husband Boris de Rachewiltz, the parents of his two grandchildren back in Italy.

330 *chiao*¹: jiao [M694], "arrogant." From chapter twelve of the *Edict*, "On Education."

356 *Yao*: The "two lovelies" are Yao's daughters.

361 *Hsiang i hsiang*: "Think it over."

364 *hsiao⁴*: "Put into circulation."

365 *tsou (four)*: "Memorialize the emperor."

366 *k'ao ch'eng*: "Settlement between a superior and a subordinate."

369 *Thiers . . . Talleyrand*: Louis-Adolphe Thiers (1797–1877) was one of the few major French politicians to oppose war with Prussia in 1870; he became the provisional president of the Third Republic in 1871. Talleyrand: cf. Canto LXX.1–4.

371 *PANURGIA? SOPHIA*: "Knavery." "Wisdom."

379 *t'ien² ti⁴*: "Land," "soil."

380 *liang²*: "Taxes in kind."

401 *Yong*: The Yongzheng Emperor, son of Kangxi, author of the *Wen-li*.

402–3 Elkin Mathews (1851–1921) was Pound's early publisher in London; W. L. Courtney (1850–1928) was the editor of the (apparently well-paying) *Fortnightly Review*.

404 *The State is corporate*: Mussolini's term for the government regulation of business and labor was the "corporate state."

406 *Chou rite*: Cf. the translation of the Confucian *Book of Rites* in Canto LII.

419 *manesco*: "rough, brutal."

419–30 These lines, broadcast over a radio in Italian translation, provide the voiceover for the end of Pier Paolo Pasolini's film *Salò, or the 120 Days of Sodom* (1975), amid scenes of obscene violence.

437 *yo el Rey*: "I, the king" (i.e. the Yongzheng Emperor).

441–42 *nung/sang*: "To cultivate mulberry trees."

451 [IDEOGRAM]: zhao (ch'ao⁴) [M247], "omen."

454 *ch'ang²*: "To show respect."

456 *chu four*: zhu (chu⁴): "To assemble or meet together."

462 *wu² mu . . . li⁴*: "Do not." "Love ardently." "Wonderful." "Profit." "Double profit." "Interest on money."

466 *Byzance did better*: Pound was convinced that the reason that the Byzantine Empire outlasted the Manchu Dynasty was its low interest rates.

469 *vide Michelet & Ambrose*: Jules Michelet (1798–1874), French historian and critic of usury. St. Ambrose (c.340–397), bishop of Milan and doctor of the Church; his commentary on the *Book of Tobias* denounces usury.

472 *que ça doure*: From "pourvou que ça doure" ("as long as it lasts"), attributed to Napoleon's mother, Letizia, commenting on her upstart son's reign.

478 *thundering phalloi*: Pound's visual "mistranslation" of the character nuo (no⁴) [M4750], composed of the (left-hand) radical for "heart" (misinterpreted as "phallus") and a right-hand component misread as "thunder." The character actually means weak, cowardly.

482 *stimulate anagogico*: The "anagogic," the highest of four allegorical levels of meaning as described by Dante, is related to a spiritual interpretation of the Bible.

485 [IDEOGRAM]: En¹ [M1743–3]. "Bound by mutual ties, on the one side grace and on the other loyalty." Pound used this character as part of the title-page seal of the original edition of *Thrones* published by Scheiwiller in Milan.

508 *the four TUAN*: The four principles of *Confucianism*: ren (jen²), humanity; yi (i⁴), equity; li (li²), propriety; zhi (chih⁴), wisdom.

523 *fu jen*: "Wise man."

from DRAFTS AND FRAGMENTS OF CANTOS CX–CXVII (1969)

First "freaked" into print in 1967 as Cantos 110–116 by "the FUCK YOU press at a secret location in the lower east side." This pirated edition forced James Laughlin to publish (initially against Pound's wishes) an official New Directions edition in 1969 (followed by Faber's in 1970).

FROM CANTO CXII

1–2 *owl . . . fire-fox*: Among the birds and animals which grew purified in the Naxi Muan Bpö ceremonies described by Joseph Rock. *Huo³-hu²*: Bay or sorrel horse.

3 *Amṛta*: "Nectar of immortality," or Beauty, the pure, limpid distillation of nine different medicines alchemically sublimated over the course of the purification ceremonies.

8 *²La ²mun ³mi*: a female Tibetan lama-like figure (or muse) involved in the creation of the Beauty that is the nectar Amrta.

9 *²Ndaw ¹bpö*: The Naxi rite known as "Sacrifice to Earth."

17–23 *Li Chiang*: Lijiang, town in northwestern Yunnan province, near the Tibetan border, center of Naxi culture. To the north of the town lies Elephant Mountain ("Hsiang Shan"); the "Lung Wang" or Dragon King Temple was built near the springs feeding the Jade Stream that runs along the streets of the town like the canals of Venice.

24–25 [IDEOGRAMS]: Yu (Yu⁴) [M7666], "jade." He (Ho²) [M2111], "stream."

26–28 *Artemisia/Arundinaria*: Two plants much used in the purification ceremonies: Artemisia, or wormwood, may derive from Artemis the moon goddess (because of the dream-state induced by the herb). Or it may refer to Artemis, wife and sister of King Mausoleus (and architect of his posthumous Mausoleum), hence, a tomb-goddess. Arundinaria is a kind of small bamboo used in the weaving of the ceremonial winnowing tray pictured below in two lunar phases.

29–30 *neath/luna*: The whole nocturnal domain ruled over by Artemis/Diana/Luna, as well as the various (self-)sacrifices involved in her ceremonial service.

CANTO CXIII

1–6 *12 Houses of Heaven . . . Fortuna's*: The twelve signs of the Zodiac through which the sun ("Pater Helios") turns like the wheel of the goddess Fortuna. *"Mortal praise has no sound in her ears"*: *Inferno* VII, 92, in the fourth circle of Hell (Avarice and Prodigality), describing Fortune's indifference to human opinion of her. Fortune in Dante represents (economic) Necessity, and "the whole sublunar world is Fortune's realm" ("tutto l'oro ch'è sotto la luna"). Cf. Canto CXII.29 ("neath/luna").

7 θρῆνος: "thrênos" (Greek lament for the dead).

10 *to walk with Mozart*: Companions in paradise: The Austrian Wolfgang Amadeus Mozart (1756–1791), for his playful sense of form; the Swiss-born comparative zoologist Louis Agassiz (1807–1873), for his counter-Darwinian eye; the Swedish botanist Linnaeus (1707–1778), for the taxonomic precision of his coinage of names.

13 *And to this garden, Marcella*: Marcella Joyce Spann (b. 1932), a regular young Texan presence at St. Elizabeths. Pound's secretary and late muse, she sailed back to Italy with him and

wife Dorothy in June, 1958 and stayed with them at his daughter's castle, Schloss Brun-
nenburg, in the South Tyrol (hence perhaps the triangulations of "pride, jealousy and
possessiveness" of l. 43 below). She also edited with Pound the anthology (or "Spannthol-
ogy," as he called it) *Confucius to Cummings* (New Directions, 1964).

15–16   *Li Chiang . . . Rock's world*: "Rock's world" is the region around Lijiang in Yunnan
province. A landscape at once natural and mental, its paradisal Himalayan heights here
inform the Alpine air of Brunnenburg.

18–19   *Paré . . . Donnelly*: Representative medical men and/or healers: Ambrose Paré (c.1510–
1590), considered the inventor of modern surgery; Francis Twedell (b.1863–?), prominent
American baby-doctor around the turn of the century; Leo Donnelly (d.1958), friend of
Pound's who served as an orthopedic surgeon in France in WWI, later founded the So-
cial Credit Party in Detroit.

20–21   *old Pumpelly*: Raphael Pumpelly (1827–1923), American geologist who made two expedi-
tions into Turkestan funded by the Carnegie Institute in order to test the theory of Aryan
migration. "No horse, no dog, and no goat" is his description of the lowest level of his ar-
cheological dig, revealing a pre-historical culture with no evidence whatsoever of domes-
tic animals.

22–23   *"I'd eat his liver . . .*: Anecdote from Pumpelly's travelogue *Across America and Asia* (1869):
a gold-miner in the outback of Australia taking revenge on an enemy by cooking and eat-
ing his liver. Cf. the cannibalism of Canto IV.21.

24   *17 Maggio*: May 17 1959, Pound's first spring as a free man in fourteen years, traveling to
sacred places such as Lake Garda with Marcella Spann.

28   *H.D.*: Hilda Doolittle (1886–1961), Pound's earliest (and comparably lithe) American muse,
who used the term "serenitas" in reference to a translation of Sappho's poem "Atthis."
Pound plays a prominent role in H.D.'s *Tribute to Freud* (1956), her late poem "Winter
Love," and her posthumous memoir, *End to Torment* (1979). *Dieudonné's*: a London res-
taurant frequented by Pound and the Imagistes before WWI.

40   *The Gods have not returned*: Cf. "The Return," p. 31.

45   *garofani*: Carnations or clove-trees.

46   *Portofino*: Harbor town just beyond Rapallo.

47   *apples from Hesperides*: The golden apples of the sun.

49–55   *The old Countess . . . Pétain warned 'em*: Interwar history of Poland, as refracted through
the reminiscences of Pound's longtime friend Stephanie Yankowska ("Stef"). General
Ian Hamilton (1853–1947) was an acquaintance of Yeats's, Irish commander of the Brit-
ish Mediterranean Expeditionary Forces in WWI, and later foreign affairs advisor who
assured the Poles that if Germany invaded they could expect help from the Black Sea.
French Marshal Pétain (1856–1951) warned the newly independent Poles against march-
ing into the Ukraine in 1920.

59   *Kalenda Maja*: Defined by Pound as the "Feast of Venus Genetrix, which survives as May-
day," the ritual core of troubadour eros. Cf. Canto LXXVI.221.

60   *Li Sao*: "Encountering Sorrow," famous elegiac sequence by the poet Qu Yuan (c.343–278
B.C.E.), in which he evokes his unrequited loyalty to his king and bemoans his unjust exile,
while dreaming of a more understanding ruler. Qu Yuan drowned himself in a river: the
Dragon Boat Festival, held during the fifth day of the fifth month of the Chinese lunar
year, originated as a search for the poet's body.

68   *Schwundgeld*: "Disappearing money," a form of currency devised by the economist Silvio
Gesell that loses its value if not spent. Here compared to the Continental currency used
to finance the American Revolution.

83   *Washington Bridge, N.Y.C.*: Memories of Pound's childhood visits to New York City to visit
relatives.

89   *Yeats noted the symbol*: Yeats observing the Rosicrucian import of the rose window in the western façade of Notre Dame cathedral in Paris.

91   *And the bull*: Cf. Canto XLVII.41.

95   *(Sac. Carioli . . . giusto)*: L. P. Carioli, author of *Il Giusto Prezzo Medioevale: Studio Economica Politica* (1913), a study of medieval canon law's concept of the "just price."

96   *Giustizia*: "Justice." The inscription over its gates explicitly states that God was moved to create Hell by Justice (*Inferno* III, 7).

104   *Article X*: The Tenth Amendment of the U.S. Constitution reads: "'The powers not dele- gated to the United States by the Constitution, nor prohibited by it to the States, are re- served to the States respectively, or to the people." The basis of the states' rights doctrine and, for Pound, of Social Credit: "the local control of local purchasing power."

113   *malvagità*: Orneriness.

117   *Limone*: Town on Lake Garda, visited with Marcella in May 1959.

120   *scala altrui*: The "stairs of another man." Cacciaguida says to Dante in *Paradiso* XVII, 58–60: "You will prove how salt is the taste of another's bread, how hard the way up and down the stairs of another man."

123   *Daphne*: Cf. "The Tree" (written to H.D.), p. 3.

124   *When the Syrian onyx is broken*: From Pound's "Homage to Sextus Propertius": "Nor will you be weary of calling my name, nor too weary / To place the last kiss on my lips / When the Syrian onyx is broken."

126   *Ixion*: A Beckettian variant of the wheel of Fortune: Ixion, the overthrown sun-god, bound in Tartarus to an eternally turning sun-wheel of second thoughts.

FROM CANTO CXV

3   *Wyndham Lewis*: Pound's old Vorticist ally, had gone completely blind by 1952, the year the first H-bomb was detonated by the U.S.

5   *garofani*: Carnations.

7   *Mozart, Linnaeus, Sulmona*: Cf. Canto CXIII.10. *Sulmona*: Birthplace of Ovid in the prov- ince of Aquila.

19   *In meiner Heimat*: "In my homeland." Identified by Pound as "roughly Rapallo."

CANTO CXVI

7   *Muss.*: Mussolini.

12   *cuniculi*: Prehistoric "canals" or irrigation, discovered by the Italian archaeologist Del Pelo Pardi near Rome.

15   *The vision of the Madonna*: Above the portal of Santa Fosca, a Byzantine chapel at Torcello in the lagoon of Venice.

19   *mucchio di leggi*: "A haystack of laws." Re Mussolini.

20   *Litterae nihil sanantes*: "Literature which cures nothing," the retired John Adams in a 1813 letter to the retired Thomas Jefferson.

21   *Justinian's*: The code of law of the Byzantine emperor Justinian.

35   *"plus j'aime le chien"*: A quip by Voltaire's mistress Mme Roland: "the more I know men, the more I like dogs."

37   *Disney*: Pound was quite taken by Disney's film about a squirrel, Perri, when he saw it in 1958.

38   *Jules*: Jules Laforgue (1860–1887), French symbolist whose prose Pound translated in 1918.

39   *Spire*: Andé Spire (1868–1966), French poet and fierce proponent of modern free verse, here thanking Pound specifically (*in proposito*) for his early championing of Laforgue's *vers libre*.

44   *chi crescerà i nostri*: From *Paradiso* V, 105: "Behold the man *who will increase our loves*."

45–48   *that terzo*: The heaven (or sphere) of Love (Venere) in Dante's *Paradiso*, inhabited by Cunizza.

64–65   *al poco giorno . . . d'ombra*: Dante, *Rime* I, 1: "In the small hours with the darkness describing a huge circle."

68   *al Vicolo d'oro*: Gold Lane, street in Rapallo, situated on the gulf of Tigullio.

NOTES FOR CXVII ET SEQ.

Some scholars argue that the *Cantos* proper end with Canto CXVI (at the closural "A little light, like a rushlight/to lead back to splendour"), with the remaining text but fragments shored against ruin. Others read these "Notes" for Canto CXVII and the following ("et seq.") as Cantos in their own right, implicitly numbered (as we have here) CXVII, CXVIII, CXIX, CXX.

[CANTO CXVII]

2   *benedetta*: "Blessèd."

6   *Brancusi's bird*: Pound wrote admiringly of the Rumanian sculptor's work in the *Little Review* in 1921. He noticed that the shape of his "Golden Bird" (1919) was reproduced in a tree trunk on the lawn of St. Elizabeths.

10   *Rupe Tarpeia*: The Tarpeian Rock, site on the Capitoline Hill in Rome from which criminals were thrown to their deaths.

13   *Zagreus*: Ritual name of Dionysus, son of Semele.

[CANTO CXVIII]

1   *M'amour, m'amour*: "My love, my love."

8–9   *paradiso/terrestre*: "Earthly paradise." Located by Dante at the summit of Mount Purgatory.

[CANTO CXIX]

In the New Directions editions of *The Cantos* immediately after Pound's death in 1972 (but not in the Faber editions), this fragment was added as the final text in the poem, which thereby concluded on a note of remorse. It was moved into penultimate position in editions after 1991.

[CANTO CXX]

1   *La faillite de François Bernouard*: "The bankruptcy of" François Bernouard (1884–1948), a publisher friend of Pound's in Paris who went bankrupt during the world crash of 1929.

2   *field of larks at Allègre*: Glimpsed by Pound in the Auvergne during his walking tour of the roads of southern France in the summer of 1912.

3–5   *"es laissa cader . . . sas alas"*: From Bernart de Ventadorn's poem "The Lark," translated by Pound in 1910 as "When I see the lark a-moving/*For joy his wings* against the sunlight,/Who forgets himself and *lets himself fall*."

7   *Two mice and a moth*: According to Olga Rudge's unpublished notes on these Cantos, three creatures Pound saw attempting suicide in Rapallo and Venice in the early 60s.

8–10   *farfalla gasping . . . the kings*: A dying butterfly's wing-beat witnessed on the terrace of Brunnenburg. Cf. the butterflies of Cantos XC.99 and XCII.54–58. The "kings" would be those monarch butterflies who live on poisonous milkweed and migrate from arctic Canada in mid-September.

TRANSLATIONS (1954–1964)

from THE CLASSIC ANTHOLOGY DEFINED BY CONFUCIUS (1954)

The *Shi Jing*, or *Book of Odes*, is an anthology of 305 poems whose compilation is attributed to Confucius. In the Chinese tradition, knowledge of the *Odes* was deemed essential to any meaningful participation in government. Pound initially read this foundational compilation of folk-wisdom in the Latin prose translation of Alexandre de Lacharme's *Confucii Chi-King Sive Liber Carminorum* (1830) and planned an English version as early as 1929. In May 1947, now incarcerated for two years, he returned to the project. Aided by the romanizations provided in the glosses to the *Odes* of the Swedish sinologist Bernhard Karlgren and by Veronica Sun, a student at Catholic University in Washington, D.C., Pound compiled a 588-page "singing key" to guide the oral chanting of the poems. This "singing key" as well a rubbing of the Stone Classics text and the text written in ancient seal script were to accompany Pound's English translation in the ambitious "scholar's edition" of the *Book of Odes* that he envisioned—but on which Harvard University Press, the eventual publisher of *The Classic Anthology Defined by Confucius* (Cambridge, 1954), reneged. This edition was republished in paperback by New Directions in 1959 under the title *The Confucian Odes*. The following selection has been guided by Pound's own choice of poems for his 1970 recording of *The Confucian Odes* (now available on the web at PennSound).

"RABBIT GOES SOFT-FOOT . . ."
13–14 *Aliter/Ole Brer Rabbit: Aliter*: "Otherwise." *Brer Rabbit*: Pound and his friend, T. S. Eliot (the "Possum") had a lifelong affection for Joel Chandler Harris's (Amerindian) trickster-figure, Brer Rabbit, from his Uncle Remus stories, published in eight collections beginning in 1880.

JE BOIS DANS MON VERRE
TITLE "I drink in my glass." From Alfred de Musset, "My glass is not large, but I drink in my glass."
12 *Who can plumb another man's thought?*: Cf. Canto CXIII.120.

"PICK A FERN . . ."
1 *Pick a fern*: Translated as "Here we are, picking the first fern-shoots" in Pound's previous translation of this same poem in *Cathay* as "Song of the Bowmen of Shu," p. 55.

HUANG NIAO
TITLE "Yellow Bird." Supplied by Legge's edition of the *Odes*, with the following comment, "Lament for three worthy brothers of Ch'in who were buried alive in the same grave with Duke Mu."

CHORUSES FROM SOPHOKLES' WOMEN OF TRACHIS (1956)

Rereading the Fenollosa Noh plays while helping Hugh Kenner to prepare the 1953 edition of his collected *Translations*, Pound decided to attempt a "Noh" version of Sophocles' *Women of Trachis*, a (self-)revenge tragedy focused on the erotic infidelity and subsequent remorse and madness of the solar superhero Herakles. In the spring of 1954, it was performed on the BBC's Third Programme and at the New School in New York City (with a cast that included the young James Dean as Herakles's son). First published in book form in London in 1956 (Neville Spearman) and by New Directions the following year. Its choruses were included in New Directions editions of Pound's *Selected Poems* after 1957 on the strength of T. S. Eliot's blurb: "Pound's handling of the verse, especially in the choruses of the play, seems to me to be masterly. His ear is as faultless as ever."

from TRANSLATIONS (1964)

Hugh Kenner's 1953 edition of *Translations of Ezra Pound* for Faber and Faber was augmented in the enlarged 1964 New Directions paperbook edition by the addition of forty pages, including the material below:

The Rimbaud versions appeared in book form in Scheiwiller's *Rimbaud* (Milan, 1957). "Conversations in Courtship" was initially published in periodical form in 1960 in *Wort und Wahrheit* (Freiburg im Breisgau), *A Quarterly Review* (London), and *National Review* (New York). The three translations from Horace's *Odes* were first published in *Agenda* (U.K.) in 1964. The Marquise de Boufflers's "Air: Sentir Avec Ardeur" ("Feel with Ardor") comes from the Pound/Spann *Confucius to Cummings* (1964).

Appendix

Selecting Pound

When T. S. Eliot signed on as a director of the fledgling firm of Faber and Gwyer in 1925, his first editorial act was to have the new house bring out his own collected *Poems 1909–1925*. His second was to invite his old friend Ezra Pound, *il miglior fabbro* (as he now referred to him in the most recent dedication of the The *Waste Land*), to join the establishment with a British edition of his *Selected Poems*, edited and introduced by Eliot himself. This 1928 *Selected Poems*, initially issued in 1000 copies, would stay in print at Faber through various covers, hard and soft, until the early 70s and both its contents and Eliot's persuasive introduction in very large measure determined the reception of Pound's poetry in England for over forty years. Pound's more official entry into the Faber canon came in 1933, with Eliot's (surprisingly bold) marketing decision to place his *ABC of Economics* on the spring list as a preparatory advertisement for the fall appearance of the long-awaited trade edition of *A Draft of XXX Cantos*. It was also in 1933 that Faber and Faber published Pound's *Active Anthology*—an extraordinarily prescient transatlantic gathering of experimental poetries, anchored on the American side by William Carlos Williams, Louis Zukofsky, George Oppen, Marianne Moore, and e. e. cummings, and, on the British, by Basil Bunting and Eliot (who was represented by the only piece of his that Pound cared for after *The Waste Land*, the demotic "Fragment of a Prologue" from his play *Sweeney Agonistes*).

Pound spent a good portion of the preface to his *Active Anthology* attacking the academic (indeed "gongorist") bent of Eliot's recent volume of *Selected Essays 1917–1932*, while taunting him about his "flattering obeisance" to the British "bureaucracy of letters" — Eliot would reply the following year in *After Strange Gods* with a pontifical rebuke of the *Cantos*. But much as Pound despised the literary London over which, at least in matters high modernist and high church, the "Reverend" Eliot (as he called him) now seemed to reign supreme, the house of Faber provided him with his only stable publishing venue in the English language over the course of the 1930s. As if to make amends for his omission of *Homage to Sextus Propertius* from the 1928 selection, Eliot arranged for it to be published as a separate book in 1934, in tandem with Pound's volume of literary essays, *Make It New*. Pound's increasingly intemperate prose was in turn humored by his confrere with the Faber publication of *Polite Essays* in 1937 and *Guide to Kulchur* in 1938. Meanwhile, the firm continued faithfully to follow his Odyssean work-in-progress wherever it might lead, bringing out *A Draft of Cantos XXXI–XLI* in 1935, *The Fifth Decad* in 1937, and *Cantos LII–LXXI* in 1940 — its entire Pound offerings somewhat predicated upon the ongoing sales of his *Selected Poems* to the more general reader just discovering his work.

In 1935, Allen Lane inaugurated the paperback revolution in England by founding Penguin Books, initially published as an imprint of Bodley Head, the firm founded by his uncle John Lane, erstwhile associate of Pound's first British publisher, Elkin Mathews, who in 1900 had pioneered the marketing of inexpensive volumes of "quality" literature with his Vigo Cabinet Series editions of Synge's plays, Yeats's stories and Masefield's ballads. By mid-1936, one million Penguins, priced at 6d. (roughly the price of a packet of cigarettes), were already in print. Faber and Faber decided to follow suit, issuing a series of cheaply produced editions from its trade list under the name of Sesame Books. The first of these popularizations was Eliot's *The Waste Land and Other Poems*, published in early 1940; this was followed that same year by a much condensed *Selection of Poems by Ezra Pound*, priced at 2s. 6d. (a third of the price of the earlier hardcover version), in an edition of 7,100 copies — the poet's largest print-run to date and, as fate would have it, arriving just in time for the near total eclipse of his reputation as a result of his wartime radio broadcasts from Mussolini's Italy and subsequent indictment by the U.S. government for treason. Eliot's stock, by contrast, continued to rise with his repositioning within the broader culture of the paperback: in 1948, the year he was awarded the Nobel Prize in Literature, Penguin issued his *Selected Poems* at 1s. 6d. in an edition of 50,000 copies, no doubt the century's high-water mark for the mass-market distribution of "difficult" modernist poetry. As for *il miglior fabbro*, now institutionalized in a mental hospital in Washington, D.C., when Faber resurrected the 1928 edition of his *Selected Poems* (with Eliot's introduction) in 1949, it released a conservative 2,300 copies.

Through the personal loyalties of Eliot and fellow director F. V. Morley, Faber & Faber provided Pound with a regular outlet for both his *Cantos* and critical prose throughout the 30s, while conferring upon him a mantle of respectability as an authority (however wayward) on matters poetical, cultural, and economic. Compared to the continuity and capaciousness of his arrangement with Faber, Pound's relations with his American publishers had always been more fraught. His first venture into the U.S. trade market was his 1917 volume *Lustra*, which his New York patron and agent John Quinn had recommended to the newly founded house of Alfred A. Knopf. Providing the first full-scale selection of his poetry from his earliest work through his recent *Cantos*, *Lustra* was the volume that would define Pound to the postwar generation of American poets that mattered. To bolster its sales, Knopf even brought out a promotional brochure entitled *Ezra Pound His Metric and Poetry*, anonymously penned by the virtually unknown T. S. Eliot in gratitude for Pound's signal efforts on behalf of the publication, that very same year, of *Prufrock and Other Observations* in London. Pound had kept the whole operation secret because, as he wrote to Quinn, "I want to boom Eliot and one can't have too obvious a ping-pong match at that sort of thing." Publication by Knopf briefly placed expatriate Pound in the commercial vanguard of New York publishing, but after the scathing reviews of his prose volume, *Pavannes and Divisions*, and the lamentable sales of his edition of Fenollosa's *"Noh" or Accomplishment: A Study of the Classical Stage of Japan*, he was unceremoniously ushered out of Knopf's stable of modern authors—but not before he had made sure that the house published the first American edition of his friend Eliot's *Poems* in 1920.

After this setback, the ever-resourceful Quinn steered Pound's next book of prose, *Instigations* (which included Fenollosa's essay on the moving pictures of Chinese poetry) toward Horace Liveright of Boni and Liveright, the jazz-age publisher of John Reed, Eugene O'Neill, and Theodore Dreiser, and deviser of the very profitable Modern Library series of counter-classics (Nietzsche, Wilde, Ibsen etc.). Liveright subsequently brought out Pound's *Poems 1918–1921*: the inclusion of dates in the title, unusual at that point for the work of a contemporary poet, gave the book—divided into "Three Portraits" and "Four Cantos"—the glitz of a fashionable gallery opening on lower Fifth Avenue. The appearance of this collection of Pound's most "advanced" work coincided with Liveright's visit to its author in Paris, where a meeting was arranged in January 1922 with Eliot and Joyce to devise a common strategy for the publication of *Ulysses* and what would eventually become, after Pound's extensive editorial midwifery, *The Waste Land*. Though censorship problems delayed the trade edition of Joyce's masterwork in the U.S. for a number of years, Eliot's *Waste Land* was published by Liveright in book form (and for the first time with notes) in December 1922, bringing this annus mirabilis of modernism—largely stage-managed by Pound—to a close. Four years later, now installed in Rapallo, Italy and having just published a limited deluxe edition of his *A Draft of XVI Cantos* in Paris, Pound decided to gather his Collected Shorter Poems into a handsome volume for Liveright.

Entitled *Personæ* (Latin for "masks"), the book definitely exuded an aura of retrospect: not only was his most celebrated poem to date, "Hugh Selwyn Mauberley," presented as "distinctly a farewell to London," but the volume as a whole marked Pound's abandonment of the shorter, anthologizable forms of the lyric in favor of the open-ended, serial shape of his *Cantos*. These latter he eventually managed to place on the U.S. market in 1933 with the firm of Farrar and Rinehart — where his editor was that master of light verse, Ogden Nash, a far cry from Faber's Eliot. After lackluster sales, the firm dropped the *Cantos* from its list in 1939.

It was at this point that Pound's most recent disciple appeared on the scene to salvage the publication of his oeuvre in the U.S. As a Harvard undergraduate, James Laughlin had made the pilgrimage to Rapallo in 1933 to sit at the master's feet and soak up the lessons of the Ezuversity (which included a strong dose of Social Credit economics, to which the young steel heir became converted). Upon his return to Cambridge, Laughlin prevailed upon the *Harvard Advocate* to buy the publication rights to one of Pound's recent Cantos and played with the idea of importing the Faber *Active Anthology* to the States in a "student edition" priced at 50 cents. By 1936, Laughlin had gotten his magazine *New Directions in Prose and Poetry* up and running (with Pound's Canto about the 1694 founding of the Bank of England as its centerpiece) and in 1938 he imported the English sheets of Faber's *Guide to Kulchur* for American distribution. In contradistinction to the now established Faber & Faber and the readership it had cultivated, Laughlin conceived New Directions as a brash venture aimed at the American youth — or, more precisely, college student — market, exactly the audience that Pound had long hoped but had largely failed to reach with such didactic works as *How To Read* or *ABC of Reading*, neither of which Faber published initially — whereas Yale University Press, sensing classroom potential, issued both *ABC of Reading* and *Make it New* in 1934. Remembering the youth appeal of Liveright's Modern Library series (later absorbed by Random House), and aware of Allen Lane's populist shake-up of the British publishing industry, Laughlin corresponded with Pound in 1940 about launching a series of books to be entitled the New Classics, priced at an affordable one dollar a piece: the first volumes were to be devoted to the work of Pound and his old college friend William Carlos Williams; further volumes, so Pound instructed Laughlin from Rapallo, should be devoted to student editions of Mencius, selections from the works of American Founding Fathers, and Social Credit primers.

Although sympathetic to Pound's economic views (but increasingly alarmed by his paranoid fixation on Jewish bankers and financiers), Laughlin replied to his mentor that he was above all interested in publishing "literchoor," not political pamphlets. Sensing Farrar's flagging commitment to the *Cantos*, he managed to secure the rights for New Directions and published its latest Chinese History/

Adams Dynasty section in 1940, complete with a packet of pedagogical material explaining themes and versification pasted inside the back cover, *ad usum delphini*. But Laughlin's most pressing project—a cheap one-dollar student edition of Pound's *Selected Poems* on the order of Faber's 1940 Sesame Book edition—continued to elude him, for the Liveright Company refused to relinquish the rights to *Personæ* until it had gone into its sixth impression in 1944. Only when Laughlin had taken ownership of all of Pound's early poetry in addition to the Cantos was he in a position to play the same role in the American marketing of Pound as Faber had in England. When Pound was returned to Washington D.C. to stand trial for treason in the fall of 1945, it was therefore Laughlin who arranged for his legal defense and began orchestrating what he called a "propaganda campaign" to generate a "counter-swing" against all the negative publicity that had attended the poet's so-called "trial." He approached *Poetry* magazine about doing a special issue on Pound, offering an excerpt from one of the extraordinary Cantos he had written while in the U.S. Army prison at Pisa, and contacted Eliot about writing "the cornerstone essay" for the number. Eliot obliged in 1946 with a remarkably moving tribute, but it was now clear that it was New Directions, and no longer Faber, that was becoming the primary custodian of Pound's reputation.

With the manuscript of the *Pisan Cantos* in hand and full control over the bulk of his published work (including the recently acquired *Personæ*), Laughlin set out to reinvent Pound for a generation of postwar American readers, many of them newly enrolled in college under the G.I. Bill, starting with an inexpensive "New Classic" selection that would provide (unlike *Personæ* and unlike Eliot's Faber selection) a representative mix of both early poems and later Cantos. In July 1946, with Pound now having been officially declared mentally incompetent to stand trial for the charge of treason, Laughlin approached John Berryman to compile and introduce the selection: Berryman, then at Princeton, was part of the loose fraternity of university poets and New Critics such as R. P. Blackmur, John Crowe Ransom, Randall Jarrell, and Delmore Schwartz whom Laughlin had drawn into the ambit of New Directions during the early '40s. Overawed at having to compete with Eliot's authoritative introduction to the Faber *Selected*, Berryman promptly blocked, turning his attention instead to a cycle of love sonnets on the theme of adultery (treason again) and sketching out an early draft of his (very Poundian) *Homage to Mistress Bradstreet*. After a visit to the poet in the madhouse of St. Elizabeths in November 1948, Berryman put the finishing touches on his edition—at the same moment that the Fellows in American Literature at the Library of Congress (who included that year's Nobel, T. S. Eliot, W. H. Auden, Robert Lowell, Katherine Anne Porter, Allen Tate, and Robert Penn Warren) were meeting to award the first annual Bollingen Prize of $10,000 to Pound for the *Pisan Cantos*, published by Laughlin earlier that year.

When the Bollingen Prize was finally announced the following February, controversy erupted. Although the committee had stated that its award was based solely on the "objective perception of value" and in exclusive consideration of Pound's "poetic achievement," to the popular press it seemed incredible that one arm of the U.S. Government could thus be honoring a citizen whom another arm (the Department of Justice) deemed dangerous enough to keep under lock and key as both a lunatic and a traitor. As The New York Times headline put it: "POUND IN MENTAL CLINIC / WINS PRIZE FOR POETRY / PENNED IN TREASON CELL." Another vocal group of critics simply resented the fact that the Bollingen had been fobbed off on the credulous American public by what amounted to a literary conspiracy headed by the British Nobel Laureate T. S. Eliot and his various U.S. minions. George Orwell attempted to raise the tone of the argument by observing that Eliot and his associates had in fact taken an "art for art's sake position" by choosing to isolate the sphere of the aesthetic from that of the political or ethical—from the opposite fringe of the political spectrum, Pound would have completely agreed. In the end, fed up with the entire affair, the U.S. Congress simply announced that it would henceforth get out of the poetry prize business altogether—and there the matter rested.

The New Directions Selected Poems appeared in the fall of 1949, just as the Bollingen controversy was blowing over. It was pretty much the volume Laughlin had wanted all along: a New Classics clothboard, priced at $1.50, 184 pages in all, almost half of which were devoted to the Cantos. In its first year, he managed to sell 10,000 copies. Berryman was primarily responsible for the choice of the shorter poems, which emphasized Pound's early lyrics and dramatic monologues, and some of the better known Cantos, while Laughlin, a deeper student of the poem, made sure that the more didactic and historical regions of the epic (Confucian China, Renaissance Italy, and the early American Republic) were drawn in. Pound objected to Berryman's initial selections from the Pisan Cantos as a "hash" and "just a mess of snippets"—which Laughlin rectified by "adding some fat on the sides of the bones." But the long and scholarly introduction that Berryman had written for the volume (in which he argued that all of Pound's poetry was essentially autobiographical in inspiration, comparing the Cantos to Wordsworth's Prelude) was immediately rejected by both publisher and poet: the former felt that it was too specifically aimed at a "special high brow audience," while the latter dismissed Berryman's piece as "a lot of damn argument mostly with 2nd/rate critics," certainly "NOT a preface," and certainly "NOT whetting anyone's appetite for the text." The introduction was discreetly relegated by Berryman to the pages of the Partisan Review.

At Pound's suggestion, Rolfe Humphries (who had written a positive review of the Pisans for another left-wing journal, The Nation) was approached by Laughlin to supply a replacement essay aimed at the more general reader. This too fell upon Pound's disfavor, Humphries having insisted on making it clear in his otherwise very laudatory and accessible introduction that while he admired Pound's poetry, he could in no way condone "the anti-Semitic remarks that can be found, if not in this selection, here and there in the Cantos." Feeling that these questions had no place in a brief overview of his lifetime achievements as a poet, Pound asked Laughlin to axe Humphries' piece as well. In the end, the *Selected Poems* appeared with no other apparatus than a preliminary one-page "Autobiography." Part curriculum vitae, part legal brief for the defense he was never allowed to mount because judged *non compos mentis*, Pound here lays out to an imaginary jury his career as a conscientious objector: "1918 began investigation of causes of war to oppose same. . . . 1939 first visit to U.S. since 1910 in endeavor to stave off war. 1940 after continued opposition obtained permission to use Rome radio for personal propaganda in support of U.S. Constitution, continuing after America's official entry into the war only on condition that he should never be asked to say anything contrary to his conscience or contrary to his duties as an American Citizen. Which promise was faithfully observed by the Italian Government."

Although this bit of political theater continued to figure in all subsequent New Directions editions, Pound never had his day in court. Ruling that the elderly poet would never be able to understand the nature of the charges against him (which was quite true), the U.S. government declared him permanently unfit to stand trial and dismissed his treason indictment in 1958, leaving him free to return to Italy, where he lived out the remainder of his years. His work by this point was beginning to enter the college curriculum and his Pisan sequence had earned the emulation of another generation of American poets. While formalists such as Berryman, Schwartz, and Lowell tended to his stock in the Ivy League, Charles Olson and his Black Mountain School joined with the poets of San Francisco to keep his work in circulation at the avant-garde margins. When the *Selected Poems* went into a cheap $1.15 paperback edition in 1957, the sales took off and remained steady thereafter, with New Directions reprinting year after year. In 1959 Faber followed suit by issuing Eliot's 1928 selection of early Pound in paper covers. After Eliot's death in 1965, this edition lapsed quietly, to be replaced in 1975 by a new Faber paperback of Pound's *Selected Poems 1908–1959*, identical in many ways to the New Directions selection. In 1967, however, Faber took precedence in originating a paperback *Selected Cantos* in an ambitious edition of 34,000 copies—a companion volume to Eliot's cullings from the early poetry. Pound had chosen the texts himself after having met with Faber editor Peter de Sautoy while in London in late 1965 to attend Eliot's memorial service at Westminster Abbey (it was apparently during this meeting that the eighty-year-old Pound, depressed about his inability to bring the poem to a close, asked de Sautoy to "abolish" the *Cantos*). The edition bore a dedication to his companion Olga Rudge, with the indication that despite the silence that had now descended over him, it was nonetheless time to speak out — "Tempus loquendi" — if only to honor the shade of Eliot.

This memorial to Eliot was not, however, to be the swansong of the *Cantos*. Unbeknownst to either Faber or New Directions, a samizdat version of their "ending" had also appeared in 1967, distributed in typewritten reproduction as *Cantos 110–116*, "printed & published by the FUCK YOU press at a secret location in the lower east side." Laughlin quickly moved to enforce New Directions's copyright on this leak of the poem's latest manuscripts into the bardic counter-culture gathered around Allen Ginsberg. A year and a half later an official edition of Pound's *Drafts & Fragments of Cantos CX–CXVII* duly appeared — with the poet's tacit imprimatur — to warm critical reception both in the U.S. and Great Britain, late-sixties readers discovering in its luminous shards a confessional authenticity not heard since the *Pisans*. These *Drafts & Fragments* — surely one of the most arresting examples of Late Style in twentieth-century poetry — have been poorly served in selection: Laughlin tacked on a few pages of them in his New Directions *Selected Cantos* (1970), while another four appeared at the end of the 1977 expanded Faber paperback of the *Selected Poems 1908–1969*. It is hoped that in this new edition of his selected poetry they will take pride of place alongside his late translations.

Introduction: 1928

BY T.S. ELIOT (1929/1948)

Mr. Ezra Pound recently made for publication in New York a volume of 'collected poems' under the title of *Personæ*.[1] I made a few suggestions for omissions and inclusions in a similar collection to be published in London; and out of discussions of such matters with Pound arose the spectre of an introduction by myself.

The poems which I wished to include, from among those which the author had omitted, are found together at the back of the book[2]. The order followed throughout the book is, with the exception mentioned, that of original publication of the scattered volumes from which the poems are drawn.

Mr. Pound intended his collection to consist of all of his work in verse up to his *Cantos*, which he chooses to keep in print. This book, so far as I am responsible for it, is not intended for quite that role: it is not a 'collected edition' but a selection. Some of the poems omitted by Pound, as well as some of those omitted by myself, seem to me well 'worthy of preservation.' This book is, in my eyes, rather a convenient Introduction to Pound's work than a definitive edition.

[1]That title could not be given to the present book, because it would led to confusion with the American volume, and with the original *Personæ* published in 1909 by Elkin Mathews.
[2] The "early Poems Rejected by the Author and omitted from his collected Edition" include "In Tempore Senectutis," "Comeraderie," "An Idyl for Glaucus," "Canzon: The Yearly Slain," "Koré," and "Canzone: Of Incense" [ed.].

The volumes previously published represent each a particular aspect or period of his work; and even when they fall into the right hands, are not always read in the right order. My point is that Pound's work is not only much more varied than is generally supposed, but also represents a continuous development, down to *Hugh Selwyn Mauberley*, the last stage of importance before the *Cantos*. This book would be, were it nothing else, a text-book of modern versification. The *Cantos* 'of a poem of some length' are by far his most important achievement; owing to their scarcity and their difficulty, they are not appreciated; but they are much more comprehensible to a reader who has followed the author's poetry from the beginning.

I remarked some years ago, in speaking of *vers libre*, that 'no *vers* is *libre* for the man who wants to do a good job'. The term, which fifty years ago had an exact meaning, in relation to the French alexandrine, now means too much to mean anything at all. The *vers libre* of Jules Laforgue, who, if not quite the greatest French poet after Baudelaire, was certainly the most important technical innovator, is free verse in much the way that the later verse of Shakespeare, Webster, Tourneur, is free verse: that is to say, it stretches, contracts, and distorts the traditional French measure as later Elizabethan and Jacobean poetry stretches, contracts and distorts the blank verse measure. But the term is applied to several types of verse which have developed in English without relation to Laforgue, Corbière, and Rimbaud, or to each other. To be more precise, there are, for instance, my own type of verse, that of Pound, and that of the disciples of Whitman. I will not say that subsequently there have not appeared traces of reciprocal influence of several types upon one another, but I am here speaking of origins. My own verse is, so far as I can judge, nearer to the original meaning of *vers libre* than is any of the other types: at least, the form in which I began to write, in 1908 or 1909, was directly drawn from the study of Laforgue together with the later Elizabethan drama; and I do not know anyone who started from exactly that point. I did not read Whitman until much later in life, and had to conquer an aversion to his form, as well as to much of his matter, in order to do so. I am equally certain — it is indeed obvious — that Pound owes nothing to Whitman. This is an elementary observation; but when dealing with popular conceptions of *vers libre* one must still be as simple and elementary as fifteen years ago.

The earliest of the poems in the present volume show that the first strong influences upon Pound, at the moment when his verse was taking direction, were those of Browning and Yeats. In the background are the 'Nineties in general, and behind the 'Nineties, of course, Swinburne and William Morris. I suspect that the latter influences were much more visible in whatever Mr. Pound wrote before the first of his published verse; they linger in some of his later work more as an emotional attitude than in the technique of versification: the shades of Dowson, Lionel Johnson and Fiona flit about.[1] Technically, these influences were all good; for they combine to insist upon the importance of *verse as speech* (I am not excepting Swinburne); while from more antiquarian studies Pound was learning the importance of *verse as song*.

It is important at this point to draw a simple distinction which is overlooked by nearly all critics who are not verse-makers themselves, and by many who are: the distinction between form and substance, and again between material and attitude. Such distinctions are constantly drawn, but are often drawn when they should not be, as well as ignored when they should be observed. Modern verse is often associated where it is different, and distinguished where it is the same. People may think they like the form because they like the content, or think they like the content because they like the form. In the perfect poet they fit and are the same thing; and in another sense they *always* are the same thing. So it is always true to say that form and content are the same thing, and always true to say that they are different things.

Pound, for example, has been accused of exactly opposite faults, because these distinctions are seldom observed in the right place. He is called objectionably 'modern', and objectionably 'antiquarian'. Neither is true at the point at which it is supposed to be true.

I should say first that Pound's versification is objectionable to those who object to it as 'modern', because they have not sufficient education (in verse) to understand development. Poets may be divided into those who develop technique, those who imitate technique, and those who invent technique. When I say 'invent', I should use inverted commas, for invention would be irreproachable if it were possible. 'Invention' is wrong only because it is impossible. I mean that the difference between the 'development' and the 'sport' is, in poetry, a capital one. There are two kinds of 'sports' in poetry, in the floricultural sense. One is the imitation of development, and the other is the imitation of some Idea of originality. The former is commonplace, a waste product of civilization. The latter is contrary to life. The poem which is absolutely original is absolutely bad; it is, in the bad sense, 'subjective' with no relation to the world to which it appeals.

Originality, in other words, is by no means a simple idea in the criticism of poetry. True originality is merely development; and if it is right development it may appear in the end so *inevitable* that we almost come to the point of view of denying all 'original' virtue to the poet. He simply did the next thing. I do not deny that *true* and *spurious* originality may hit the public with the same shock;

[1] Mr. Pound, it must be remembered, has written an excellent brief study of the verse of Arthur Symons, and has edited a volume of the poems of Lionel Johnson, some few copies of which contained an introduction by the editor, hastily withdrawn from circulation by the publisher and now a bibliophile's rarity.

indeed spurious originality ('spurious' when we use the word 'originality' properly, that is to say, within the limitations of life, and when we use the word absolutely and therefore improperly, 'genuine') may give the greater shock.

Now Pound's originality is genuine in that his versification is a *logical* development of the verse of his English predecessors. Whitman's originality is both genuine and spurious. It is genuine in so far as it is a *logical* development of certain English prose; Whitman was a great prose writer. It is spurious in so far as Whitman wrote in a way that asserted that his great prose was a new form of verse. (And I am ignoring in this connexion the large part of clap-trap in Whitman's content.) The word 'revolutionary' has no meaning, for this reason: we confound under the same name those who are revolutionary because they develop logically, and those who are 'revolutionary' because they innovate illogically. It is *very* difficult at any moment, to discriminate between the two.

Pound is 'original', in the way which I approve, in another sense. There is a shallow test which holds that the original poet goes direct to life, and the derivative poet to 'literature'. When we look into the matter, we find that the poet who is really 'derivative' is the poet who *mistakes* literature for life, and very often the reason why he makes this mistake is that—he has not read enough. The ordinary life of ordinary cultivated people is a mush of literature and life. There is a right sense in which for the educated person literature *is* life, and life *is* literature; and there is also a vicious sense in which the same phrases may be true. We can at least try not to confuse the material and the use which the author makes of it.

Now Pound is often most 'original' in the right sense, when he is most 'archæological' in the ordinary sense. It is almost too platitudinous to say that one is not modern by writing about chimney-pots, or archaic by writing about oriflammes. It is true that most people who write of oriflammes are merely collecting old coins, as most people who write about chimney-pots are merely forging new ones. If one can really penetrate the life of another age, one is penetrating the life of one's own. The poet who understands merlons and crenelles can understand chimney-pots, and vice versa. Some men can understand the architecture of the cathedral of Albi, for instance, by seeing it as a biscuit factory; others can understand a biscuit factory best by thinking of the cathedral of Albi. It is merely a subjective difference of method. The mole digs and the eagle flies, but their end is the same, to exist.

One of Pound's most indubitable claims to genuine originality is, I believe, his revivification of the Provençal and the early Italian poetry. The people who tire of Pound's Provence and Pound's Italy are those who cannot see Provence and medieval Italy except as museum pieces, which is not how Pound sees them, or how he makes others see them. It is true that Pound seems to me to see Italy through Provence, where I see Provence through Italy (the fact that I am totally ignorant of Provençal except for a dozen lines of Dante, has nothing to do with the matter). But he does see them as contemporary with himself, that is to say, he has grasped certain things in Provence and Italy which are permanent in human nature. He is much more modern, in my opinion, when he deals with Italy and Provence, than when he deals with modern life. His Bertrand de Born is much more living than his Mr. Hecatomb Styrax (*Mœurs Contemporaines*). When he deals with antiquities, he extracts the essentially living; when he deals with contemporaries, he sometimes notes only the accidental. But this does not mean that he is antiquarian or parasitical on literature. Any scholar can see Arnaut Daniel or Guido Cavalcanti as literary figures; only Pound can see them as living beings. Time, in such connexions, does not matter; it is irrelevant whether what you see, really see, as a human being, is Arnaut Daniel or your greengrocer. It is merely a question of the means suited to the particular poet, and we are more concerned with the end than with the means.

In Pound's earlier poems then, we must take account first of the influence of certain predecessors in English poetry, and second of the influence of Provençal and Italian. In each of these influences we must distinguish between influence of form and influence of content; but, on the other hand, no one can be influenced by form or by content without being influenced by the other; and the tangle of influences is one which we can only partially resolve. Any particular influence of one poet on another is both of form and content. The former is perhaps the easier to trace. Certain of the early poems are obviously affected by the technical influence of Yeats. It is easier to trace the influence of the exact and difficult Provençal versification, than to distinguish the element of genuine revivification of Provençal, from the element of romantic fantasy which Pound acquired, not from Arnaut Daniel or Dante, but from the 'Nineties. But it must be remembered that these things are different, whether we are competent to perform the analysis or not.

There is a definite advance in *Riposte* of 1912 beyond *Personæ* of 1910. Some indications of the point of view of this period are found in notes reprinted in a prose book, *Pavannes and Divisions* (Knopf, 1918), entitled 'Retrospect', and a note on 'Dolmetsch and Vers Libre'. Probably the most important poem in this group is the version of the Anglo-Saxon 'Seafarer'. It is a new assimilation, subsequent to the Provençal, and with that a preparation for the paraphrases from the Chinese, *Cathay*; which in turn is a necessary stage in the progress towards the *Cantos*, which are wholly himself. Throughout the work of Pound there is what we might call a steady effort towards the synthetic construction of a style of speech. In each of the elements or strands there is something of Pound and something of some other, not further analysable; the strands go to make one rope, but the rope is not yet complete. And good translation like this is not merely translation, for the translator is giving the original through himself, and finding himself through the original. And again, in following the work of Pound, we must remember two aspects: there is the aspect of versification, traced through his early influences, through his work on Provençal, Italian and Anglo-Saxon, on the Chinese poets and on Propertius; and there is that aspect of deeper personal feeling, which is not invariably, so far, found in the poems of most important technical accomplishment. The two things tend in course of time to unite; but in the poems under consideration they often are distinct, sometimes imperfectly united. Hence those who are moved most by technical accomplishment see a steady progress; those who care most of the personal voice are apt to think that Pound's early verse is the best. Neither are quite right; but the second are the more wrong. *Ripostes* is, I think, a more personal volume than the earlier *Personæ* and *Exultations*; some poems in *Lustra* continue this development and some do not; *Cathay* and *Propertius* are more directly important on the technical side, as is *The Seafarer*; it is not until we reach *Mauberley* (much the finest poem, I believe, before the *Cantos*) that some definite fusion takes place. The reader should compare some of the lovely small poems in *Ripostes* with the poems in *Canzoni*, *Personæ*, and *Exultations* which are of more manifest technical interest, and on the other hand with *Mauberley*. Meanwhile, in *Lustra* are many voices. In the beautiful 'Near Perigord' in *Lustra* there is the voice of Browning. There is also

> There shut up in his castle, Tairiran's,
> She who had nor ears nor tongue save in her hands,
> Gone—ah, gone—untouched, unreachable!
> She who could never live save through one person,
> She who could never speak save to one person,
> And all the rest of her a shifting change,
> A broken bundle of mirrors. . . .

These verses are not Browning, or anybody else but Pound; but they are not the final Pound either; for there is too much in the phrasing that might have been constructed by a various number of good poets. It is fine poetry; it is more 'personal' than *Cathay*; but the syntax is less significant. In *Ripostes* and in *Lustra* there are many short poems of a slighter build than this, equally moving, but in which also the 'feeling' or 'mood' is more interesting than the writing. (In the perfect poem both are equally interesting, and being equally interesting are interesting as one thing and not as two.)

A GIRL

> The tree has entered my hands,
> The sap has ascended my arms,
> The tree has grown into my breast—

Downward,
The branches grow out of me, like arms.

Tree you are,
Moss you are,
You are violets with wind above them,
A child—so high—you are,
And all this is folly to the world.

There, you see, the 'feeling' is original in the best sense, but the phrasing is not quite 'completed'; for the last line is one which I or half a dozen other men might have written. Yet it is not 'wrong', and I certainly could not improve upon it.

As for *Cathay*, it must be pointed out that Pound is the inventor of Chinese poetry for our time. I suspect that every age has had, and will have, the same illusion concerning translations, an illusion which is not altogether an illusion either. When a foreign poet is successfully done into the idiom of our own language and our own time, we believe that he has been 'translated'; we believe that through this translation we really at last get the original. The Elizabethans must have thought that they *got* Homer through Chapman, Plutarch through North. Not being Elizabethans, we have not that illusion; we see that Chapman is more Chapman than Homer, and North more North than Plutarch, both localized three hundred years ago. We perceive also that modern scholarly translations, Loeb or other, do not give us what the Tudors gave. If a modern Chapman, or North or Florio appeared, we should believe that he was the real translator; we should, in other words, do him the compliment of believing that his translation was translucence. For contemporaries, no doubt the Tudor translations were translucencies; for us they are 'magnificent specimens of Tudor prose'. The same fate impends upon Pound. His translations seem to be—and that is the test of excellence—translucencies: we *think* we are closer to the Chinese than when we read, for instance, Legge. I doubt this: I predict that in three hundred years Pound's *Cathay* will be a 'Windsor Translation' as Chapman and North are now 'Tudor Translations': it will be called (and justly) a 'magnificent specimen of XXth Century poetry' rather than a 'translation'. Each generation must translate for itself.

This is as much as to say that Chinese poetry, as we know it to-day, is something invented by Ezra Pound. It is not to say that there is a Chinese poetry-in-itself, waiting for some ideal translator who shall be only translator; but that Pound has enriched modern English poetry as Fitzgerald enriched it. But whereas Fitzgerald produced only the one great poem, Pound's translation is interesting also because it is a phase in the development of Pound's poetry. People of to-day who like Chinese poetry are really no more liking Chinese poetry than the people who like Willow pottery and Chinesische-Turms in Munich and Kew like Chinese Art. It is probable that the Chinese, as well as the Provençals and the Italians and the Saxons, influenced Pound, for no one can work intelligently with a foreign matter without being affected by it; on the other hand, it is certain that Pound has influenced the Chinese and the Provençals and the Italians and the Saxons—not the matter *an sich*, which is unknowable, but the matter as we know it.

To consider Pound's original work and his translation separately would be a mistake, a mistake which implies a greater mistake about the nature of translation. (Cf. his 'Notes on Elizabethan Classicists' in *Pavannes and Divisions*, pp. 186 ff.) If Pound had not been a translator, his reputation as an 'original' poet would be higher; and this is all irrelevant.

Those who expect that any good poet should proceed by turning out a series of masterpieces, each similar to the last, only more developed *in every way*, are simply ignorant of the conditions under which the poet must work, especially in our time. The poet's progress is dual. There is the gradual accumulation of experience, like a tantalus jar: it may be only once in five or ten years that experience accumulates to form a new whole and finds its appropriate expression. But if a poet were content to attempt nothing less than always his best, if he insisted on waiting for these unpredictable crystallizations, he would not be ready for them when they came. The development of experience is largely unconscious, subterranean, so that we cannot gauge its progress except once in every five or ten years; but in the meantime the poet must be working; he must be experimenting and trying his technique so that it will be ready, like a well-oiled fire-engine, when the moment comes to strain it to its utmost. The poet who wishes to continue to write poetry must keep in training; and must do this, not by forcing his inspiration, but by good workmanship on a level possible for some hours' work every week of his life.

What I have just said should serve as an introduction, not only to the translations, but to a class of Pound's poems which may be called the Epigrams. These occur *passim* throughout *Lustra*. I have included most of them in this edition. There is, of course, acquaintance with Martial as well as with the epigrammatists of the Greek Anthology. Among 'poetry lovers' of the present time a taste for Martial is still more rare than a (genuine) taste for Dryden; what 'poetry lovers' do not recognize is that their limitation of poetry to the 'poetical' is a modern restriction of the romantic age: the romantic age has decided that a great deal of prose is poetry (though I dare say that Burton, and Browne, and De Quincey, and other idols of the poetry-prose romanticists presumed that they were writing prose); and conversely that a good deal of poetry is prose. (To me, Pope is poetry and Jeremy Taylor is prose.) The reader must not be hasty in deciding whether Pound's epigrams 'come off'; for he should first examine his own soul to find out whether he is capable of enjoying the very best epigram as poetry. (Mackail's selections from the Greek Anthology are admirable except for being selections: that is, they tend to suppress the element of wit, the element of epigram, in the anthologists.) The reader who does not like Pound's epigrams should make very sure that he is not comparing them with the *Ode to a Nightingale* before he condemns them. He would do best to try to accept them as a peculiar genre, and compare them with each other—for some are indeed better than others, and I have even omitted one on Mr. Chesterton—before he compares them with anything else. No one is competent to judge poetry until he recognizes that poetry is nearer to 'verse' than it is to prose poetry.

I am not prepared to say that I appreciate epigrams: my taste is possibly too romantic. All that I am sure of is that Pound's epigrams, if compared with anything contemporary of similar genre, are definitely better. And I am sure also of this, that Pound's occupation with translations and paraphrases, and with the lighter forms of serious verse, provide evidence of the integrity of his purpose. One cannot write poetry all the time; and when one cannot write poetry, it is better to write what one knows is verse and make it good verse, than to write bad verse and persuade oneself that it is good poetry. Pound's epigrams and translations represent a rebellion against the romantic tradition which insists that a poet should be continuously inspired, which allows the poet to present bad verse as poetry, but denies him the right to make good verse unless it can also pass as great poetry.

This introduction will serve its purpose if it makes clear to the reader one point: that a poet's work may proceed along two lines on an imaginary graph; one of the lines being his conscious and continuous effort in technical excellence, that is, in continually developing his medium for the moment when he really has something to say. The other line is just his normal human course of development, his accumulation and digestion of experience (experience is not sought for, it is merely accepted in consequence of doing what we really want to do), and by experience I mean the results of reading and reflection, varied interests of all sorts, contacts and acquaintances, as well as passion and adventure. Now and then the two lines may converge at a high peak, so that we get a masterpiece. That is to say, an accumulation of experience has crystallized to form material of art, and years of work in technique have prepared an adequate medium; and something results in which medium and material, form and content, are indistinguishable. A semi-metaphorical account like this must not be applied too literally; even if it could be applied to the work of all poets, the work of each individual poet would exhibit some deviation from it. I posit it only as an introduction to the work of *some* poets, of whom Pound is one. It should help us to analyse his work, to distinguish his work of the first, second and third degree of intensity, and to appreciate the value of the lower degrees.

At this point the objection may be raised: even if the account of the process is correct, is it justifiable for a poet to publish any of his work but that in which perfection of form unites with significance of feeling; any, that is, but his very best? There are several rejoinders to this objection, both theoretical and practical: one of the simplest being that if you apply it you must apply it both ways, and the result would be to censor a larger part of the published work of most of the accepted poets. It might also expunge several excellent poets altogether. I have met but very few people in my life who really care for poetry; and those few, when they have the knowledge (for they are sometimes quite illiterate people), know how to take from every poet what he has to give, and reject only those poets who whatever they give always pretend to give *more* than they do give; these discerning people appreciate the work of Pope and Dryden (indeed it might be said in our time that the man who cannot enjoy Pope as poetry probably understands no poetry: incidentally, I remember that Pound once induced me to destroy what I thought an excellent set of couplets; for, said he, 'Pope has done this so well that you cannot do it better; and if you mean this as a burlesque, you had better suppress it, for you cannot parody Pope unless you can write better verse than Pope—and you can't'). I have just described the relation of a poet's technical development and his personal development as two curves on a graph which sometimes meet. But I should add that the metaphor is deceptive if it makes you suppose that the two things are quite distinct. If we only knew 'perfect' poetry we should know very little about poetry; we cannot say even who are the twelve, or the six, or the three, or the two 'greatest' poets. But if we really love poetry, then we know and must know all its degrees. The distinction between technique and feeling—a distinction necessarily arbitrary and brutal—will not bother us: we shall be able to appreciate what is good of its kind; we shall be able to appreciate the meeting of the peaks, the fusion of matter and means, form and content, on any level; and also we shall appreciate both poetry in which technical excellence surpasses interest of content, and poetry in which interest of content surpasses technique.

In this volume you will find poetry of all three kinds. In some of the verse I believe that the content is more important than the means of expression; in others the means of expression is the important thing; some combines both. Most people will find things that they like in this book, and things that they dislike; only persons who like poetry and have trained themselves to like poetry will like it all. And of such persons there are not many.

The closest approximation—I mean the most nearly continuous identification—of form and feeling in Pound's poetry, I find is his *Cantos*, of which I can say but little, as I am not permitted to print them in this book. (At least they are the only 'poem of some length' by any of my contemporaries that I can read with enjoyment and admiration; at most, they are more than I could deal with anyway in this essay: in any case, they are a mine for juvenile poets to quarry; and in any case, my disagreement with their 'philosophy' is another affair.) But concerning the contents of this book, I am quite certain of *Mauberley*, whatever else I am certain of. I have omitted one long poem, which Mr. Pound might himself have included: the *Homage to Sextus Propertius*. I was doubtful of its effect upon the uninstructed reader, even with my instructions. If the uninstructed reader is not a classical scholar, he will make nothing of it; if he be a classical scholar, he will wonder why this does not conform to his notions of what translation should be. It is not a translation, it is a paraphrase, or still more truly (for the instructed) a *persona*. It is also a criticism of Propertius, a criticism which in a most interesting way insists upon an element of humour, of irony and mockery, in Propertius, which Mackail and other interpreters have missed. I think that Pound is critically right, and that Propertius was more civilized than most of his interpreters have admitted; nevertheless, I have thought best to omit the poem — though it is a most interesting study in versification, and one of the necessary prolegomena to the *Cantos*. I felt that the poem, *Homage to Propertius*, would give difficulty to many readers: because it is not enough a 'translation', and because it is, on the other hand, too much a 'translation', to be intelligible to any but the accomplished student of Pound's poetry.[1]

It may give surprise that I attach so much importance to *Hugh Selwyn Mauberley*. This seems to me a great poem. On the one hand, I perceive that the versification is more accomplished than that of any other of the poems in this book, and more varied. I only pretend to know as much about versifying as my carpenter knows about woodwork, or my painter knows about distemper. But I know very well that the apparent roughness and *naïveté* of the verse and rhyming of *Mauberley* are inevitably the result of many years of hard work: if you cannot appreciate the dexterity of *Altaforte* you cannot appreciate the simplicity of *Mauberley*. On the other side, the poem seems to me, when you have marked the sophistication and the great variety of the verse, verse of a man who knows his way about, to be a positive document of sensibility. It is compact of the experience of a certain man in a certain place at a certain time; and it is also a document of an epoch; it is genuine tragedy and comedy; and it is, in the best sense of Arnold's worn phrase, a 'criticism of life'.

I wish that it were suitable and permissible for me to proceed to discuss the *Cantos*, and Pound's philosophy. But in any case it is not desirable for me to expound these matters except with those who accept his poetry as I accept it.

I must repeat that although this edition differs from Mr. Pound's collection in only one important respect — the omission of *Sextus Propertius* — the responsibility is wholly mine. Mr. Pound still disapproves of my additions, which have

---

[1] It is, in my opinion, a better criticism of Propertius than M. Benda's *Properce*. I observe in passing that it was Mr. Pound who introduced Benda to England and America.

accordingly been segregated at the end of the book. On the other hand, I have not omitted any poems merely because they did not happen to please me. I omitted *The Goodly Fere* because it has a much greater popularity than it deserves, and might distract some readers from better work of the same period. I have omitted a small number of epigrams and translations merely in order to concentrate attention on the best ones. And I have omitted *Propertius* because I thought it better for the reader to form an opinion of Pound's poetry before reading that poem, or the *Cantos*. *Propertius* may be read in the American *Personæ*, published by Boni and Liveright, or in the volume *Quia Pauper Amavi*, published by The Egoist and taken over by the firm which was then Faber & Gwyer. The 'Draft of XVI Cantos for the Beginning of a Poem of some Length' was published in a limited edition by The Three Mountains Press in Paris.

POSTSCRIPT: 1948

This Introduction, written over twenty years ago, still seems to me to serve its purpose better than would a new introduction to the same selection of poems. The contemporary of the author of the later *Cantos* cannot alter the introduction written when he was a contemporary of the author of *Lustra* and *Hugh Selwyn Mauberley*. Certainly, I should now write with less cautious admiration of *Homage to Sextus Propertius*; but such changes of opinion are not enough to require a new introduction to the reprint of a volume from which it was omitted. There is no place for a new 'selection'; the complete early poems will be necessary when we have the complete *Cantos*. In the work of any major poet who does not repeat himself, the earlier part is necessary for understanding the later, and the later for understanding the earlier; but until Pound's complete works are assembled, there is still a place for a selection of the earlier poems up to and including *Mauberley*.

The Poetry of Ezra Pound

BY JOHN BERRYMAN (1949)

Since Pound has been for several generations now one of the most famous of living poets, it may occasion surprise that an *introduction* to his poetry (such as I was lately invited to make for New Directions) should be thought necessary at all. It may, but I doubt that it will. Not much candour is wanted for the observation that, though he is famous and his poetry is famous, his poetry is not familiar, that serious readers as a class have relinquished even the imperfect hold they had upon it fifteen years ago and regard it at present either with hostility or with indifference. The situation is awkward for the critic. Commonly, when the object of criticism is at once celebrated, unfamiliar, and odious, it is also remote in time; the inquiry touches no current or recent passion. Our case is as different as possible from this enviable condition.

> In a few years no one will remember the *buffo*.
> No one will remember the trivial parts of me,
> The comic detail will be absent.

After thirty-five years neither comic nor tragic detail is absent. Whatever the critic may wish to say of the poetry runs the risk of being misunderstood as of the poet; one encounters *eager* preconceptions; and no disclaimer is likely to have effect. I make, however, no disclaimer just yet. Let us only proceed slowly — remembering that it is the business of criticism to offer explanations — toward the matter of hostility, beginning with the matter of indifference.

It *is* very surprising, perhaps, that readers of poetry should remain indifferent to the verse of a poet so influential as Pound has been. As one of the dominant, seminal poetries of the age, one would expect readers to want to become acquainted with it as a matter of course. That many do not want to suggests that they do not in fact so regard it, or regard it as only in some special sense an influence; and I think this is the case. They regard *Pound* as a dominant influence. They are quite right, of course. But even this is often disputed or ignored, so we cannot avoid some discussion. It is necessary to see Pound under two aspects: as he worked upon poetry and as he worked upon the public. The notion of him as publicist for Joyce, Eliot, Frost, a hundred others, being still current, I feel free to select instances displaying rather the first aspect, and take his relations with W. B. Yeats, with Imagism, and with *The Waste Land*—with the major poet, that is, the major movement, and the major poem, of the century so far.

Pound went to London in 1908, at twenty-three, to learn from Yeats how to write poetry, in the belief that no one then living knew more about it. Swinburne was just alive (when he died the following April, "I am the King of the Cats," said Yeats to one of his sisters meeting her in the street), inaccessible behind Watts-Dunton.

> Swinburne my only miss
> *and* I didn't know he'd been to see Landor
> > and they told me this that an' tother
> and when old Mathews went he saw the three teacups
> > two for Watts Dunton who liked to let his tea cool
> So old Elkin had only one glory
> > He did carry Algernon's suit *once*
> when he, Elkin, first came to London.
> > But given what I know now I'd have
> > got thru it somehow . . . Dirce's shade
> > > or a black jack.   (Canto LXXXII)

Pound was a most odd disciple; he regarded himself as the heir of Browning, he was stirring free of Fitzgerald and the nineties, he had already begun the war on the iamb and the English heroic line that would never end (consider the two opening dactyls here and then the spondee-two-dactyls-and-trochee of the beautiful sixth line), he was full of the Troubadours, and he was becoming obsessed with the concept of verse-as-*speech*. He had as much energy as Yeats. The older poet has recorded his debt to the younger for advice against abstractions, underlinings of them, help in revision, and so on. But the change that began to move in Yeats's verse about this time was toward speech, the beginning of his famous development, and like one or two others I have always supposed Pound the motor. What seems to have happened was this: Pound was going in the afternoons to see Ford Madox Hueffer (Ford), and in the evenings to see Yeats; the older men did not get on. Of four "honourable debts" he acknowledged later, the chief was Hueffer, who "believes one should write in a contemporary spoken or at least speakable language"—not the same thing, it will be observed, as Pound's famous earlier formulation of "Mr. Hueffer's realization that poetry should be written at least as well as prose." So old Ezra had only one glory here, that he passed on without source in the evening what he had heard in the afternoon.

Then Imagism. There were two "Imagist" movements (besides a dilution of the second, conducted by Amy Lowell, which reached the public), both in London. The first was started in March 1909 by T. E. Hulme, who was insisting on "absolutely accurate presentation and no verbiage," F. S. Flint, who had been advocating "vers libre," Edward Storer, who was interested in "the Image," and others, all strongly under the influence of French Symbolist poetry. Pound joined the group on 22 April—Elkin Mathews had published the week before a third collection of poems, *Personæ*, his first book proper, which would establish him. Pound read out to the startled Soho café a new poem, "Sestina: Altaforte." *Exultations*, issued later that year, and *Canzoni* (1911), continuing his Provençal investigations, display no Imagist affiliation; *Ripostes* (1912) does, and at the end of it he printed Hulme's five poems and named the movement, which had passed away meanwhile, perhaps because none of its other members could write poetry. Through Pound personally, the first movement reached the second. The second consisted of H.D. and Richard Aldington, who were inspired not by French but by Greek verse, in 1912; Pound got their work printed, wrote the movement's essential documents (in *Poetry* for March 1913, "A Few Don'ts" and an interview with him signed by Flint), and edited *Des Imagistes*, which appeared in March of 1914. By the time Miss Lowell arrived with her retinue that summer, Pound, joined now with Wyndham Lewis and the sculptor Gaudier-Brzeska, had launched Vorticism, in the opening *Blast*. The importance of literary movements is readily exaggerated; conceivably in the end Imagism will seem valuable above all as it affected Pound's verse. Still, with a doubtful exception for the unnamed movement of the Auden group about 1930, it is the migration to a new position, for our time, that retains most interest, and is a fair sample of Pound's activity.

His now celebrated operation some years later upon *The Waste Land*, disengaging that work as we know it from what its author describes as a sprawling, chaotic poem twice as long, is another. Keeping our wits and facts in order, we need not follow a critic sometimes so penetrating as Yvor Winters in seeing Pound as the "primal spirit" behind every gesture, every deplorable gesture, of the deplorable Eliot. "The principal influence" upon Eliot's verse, Winters writes, "is probably that of Laforgue, whose poetry Pound had begun to champion at least as early as 1917." This is very early indeed, only seven years after Eliot's "Humouresque, After J. Laforgue" in the *Harvard Advocate*. No, Eliot started alone. The two poets met first, and Pound persuaded *Poetry* to print "The Love Song of J. Alfred Prufrock" in 1915, by which date Eliot was nearly through with Laforgue. Winters's remark neglects also the serial character of the influences on Eliot's poetry, which include Laforgue, Webster, James, Baudelaire, Pound, Gautier, Joyce, Apollinaire, Dante. It is emphatically not a mistake, however, to regard Pound's personal influence as great from 1915 on; and great on the period as a whole.

The reader who is not a student of poetry has another ground for indifference. Pound, he has always heard, has no "*matter*." Granting the "importance" of his verse, granting the possibility that having been for poets fertile it might prove on acquaintance agreeable or beautiful, what has he to do with this sport, a matterless poetry? This is a much more sophisticated dissatisfaction, and can claim the highest critical support. "I confess," Eliot once wrote, "that I am seldom interested in what he is saying, but only in the way he says it"; and R. P. Blackmur, "He is all surface and articulation." We notice Eliot's qualification ("seldom") and we are puzzled by an ambiguity in Blackmur's "articulation" (is this jointing or merely uttering?); but on the whole they put authoritatively the established view. Now there can be no question of traversing such authorities directly. But it is a violent and remarkable charge; I think we are bound to look into it a little.

If his critics are right, Pound himself misconceived his work from the beginning and has continued to do so. This is of course not impossible; in fact, I shall be arguing presently, in another sense, that it is just what he has done. But let us hear what he has said. In a very early poem, "Revolt, Against the crepuscular spirit in modern poetry," he says:

> I would shake off the lethargy of this our time, and give
> For shadows—shapes of power
> For dreams—men.

If the poem is bad, the programme is distinct. Then one of his debts, he records later, "may be considered as the example of or hint from Thomas Hardy, who, despite the aesthetic era, has remained interested in his subject, i.e., in distinction to being interested in 'treatment.'" Among other passages to the same effect, I give one more, later still, which readers must have come on with surprise. Speaking of Eliot and Miss Moore, Pound remarks, "Neither they nor anyone else is likely to claim that they have as much interest in life as I have, or that I have their patience in reading."

The "literary" or "aesthetic" view taken of Pound now for many years will not be much disturbed by such assertions, until we observe how oddly they are confirmed by the opinions expressed in 1909 about *Personæ*. These opinions are worth attention, because Pound's literary personality became known as a leader's thereafter, and most reviews his books have received since show the impress of this knowledge; they are impure. It is hardly too much to say that the first *Personæ* was the last volume of Pound's that was widely judged on its merits. What did the old reviewers say? "He writes out of an exuberance of incontinently struggling ideas and passionate convictions . . . He plunges straight into the heart of his theme, and suggests virility in action combined with fierceness, eagerness, and tenderness"—so R. A. Scott-James, whose excitement, by the way, about "the brute force of Mr. Pound's imagination" did not prevent his noticing the unusual spondee-dactyl use, which he exemplified with a lovely line from "Cino":

Éyes, dréams, / líps, and the / níght góes.

It is absolutely unnecessary, and appears to a scholar probably very ridiculous, to patronize the reviewers of an earlier age. "The beauty of ["In Praise of Ysolt"] is the beauty of passion, sincerity and intensity," wrote Edward Thomas, "not of beautiful words and images and suggestions . . . the thought dominates the words and is greater than they are." One hardly recognizes here the "superficial" or "mindless" Pound whom critics have held up to us since. Faced with a welter of Provençal and Browning and early Yeats, not to mention Villon, the reviewers nevertheless insisted upon the poet's strong individuality: "All his poems are like this, from beginning to end, and in every way, his own, and in a world of his own." Faced with this learning (the notes quote Richard of St. Victor, etc.), they admired "his fearlessness and lack of self-consciousness," the "breath of the open air." "He cannot be usefully compared," Thomas went on, "with any living writers . . . full of personality and with such power to express it, that," and so on. The Oxford *Isis* agreed that "physically and intellectually the verse seems to reproduce the personality with a brief fullness and adequacy." Instead of pursuing the engaging themes thrown up by this medley of exaggeration and justice, culled mostly from the back leaves of *Exultations*, let me pass to a third, more serious difficulty with the view that Pound has no "matter."

Pound's poetry treats of Provence, China, Rome, London, medieval living, modern living, human relationships, authors, young women, animals, money, games, government, war, poetry, love, and other things. This can be verified. What the critics must mean, then, is that they are aware of a *defect*, or defects, in the substance of the poetry. About one defect they have been explicit: the want of originality of substance. Pound has no matter *of his own*. Pound—who is even in the most surprising quarters conceded to be a "great" translator—

is best as a translator. "The *Propertius* is a sturdier, more sustained, and more independent poem than *Mauberley*," writes Blackmur. "Craftsmanship may be equally found in both poems; but Mr. Pound has contributed more of his own individual sensibility, more genuine personal voice, in the *Propertius* where he had something to proceed from, than in *Mauberley* where he was on his own . . . This fact, which perhaps cannot be demonstrated but which can be felt when the reader is familiar enough with the poems, is the key-fact of serious judgment upon Mr. Pound." I do not feel sure that time is bearing out the first part of this careful judgment; the finest sections of Pound's postwar farewell to London, where the grotesquerie of Tristan Corbière is a new element in the complex style, naïve and wily, in which he celebrates the modern poet's difficulties and nostalgia, seem to me somewhat more brilliant, solid, and independent than the finest sections of the Roman poem. But my objections to the point of view begin well behind any value judgment. *All* the ambitious poetry of the last six hundred years is much less "original" than any but a few of its readers ever realize. A staggering quantity of it has direct sources, even verbal sources, in other poetry, history, philosophy, theology, prose of all kinds. Even the word "original" in this sense we find first in Dryden, and the sense was not normalized till the midcentury following. A few hours, or days, with several annotated editions of *Lycidas* will transform the reader's view of this matter, especially if he will bear in mind the likelihood that the serious modern poet's strategy resembles Milton's—exceptional as Milton was—far more closely than his (the reader's) attitude and knowledge resemble Milton's contemporary reader's attitude and knowledge. Poetry is a palimpsest. "The old playwrights took old subjects," remarks a poet who has not been accused of want of originality, "did not even arrange the subject in a new way. They were absorbed in expression, that is to say in what is most near and delicate." So Yeats; but our literary criticism, if at its best it knows all this well enough, even at its best is inclined to forget it and to act as if originality were not regularly a matter of *degree* in works where it is worth assessing at all. A difficulty is that modern critics spend much of their time in the perusal of writing that really is more or less original, and negligible. This African originality is very confusing. One of the writer's favorite poems is perfect Thomson in manner as well as perfect Wordsworth, the substance is all but purely Wordsworth's, and how are we accustomed to deal with this? The answer is that we are not. It clearly troubles Eliot that the two first sections of "Near Perigord" resemble Browning, Pound's master, though the poem seems to him (as to me) beautiful and profound; this poem is extremely original in substantial development. Now, though Blackmur is preferring derivation and Eliot is deprecating it, they appear to illustrate an identical disorder of procedure, that of a criticism which is content to consider in isolation originality of either matter *or* manner, without regard to the other, and with small regard to degree.

I term this a disorder rather than a defect, because with regard to a poetry as singular as Pound's, and with such diverse claims upon our attention, it is all but fatal to criticism. The critics were writing, one fifteen years ago, the other twenty, but I do not know that our situation has much improved, and it goes without saying that the best criticism of the period has addressed itself almost exclusively to manner, except for the proliferation in the last decade of an exegetical criticism similarly limited and comparatively abject. Until we get a criticism able to consider both originalities, in degree, Pound's achievement as a poet cannot be finally extricated from the body of his verse; and prepossessions should be avoided. That he has translated so much has no doubt cost him many readers, who (despite Dryden and Pope) cannot imagine that a "real poet" would be content to translate so much; but criticism should be wiser.

Why *has* Pound translated so much? The question is an important one, and the answers usually given ignore the abyss of difference between his just-translations, like the Cavalcanti (the Canzone aside, of which his final version opens Canto XXXVI), such as might have been made by another poet of superlative skill, and renderings like those in *Cathay* and *Propertius*, which are part of Pound's own life-poetry. The first class may be considered as exercise, propaganda, critical activity, taken in conjunction with his incoherent and powerful literary criticism. The second class requires a word about Pound's notion of *personae* or masks, which issued successively in the masks of Cino, Bertran de Born, various Chinese poets, Propertius, Mauberley, fifty others. They differ both from Yeats's masks and from the dramatizations, such as Prufrock and Auden's "airman," that other poets find necessary in a period inimical to poetry, gregarious, and impatient of dignity.

We hear of the notion in two of his earliest poems, a sonnet "Masks" about

> souls that found themselves among
> Unwonted folk that spake a hostile tongue,
> Some souls from all the rest who'd not forgot
> The star-span acres of a former lot
> Where boundless mid the clouds his course he swung,
> Or carnate with his elder brothers sung
> E'er ballad makers lisped of Camelot . . .

and "In Durance":

> But for all that, I am homesick after mine own kind
> And would meet kindred even as I am,
> Flesh-shrouded bearing the secret.

The question is, what the masks are *for*.

Does any reader who is familiar with Pound's poetry really not see that its subject is the life of the modern poet? It is in "Famam Librosque Cano" and "Scriptor Ignotus" of *Personæ*—

> And I see my greater soul-self bending
> Sibylwise with that great forty-year epic
> That you know of, yet unwrit
> But as some child's toy 'tween my fingers . . .
>
> If my power be lesser
> Shall my striving be less keen? . . .

It is in "Histrion" of *Exultations*—

> 'Tis as in midmost us there glows a sphere
> Translucent, molten gold, that is the "I"
> And into this some form projects itself . . .
>
> And these, the Masters of the Soul, live on.

It is in one of the few good lines of *Canzoni*—

> Who calls me idle? I have thought of her.

It is in "N.Y." of *Ripostes* (1912), the volume in which Pound established his manner and the volume with which modern poetry in English may be felt to have begun—

> My City, my beloved, my white! Ah, slender . . .
>
> Delicately upon the reed, attend me!
>
> Now do I know that I am mad,
> For here are a million people surly with traffic:
> This is no maid.
> Neither could I play upon any reed if I had one.

It is everywhere (as well as the Chinese work) in the more "original" poems and epigrams of *Lustra*, written 1913-16. (A lustrum is "an offering for the sins of the whole people, made by the censors at the expiration of their five years of office." It has not perhaps been sufficiently observed that Pound is one of the wittiest poets who ever wrote. Yet he is serious enough in this title. In certain attitudes—his medieval nostalgia, literary anti-Semitism, others—he a good deal resembles Henry Adams; each spent his life, as it were, seeking an official post where he could be used, and their failure to find one produced both the freedom and the inconsequence that charm and annoy us in these authors.) It is in the elaborate foreign personae that followed, *Cathay* (1915)—

> And I have moped in the Emperor's garden, awaiting
> an order-to write!

and *Propertius* (1917)—

> I who come first from the clear font
> Bringing the Grecian orgies into Italy
> and the dance into Italy.

It is in *Mauberley*, of course—

> Dowson found harlots cheaper than hotels;
> So spoke the author of "The Dorian Mood,"

> M. Verog, out of step with the decade,
> Detached from his contemporaries
> Neglected by the young,
> Because of these reveries.

Meanwhile, Pound's concept of method had been strongly affected by Ernest Fenollosa's essay *The Chinese Written Character as a Medium for Poetry* ("Metaphor, the revealer of nature, is the very substance of poetry . . . Chinese poetry gets back near to the processes of nature by means of its vivid figure . . . If we attempt to follow it in English we must use words highly charged, words whose vital suggestion shall interplay as nature interplays. Sentences must be like the mingling of the fringes of feathered banners, or as the colors of many flowers blended into the single sheen of a meadow . . . a thousand tints of verb") and for years he had been trying to work out a form whereby he could get his subject all together; by the time of *Mauberley* he had succeeded, in the final version of the opening Cantos. And it is, as we shall see, in the *Cantos* also.

Above all, certain themes in the life of the modern poet: indecision-decision and infidelity-fidelity. Pound has written much more love poetry than is generally realized, and when fidelity and decision lock in his imagination, we hear extraordinary effects, passionate, solemn. A lady is served her singer-lover's heart, eats, and her husband tells her whose:

> "It is Cabestan's heart in the dish."
> "It is Cabestan's heart in the dish?
> "No other taste shall change this." (Canto IV)

She hurtles from the window.

> And in south province Tchin Tiaouen had risen
> and took the city of Tchang tcheou
> offered marriage to Ouang Chi,
> who said: It is an honour.
> I must first bury Kanouen. His body is heavy.
> His ashes were light to carry
> Bright was the flame for Kanouen
> > Ouang Chi cast herself into it, Faithful forever
> > High the hall TIMOUR made her. (Canto LVI)

"His body is heavy." The theme produces also the dazzle and terror of the end of "Near Perigord," where we finally reach Bertran *through Maent*, whom we'd despaired of. If there are a passion and solemnity beyond this in poetry —

> Soul awful! if the Earth has ever lodg'd
> An awful soul —

we have to go far to find them. If Pound is neither the poet apostrophized here nor the poet apostrophizing, not Milton or Wordsworth, his place will be high enough. These themes of decision and fidelity bear on much besides love in his poetry, and even — as one would expect with a subject of the poet-in-exile (Ovid, Dante, Villon, Browning, Henry James, Joyce, Pound, Eliot, as Mann, Brecht, Auden) whose allegiance is to an ideal state — upon politics:

> homage, fealty are to the person
> can not be to body politic . . . (Canto LXVII)[1]

[1] Without allusion to the poet's personal situation (in 1949), which is rather a matter for courts, which have reached no verdict, and psychiatrists, who have declared the poet insane, that when the Irish patriot Sir Roger Casement was tried for treason a war ago, he had to be tried under a statute centuries old, the charge being based upon a conventional oath of personal loyalty to the King made when Casement was knighted for services "to the Crown" as a civil servant investigating atrocities in the Putomayo.

Of course there are other themes, strong and weak, and a multiplicity of topics, analogies to the life of the modern poet, with or without metaphor the interests of the poet. But this would appear to characterize any poet's work. I mean more definitely "Life and Contacts," as the subtitle of *Hugh Selwyn Mauberley* has it.

It is not quite Ezra Pound himself. Yeats, another Romantic, was also the subject of his own poetry, himself-as-himself. Pound is his own subject *qua* modern poet; it is the experience and fate of this writer "born/In a half savage country, out of date," a voluntary exile for over thirty years, that concern him. Another distinction is necessary. Wallace Stevens has presented us in recent years with a series of strange prose documents about "imagination" and "reality." If Stevens's poetry has for substance imagination, in this dichotomy, Pound's has for substance reality. A poem like "Villanelle: the Psychological Hour" or the passage I have quoted about Swinburne could have been made only by Pound, and the habit of mind involved has given us much truth that we could not otherwise have had. Two young friends did not come to see the poet! The poet missed a master! This is really in part what life consists of, though reading most poetry one would never guess it.

> And we say good-bye to you also,
> For you seem never to have discovered
> That your relationship is wholly parasitic;
> Yet to our feasts you bring neither
> Wit, nor good spirits, nor the pleasing attitudes
> Of discipleship.

It is personal, but it is not very personal. The "distance" everywhere felt in the finest verse that treats his subject directly has, I think, two powerful sources, apart from the usual ones (versification and so on). First, there is the peculiar detachment of interest with which Pound seems to regard himself; no writer could be less revelatory of his passional life, and his friends have recorded—Dr Williams with annoyance—the same lifelong reticence in private. Second, his unfaltering, encyclopedic mastery of tone—a mastery that compensates for a comparative weakness of syntax. (By instinct, I parenthesize, Pound has always minimized the importance of syntax, and this instinct perhaps accounts for his inveterate dislike for Milton, a dislike that has had broad consequences for three decades of the twentieth century; not only did Milton seem to him, perhaps, anti-romantic *and* anti-realistic, undetailed, and anti-conversational, but Milton is the supreme English master of syntax.) Behind this mastery lies his ear. I scarcely know what to say of Pound's ear. Fifteen years of listening have not taught me that it is inferior to the ear of the author of *Twelfth Night*. The reader who heard the damage done, in my variation, to Pound's line—*So old Elkin had only one glory*—will be able to form his own opinion.

We write verse—was it Lautrec, "I paint with my penis"—we write verse with our ears; so this is important. Forming, animating, quelling his material, that ear is one of the main, weird facts of modern verse. It imposes upon the piteous stuff of the *Pisan Cantos* a "distance" as absolute as upon the dismissal of the epigram just cited. The poet has listened to his life, so to speak, and he tells us that which he hears.

Both the personality-as-subject and the expressive personality are nearly uniform, I think, once they have developed. In Yeats, in Eliot, we attend to re-formations of personality. Not really in Pound; he is unregenerate. "*Toutes mes pièces datent de quinze ans,*" he quoted once with approval from a friend, and the contrast he draws between the life of the poet as it ought to be (or has been) and as it is, this contrast is perennial. But if this account of the poet's subject is correct, what can have concealed it from most even sympathetic and perceptive critics and readers? With regard to critics, two things, I believe. All the best critics of Pound's work themselves write verse, most of them verse indebted to Pound's, much of it heavily; they have been interested in craft, not personality and subject. Also, they have been blinded, perhaps, by the notion of the "impersonality" of the poet. This perverse and valuable doctrine, associated in our time with Eliot's name, was toyed with by Goethe and gets expression in Keats's insistence that the poet "has no identity—he is continually in, for, and filling some other body." For poetry of a certain mode (the dramatic), this is a piercing notion; for most other poetry, including Pound's, it is somewhat paradoxical, and may disfigure more than it enlightens. It hides motive, which persists. It fails to enable us to see, for instance, that the dominant source of inspiration in Keats's sonnet on Chapman's Homer is *antagonism*, his contempt for Pope and Pope's Homer. (This view, which I offer with due hesitation, is a development from an industrious and thoughtful biography of the sonnet by a British scholar in *Essays and Studies* for 1931.)

The reader is in one way more nearly right than the majority of critics. He is baffled by a heterogeneity of matter, as to which I shall have more to say in a moment, but he hears a personality in Pound's poetry. In fact, his hostility—we reach it at last—is based upon this. The trouble is that he hears the personality he expected to hear, rather than the one that is essentially there. He hears Pound's well-known prose personality, bellicose, programmatic, positive, and he resents it. Pound is partially responsible. This personality does exist in him, it is what he has lived with, and he can even write poetry with it, as we see in "Sestina: Alaforte" and elsewhere early and late. A follower of Browning, he takes a keenly *active* view of poetry, and has, conceivably, a most imperfect idea both of just what his subject is and of what his expressive personality is like.

This personality is feline, supra-delicate, absorbed. If Browning made the fastest verse in English, Pound makes the slowest, the most discrete and suave. He once said of a story in *Dubliners* that it was something better than a story, it was "a vivid waiting," and the phrase yields much of his own quality. There is restlessness; but the art of the poet places itself, above all, immediately and mysteriously at the service of the passive and elegiac, the nostalgic. The true ascendancy of this personality over the other is suggested by a singular fact: the degree in which the mantic character is absent from his poetry. He looks ahead indeed, looks ahead eagerly, but he does not *feel* ahead; he feels back. (Since writing the sentence, I come on the phrase in Fenollosa, an impressive remark, "The chief work of literary men in dealing with language, and of poets especially, lies in feeling back along the ancient lines of advance.") It is the poetry of a late craftsman; of an expatriate —

> Moaneth alway my mind's lust
> That I fare forth, that I afar hence
> Seek out a foreign fastness. ("The Seafarer")

> Here we are, picking the first fern-shoots
> And saying: When shall we get back to our country? . . .

> Our sorrow is bitter, but we would not return to our
> country. (*Cathay's* first lines)

— of a failing culture. The personality is full already in "The Return" from *Ripostes* — return of the hunters, or literary men, for like others of Pound's poems this is a metaphor: those who in an earlier poem had cried

> "'Tis the white stag, Fame, we're ahunting,"

now come back illusionless.

The *Cantos* seem to be a metaphor also. This immense poem, as yet untitled and unfinished, is seriously unfinished: two cantos are missing and sixteen are to come, if the poet recovers sufficiently to be able to write verse again. Since Canto LXXIV alone is twenty-five pages long, it is clear that the last sixteen of the hundred may alter radically views we have formed of the work as a whole from the part we know; and we want to avoid the error (if it was one) of Pound when he hazarded in 1933, of the still untitled and unfinished *Finnegans Wake*, "It can hardly be claimed . . . that the main design emerges above the detail." Nevertheless, I must say something of the subject and form of this epic. I believe the critical view is that it is a "rag-bag" of the poet's interests, "a catalogue, his jewels of conversation." It can be read with delight and endless profit thus, if at any rate one understands that it is a work of versification, that is, poem. The basal rhythm I hear is dactylic, as in the Swinburne and Ouang Chi passages and in the opening line, "And then went down to the ship," — in this line we see the familiar tendency of English dactyls to resolve themselves into anapests with anacrusis, but the ambiguity seems to me to be progressively avoided as the poem advances. But the rag-bag view depends for support upon lines that Pound cut out of the primitive printed versions of the earliest cantos; the form greatly developed, the form *for the subject*. For a rag-bag, the poem sets out very oddly. I will describe the first three cantos.

1. The Poet's, the Hero's, physical and mental travel: what can "I" expect? Persona, Odysseus-in-exile; antagonist, Poseidon (the "godly sea" — an ironic pun). Material: escape-from-transformation, sacrifice, descent to Hell, recognition of and obligation to the Dead (parents, masters), prediction of return *alone* over the seas, "Lose all companions." (This is exactly, thirty years later, what happened to the poet.) Form: a depth-introduction, heroic Greek (*Odyssey*, xi) through Renaissance Latin (Divus) in old-heroic-English style as modified by modern style. So the first canto, about sacrifice to the enemy, acknowledgment of indebtedness, and outset.

2. The orchestra begins, the poet's nineteenth-century English master to Provençal to Chinese to ancient British to modern Spanish (another exile) to ancient Greek, very rapidly; then the Poet's theme and temptation, Beauty, a faithless woman (Helen); then an exquisite, involved color and sense lyric (the first of dozens) in honor of Poseidon's beloved; then the canto proper, about *betrayal*, the metamorphoses into "Sniff and pad-foot of beasts" of all those who do not recognize and wish to *sell* (sell out) the God — Dionysus and Poseidon are linked as having power each over the sea, and those false to them are the "betrayers of language" of Canto XIV, Mr. Nixon of *Mauberley* — "I" (Acoetes, the persona) alone have not. Exilic Ovid is the fable's source.

3. Three themes: (1) A stronger sea ceremony than sacrifice, *embracing* of difficulties, the Venetian "*sponzalizio del mar*" ("to wed the sea as a wife," Canto XXVI), "*voce tinnula*" below being Catullus' "with ringing voice" for nuptial songs; (2) enmities and poverty that beset the Poet or Hero (persona, the Cid), *proscription*; (3) artistic mortality, a Mantegna fresco flaking, and just before, an opposite example, Ignez da Castro stabbed by her lover's order (Pedro I of Portugal) in 1355, then avenged by her son, exhumed and crowned ("here made to stand") —

> Time is the evil. Evil.
>
> A day, and a day
> Walked the young Pedro baffled,
>   a day, and a day
> After Ignez was murdered.
> Came the Lords in Lisboa

a day, and a day

In homage. Seated there

dead eyes,

Dead hair under the crown,

The King still young there beside her. (Canto XXX)

This kind of interpenetration of life and art, in metaphor, is one of the poem's triumphs, a Coleridgean "fusing."

Such, according to the notes I once made in my margin, is the beginning of this famous "formless" work, which is, according to one critic of distinction, "not about anything." Reviewers of the *Pisan Cantos* have showed surprise that they were so "personal," and yet very fine, — it is the most brilliant sequence indeed since the original thirty. The *Cantos* have always been personal, only the persona increasingly adopted, as the Poet's fate clarifies, is Pound himself. The heterogeneity of material, every reader remarks, seems to have three causes. The illusion of Pound's romanticism ("—if romanticism indeed be an illusion!" he exclaims in *Indiscretions*) has given him an inordinate passion for ages and places where the Poet's situation appears attractive, as in the Malatesta cantos, where Sigismondo is patron as much as ruler and lover (VIII–XI), and the Chinese cantos (XIII, XLIX, LII–LXI); here he is sometimes wonderful but sometimes ungovernable. Then he is anxious to find out *what has gone wrong*, with money and government, that has produced our situation for the Poet; several of the money cantos, XLV and LI, are brilliant, but most of the American historical cantos (XXXI–IV, XXXVII–VIII, LXII–LXXI) are willed, numb, angry—the personae Jefferson and John Adams are not felt and so the material is uncontrolled. The rest of his heterogeneity is due to an immoderate desire, strong in some other modern artists also, for mere conservation—

And lest it pass with the day's news

Thrown out with the daily paper. (Canto XXVIII)

Once the form, and these qualifications, are understood, Pound's work presents less difficulty than we are used to in ambitious modern poetry. Pieces like "A Song for the Degrees" (an anti-Psalm) and "Papyrus" (a joke, for that matter, a clear and good one) are rare. Occasionally you have to look things up if you don't wish to be puzzled; and it does no harm to use the index volume of Britannica 11th, and various dictionaries, and to be familiar with Pound's prose, when you read the *Cantos*; the labour is similar to that necessary for a serious understanding of *Ulysses*, and meditation is the core of it. To find out what a modern poet has done, we have often to ask *why* he did it.

The poet's own statements must be accepted with a certain reserve, which neither his admirers nor his detractors have always exercised. Thus the *Cantos* are said to be written in an equivalent for ideogram. We have recognized their relation to parts of Fenollosa. But Fenollosa's technical center is an attack on the copula; I observe that four of the lines about Ouang Chi successively employ the copula without loss to characteristic beauty, and I reason that we must inquire into these things for ourselves. More interesting, far, are the equivalents for musical form, and the versification. So with Pound's remark that the *Cantos* are "the tale of the tribe"; they seem to be only apparently a historical or philosophical epic, actually a personal epic—as he seems to understand himself elsewhere in *Guide to Kulchur* when he suggests that the work may show, like Beethoven's music, the "defects inherent in a record of struggle." Pound, too, may really, like his critics, regard the work as nearly plotless and heroless. Writing of Dr. Williams, he says, "I would almost move . . . to the generalization that plot, major form, or outline should be left to authors who feel some inner need for the same; even let us say a very strong, unusual, unescapable need for these things; and to books where the said form, plot, etc., springs naturally from the matter treated." "Almost," and he is not speaking of the *Cantos* directly, but the passage is a very striking and heretical one. I put in evidence against it his long labours on the opening cantos, and the cantos themselves in my simple analysis, where the arraying of themes is quite different from casualty. The Hell allusions in the first half of the work, with the allusions to Heaven in recent cantos, also strongly imply a major form. But all present discussion must be tentative. I have the impression that Pound allowed, in whatever his plan exactly is (if it exactly is, and if it is one plan), for the drift-of-life, the interference of fate, inevitable in a period of violent change; that this may give us something wholly unpredictable in the cantos to come, as it has given us already the marvellous pages of the *Pisan Cantos*. Here we feel the poet as he felt D'Annunzio in 1922: D'Annunzio, he wrote from Paris to *The Dial*, "lies with a bandaged eye in a bombarded Venice, foaming with his own sensations, memories, speculations as to what Dante might or might not have done had he been acquainted with Aeschylus." Foaming, yet always with the limpidity, *clarté*, the love against rhetoric, for which his poetry is our model in this century. It would be interesting, if the *Cantos* were complete, to compare the work with another poem, not more original in conception, exhibiting, if a smaller range of material and technical variety, greater steadiness, a similar substance, and a similar comprehensive mastery of expression, *The Prelude*; but the argument of my very limited essay is ended. Let us listen to this music.

INDEX OF TITLES